Girl Talk

"The Consequences Of Sexual Promiscuity!"

What your girlfriends don't or won't tell you, and what your mother should have told you.

Marquíta E. Waters

outskirts press
Denver, Colorado

Copyright Authorization

Girl Talk
The Consequences Of Sexual Promiscuity

v3.0

Outskirts Press, Inc.
http://outskirtspress.com

PB ISBN 978-1-4327-7621-3
HB ISBN 978-1-4327-8096-8

PRINTED IN THE UNITED STATES OF AMERICA

Cautionary Note

The stories in this book are true. The names were changed to protect the innocent and the not so innocent. Any similarities referenced in this book are strictly coincidental.

Table of Contents

Table of Contents

Acknowledgements

Acknowledgements

I thank my Father in Heaven, the Lord Jesus Christ, and the Holy Spirit (the Triune God) for giving me courage to write this book, and enabling me to fulfill my purpose. I give You all the glory and praise forever and ever. Amen.

There were so many people who crossed my path and contributed to my life's experiences – some bad, but mostly good. However, my life has been truly enriched through all of them and through all of my experiences.

I wish to thank all of those who inspired me, encouraged me, loved me, lifted me up when I was down, provided financial support to help get this project off the ground, and who prayed with me and for me.

I am truly blessed.

– Marquíta E. Waters

Dedication

Dedication

This book is dedicated to my mom, Eunice Mabel Morgan, who did the very best she could under the most horrendous circumstances for a young, beautiful, Blackfoot Indian/African American woman, and who raised four children on her own in the 1950s and '60s. I believe, unbeknownst to her, she did a good job and I love her for it. She, with God's help, made us four kids grow up strong enough to live this life. I didn't understand it at first, didn't like her methods, did not like her on occasion, and in her shoes I would have done some things differently, but I understand the method of the madness. I get it!

I also dedicate this book to my small circle of family and friends who are the most beautiful people in the world in all areas of life [Forrest Joseph Celestine, III, Elena Denise Celestine, Daniella Marie Celestine, Michael R. Magasin, Sharon Jones, Drucie & Tim Riley, Emalean Rowland, Janelle Jenkins-Stewart, Andrea Kipp, Marjorie Reed, Gayle Savonne, Michelle Pleasant, and Caroline & Mark Kuperstock]. They have loved and cared for me in so many ways over the years and I thank God for them. They have been with me through husbands, children, misguided friends, loss of jobs, financial difficulties, and personal insecurities. They always listen and understand no matter what the situation. They believe in God with all their hearts, and they believe in me. They stand in agreement with me in prayers.

I also gratefully dedicate this book to my pastor, Pastor Tom Pickens, Jr., and his beautiful and wonderful wife, Minister Donna Pickens, who not only teach the Word of God without hesitation, but who are inspiring examples for us all to emulate. Their teaching is definitely not in vain.

I love them all and love the Lord for enriching my life through them.

– Marquíta E. Waters

Introduction

Introduction

This book is written to all ladies – young girls, teenage girls, young women and even older women. It's written to really open one's eyes to the truth and the actual consequences of being sexually promiscuous. Sexual promiscuity is a symptom of a more serious problem, not the problem itself.

The contents of this book present various consequences as a result of sexual promiscuity. It also presents man's laws and God's laws regarding sexual promiscuity.

This book is based on real and actual events and their related consequences experienced by women of all ages. The stories within the chapters are real, and the names were changed to protect the not so innocent. Medical information provided in this book also evidences the consequences of sexual promiscuity. Everyone who has indulged in sexual promiscuity has come to the same conclusion that the consequences of ignorance, low self-esteem, wrong thinking and bad choices are always the same, with little variation.

We must count the costs before we make decisions in all areas of our lives, but especially in the area of sexual promiscuity because life is really not a game. There are very serious reasons why ladies of all ages should think things through, first, before engaging in any unhealthy, unsafe, and ungodly activities. Although there are so-called precautions one can take for "protective" sex, there is a price to pay for not lining up one's thinking and actions with the Word of God. The laws, statutes, principles and consequences in the Bible are real, alive, and are continually active. God is not mocked. God says what He means and He means what He says. He's no respector of person.

It's not about what you think or what your girlfriends think may or may not happen if you make the wrong choices. The choice determines the consequence – good or bad. No one is immune. It doesn't matter who you are, where you come from, whether you're rich or poor, what color your skin is, how educated you are, or what religious affiliation you have. There are real and harsh consequences for the sexually promiscuous woman, and these consequences can follow throughout her entire life. Some consequences can even shorten a person's life.

Commercialism encourages, promotes, applauds, and makes billions of dollars from sexual promiscuity. It encourages sleeping around with every Tom, Dick, Harry, Mary, and the married. It even promotes dressing, walking, and talking provocatively, and society buys into it. Commercialism doesn't care about the destructive results that follow sexual promiscuity, and it never shows the real life consequences.

If reading this book convinces and persuades even one young girl, one teenager, or one woman to be aware of the consequences before making a bad decision, to be aware of the value she has to God and to herself, and to think before she acts so she can make the right decisions to receive the best results in her life, then this book has accomplished its purpose.

– Marquíta E. Waters

Chapter 1

Seven Things That Will Be With You All Of Your Life

Chapter 1

Seven Things That Will Be With You All of Your Life

(1) *Your Reputation – A Good Name*
(2) Your Children
(3) Your Health
(4) Your Credit
(5) Your Criminal Record
(6) Your Self-Worth/Value
(7) Your Conscience

Your Reputation – A Good Name

Your reputation is your standing in society by the quality of your character as seen by others over a period of time. A person's character is a combination of qualities, habits, mannerisms and attributes that distinguish one person from another and is developed over a period of time as others view that person as she relates to people in different environments such as at home, in school, at work, or in public places. It's her mode of operation.

I'm sure you have heard the saying: "You are known by the company you keep." This is a very real and true statement. When you least expect it, your reputation can either praise you or degrade you.

There is also another familiar and somewhat popular statement: "Perception is reality." Although other people's perception of you may not be the real you, their view of you may be based on their own prejudices and idiosyncrasies, based on your reputation, or based on your character. Other people's perception of you can be your reality – good or bad. It may not be true, and nine times out of ten it isn't true, but it is true and real to them. For example, if you are known to people to lie on occasion, people will view you as a person whose word cannot be trusted. If you do not have a healthy perception of yourself due to self-esteem issues, you can tarnish your own reputation and character.

If you were known by the boys in elementary, junior high or high school to be a "loosey-goosey", "easy", a "tramp" or a "slut", that stain on your character stays with you like a huge pimple or scar on your face that makeup just cannot hide no matter what you do. Unless all those guys you were sleeping around with, or those who heard about you sleeping around, died off (slim chance), it will be hard for you to erase this stigma while in the environment (school for example) where you created your reputation. Sometimes the reputation you created will follow you into other environments. It only takes one time for a guy to say that he "had" you.

You may not care what is said about you or you may not even know the meaning of the words that label you early on, but over time these labels tend to stick to you and wear on you. Negative labels can wear you down to the point of you believing you really are worthless, you have no value, you are an easy lay to men, no one will want you, and no one will respect you. You have no idea how to fix the problem you created, so you end up accepting your fate and you continue to act the part. Yeah, you can say the same about the guys you were sleeping around with, but it just doesn't have the same meaning or effect, and their wrong-doing will fade away much quicker than yours. Your name is dragged through the mud and you will have a very difficult time cleaning it up. *"A good name is better than precious ointment." (Ecclesiastes 7:1)*

Have you heard the one about the guy who goes into a bar, gets drunk, staggers out of the bar, falls into the gutter, and sleeps it off? He wakes up, goes home, takes a shower, gets dressed up in a suit, and goes down the street near the bar. Everyone who sees him calls him "Mister." We, as women, cannot do that same thing and get away with it; we just don't get that same respect. We will be called everything but a child of God. There is still a double standard, which can definitely be harmful to your reputation.

In this society, a teenage boy or a young man who is able to "score" with you in the area of sex is looked upon favorably by his peer group – other males. What he did may be morally wrong, but the male society in general believes that a man must get his experience some way, somehow, and from someone. Who is he going to get his experience from? From you, if you are stupid enough to let him "use" you. The operative word here is "use." After he has got the "hang of it" with you, he will then go on to use someone else. You are considered training ground for him, nothing more and nothing less. Yeah, he will know the words to say to sweeten you up, he will talk to you and give you the attention you find yourself craving for, but his main objective at such a young stage in his life is to score at your expense. He probably will not remember your name a few weeks from the "big moment" unless you let him "experiment" on you again. He certainly will not marry you because you've been used already – by him. You're no longer a virgin, and you've been "had." He's looking to marry someone who is pure, a virgin, unspoiled, of no reputation, untainted, and a person who respects herself too much to be involved in sex prior to marriage. He's not going to bring you home to meet his parents and announce to them that he plans to marry you. He's just testing out his equipment with your equipment to see if and how his equipment works, that's all. If confronted about getting you pregnant or giving you a sexually transmitted disease (STD), more than likely he will blame you, claiming that you seduced him, that you gave him the STD, that you slept around with other boys, and that you have a reputation, etc. He will emphatically dismiss the fact that you got an STD from him. Get the picture?

After having sex with you, that teenage boy or young man will not be looked upon as a whore or a tramp amongst his peer group of guys, but as one who "conquered" and who "got over" at your expense. After he has told all of his friends that he scored with you, guess what? They will more than likely want to score with you, too. After a few times with you, he will go on to other girls who he feels he can also score. Although the girls may be innocent or unaware, have low self-esteem, or are ugly in their own view and would welcome the attention that he gives them, he will sleep with them to (1) get his pleasure, (2) to compare any differences in having sex with them as opposed to having sex with you, and (3) to see if he can have sex more frequently without any complications. He's not looking for a serious relationship or to get married, although he may say things along those lines. He certainly does not want to get anyone pregnant, but he's reluctant to use any type of contraception (rubbers/condoms). Most boys and men believe that birth control is the responsibility of the females, not them.

In a conversation I once had with some co-workers during a break, we discussed the latest "trash trade" newspaper article about the latest young male celebrity who was sleeping around town with yet again another female celebrity and who all the girls swooned over because he was so good-looking. I gave my observation that the male celebrity acted like a whore. I stopped short of actually calling him a whore, although he was definitely one by definition. I only stated that he "acted" like one. The reaction I received was a bit startling – in fact amazing! The women in the group were at first puzzled by my statement and then they laughed, but the guys who were involved in the conversation heard my statement and were downright insulted. How dare I call a guy a whore, although he was doing the same thing in line with the definition of a whore. Isn't it true that if it walks like a duck, quacks like a duck, and acts like a duck, it's got to be a duck? So what's up with the double standard? Unfortunately, that double standard has prevailed for centuries.

Doesn't the term "perception is reality" ring true concerning a guy as well as a gal? Nope! Why not?! Unfortunately, there is that underlying double standard that females still suffer from to this day. We must guard our reputations in all areas and at all times.

For example, after having a reputation for being sexually promiscuous with the guys, you then grew up, moved away from home, went to college, got a degree, got a professional job, found someone who you fell in love with, married him, and now you and he are happily raising a family in suburbia. Then, all of a sudden, your husband decides to go into politics and run for a public office. Because of your past reputation "back in the day" in your hometown, you are now concerned because there is always someone who remembers **"you"** when you were not so pure and upstanding as you appear to be now. You tell your husband about your past before he finds out from someone else, and he now has to deal with your past as well as trying to get elected into some political office representing the "good, wholesome, upstanding, righteous people." The damage is done in your marriage, and if he pursues the political office, he will have to deal with that on top of other issues. You can't fix it or turn back time. Get the point?

The damaging effects are basically the same for alcoholics, drug addicts, all sorts of criminals, etc. If you were engaged in or are currently engaged in any of these destructive activities, you could expect similar consequences.

If you keep playing with fire, you will definitely get burned. If you allow yourself to be promiscuously used, something that you did not plan for or expect will definitely happen – and something always happens.

You have got to begin **early** to think about yourself, who you are, what you mean to God, what you mean to yourself, how you value yourself, what you want to be and where you want to be two, five, or even ten years from now. You must think things through before you make decisions, which will determine your actions, which create your consequences. **You must think about how the consequences will affect your future before you create the consequences.**

Be aware of your thoughts, decisions, actions, and the consequences of those actions, and then control yourself accordingly. You cannot control other people, their actions, or what they say or think. However, you must care enough about you to make the right decisions for you at all times so that you will have a good reputation now and in your future. It really does matter how others see you. It matters that they view you in a positive way and not in a negative way.

You may not get the positive reinforcement from your parents or those closest to you while growing up because they probably have their own issues. However, you must think and consider **YOU** at all times. Call it being "selfish", if you like, but it's important. It's important to think about **YOU.** It's important to make the right decisions to obtain the right results or best consequences for **YOU**.

Remember that a good reputation is built over a period of time, and so is a bad reputation. If you are known to do the same bad or wrong things over and over again that everyone can identify you by, you have somewhat solidified your negative reputation. You cannot just say you don't care and do what you want because you will care later on. The bad consequences will be borne by you, and you alone.

Your reputation is always at stake! You must care enough about yourself to stop and think things through before you do something stupid! It only takes a moment to make a bad choice and suffer the consequences throughout your whole life.

You may have made a bad decision in the past because you did not think that decision through before you acted on it or committed to it. This means that you did not think enough of yourself to think things through and weigh the consequences. You must always count the cost before paying the price.

Side Trip: When I was in elementary school, my father got into a lot of trouble with the law – a lot of felony, criminal trouble. I don't know why nor do I remember all of the circumstances. I just know that he was in jail more than he was out.

One time when I was about seven years old, a lot of Sheriffs came to our home around 5:00 a.m. They practically broke down the front door and came inside. A scuffle ensued, curse words were blazing through the air, holes went into walls, and furniture was tossed to and fro. My father was eventually subdued, handcuffed, ankle-cuffed, dragged out of our home, thrown into the back seat of a patrol car, and driven off to jail. This took place in the midst of a crowd of our neighbors who heard all the commotion that morning, and who came over to see the action, so to speak. When all the patrol cars left, the neighbors left. No one came to see about my mother or us kids.

Later that morning, my mom fed us breakfast, dressed us, and sent us off to school as if nothing had happened, and she offered no explanation. Since all of the children in my neighborhood went to the same elementary school, they apparently knew from their parents what happened at our home earlier that morning. The news spread like wildfire throughout the school. By mid-morning, I, my sister, and my two brothers were given the label of "Jailbird Kids." We cried all the way home from school that day. We told our mom what was said about us at school, but there was nothing she could do about it except to say that we were to pay them no attention. That label hurt us very deeply. Kids can be so cruel. That reputation stuck with us throughout the rest of our stay in elementary school, most of junior high school, and some of high school. The Sheriffs arrested our dad, not us, but we bore the brunt of what the neighbors saw and surmised because we were his children. All of a sudden, we got a bad reputation because of our father. To this day, I still don't know what he did that morning to get himself arrested and jailed.

The adult neighbors no longer spoke to our mother, but they talked about her and us, and they turned up their noses when they saw us coming. Some of the neighbors even laughed at us in our faces. The kids constantly teased us calling us Jailbird Kids, and no one wanted to play with us anymore. We were outcasts.

During that time, our mother encouraged us. We excelled in school, received awards, stayed out of trouble, graduated from high school and went to college. That label that was put on us did not stick because we gave it no credence. If we acted like our father, that label probably would have stuck with us throughout our adult life. My mom knew that label on her children was not true and she taught us not to believe it. We also learned not to follow in our father's footsteps for we had first-hand knowledge of the consequences my father suffered behind his decision to do wrong.

Apparently, my father did not think things through before he made his decisions, before he acted, and before he suffered his consequences. He did not think about the consequences of his actions that affected his family and that his family had to endure. He did not control himself, nor did he seem to care enough about himself or about his family to control himself. He did not think enough about himself or his family.

My mother taught us that our destinies were our own to make, and that our destinies were not doomed as a result of our father's decisions, actions and consequences. But, in those early years, we really suffered behind our father's actions and his ensuing consequences.

Now, bear in mind that even though we did not have anything to do with what our father did, we bore the brunt of the reputation he created for himself in our early years of growing up. He went to jail for a long time, so we never really knew him and he never really knew us. He had no idea of what we went through because of him. Some people thought we were all going to grow up and raise hell like he did, but we didn't.

It was very difficult growing up back then. My mother was a homemaker and a housewife. Not many women worked outside the home in the 1950s. So, when the income was gone because my father went to jail, my mother could not pay the mortgage, utilities, or put food on the table. We ended up receiving state assistance (welfare) because my mother could not work outside the home and raise four children at the same time because we were too young.

We had no transportation after my father went to jail. The brand new car (DeSoto) he purchased was repossessed. We were kind of glad the car was gone because we always had to clean it, but rarely got a chance to ride in it. When we cleaned the car, we found other women's cigarette cases, cigarette butts, and lipstick cases in the car. We did not know what that meant at the time. Dummy us would bring the shiny cigarette and lipstick cases to our mom and say, "Look what we found. Isn't it pretty and shiny?" How dumb we were. We didn't know our father was cheating on our mother. Our mom was thoughtful, but she was hurting inside.

Anyway, a few weeks after the incident with the Sheriffs, we moved out of our new home and moved into a shack that was located outside of the pretty neighborhood we use to live in. We were in the ghetto. The shack had a living room, two bedrooms, one bathroom, a large kitchen, a small dining room and a rickety back porch. The backyard was long (deep) that went into a gully.

Since we were on welfare, we gained another label. Yep, you got it! Not only were we called "Jailbird Kids", but now we were called "Welfare Rats", too! That information also spread like wildfire throughout school.

I remember being very afraid and very unhappy when my father was living with us. I only have one good memory of him, and I will keep that memory until the day I die. All the other memories we, his children, had were dreadful. My father was a big man (football linebacker type). He was about 6 feet, 4 inches, weighed almost 300 pounds, and he was always yelling and cursing. We were intimidated by his yelling to the point of stuttering. We stuttered a long time after he went away. We feared him terribly and we always hid from him when he was home. He physically and verbally abused our mother. Before the Sheriffs took my father away, we saw him on numerous occasions beat our mother almost unrecognizable. He threw her over many pieces of furniture, called her everything but a child of God, and tried and almost succeeded in physically, emotionally and mentally breaking and destroying her. We were all too small and too frightened to do anything, except cry and hide. We were paralyzed by our fear of him. This went on for what seemed like an eternity until the Sheriffs got him. I have to say that when the Sheriffs came, I felt a great relief, even at such a young age. We all slept very peacefully at night afterwards.

My mother divorced my father while he was in jail, and we lost touch with him for he did not write. We probably would not have written to him, either, because we didn't like him. We learned many years later that my father lived a dreadful life when he got out of prison, and then he died in his mid-50s. None of us went to his funeral because we had no knowledge of when he died or where he was living at the time of his death.

My father had a hell of a reputation for being a bad ass, a gangster, a tough guy, and a hoodlum. There was no honor in his life, except for his wife and his four children. He didn't even know about the honor we brought him – in spite of him. Now that he's gone, we will never know why he was the way he was and why he lived the type of life he chose to live. But, us four kids have grown up and we all have our own families. None of us do what our father did. We do not believe in physical abuse, we do not curse our mates or our children, and none of us allow any yelling in our homes. As adults, we are no longer known as Jailbird Kids or Welfare Rats.

What my father did was by his choice, and his choice alone. He paid the consequences for his choices. I believe he regretted the choices he made in his life. His children made different choices, better choices.

We must strive to make good choices in our lives so we don't live in regret. Good choices come from reading and meditating on the word of God to gain wisdom, understanding, discernment and guidance.

This was a rather extreme example of one with a reputation and how it affected others, but all of it was true. <u>End of side trip</u>.

It takes a long time to overcome a negative reputation. Some things keep trying to stick on you. But, if you believe in God, if you believe that He can change your circumstances, if you put your trust in Him by accepting His Son, Jesus Christ, as your Lord and Savior, and if you read the Bible to see what God, Himself, says about you and His promises to you and for you, you will overcome your negative reputation. As God's kids, we are overcomers.

When you change how you feel and think about you, knowing that God has got your back, your reputation will change, too. A reputation of sexual promiscuity can be overcome, but it takes time. Your bad reputation can be overcome by you recognizing the problem and by making the necessary changes in your life to revamp your reputation. To do this, you line up your thoughts, decisions and actions with the word of God. You think things through all the way before you act on them. It's a process and it takes time, but it's worth it and it works.

Remember always that God loves you, He forgives you, and He will bring you through. God loves the sinner. He does not love the sin, but He definitely loves the sinner. He will change the sinner if allowed to do so by the sinner surrendering to Him.

Be strong. Stand! And having done all, still stand. Don't be concerned about what others say about you. Be concerned about what God says about you. Your reputation with Him is what really counts.

You are valuable and wonderful to God. Tell yourself that you are wonderful, that you have value, and that God loves and values you. In essence, you must love yourself. Even if no one else says they love you, you must say to yourself that you love you and that God loves you. Tell yourself daily that you are loved, you are Jesus Christ's heir to the throne, and you are the righteousness of God. *Romans 8:31* states: *"What then shall we say to these things? If God is for us, who can be against us?"* God has got your back. He is for you. Ask the Lord Jesus to come into your life and to forgive you of your sins. He will forgive you and He will save you. He did not come to save the righteous, but to save the sinner. *Matthew 9:11-13* states: *"And when the Pharisees saw it, they said to His disciples, 'Why does your Teacher eat with tax collectors and sinners?' When Jesus heard that, He said to them, 'Those who are well have no need of a physician, but those who are sick. 'But go and learn what this means: I desire mercy and not sacrifice.' For I did not come to call the righteous, but sinners, to repentance.'"*

Most importantly, you must know in your heart that you are loved by God way beyond your imagination. In *Jeremiah 29:11-12,* God says: *"For I know the thoughts that I think toward you, says the Lord, thoughts of peace and not of evil, to give you a future and a hope. Then you will call upon Me and go and pray to Me, and I will listen to you. And you will seek me and find Me, when you search for Me with all your heart."* You must believe that you are loved. Have faith that God loves you. Tell yourself that you have value, you are worthy, you are beautiful, you are a child of God, and that you are His creation.

The Creator, who made you, did not make a mistake, He does not make junk, but He made something very beautiful and special when He made you. *"Therefore if any man [woman] be in Christ, he [she] is a new creation: old things are passed away; behold, all things are become new." (2 Corinthians 5:17)* This pertains to you having a new reputation, too. Begin acting like the new creation that you are – you are loved. Hold your head up high, fix yourself up, and smile! Before you know it, you will be walking in love and your reputation will be of good report.

Remember that God has plans for you, and He has a purpose for you on this earth. You are a new creation, created by God, Himself, the One who created the universe, the One who created all things, the One who spoke things into existence when they didn't even exist.

Your Children

Psalm 127:3-5 states: *"Behold, children are a heritage from the Lord, the fruit of the womb is a reward. Like arrows in the hand of a warrior, so are the children of one's youth. Happy is the man who has his quiver full of them; they shall not be ashamed, but shall speak with their enemies in the gate."*

When you have children, they will always be with you through thick and thin. *Proverbs 22:6* states: *"Train up a child in the way he [she] should go, and when he [she] is old he [she] will not depart from it." Proverbs 20:11* states: *"Even a child is known by his [her] deeds, whether what he [she] does is pure and right."* Your children will need you and you will need them throughout their entire life until either you or they go to be with the Lord. If you love them and cherish them, they will never leave you. Even when they get married, they will be there for you. They will respect you. They will defend you. They will help provide for you when they are grown and you are old. As you have made your children part of your life, they will include you in their lives. *Proverbs 31:28* states: *"Her children rise up and call her blessed;"*

However, if you forsake your children, do not show love to your children, do not appreciate your children, do not teach your children right from wrong, do not instill self-assurance and confidence in your children, do not affirm your children, do not provide for your children, do not keep your children in a safe environment, or do not defend and protect your children, they will grow up insecure, having low self-esteem, having no confidence, having no sense of right and wrong, having no sense of allegiance to you or anyone or anything, hard-hearted, selfish, defensive, angry, non-caring, and vulnerable to those trying to take advantage of them.

Children tend to emulate their parents. Your children may grow up making almost the same mistakes you made because you did not teach them any better. Some children will grow up being very angry and bitter and not even know why. They will not love you or anyone else because you did not teach them how to love and you didn't show them love. They will not give their allegiance to you and be faithful to you because you were not faithful to them. They will grow up disrespecting you because you did not respect them. You called them out of their names using derogatory and gutter names such as bitch, whore, bastard, etc., when you were angry with them, or just in general as they grew up. Or, you dismissed and ignored them when they really needed you. They may be defiant in the world, or they may fear the world because they did not learn from you how to cope in the world. They will not take care of you in your old age and they will not care about you because you did not care about them when they were growing up. They won't care that you suffer physically or financially now that you're old because they suffered because of you as they grew up. Your adult children may even be physically and/or verbally abusive to you because you were physically and/or verbally abusive to them as they were growing up. In essence, they may grow up treating you the same way you treated them. That can be a good thing or a bad thing for you because children remember their childhoods.

You are accountable to God for how you raise your children. Did you bring them up in the admonition (correction and teaching) of the Lord? Did you help them to fulfill their purpose in their lives that God has provided for them? Did you give them love and confidence where they have no fear of anything?

Your children are your special gifts given to you by God. He included you in their future to help them fulfill their purpose that He instilled in them. It's by the grace of God that children are in this world and that we are able to conceive, deliver and raise them. It doesn't matter under what circumstances they came to you. It doesn't matter that you had a child out of wedlock, or had a child through rape or incest. As harsh as those particular circumstances are, you must remember that God is in control and that He works all things out for good to those of us who love Him, and who are the called according to His purpose. *Romans 8:28* states: *"And we know that all things work together for good to those who love God, to those who are the called according to His purpose."* We really must get a grip on this issue.

We don't have children to fulfill our unmet desires, to snag a man, to keep a man, to get extra money from a government welfare program, to get a tax deduction, to get extra child support from a husband who has left his family, or to get child support from a boyfriend who has left the relationship. We don't have children to use as slaves, whipping boys, or as labor to bring in extra income to support the family when we, as parents, refuse to work. Again, our children are our special gifts from God and they are for His purpose. Our children do not owe us anything except respect, provided we do our part as unto the Lord.

Not everyone can have a child. It is truly a blessing to be chosen by God to have a child, no matter how the child comes into being. It's a blessing to be a participant in God's miracle creation of life inside our bodies. It is an honor that God has chosen you to birth, raise, and steer your child in the right direction to fulfill God's purpose in his or her life.

God has a purpose and a destiny for each child born into this world, and for each child born into your life. He has a definite purpose for a child who is born with or who has developed a challenge physically, emotionally, or mentally.

Some people say that you must have sinned somewhere down the road to birth a less-than-perfect child (in the world's view). This is not for them to judge. It doesn't matter that the child has come to you in a less than perfect package – challenged in their health and/or abilities. What matters is that you, as the child's parent, are to ask God what His plan and purpose are for your child and for you in the raising of your child. You must seek Him to find out what role you play in that child's life so you can help him or her fulfill their purpose, plan, and destiny that God has given them. In fact, you should seek God's wisdom concerning raising any children you help bring into this world.

Remember that God knows what He's doing. He has a purpose, a plan, and a destiny for every child. Look to God for the answers. Don't look to yourself or to other humans, especially not those who have no knowledge of God, or those who have the wrong knowledge of God, or those who have never had children, or those people who have a negative attitude concerning your child's challenges.

In the Gospel of *John*, Chapter 9:1-3, the Lord Jesus clarifies the issue of a child being born in a less-than-perfect condition by the world's standards. *John 9:1-3* states: *"Now as Jesus passed by, He saw a man who was blind from birth, and His disciples asked Him, saying, 'Rabbi, who sinned, this man or his parents, that he was born blind?' Jesus answered, 'Neither this man nor his parents sinned, but that the works of God should be revealed in him.'"* Jesus healed the blind man and he received his sight in Verses 6 and 7 of Chapter 9: *"When He [Jesus] had said these things, He spat on the ground and made clay with the saliva; and He anointed the eyes of the blind man with the clay. And He said to him, 'Go wash in the pool of Siloam (which is translated, Sent).' So he [the blind man] went and washed, and came back seeing."* Apparently, God was even involved in guiding the blind man to the pool to wash.

It doesn't matter if a child is born in abject poverty, filthy wealth, or in a middle-class family. God is in control of that child's purpose, plan, and destiny. We do not have the mind of God. Heaven forbid that we think we are as smart as God!

It doesn't matter that you're an unwed teenager and the boy who got you pregnant has denied impregnating you. It doesn't matter that your parents may be very angry with you being pregnant and are talking of disowning you, or they may actually have thrown you out of their home – the home that was once your home. You will survive. All of the pain and uncertainty of your future and your child's future will be answered by the Lord for He has a plan for you and for your child under even these circumstances.

Two people engaged in the act of having sex outside of marriage have committed the sin of fornication. However, if a child is born as a result of that sin, the child is not the sin and should not be discredited. The parents, by their actions, helped to bring the child into existence. Therefore, parents who had sex out of wedlock performed an illegitimate action that created the pregnancy that resulted in the birth of a child. God was the One who ordained the pregnancy and the birth of the child for His purpose. He did not ordain the illegitimate act of fornication. If a child is born on this earth, he or she is here on purpose – God's purpose.

If you become pregnant out of wedlock, remember that your child is a gift from God, and she or he is not to be identified as a "bastard." No child should ever be called a bastard because he or she is not illegitimate. People who accuse and/or label a child who was born out of wedlock as a bastard are guilty of false accusations. No one has the right to accuse anyone of a sin for no one is perfect. In the Gospel of John in the New Testament of the Bible, the Pharisees and the scribes caught a woman in the act of adultery. They brought her to Jesus to see what He would do. They were trying to discredit the Lord Jesus and His teachings. *John 8:7* states: *"So when they continued asking Him, He raised Himself up and said to them, 'He who is without sin among you, let him throw a stone at her first.'"*

Children who are born with a handicap or medical condition are all gifts from God, and they all have a purpose ordained by God.

Psalm 127:3-5 states: *Behold, children are a heritage from the Lord. The fruit of the womb is a reward. Like arrows in the hand of a warrior, so are the children of one's youth. Happy is the man who has his quiver full of them; they shall not be ashamed, but shall speak with their enemies in the gate."* In *Matthew 18:10*, the Lord Jesus states: *"Take heed that you do not despise one of these little ones, for I say to you that in heaven their angels always see the face of My Father who is in heaven."* All children have a number of angels protecting them and representing them before God in heaven. In *Matthew 18:12-14*, the Lord Jesus states: *"What do you think? If a man has a hundred sheep, and one of them goes astray, does he not leave the ninety-nine and go to the mountains to seek the one that is straying? And if he should find it, assuredly, I say to you, he rejoices more over that sheep than over the ninety-nine that did not go astray. Even so, it is not the will of your Father who is in heaven that one of these little ones should perish." Mark 10:13-16* states: *"Then they brought little children to Him that He might touch them; but the disciples rebuked those who brought them. But when Jesus saw it, He was greatly displeased and said to them, 'Let the little children come to Me, and do not forbid them for such is the kingdom of God. Assuredly, I say to you, whoever does not receive the kingdom of God as a little child will by no means enter it.' And He took them up in His arms, laid His hands on them, and blessed them."*

It's up to the parents to assist their child in fulfilling his or her purpose no matter what obstacles exist, both physically and emotionally. The child's purpose may very well be to change his or her parents' mindset, to bring something good out in the parents, to help the parents see God through the circumstances and conditions, and to show his or her parents how to trust God and to know that God is continually involved and will see all of them through. We have to look beyond the obvious to see the gem that He has created for us to care for and cherish.

Not everyone can have a child. However, if it's truly a desire of your heart, get in line with God's word and He will give you the desire of your heart. If you are unable to have a baby by conventional means, He has provided other opportunities for you to have a child through the advancement of science and medicine utilizing in vitro fertilization and surrogacy. Plus, there's always adoption. Remember that God is in control of your future, and He has a good reason for everything. Things happen or don't happen for a reason, His reason. Nothing is coincidental. If you stay in His word and ask Him to reveal it to you, He will. Also, things are never done according to your timing, but according to His timing. God doesn't need to own a timepiece; He created time.

Even though things may not have turned out as you planned, it doesn't mean that raising the gift that God has given to you was not your purpose in the first place. Who knows, you may be raising the next leader of a country, the next Super Bowl Champion, the next female president of a corporation, or the next scientist who discovers the cure for cancer or AIDS. In spite of the obstacles, aim high. Look for the best in every situation and focus on the good. God will unfold His purpose in your child and in your participation in your child's life. But, you've got to hang in there and trust Him. Remember *Romans 28: "And we know that all things work together for good to those who love God, to those who are the called according to His purpose."*

In sexual intercourse, the woman receives sperm from the man through the penetration of the vagina by the penis. A discharge (ejaculation) of fluid (sperm) by the man enters into the woman's vagina as a result of the man being sexually aroused during the physical act of sexual intercourse. The sperm then mates with an egg from the woman's ovaries. However, it takes God's miracle touch that makes the sperm to be able to penetrate through the two highly protective walls of the egg, mate with the egg, and create an embryo that develops into a child. Without the sperm, the egg, and God's miracle touch, a woman would not get pregnant. It is God's decision and His action that causes the mating of the sperm with the egg creating conception by the woman. God definitely has a plan and a purpose for that child to be born through those two people, at that particular time. It's not whether you did things right which brought that child into the world. The issue is what are you going to do to help ensure that the child fulfills God's purpose for his or her life? The ability to get pregnant and have a baby really is a perfect immaculate conception. We should not take this miracle for granted.

You should always want God's best for you and for your children that you help bring into this world. That's why it's so important to do things in your life the right way, God's way, so that your child will not have to suffer and face unnecessary obstacles early on in life in order to accomplish what God has for him or her. Bear in mind that God will get the child through the obstacles in order to accomplish His plans, but it would be so much easier for the child if he or she starts off the right way in the right environment, which includes right-thinking parents.

Being married before you engage in sexual intercourse creates a perfect union to bring into this world that wonderful miracle – a child. Bringing a child into the world by any other means creates hardships for the child, the mother, and the father in a variety of forms. It is unfair to the child to not do it God's way.

Your Health

Be sure, the truth will find you out. Be sure your health will find you out. You only get one body in this life; use it wisely. There are no 'HBP' (Human Body Parts) Stores where one can purchase spare body parts to replace worn out or diseased parts. Yes, there have been strides made in the medical field concerning some transplants.

Doctors can transplant livers, hearts, lungs, kidneys and a few other body parts, but there's no guarantee the transplants will be readily available, or won't be rejected by the body. In fact, nothing is guaranteed. Only God's word is guaranteed.

There are at least 39 known major diseases, and an untold number of variations of those diseases. By engaging in unsafe, dangerous health practices, you can certainly increase your risk of catching something that doctors and modern day medicine may or may not be able to fix or cure.

A lot of young ladies do not realize that even kissing a guy who has Herpes on his lips (for example) can have life-long negative effects and can be dangerous to their future with a prospective husband. Without even realizing it, you could be putting your health in jeopardy by getting out of God's order and being sexually active before marriage because you acted on your emotions and your flesh, and you did not think things through or care about yourself enough to weigh the consequences of your actions before you acted.

There are far too many young girls who do not think things through before they give all of themselves totally away (body, soul, and mind) because some boy gave them a little attention, and maybe even told them they "liked" them (not loved them, but just "liked" them).

The word "love" carries such a high degree of responsibility when it comes to matters of the heart. The word "like" has no responsibility at all when it comes to matters of the heart. Merriman-Webster's definition of love in this instance is strong affection arising out of kinship and personal ties. It's attraction based on sexual desires, which include affection and tenderness felt by lovers. There must be time invested to know a person long enough so you can possibly reach the stage of love. You can't just hop in the bed with someone first, and then determine whether you "like" or "love" the person. This is backwards! You have to spend time getting to know the person, finding out if you are compatible with one another in all other areas of social interfacing, and finding out whether you want to commit all of yourself (emotionally and physically) to that person for the rest of your life. There's got to be some strong glue that binds you together with a person in all areas of a relationship, and it's got to be much more than the physical exercise of sex. The emotional and physical risks are just too great not to invest time in knowing someone to the point where you actually love that person. If your love for the person is not as strong as Super Glue, where the ties will not be easily broken, your relationship will eventually break and it will be next to impossible to put the pieces back together because the edges are so jagged due to the splintering of the pieces.

You can't let your bottom rule your head when it comes to sex because you will be bound to that person emotionally after having physical sex with him the first time. The emotional bond is a hard thing to turn off because of the chemical juices in your body that will be activated. The juices create somewhat of an addiction to where you will want more sex and more emotional closeness from the person. That's the reason why it's so much better to first be married to the person you care about before having sex with him. Remember, females are more emotional than males, and this comes into serious play in relationships, no matter how brief they are.

These days, teenage girls and women sleep around with a lot of men, and they tend to lose their sensitivity about what sex is all about. It's almost like they have a callousness toward the person they are having sex with; they are involved in physical sex for just that – physical sex, and they don't care about the dangers of contracting a sexually transmitted disease or getting pregnant, or both. Maybe when they gave themselves to someone the first time, they were disappointed when they realized the other person did not feel the same way about them and did not want to spend the rest of their lives with them. They felt used and now want to use someone else in the same way.

Young girls from an early age have cheapened their own value by engaging in sex prior to marriage because they do not know who they are and what value they have to God and to themselves. They end up with all sorts of medical problems from sleeping around with guys. They don't think enough of themselves to "**Just Say No!**" Instead, because of their ignorance, low or no self-esteem, and insecurities because of various things that have happened in their lives, they don't think things through. They give all they have, their total being, to some boy or man who could care less about them. He only cares about what he can get from them sexually, and he doesn't care that he's passing on a sexually transmitted disease to them. These young girls will suffer the consequences of dealing with health, emotional, and self-esteem issues throughout their whole lives.

Your Credit

Have you heard the one about the guy who was dating a young lady and after a few dates, he asked her to co-sign for him to purchase a car? After the car was purchased, he dumped her, stopped paying the car note, kept the car and moved on to another woman. Because she co-signed for him and he stopped paying the car note, she now has to make the payments. If she doesn't, the car will be repossessed and her credit will be trashed. She will not be able to purchase a vehicle in her own name for a long time. Have you ever wondered why a person asks another person to co-sign? It's because they are not responsible enough to keep their own credit intact.

Have you heard the one about the guy who was dating a woman for a while, then he asked to use her credit card to make a purchase, and he promised to pay her back? He never did. Her money is gone.

Have you heard the one about the guy who was dating a woman, stole her credit card(s) out of her wallet, made several large purchases with the credit cards, dumped her and disappeared? She doesn't have the merchandise to return so she has to either fight the credit card companies or pay the bills created by the guy. The burden of proof is on her. Her credit is possibly ruined.

Have you heard about the woman who had a so-called "Bad Boy" for a boyfriend? She thought he was so cool and sexy as a "Bad Boy." He got in trouble with the law, went to jail and called her to bail him out. His bail was $25,000, which meant that she could get him bailed out with $2,500 (non-refundable) provided he showed up for his court appearance. He bailed out on her money and did not show up for the court appearance. She became accountable for the full $25,000 less the $2,500 she already paid. If she put her home up for collateral on the bail, there would now be a lien against her property for $22,500. Her credit is ruined, she's got a lien on her property, and her bank account is drained.

Guys like the ones described above will take advantage of a pretty girl, a not-so-pretty girl, a naive woman or a not-so-pretty and silly older woman. They use them for what they can get from them – money, cars, and credit. If these women don't have money, they somehow know how to get it for their 'man.' This type of guy can sense, smell, and will take advantage of a desperate, low self-esteem, gullible, shy, quiet, and insecure female – young or old. He's slick, smooth, conniving, convincing, ruthless and underhanded. He cares that her credit is good enough for him to use, and he'll use her, too. It happens to the best of women as well as young and innocent women and teenage girls. Nowadays, it frequently happens to girls whose parents give them credit cards.

You've got to be smart about your credit and your future. If not, your financial consequences can be harsh and can last a long time. It doesn't take much to get you into financial hot water.

Say, for example, you get a new credit card with a credit limit of $2,000. If you're in college, credit cards are practically thrown at you with from $2,000 to $5,000 credit limits, advertising payback at a much later date. You get several credit cards from banks and credit card companies to high-end retail stores. You even get that infamous American Distress card that allows you a credit limit of $5,000 to $10,000. You begin to use the credit cards so freely that you forget that the bills for those cards will be coming in soon. You have expended more than you can afford to pay on the monthly minimum balances. You're now in trouble because you either made a late payment, paid less than the minimum payment, or you made no payment. Well, there goes your FICO score. [The **F**air **I**saac **CO**rporation, which is identified on the New York Stock Exchange as FICO, is a company that collects and analyzes your payment habits to create a credit score for you that lets a financial institution know whether you are credit worthy of their business by allowing you to purchase products on a time payment basis.] You then contemplate filing bankruptcy because you cannot afford to pay the monthly amounts due on your car, several credit cards, rent, utilities, cable television, entertainment, food, gasoline, car insurance, and other incidentals. Then, inevitably, Murphy's Law kicks in when you're down and out. "Murphy's Law" says if anything can go wrong, it will, and it does. Everything goes wrong. Your credit is trashed, you'll need at least five full-time jobs to pay off your debt, and you won't see any financial daylight until the year 2929. Your creditors believe in Murphy's Law, too. For example, "To err is human, but to forgive is not Company policy." So you are stuck in financial mud for a long time.

Let's take it one step further. A young man comes into your life, he establishes a friendship with you that blossoms into a deeper relationship over time, and now he wants to marry you. He proposed marriage to you and you accepted. While you both are making plans for your glorious wedding, he suggests that you and he have that "special meeting" a/k/a (also known as) that "Come to Jesus Meeting" where you both sit down and tell each other what bills you have (and other important facts about yourselves) so that you both can strategize and plan your future, financially and otherwise. Since you have trashed your credit, will he still be willing to marry you? Will he pay off your debt? Will he allow you to combine your income and debt with his? Will he help you purchase a vehicle using his credit? Will he put your name on the deed of his condominium or house? Will he put your name on any of his credit cards or on his bank accounts? Will he make major purchases with you?

I knew a couple that dated for a few years and then got married. Before they got married, however, they had that "Come To Jesus Meeting" where they both laid all of their cards on the table. In other words, they each told each other about the condition of their finances, and other issues that might have a bearing on their future together in marriage. Now, the guy had a great paying job, he accumulated a lot of money in the bank over the years, he purchased a home on his own which he had lived in for a few years, he had an old car that he used everyday to go to and from work, and he had a beautiful new sports car that he drove on the weekends to impress the ladies. This guy had a good retirement plan, good health coverage, and some good investments. His FICO score was well over 800 points, which is the highest score one can reach. He felt he worked too hard to have his financial status tarnished by anyone.

It was a different story for the woman he planned to marry. She was very honest with him, and she told him about her numerous credit cards and their high balances. She told him that her credit score (FICO) was below 600. She had outstanding doctor bills, late payments on her credit cards, absolutely no money in the bank, no investments, and no property. Although she worked, she lived from paycheck to paycheck. Her explanation for the high debt was that it costs money to look good. She expressed to him that since he was marrying her he should pay off all of her debt so they could begin the marriage with a clean slate.

Now, I ask you, was that a fair trade? Was it his fault that she had a lot of debt? Did she have a good reason for having so much debt? Was he obligated to pay off all of her debt when they got married? Did he love her enough to pay off her debt? Would he put her name on his house as co-owner knowing what he knew about her debt? Would he allow her to open new credit cards or make major purchases using his name as one of the responsible parties to pay the bills? Would he allow her to have access to his investments, bank accounts, cars, etc.? If he paid off her debt, was she willing to let him handle all of their family finances, would she bring her paycheck home and give it to him to manage, and would she accept a periodic financial allowance disbursed to her from him? Did she trust him? Did he trust her?

Was she marrying him for debt relief or was she marrying him because she loved him? Did she love him enough not to be in so much debt? Did she love him enough to wait until she was able to pay down her debt and then marry him? Did she love him enough not to ask him to pay off her debt? Did she love him enough to understand his position that since he did not create the debt, and did not share in whatever benefits that were generated by the debt, he should not be responsible or obligated to pay her debt?

He brought a lot of financial assets to the table, but she brought a lot of financial debt to the table. Did he marry her?

As it turned out, he married her with major financial strings attached. He would only marry her if they kept their finances and financial obligations separate. She accepted his demand, but then after they were married for a little while, she told him she believed he should pay off all of her debt. He refused and stood his ground. She remained in the marriage anyway, thinking she could change his mind. He married her thinking he would keep everything financially separate and that it would not be a problem. They ended up in divorce a few years later. His credit was still intact, and her debt had increased.

Now this could have happened with the woman being in good financial shape and the man in financial debt. What would you do in this situation? Would you marry a person in major financial debt and work with them to get out and stay out of debt? If you were the one with the debt, would you wait to get married until you paid off most or all of your debt? Would you love the person enough to accept his financial frailties and help him? Would the one you wanted to marry love you enough to accept your financial frailties and be willing to help you? If you were the one with heavy debt, would you be willing to change your financial spending habits for the sake of the marriage and allow your mate to manage all of your financial affairs? Would you accept a weekly, bi-weekly, or monthly allowance from your husband and allow him to handle your hard-earned income? Is any of this fair and reasonable to you? To him?

I knew a couple that got married without checking each other's financial status. The woman had a judgment against her ten years prior to her marrying her husband, but she conveniently forgot and failed to inform him before they got married. They consolidated their checking and savings account to one family checking and savings account. Over the next few years, they purchased a new car and were saving money to purchase a new home.

One Friday, the husband went to the bank to deposit his paycheck and a bonus check of over $2,500 that he received from his job. That following weekend, he went to the ATM to withdraw some of the funds to spend on his family. The ATM would not allow him to withdraw any money, so he went into the bank and spoke to a bank teller who informed him that he had no money in his account. He asked her where the money was, especially since he had deposited his paycheck the prior week. She referred him to the branch manager who informed him that there was a judgment lien on his account and that $2,500 was withdrawn. He told the branch manager he knew nothing about a judgment lien and that it was illegal for the bank to allow such a withdrawal. But the branch manager stated that the writ of execution of the judgment was legal, and the bank had no choice but to allow the money to be taken from his account. The branch manager provided him a copy of the judgment and the name of the company who collected on the judgment.

The husband contacted the company who had the judgment against his account, and he was informed that the judgment was against his wife ten years prior to their marriage. The husband informed the company representative that his wife incurred this judgment before he married her and that since they were married his money should not be taken to satisfy the judgment. The company representative stated that the judgment was legal and that it must be satisfied now that the wife had adequate resources (her husband's income) to pay it. The representative also stated that there was still an outstanding balance due on the judgment of an additional $2,500, and the representative asked him if he wanted to make payment arrangements. Needless to say, the husband was infuriated. He went home to his wife, informed her of what happened, and asked her if this was correct. She apologized stating that she forgot to tell him before they got married.

Now, I ask you, what happened in this case? Are there any more debts that the wife has not disclosed to her husband? Has the husband's trust in his wife been damaged? How can the wife make it up to the husband? Will the husband forgive his wife? Will the husband open up a new account at a new bank without adding his wife's name to his account? What would you do?

Collection companies tend to operate like King Cobra snakes, surveying a situation before striking with their venom. They are literally cold blooded (ectothermic). The cobra snake has excellent eyesight and so do collection companies. They both are highly aggressive. They both pick up the scent of their prey, track it down, and wait patiently before they strike. They both swallow their prey whole. The minute the debtor (who has the judgment against him or her) comes into some money, the collection company strikes with a vengeance. If the debtor's name is on a joint bank account and there are enough funds to satisfy the judgment, the collection company can strike at any time and withdraw the necessary amount of funds to satisfy the judgment. The collection company gets paid a percentage of the take, of course.

The mistake the husband made was to either open an account with both his and his wife's names – a joint account, or he added her name to his account. Had he not included his wife's name on his account, he would have kept his $5,000.

To begin a marriage with unresolved problematic financial situations, like the ones referred to earlier, is very difficult. A lot of premarital counseling and financial counseling are needed before you walk down the aisle of marital bliss. If not, the marriage may be short-lived because money is the first major reason for the demise of a marriage. Following at a close second cause of marital demise is adultery. Where there's no trust, there's no marriage.

Remember that your credit is like your virginity. It's something very important (almost sacred), very valuable, and is to be respected. You should ensure that your credit is intact, good, and secure prior to getting married, especially if you know your future mate's credit is soaring above 800 points. You should be able to trust the one you are marrying enough to give him your good credit in holy matrimony and vise versa.

If your credit is spotless as well as your health, etc., and you're unsure of your prospective mate's credit, health, etc., I strongly recommend you have the following done, in line with a "Come To Jesus Meeting", before you marry that man of your dreams:

(a) Criminal Background Check. Has he ever served time behind bars, even if it's for one day? What were the charges? What were the dispositions of the cases? What were his reasons for his incarcerations?

(b) Car Insurance Review. Does he carry car insurance? Is the premium high? If so, why? Any DUI's? Why?

(c) Credit Check. Get permission from him to obtain credit reports from Trans Union, Equifax, and Experian. Find out what his FICO score is from the credit reports.

(d) Medical Checkup And Medical History Check. Are there any cases of STDs in the past, etc.? Is he currently free of any STDs? What were the STDs? Does he have AIDS or is he HIV-positive? Is there any history of mental illness or debilitating diseases?

(e) Income Tax Returns. Review of federal and state income tax returns is very important. Has he failed to file any income tax returns in the past? Why? How many years are missing? Why? Does he owe the federal or state government any money? If so, how much? Has he worked out a payment plan with the IRS, how much is the monthly payment, and is he adhering to it? If not, why not?

(f) Family Background Check. Is anyone in his family habitually in jail or on death row? Is any family member in drug rehab or consistently involved in the use, sale and transportation of drugs? Does any family member(s) associate with known drug dealers or drug users? Are there gamblers in the family? Does his family frequent the racetrack or casinos recreationally or habitually? Is any family member in the insane asylum or have a history of mental illness? Is there a history of physical abuse by members of his family? Is the future mother-in-law overbearing and extremely protective of her son? Does his family respect you as his future wife? Do your future in-laws respect each other?

There are many other questions and concerns to be resolved. However, the above-listed areas are a good start to help ensure there are no surprises before you walk down the aisle of matrimony. Also, if there are any negatives, can you handle it? If you "honestly" feel you are not able to deal with any negativity in these areas, you should not marry the person. Don't try to fix the problems after you're married; it's too late then. Remember that the only person you can change is you.

Following up on the six items above will save you many tears and headaches in your future. Remember, the life you save may be your own in so many ways. You should be developing a list of concerns to discuss and resolve prior to your marriage. I strongly suggest you pray, review, discuss, and resolve these issues with your prospective marriage partner prior to getting married.

I would rather be alone and poor than have financial problems caused by someone else. I would rather be alone and have my good health. I would rather be alone and file my own tax return and expect money back from the IRS than be married to a guy who owes money to the IRS because he claimed 80 deductions and did not tell me about it. I would rather be home alone cuddled up in my bed with many pillows surrounding me as I read a good book than have to visit my mate in jail because of his so-called slickness, a/k/a/ stupidity. I would rather go shopping alone and purchase anything I wanted with my good credit and my own money than window-shop because my credit is jacked up so bad due to someone else's reckless decisions.

Your credit is your responsibility – yours alone. It's up to you how you use credit, or how it uses you. The borrower is always slave to the lender. Your credit will be with you even after you get divorced. What shape will your credit be in? If your credit gets trashed, wouldn't you rather be the one to trash it instead of allowing someone else to trash it for you? Need I say more!

Your credit stays with you whether you're married or not. If you make purchases together with the bad-credit-husband using your good credit, and he does not pay, your credit will become like his – trash! You will bear the brunt of your decision, or lack of a decision, related to your credit. By not being proactive is a decision, and there are consequences to pay.

Many years ago, I worked with a young lady who had a supervisory position in an aerospace firm. She was good to the employees in her department; everyone loved working for her. She was very pretty, she wore designer outfits to work everyday, drove the latest sports car, had great credit, had money in the bank, and she owned her own town-home – in essence, she was styling. She met a man at the aerospace company who wined and dined her. He was a young and good-looking engineer. They always had fairytale weekends; you know, the romantic weekends that we all dream about. Both she and the engineer made great money; and it seemed like they would make the perfect couple.

After a few months of dating, the engineer proposed marriage to her. All of us expected his proposal. She came into work on a Monday with a large diamond ring on her finger that was, as they say, "to die for." Everyone was very happy for her. We felt she deserved the very best because she worked really hard for what she had, and she was a sweet and kind boss. We all thought it was a match made in heaven. Little did we know . . .!

A few months down the road, they got married and honeymooned in Hawaii for a couple of weeks. When she returned to work, she appeared to be refreshed and very happy. Her future looked very bright.

Over time, though, she came to work not looking as sharp as she did formerly. She wasn't going to the beauty parlor as often as she use to go. She was not eating lunch at restaurants with some of her co-workers like she use to do, but instead bringing brown-bag lunches to work. She became sullen and not as sociable as she use to be. The excitement of life seemed to have gone out of her.

One day, one of her employees made a small mistake, and the supervisor became enraged and blew up like a volcano. Everyone in the office was shocked. Then she cried and fell crumpled to the floor. We all left our seats, ran to her and gathered her up off the floor. We consoled her as best we could, not really knowing what the problem was at the time. We all knew she was upset about something far more than the mistake our co-worker made. We all cared a lot about her and loved working for her. We became upset, too. We didn't want to see her the way she had become since getting married. We did not know what was going on in her life, but whatever it was, we didn't like it. We liked her so much, we probably would have done something, anything, to try to fix things for her. The manager came into the room and took her out of the office that afternoon to talk to her. We all left the job that day feeling sad, helpless, and wondering what was going on.

The next day the supervisor did not come into work. BUT (there's always a BUT), the manager knew we all cared about her, and with the supervisor's permission, the manager told us why she was so upset.

Apparently, although this guy wined and dined her, he gave her the "appearance" he was stable, honest, and financially secure. He certainly made good money as an engineer, but apparently he was a womanizer, a liar, a partier, and a very poor manager of his money. The truth was coming out as the marriage got underway. But the worst was yet to come.

We were paid every week at the aerospace firm. Our friend/supervisor generally handed out the paychecks to us on Fridays. However, on one particular Friday, everyone received her paycheck except our supervisor. She placed a call to the Payroll Department, and the person on the other end of the phone asked her to come to their office. That's when she learned that her paycheck was being "garnished" (a withholding of a specific sum of money from a paycheck to satisfy a creditor for what was owed them) for back taxes that her new husband owed, and he owed a lot of money to the federal and state governments. The IRS was already garnishing his wages, but he did not tell her while they were courting, nor did he tell her after they were married. She had to find out through the Payroll Department on the job. She was embarrassed, devastated, and angry after learning that her paychecks were being garnished to help pay back-taxes that he owed.

During the brief marriage, she spent most of her money (remaining after the garnishment of her wages) paying his bills and struggling to survive. She could no longer afford to go to the beauty parlor on a regular basis like she use to do. She could not do any shopping like she use to. Her lifestyle quickly changed for the worse. Her credit, combined with his bad credit, was almost totally ruined.

It took her a few months to get over the anger and hurt she experienced behind her husband not being forthright and honest with her. She also had to accept the fact that he tried to use her financially to resolve his own financial problems.

It took a while, but she was finally able to get her marriage annulled. However, it took many more months for her to get her paychecks released from the IRS and from the State. She was not reimbursed by the IRS or by the State for what she had paid while married. It took even longer for her to get her credit restored. He never apologized to her for what he put her through, nor did he pay her back for what she paid on his debts.

After a while, she looked like her old "good looking" self again. She had that million-dollar smile on her face and that pep in her step. We had our wonderful friend and great supervisor back. We were all very happy for her. All of us learned a very harsh lesson.

The sad part about this situation was that he took advantage of her. He used her to try to fix his own mess that he created. He did not care whether he could provide for her to continue in the lifestyle she was accustomed to – going to the beauty shop, shopping, and having lunch with the girls like she was use to doing on her own. He only saw her as someone who looked good, who made great money, and who he could manipulate with the right suaveness and sophistication to get what he needed to bail himself out of his financial hole. He used her and broke her heart.

Did he really love her as referenced in *Ephesians 5:25-29*, which states: *"Husbands, love your wives just as Christ also loved the church and gave Himself for her, that He might sanctify and cleanse her with the washing of water by the word, that He might present her to Himself a glorious church, not having spot or wrinkle or any such thing, but that she should be holy and without blemish. So husbands ought to love their own wives as their own bodies; he who loves his wife loves himself. For no one ever hated his own flesh, but nourishes and cherishes it, just as the Lord does the church."* I think not.

In this true situation, a little investigation on her part would have saved a lot of tears, heartbreak, anger, struggle, time and money. That "Come to Jesus Meeting" certainly would have eliminated the possibility of marriage. People and things are not always as they appear. What looks like gold isn't always gold. Perception was not the reality. It was a hard lesson to learn, but she learned it, she got through it, and she got over it. We, as her co-workers, learned that lesson, too. Be very aware. This could happen to the best of us.

Word to the wise: If a man meets you and he's attracted to you because of your beauty and you look polished [meaning that your hair is always done, your fingernails and toenails are always manicured and pedicured, your clothes are always cute, and your makeup (including those long fake eyelashes) is always perfect], he has to take you and keep you as he finds you. Keep yourself up after you get married. Your keeping yourself up was the reason he was attracted to you in the first place. If after you're married to him, he tells you that you don't need to purchase or do the things that attracted him, THERE IS DEFINITELY A PROBLEM! I learned this the hard way.

A man who is interested in you for a relationship that leads to marriage has to take you as he finds you. If you are high maintenance, as some men say, and he's attracted to you, then he has to keep you in the fashion you're accustomed to. If he's unwilling to pay for the upkeep, he should leave you alone. No woman wants to be brought down from what she was able to do for herself.

In personal injury cases, if a person who has a medical condition (back problem for example) is involved in a traffic accident where someone else's car hits her car from behind, the person who caused the accident has to take her as he found her and restore her and her property back to the way they were prior to the accident. In other words, if the victim already had a medical condition, and the car accident aggravated that condition, the person who caused the accident must pay for the additional medical relief of that aggravated condition in addition to the vehicle repair and any other associated costs to restore the person to the way she was prior to the accident as much as possible.

Your Criminal Record

The criminal record you create with the Police Department or any law enforcement agency will follow you throughout all of your life. That record, depending on its contents, can stigmatize and paralyze you, label you, and hinder your dreams and your future plans. If you have created and developed a criminal record while growing up as a teenager, unless you have it expunged and sealed, it could hold you back from any future plans you may have for entering such occupations as a police officer, a government official, or a secret service agent. Your criminal record could hinder you from obtaining a government job, running for a political office, or any type of aerospace job or aerospace subcontractor job. If you intend to work in the aerospace field, for example, your criminal record could hinder you from obtaining a security clearance, which is very important in that field. You cannot be a teacher on any grade level if you have a criminal record that involves misdemeanors or felonies such as felony speeding tickets, DUIs, public intoxication, prostitution, lewd and lascivious conduct, rape, extortion, possession of illegal fire arms, possession, use and sale of drugs, burglary, etc.

Your criminal record could also hinder you from entering into the military to serve your country and secure wonderful military benefits, which include financial assistance to go to college or trade school once you are **"honorably discharged"** from military service. It could hinder you from purchasing a home using your veterans' benefits.

If you are **"dishonorably discharged"** from military service, it's just like having a "**felony criminal record"** that will stay with you throughout your whole life. Most companies have that dreaded question on their applications for employment that ask: "Have you ever been convicted of a felony?" If your answer is "YES", you have a 50/50 chance of getting hired, depending on the company. If you lie by answering "NO" and you get hired, when they investigate that part of your application (and they always do, usually within a couple of months), you will be immediately terminated, discharged, or fired on the spot and walked off the job. You won't be able to use that employer as a reference when you seek another job.

Speeding tickets, DUIs, car accidents that you caused, etc., all add to your criminal record, which can hinder you in your future when you least expect it. It would be such a shame to go to college and get a degree for that ultimate job, only to be stopped in your tracks by your own criminal record.

It doesn't matter that your so-called friend went to jail with you behind the same nonsense. It doesn't matter that she or he was the instigator who got you in trouble. It doesn't matter that you made the wrong choice to get snotty with a Police Officer when he asked you for your identification. The choice, decision, action and consequences will be on your record, and your record will affect all of your future. True, it will be on your friend's record, too, but you should be concerned about you. Your friend may not care about her future like you should care about yours.

You are known by the company you keep. If you're always seen with people who are suspect, you will be suspect, too. Being at the wrong place at the wrong time with the wrong people for the wrong reasons will definitely put a mark on your criminal record. That combination of circumstances and people always tend to create something bad.

There's a lot of "reality shows" on television these days, and these programs are watched by the majority of young people who believe these shows to be very exciting, action packed, and entertaining. However, the sad part about "reality shows" is that the real, true, sad, harsh, and many times life altering (if not life-destroying) consequences are never shown.

Young people who do crimes and get caught tend to fall into a few categories: (1) They had no family members to teach them right from wrong, family values, or morals while they were growing up. (2) They have no concept of negative consequences for negative actions. (3) They lack self-esteem and do things destructive to themselves and to others while in search of attention by someone, anyone, who would care enough about them. (4) They don't seem to care whether they live or die; they are willing to destroy themselves because they believe there is nothing after they are dead – like they won't exist after they die. (5) They are self-centered and don't care about anybody else. And (6), they believe they are so smart and slick that they can get away with anything.

Unfortunately, reality is just that – it's real! The carjacking chases you see on the news are real, and the consequences of being locked up in jail with no possibility of getting out in less than 16 months (or more) because you failed to pull over when requested by the Police is a very hard reality. You will definitely get plenty of time behind bars to think about why you did what you did. You'll have plenty of time to determine whether it was worth it. You will have time to think about what you could have been doing with all that personal time if only you were free. Your time will now be spent being directed by someone else telling you when to get up, when to eat, when to go to the bathroom, when to exercise, etc. You won't be able to go to the movies when you want, go for a ride, visit with friends, watch television, listen to the radio, go to the beauty shop, go shopping, or do anything you want.

I understand that the court system will not even consider any possibility of going before the judge until after at least sixteen months or more are served. Think about it; sixteen months is a long time. Sixteen months breaks down to 485 days, which breaks down to 11,640 hours, which breaks down to 698,400 minutes, which breaks down to 41,904,000 seconds of your personal "free" time wasted because of a wrong choice that you, yourself, made. Evading arrest by the Police, endangering innocent people on the road, damaging property in the process that you will eventually have to pay for, wasting taxpayer money to pay the Police to chase you down, etc., all have serious consequences within the law. I'm just talking about one particular crime and its ensuing consequences that must and will be paid, but there are so many more.

I met a girl in junior high school who had the same interests in things as me. We began to hang out together, we both loved the Beatles at the time, and we cried every time we saw them on the Ed Sullivan Show back in the 1960's. (Don't ask me why we cried when we saw the Beatles; I haven't got a clue.) We even had our hair cut the same as the Beatles. She became my best friend. We would meet on the way to school and walk and talk together, we had most of our classes together, and we would go over to each other's homes on weekends to play records and hang out. We were practically inseparable. My mom liked my friend, and she didn't mind me being at my friend's house or her being over to my house. Her mother felt the same way about me.

One Saturday morning, my friend called and asked me if I would like to go to the shopping mall with her. I asked my mom and she said it was okay after I finished my chores around the house. I finished my work, took a bath, got dressed, and I was ready by 3:00 p.m. My mom gave me a couple of dollars to spend. She did not have much money, and the money she gave me was truly a sacrifice for her and a true gift to me.

My mom told me to be home within a couple of hours. So, I left and met my friend halfway to the mall for it wasn't too far from our homes. We walked through the stores together, bought penny candy, tried on clothes, looked through teen magazines, and bought Beatle cards. It was getting late and time for us to head back home, but my friend wanted to go into the Thrifty's Pharmacy to get a candy bar. I told her that I had to be home on time or my mom would not allow me to go out with her again. I went into the store with her, browsed through a few more teen magazines, and came outside to wait for her. My friend came out of the store about five minutes later, and we laughed and talked on the way home.

Halfway home, my friend pulled out of her pockets all sorts of candy, different lipsticks, an assortment of makeup, and other stuff that she had stolen out of the Thrifty's Pharmacy. She showed all of it to me and asked me if I wanted some of it. I was stunned and hurt – all at the same time. I was horrified! I knew that if she got caught shoplifting in the store while I was with her, I would be arrested, too. The Police would be called, and we would both go to jail. I knew my mother would come to the jail and sign me out. I knew I would die by the hands of my mother for being involved in theft. My father's background of being in and out of jail loomed in the back of my mind, and I definitely did not want to follow in his footsteps. I knew my mother would be deeply hurt. But most importantly, I knew I definitely did not want to have a criminal record. How dare my "so-called" friend put me in such a terrible position. Some friend!

I immediately told my friend to take all the stuff she stole back to the store, but she refused. Our friendship ended that afternoon on the way home from the mall. At times I think about my friend, and I do miss her, but the cost of her friendship was too great. My mom asked about her every now and then, but I would just tell her that we had a difference of opinion. If my mom only knew what my friend had done, she would have been very upset.

After we graduated from high school, I learned that my former friend got into some trouble with the law and actually went to jail a few times. Some of the crimes she committed and went to jail for were shoplifting; receiving and selling stolen property; and buying, selling, and using drugs. She has a criminal record that will be with her throughout the rest of her life. Each time she fills out an application for a job, she will have to check the box that acknowledges she has committed a crime (be it a misdemeanor or a felony). If she wanted to work in the aerospace, law enforcement, military or government fields, she would not be able to get a job.

Although I felt bad for my friend, I am so glad I made the right decision for myself in not taking part in her crime. I ended the friendship, which was also the right decision. She did not value our friendship enough to do the right thing, and she endangered me in the process. I believe God was definitely with me that day. He protected me. He gave me wisdom and discernment. I was still golden in my mom's eyes, and that was extremely important to me.

Young people who have no moral compass or common sense commit other stupid crimes. There are the joy riders – those who take other people's cars, drive with abandonment until they either get caught by the Police, wreck the stolen vehicle, or wind up in an accident possibly killing themselves and their passengers, or worse, injuring or killing an innocent person. There are the thieves – those who get caught because they accidentally leave something in the store that identifies them while running out with the merchandise. There are those who bully and beat up weaker people for no reason – they either put the person in the hospital or they kill them. None of these types of people have a problem engaging in these activities until the consequences set in.

I know of many parents who pay a ton of money to keep their kids out of jail on the first offense, and I strongly disagree with this line of thinking wholeheartedly! The kid should stay in jail that first time to experience the full effects of the consequences for their action(s) that led them to be arrested. If nothing else, they will think twice before going down that path again. It only takes one time in jail for an impressionable young mind to **"get it"**, and they usually do **"get it"** that first and only time – if the parents don't weaken. However, there are exceptions.

I worked for a criminal attorney for about six years, and we encountered several cases involving young teenagers and young male adults. One case in particular was very sad. This kid was about 17 years old. His parents were very wealthy. He had a brand new foreign model car, which was a sport coupe tricked out with all the bells, whistles, and plenty of NOZ gas. A lot of money went into that car. The car flashed, it dashed, and it looked like it was going 100 mph even while parked. The car was a sight to behold. Those fast car movies had nothing on this kid's car. The kid's family lived in an exclusive part of Orange County.

Late one night while racing down the freeway, this kid and his friend were clocked and caught by the CHP. They were doing over 100 mph on the San Diego Freeway around 1:00 a.m. The kid refused to cooperate with the CHP Officer, so he was hooked and booked at the jail. His hot sports car was immediately impounded.

The next morning when I arrived at work, there were several voice-messages on my phone for my boss. The messages were from the parents of the 17-year-old who was being held at the Police Station. I transcribed the messages and called my boss to inform him. He told me to call the parents and find out which jail the kid was in and to ask for the kid's bail number. I did as he requested and had the information waiting for him when he arrived in the office. My boss spoke to the parents over the phone, and he had me set an appointment for them to come into the office later that afternoon. My boss arranged to have the kid bailed out that same day as **"demanded"** by the parents. I typed up the standard retainer agreement for the parents to sign. [The retainer agreement is a contract for payment of attorney's fees and services.]

The parents picked up their son from jail, came into the office and, without hesitation, signed the retainer agreement and wrote a check for the full amount of the retainer for my boss's legal services. One of the things that caught my attention and really raised my eyebrows was the statement the father made in the meeting with my boss. The father told my boss emphatically that he did not want his son incarcerated with "those criminals." I found that statement to be very strange since his son was arrested for criminal behavior on the freeway that endangered the lives of people traveling on the same freeway. The kid was acting like a criminal. Shoot, he was a criminal. The father then told my boss that money was no object and to do everything within his power to get his son out of the mess.

My boss had me place the son in another conference room while he spoke to the parents. He then left the parents in the first conference room and went to the other conference room to speak to the teenager. The meeting with the teenager lasted about fifteen minutes. My boss emerged from the meeting very disturbed. He then went back into the conference room where the parents were, and he discussed his findings about the 17-year old with the parents. He informed them that because of their son's attitude, lack of remorse and arrogance, they should allow their son to accept whatever punishment the court deemed appropriate for his wrongful actions. He stated that their son did not understand or realize the severity of his actions, did not appear to care about the situation he was facing, and that it was very likely he would be in trouble again with the law. My boss explained to the parents that their son was uncooperative with him and with the Police Officers, very arrogant, stubborn, and unremorseful. He stated that their son needed to learn his lesson so this situation doesn't occur in the future. However, the father erupted in anger, stating that he would not have his son in with those gangbangers, drug dealers and criminals. He insisted that his son was not like them and, therefore, should not be with them. The father went on to say that he would handle his son. However, my boss stated he would do the best he could to honor the parents' wishes.

The father and the mother were very proud people from a very traditional background, but apparently their son did not hold to the traditions of his family. The wife did not speak unless she was spoken to. She said absolutely nothing, and her head was hung in shame during the whole meeting. She humbly said goodbye when the family left the office that evening.

My boss went to court on behalf of the 17-year-old and got the charges reduced, got a reasonable fine, and got community service for the teenager. The father was ecstatic. After they all left the courtroom, my boss gave the father of the teenager a strong warning.

He told the father that he feared the teen had not learned his lesson because things went so well for him in the quick bailout, in the court decision, and in the prompt payment of fines. My boss reiterated to the father that he should not have paid for his son to get out of the mess he created. A few months later the teenager turned 18 years of age.

About a year later, I was relaxing in bed with my husband while watching the 11:00 p.m. news on a Saturday night. The top story of the evening was that a vehicle was struck by another vehicle that was speeding on the freeway at a felony rate of speed. The vehicle that was hit was a van that spun out of control, flipped over and burst into flames. All occupants of the van perished in the flames (two adults and their 4 or 6 children). I felt bad about what happened. We later turned off the television and went to bed.

The following Monday when I arrived at work, I noticed that the message light on my phone was lit. I began to take the messages off the phone; there were at least 6 messages for my boss from the father of the teenager who had been in trouble over a year ago. I immediately called my boss on his cell-phone for he had not yet arrived at the office. I informed him about the messages. He immediately contacted the father of the now over 18-year old **adult**.

As things turned out, the same teenager, who my boss had helped a year earlier, was in jail for the horrific traffic accident that occurred Saturday night on the freeway where a whole family burned to death. When my boss told me, I was devastated. It was a very somber day.

My boss met with the parents that afternoon to discuss the case. Would you believe that the father still wanted to get his son out of jail at all costs! His son had turned 18 years of age and was now considered an adult. There was no way possible that this man's son was going to dodge this bullet. My boss stated that he would do what he could, but he apprised the father of the law regarding what had happened. The family was devastated.

The father did not want his son in with those criminals, but he failed to realize that his son was one of those criminals. I believe the teenager is still in prison to this day, and it's been well over 10 years. No amount of money, no amount of apologies, and no amount of time spent in jail could ever bring back the lives of those who died that Saturday night.

Needless to say, this young man's criminal record is trashed beyond repair.

Some people think they are so tough that they can do wrong and get away with it. If you are big and bad enough to do the crime, be big and bad enough to do the time. Stop running through alleys, hopping over walls and fences, and hiding in or behind trash cans and trash dumpsters, while being chased by the Police. You've been found out, you've been spotted, and an army of Police are after you with their dogs. They out-flank you by a hundred to one, with the best equipment, fastest cars, and the meanest looking dogs. It's downright stupid for you to resist. You know you're done, so why run. They got you.

I've seen so many people on the television running like frantic, scared rats after they've been targeted and they have absolutely nowhere to go. They certainly don't look so tough anymore. They should be tough enough to stand behind their actions. They were stupid to do the crime in the first place, and now that stupidity has carried them through the chase to capture and to incarceration. It was a lose-lose situation in the first place and they didn't even realize it. What's up with that?

<u>Rule Of Thumb No. 1:</u> There are mistakes that can be fixed and there are mistakes that cannot be fixed. For example, if you steal something, you can give it back, pay a fine and do the time. But, if you kill someone, you cannot bring that person back to life no matter what you do. In essence, don't do things you can't fix. Better still, don't do wrong at all. There will be consequences to pay. Can you handle it?!

<u>Rule Of Thumb No. 2:</u> If you can't do the time, don't do the crime. It doesn't matter that your friends got caught, too, doing the crime. It's you who will be sitting in that prison cell, and your friends won't be in there with you. In jail, you are not your own boss. You will be told what to do and when. There will be no air conditioning when you get hot and bothered, and no heat if you get cold. There will not be a car available to take you for a ride at your convenience. You can't watch television or movies that you want to watch, and you can't play video games when you want. You can't wear what you want or go where you want. You can't get a pizza when you want, and you can't eat what you want. You can't jump in a pool or go to the beach when you want. There's nowhere to go and nothing to do of your own free will when you're incarcerated. You're stuck, and stuck for a while. Your freedom is gone. What value do you place on your freedom?

Your Self-Worth/Value

Your ultimate value is based on how God values you. If you know how much value you have to God, you will know how to value yourself.

You are the most important person to God. As a teenage girl, a young lady, or a woman, remember that you are absolutely priceless, and what you possess within you is priceless. You were bought with a heavy price paid by the blood of Lord Jesus Christ, Himself. By not thinking of your value to God, you tarnish yourself by forgetting whom you belong to and who you are. You are allowing society (careless people, television, radio, internet websites, movies, teen magazines, glamour magazines, trash trades, etc.) to dictate who you are to be, what you are to wear, how you are to act, and what decisions you are to make without even considering the consequences, which will ultimately become your downfall as you go through life. Society won't tell you this, but you bear your consequences alone, not society.

There are many scriptures in the Bible that reflect God's love and provision for you.

John 3:16 states: *"For God so loved the world that He gave His only begotten Son that whoever believes in Him should not perish but have everlasting life."* God loves you so much that He made the ultimate sacrifice to pay for all your sins. He let His Son, the Lord Jesus Christ, die on the cross to not only pay for your sins, but by believing that He is the Son of God who was raised from the dead, you have a spot reserved for you in Heaven. Your name is written in the Lamb's Book of Life.

God loves you so much that He provides protection for you. He has given you power over anything that would try to hurt or destroy you. *Luke 10:19* states: *"Behold, I give you the authority to trample over serpents and scorpions, and over all the power of the enemy, and nothing shall by any means hurt you."* So you should not be fearful of anything. Fear includes worry, doubt, stress, nervousness, anxiousness, depression, peer pressure, failure, and anything that would hinder you. *2 Timothy 1:7* states: *"For God has not give us a spirit of fear, but of power and of love and of a sound mind."*

God loves you so much that He has forgiven all your sins, He has healed your body from diseases, He has redeemed your life from destruction, He has given you loving kindness and tender mercies, and He has satisfied your mouth with good things. God has given you all of these blessings. *Psalm 103:1-5* states: *"Bless the Lord, O my soul; and all that is within me, bless His holy name. Bless the Lord, O my soul, and forget not all His benefits; who forgives all your iniquities, who heals all your diseases, who redeems your life from destruction, who crowns you with loving kindness and tender mercies, who satisfies your mouth with good things, so that your youth is renewed like the eagle's."*

God has given you a purpose in life. He has given you a future and a hope. *Jeremiah 29:11* states: *"For I know the thoughts that I think toward you, says the Lord, thoughts of peace and not of evil, to give you a future and a hope."* You are complete in God because you are sealed. *Ephesians 4:30* states: *"And do not grieve the Holy Spirit of God, by whom you were sealed for the day of redemption."* You will complete your purpose unto the day of redemption. *Colossians 2:10* states: *"And you are complete in Him who is the head of all principality and power."*

God has given you grace as a gift. *Ephesians 2:8-9* states: *"For by grace you have been saved through faith, and that not of yourselves, it is the gift of God, not of works, lest anyone should boast."*

You are the righteousness of God. You are highly favored. *Romans 3:22-23* states: *"Even the righteousness of God through faith in Jesus Christ, to all and on all who believe. For there is no difference; for all have sinned and come short of the glory of God."*

God loves you so much that He has provided for you to ask of Him anything in the name of Jesus, in line with His Word, and you shall have it. *Mark 11:24* states: *"Therefore I say to you, whatever things you ask when you pray, believe that you receive them and you will have them."* Your requests must be made in accordance with His will and His word.

The above scriptures show God's love toward you, how He values you, and how He wants the very best for you. The Bible is riddled with scriptures concerning His love for you. Believing in God and in His Son opens up multiple blessings to you throughout your whole life until you go to be with God and the Lord in Heaven.

You definitely have value. God values you, so you should value you.

Your Conscience

In *John 8:32, Jesus says: "You shall know the truth and the truth shall make you free."* In essence, be sure the truth will find you out. Knowing the truth is not enough; you must act on the truth that you know.

In the book of Genesis, God made man and woman, and they were both naked and they were not ashamed. *(Genesis 2:20-25)* The serpent came along and tempted Eve to eat fruit from the "tree of the knowledge of good and evil" by reasoning with her. Since what the serpent said made some kind of sense to her, she did eat the fruit from the "tree of the knowledge of good and evil", but she made things worse because she also encouraged Adam to eat the fruit. Now Adam was right there with Eve as the serpent was telling her that the fruit was good and that they would become like God if they ate from the tree. Adam had an opportunity not only to chastise Eve and stop her from making a grave mistake, but he also had opportunity to not eat of the tree and to rebuke and dismiss the serpent (satan). God told Adam earlier not to eat from the "tree of the knowledge of good and evil", and He also told Adam that if he disobeyed, he would surely die. *(Genesis 2:17)* Apparently, Adam did tell Eve what God said about not eating from the "tree of the knowledge of good and evil" before she ate of it and gave Adam some of the fruit to eat. And, unfortunately, Adam did eat.

Some people just don't believe fat meat's greasy! Apparently, Adam and Eve didn't believe it either! Some people don't believe that God says what He means and means what He says. Because both Adam and Eve disobeyed God's warning and ate from the "tree of the knowledge of good and evil", they knew instantly they had sinned. God did not have to search for Adam and Eve because He already knew where they were. He knew they disobeyed Him. He knew they were hiding in their shame because of their disobedience. But God did ask Adam where he was, and Adam told Him they were hiding because they knew they were naked. When God asked who told them they were naked and did they eat from the "tree of the knowledge of good and evil", Adam blamed Eve, and Eve blamed the snake. Because of their disobedience, God gave consequences to Adam, Eve, and to the snake for their disobedience. He also banished all of them from the Garden of Eden because He did not want them to disobey again and go to eat from the "tree of life" where they would live forever. Adam and Eve's consequences for their actions in opposition to God's instructions were that Adam had to farm the dry, harsh land for food and shelter outside of Eden, and Eve had harsh labor pain in delivering her children.

Why did Adam listen to Eve instead of relying on what God, his Creator, told him earlier? Why did Eve listen to a snake in the grass, so to speak, instead of believing what Adam told her earlier? Was there a breakdown in communication between Adam and God or Adam and Eve? Adam was with Eve as she was being beguiled, seduced, and convinced by the snake. The persuasion of the serpent apparently made natural worldly sense to Eve although there were certainly other trees of fruit in the Garden of Eden that were just as tasty. Then Eve beguiled Adam into reasoning that there could be no harm in eating the fruit. They did not immediately see the consequence that they set in motion when they ate the fruit. I'm sure Adam was extremely angry with himself more than he was angry with Eve because he, himself, knew better because he was specifically and directly told by God not to eat of the "tree of the knowledge of good and evil." What was it that persuaded them both to step out of bounds with God and into the consequences of their disobedience? Adam allowed his physical senses to overrule God's word. Adam and Eve were the first to experience God's laws of reaping and sowing, as referenced in *Galatians 6:7-8,* which states: *"Do not be deceived, God is not mocked; for whatever a man sows, that he will also reap. For he who sows to his flesh will of the flesh reap corruption, but he who sows to the Spirit will of the Spirit reap everlasting life."* Adam and Eve reaped what they sowed, reaped more than they sowed, and reaped later than they sowed.

And, that's just how it's done today with disobedience. For example, some guy comes up to you and your girlfriends in the shopping mall and introduces himself to you. He shows you that special attention, he favors you above your girlfriends, and he consistently flirts with you. He asks you out on a date. He hints of enticing you to more than dinner on the date. He wants to sleep with you, and you (in your mind) want to sleep with him. You think he looks so good. He's built well with those thick abs, tight buns, and those bedroom eyes. You think it would feel so good to be with him in bed. Your mind is racing. Your girlfriends, who are with you when you meet the guy, tell you they think he's good-looking, too, and how they would love to take him off your hands if you won't take him.

You know what God's word says about having sex outside of wedlock (marriage), but you reason to yourself that this "one time" is not going to hurt, that no one will know, not even God, Himself. Your conscience is screaming at you, but you turn it off each and every time it pops up in your mind. Your eyes are fixated on this good-looking guy who is just all over you, and, oh, he smells so good, too! You can't take your eyes or your mind off of him.

The date is set. You go out to a decent dinner, and then you do it – you sleep with him. You had sex with him and now the thrill is gone and so is he. It's over. It was a one-night stand to him, and it's over. A few days go by and he doesn't even call you. A couple of weeks go by and you see him from a distance with some other woman. It hurts. You feel used and cheated.

Two more weeks go by, and you're not feeling so well in your pelvic area. You are itching in your pubic area, you've got some sort of discharge, and your pelvic area is really hurting. You make an appointment with the doctor. After being examined by the doctor, you find out that you have an STD that was given to you by that tall, dark, and handsome guy. You have entered the **"Consequence Zone**." Now you hear your conscience, which is saying, "I told you so." You turn your conscience off again because you're angry with yourself and you are convicted by your conscience. What did your conscience do but try to stop you from making that terrible mistake that you are now suffering behind.

Our conscience is built into all of us as a warning signal that tells us when we are heading in the wrong direction. It will tell us if we are about to do something stupid or flat out wrong. Our conscience gives us fair warning ahead of time. Our conscience will also convict us after we disobey.

The problem is that we don't always listen to what God is telling us through our conscience. We listen more to our flesh. We give our flesh way more credit and power than it should ever have. We listen to the five senses of the flesh (hear, taste, smell, touch, and see). We also listen to our friends that can be identified as another type of sense – nonsense. We listen to what we can imagine in our minds by doing the things that entice us, tempt us, and sway us in our minds. We deceive ourselves long before we do the act. Then we go for it, not thinking or realizing the ensuing consequences of our decisions that our actions have set in motion.

Before you make a decision and act on it, you're in control of your situation and any accompanying consequences. **However, once you act on your decision, you are no longer in control of the ensuing consequences.** The consequences are now in control of you, and there's nothing you can do about what consequences come to you. You cannot choose what consequences you will deal with and what consequences you won't deal with. You cannot choose how long the consequences will last. Your hands are tied. You have set things in motion that you no longer control; these things now control you. In *James 1:14-16,* the Apostle James states: *"But each one is tempted when he [she] is drawn away by his [her] own desires and enticed. Then, when desire has conceived, it gives birth to sin, and sin, when it is full grown, brings forth death. Do not be deceived, my beloved brethren."* As you can see by this scripture, you are the one who makes the final decision, based on what enticed, seduced, swayed or tempted you, and you are the one who will bear the consequences.

So, when you're with a guy and he's getting your flesh all enflamed by enticing and seducing you through physically touching and kissing you, and you know this is leading to having sex with him, this is the critical time to ask yourself the following questions:

1) Is God with me right now and is He watching me?

2) Can I really do this in front of God?

3) Is this something I really need right now or can I wait to do things God's way?

4) Does this guy mean more to me than God?

5) Is this guy worth me disobeying God's Word?

6) Am I willing to pay the consequences that will come from this situation?

7) Am I willing to alter my life and my plans forever for one moment of physical pleasure?

8) Is this guy really what I want in my future? Does he want me in his future?

9) Is this guy really looking out for my best interest, or is he looking out for his own physical satisfaction?

10) Why can't I wait?

Part of the reason most marriages don't last (secular and religious) is because of premarital sex. A man who proposes marriage to a woman is called a fiancé. His title means that he makes a promise of marriage to a woman; he proposes a trust that he will marry her and stay married. The woman he proposes marriage to is called his fiancée, or a woman engaged to be married. This means she is unavailable and no longer on the market for other men to date her.

A woman, who is a virgin, who has been proposed to by a man for marriage, tends to believe that fulfilling the man's request for premarital sex will definitely ensure that he will take her to the alter, marry her, and stay married to her. WRONG, WRONG, WRONG!!!! After she has given herself to him so easily prior to the wedding (even a few days prior), his value of the marriage is now somewhat diminished. His thinking may now be that he really was able to conquer her before marriage. He won! Now that the man has conquered the woman before the marriage, does he really need to get married? Hmm?!!! The idea of marriage now takes on a whole different twist. Even the vows in the marriage ceremony take on a different tone in both the groom and the bride because there is no longer any purity. The question now becomes whether he will be at the altar to get married, and, if he gets married, will he stay married? Remember, men are conquerors and after they have conquered, they go on to other things.

Why couldn't she wait until after she was married? She was the one definitely **in control** in the area of sex at the time. Of course, her conscience was telling her to wait, but she got caught up in the fantasy of the marriage and in the bling of the ring instead of relying on God's word concerning marriage. She lost her focus on the right thing to do, and she put her focus on doing the wrong thing by succumbing to her fiancé's wishes prior to marriage (having premarital sex). **IF EVER THERE IS A TIME TO HOLD OUT, IT IS DEFINITELY BEFORE YOU GET MARRIED!!!!!!!!!!!!!!**

A man realizes how very special you are when you walk down that aisle as a virgin to marry him on the wedding day. Vows are spoken between the two of you and to God, for He is in the midst of your union. Your vows mean that you have made a covenant (contract) and a commitment (obligation) to God and to each other to stay together in love for one another and for the love of God. *Ecclesiastes 5:4-5* states: *"When you make a vow to God, do not delay to pay it, for He has no pleasure in fools. Pay what you have vowed. Better not to vow than to vow and not pay."* Your marriage should last with the understanding of the vows you made to one another and to God.

On that wedding night when you present yourself in purity to your husband, he will feel honored and you will be so very glad you waited. He'll be appreciative that you saved yourself just for him, and for him alone. During the marriage, there will be a stronger bond between the two of you because he knows you totally belong to him, and you gave him that special gift out of your love for him. He will honor and treasure you because you were his virgin.

Men are looking for that special thing that sets the marriage in place for them, and that set's his wife apart from all other women he's had in the past. That special thing is your virginity. Although most men feel it's okay for them to get their experience in the bed, most men don't feel the same way about the woman they are marrying. Virginity is an extremely crucial factor in marriage. Men believe it is, and we should, too. If you value yourself and listen to your conscience, you will remain pure until you say "I DO."

There is power and blessings in being obedient to God, in following your conscience, and in living a disciplined life. Protect your sexual integrity. Don't sacrifice your virtue to prove your love to someone who may just lust after you, but not love you.

We should always be aware of our conscience in all that we think, say, and do in order to make the right decisions that create the right actions to get the best results. That's why it's important to meditate on the word of God, which changes and molds our minds, and keeps us from making mistakes.

One particular sin that is on the rise and taking hold of teenage girls' and women's minds is pornography. Just the sight of a pornographic image instantly burns into your mind, and it stays there. You can become addicted to pornography just as easily as you can become addicted to drugs, alcohol, sex, gambling, and other vices. Pornography is seen through your eye-gate and goes directly into your mind. Not only that, pornography instantly activates all of your senses. *1 John 2:16* states: *"For all that is in the world – the lust of the flesh, the lust of the eyes, and the pride of life – is not of the Father, but is of the world."* Jesus says in *Matthew 5:29: "If your right eye causes you to sin, pluck it out and cast it from you; for it is more profitable for you that one of your members perish, than for your whole body to be cast into hell." Matthew 18:9* states: *"And if your eye causes you to sin, pluck it out and cast it from you. It is better for you to enter into life with one eye, rather than having two eyes to be cast into hell fire."* These last two scriptures spoken by Jesus, Himself, let's you know how serious this sin is and to not allow your eyes to look on such things of the world that will destroy you. Don't go plucking your eyes out if you are guilty of this particular sin, but repent (ask forgiveness of God, change your mind and your heart, and go a different direction – just stop doing it). God will forgive you. *Romans 13:14* states: *"But put on the Lord Jesus Christ, and make no provision for the flesh, to fulfill its lusts." 1 Peter 2:11* states: *"Beloved, I beg you as sojourners and pilgrims, abstain from fleshly lusts which war against the soul."*

Indulging in pornography will lead you in the wrong direction, which will eventually destroy you. The Apostle Paul states in *Galatians 5:16-21: "I say then: Walk in the Spirit [the Holy Spirit], and you shall not fulfill the lust of the flesh. For the flesh lusts against the Spirit, and the Spirit against the flesh; and these are contrary to one another so that you do not do the things that you wish. But if you are led by the Spirit, you are not under the law. Now the works of the flesh are evident, which are: adultery, fornication, uncleanness, lewdness, idolatry, sorcery, hatred, contentions, jealousies, outbursts of wrath, selfish ambitions, dissentions, heresies, envy, murders, drunkenness, revelries, and the like; of which I tell you beforehand, just as I also told you in time past, that those who practice such things will not inherit the kingdom of God."* So, if you are allowing your eye-gates (your eyes) to receive the images of pornography, if you are reading pornographic material, if you are watching pornography on television, or if you are engaging in pornographic activities, you will not enter the kingdom of God. If any such thing enters your senses and your emotions, your conscience will immediately let you know, and that's the time to remove yourself totally from it and rebuke satan and his tactics "in the name of Jesus."

Don't give entrance to any pornography in any place in your life. Don't allow it in your eyesight, your hearing, or any of your senses. Don't allow it in your mind. *Galatians 6:7-8* states: *"Do not be deceived, God is not mocked; for whatever a man [woman] sows, that he [she] will also reap. For he [she] who sows to his [her] flesh will of the flesh reap corruption, but he [she] who sows to the Spirit will of the Spirit reap everlasting life."*

Your conscience tells you that you know better, but the Holy Spirit tells you why. God has sent a helper to those of us who have accepted Jesus Christ as our Lord and Savior. God has sent us the Holy Spirit, who is a person who dwells within us and who works with our conscience. The Holy Spirit is part of the Trinity – The Father, The Son, and The Holy Spirit. In *John 14:16-17,* Jesus says: *"And I will pray the Father, and He will give you another Helper, that He may abide with you forever – the Spirit of truth, whom the world cannot receive, because it neither sees Him nor knows Him, but you know Him, for He dwells with you and will be in you."*

The Holy Spirit helps you by working with your conscience to give you truth, discernment, wisdom and understanding. So, with the Holy Spirit, you know beforehand whether your thoughts, motives, plans, and your will line up with God's word and His will for your life. The Holy Spirit works with your conscience to let you know whether you're about to do wrong. You can also silence the Holy Spirit by consistently ignoring Him. This is known as having a "reprobate mind." Don't allow your flesh, feelings, and emotions to lead you astray. Be led by the Holy Spirit of God.

We are always to look to please God in our thoughts and in our actions. In *Acts 24:16*, the Apostle Paul states: *"This being so, I myself always strive to have a conscience without offense toward God and men."* In essence, strive to do right by God and by men with the assistance of the Holy Spirit and your conscience.

Summary

In summary, your reputation, children, health, credit, criminal record, your self-worth, and your conscience all play major roles in the successes or failures in your life. All of these elements play upon and intersect one another throughout your life. How you consider them in your daily thinking, decisions, and actions will determine your resulting consequences, good or bad. These elements will determine how successful you will be in the direction you're going, the achievements you're able to attain or unable to attain, how well you lead a peaceful and productive life, and whether or not you're able to fulfill God's purpose in your life.

Chapter 2

Appearance Is Everything!

Chapter 2

Appearance is Everything!

You've Got What It Takes – What The World Takes!

Yes, you have got what it takes! In the world, you've definitely got what it takes for the world. You're young, you're naive, you're attractive, you have a nice shape, and you have a nice smile. You have some money, you have good credit, and you have a car. You're basically doing well for yourself.

You look good to others from their view of you. They want to be around you, they want to invite you to their social activities, and they think you look good being with them. In fact, they think you enhance them by your presence. They believe they have value in other people's eyes because they have you with them. You make them feel good about themselves when you're with them. They like you so much that they want you to follow them and do what they do.

The question is, though, why are you with them? Do they provide some value to you? Do they enhance your presence? Do they make you feel good about yourself when they are with you? Are you going along with their program because you're getting something out of it? Does being with them validate you? Are you going to their social activities because of you or because of them?

Because you are physically attractive to others, are you allowing others to exploit you by telling you what looks good on you, and even buying you provocative clothing because they say you look good in the clothing? Are you purchasing provocative clothing for yourself because you want attention? Are these people showing you off to their friends and associates as if you are a shiny new car they just purchased? Are you allowing others to treat you as a sexual toy to play with and then when they're through with you (they "had" you), you are no longer of interest to them and are tossed aside?

Are you allowing people to take pictures of you in sexually provocative clothing, and then putting your pictures on the Internet? Do you know for sure whether they are doing this? Are you allowing people to take pictures of you in the nude and then putting your nude pictures on the Internet? Do you know for sure whether they are doing this? Are you putting your own provocatively dressed or nude pictures on the Internet or on your cell-phone or on someone else's cell-phone? Do you know how to get your provocative or nude photos out of the Internet or out of your cell-phone? Are you aware there are state and federal laws concerning the use of the Internet, which is under the jurisdiction of the Federal Communication Commission (FCC)? Do you know what the FCC regulations and state laws are for transmitting sexually provocative photos through your cell-phone over cyberspace? Can you say JAIL TIME?????

Or, maybe you're not that physically attractive, but you are ever so grateful to receive others' attention. Do you go along with their program, whatever it is? Do you base how much value you have or don't have on your physical appearance? Do you think others see you as you see yourself? Do you find that you're lacking in areas, such as physical beauty, and you feel you deserve not to be noticed because of it? Do you allow people to treat you poorly because of your physical appearance?

Are you overweight and feel less than human because of it? Do you feel you deserve less attention, less respect, less anything because you feel you're unworthy because you don't fit the mold, whatever that is? Are you allowing people to treat you disrespectfully because of the poor view you have of yourself?

Because you come from a wealthy family, is that so-called friend or that group of so-called friends staying around you because of who you are or because of what they can get from you? Being in a wealthy family definitely requires great responsibility, even greater accountability, greater wisdom, and greater discernment so you can make the right decisions for the right reasons. You need the ability to see people for who they really are, whether their motives are true and correct in their dealings with you, and whether your motives are the same.

Because you have a car, and your so-called friends don't, do they bum rides from you and involve you in their social activities, with you driving?

Does your so-called friend ask to borrow your car to run an errand, but gets speeding and parking tickets and doesn't inform you? Your car registration is due, so you go to register your vehicle and find out at the DMV (Department of Motor Vehicles) that you've got a number of parking tickets that must be paid before you can register your car. You then learn that there is a warrant issued for your arrest because of the speeding tickets that did not get paid in a timely manner because you knew nothing about them. The friend who borrowed your car told the Police Officer who stopped her that she was you and she forgot to bring your driver's license with her. Since you have a clean record, the Police Officer just gave her an additional ticket for not carrying your identification with her, and he let her go.

Does your so-called friend borrow your car and is later involved in a car accident? Your car insurance drops your coverage after it pays the claim, or not, because your friend was not on your insurance policy, which invalidates your insurance coverage. You seek out other car insurance, but now your insurance rates have doubled. Does your friend help pay to restore your vehicle? Does he help pay the high insurance premiums that you are now responsible for?

Do your so-called friends help pay for the gas in your car, yet run all of the gas out as you take them all over town to where they want to go?

Do you know if your friends will sue you if you get into a car accident while taking them where they want to go? Although the accident was not your fault, they were injured. Although your car insurance covers everyone in the vehicle, they know that if they got their own attorney, they could possibly collect double for their trouble from your car insurance and from the other driver's car insurance. Or, they could try to sue you beyond your policy limits and obtain a judgment against you. That judgment could be attached to everything you own, and/or the judgment could attach to any future earnings or future property you may acquire until it's satisfied (paid in full). If your parents have you on their car insurance policy, your parents could possibly be sued beyond policy limits, too, and lose everything they have worked for all their lives.

Maybe you have worn your vehicle and yourself out taking your so-called friends all over town. Will your friends help pay for the repair of your vehicle if it breaks down? Will they help in the cost of upkeep of your car and pay for a car wash or two?

Suppose your friends invite another person, who you do not know, to ride in your car with them and you. You do not question your friends or the stranger now riding with you because you are just dropping him or her off down the street on your way to the mall or to the movies. The Police pull up behind you, they follow you for a few miles, and then they flash their lights signaling you to pull over. You don't know why you're being pulled over by the Police, but you comply. Apparently, the Police had that person (the stranger to you) under surveillance, who you picked up at the request of your friends. That person has a police record, and he or she had been in jail for possession and sale of narcotics and other related crimes.

While you're pulled over waiting for the Police Officer to come to your door and speak to you, that person takes something out of his or her pocket and stuffs it under the seat. The Police Officer notices that person's uneasiness, and the uneasiness of your other passengers as he speaks to you. The Police Officer then calls for backup. When backup arrives, the Officer orders all of you out of the vehicle.

As a courtesy, the Officer asks you for permission to search your vehicle, although he doesn't have to because he has probable cause because of the company you have in your car. The Officer doesn't know whether you're involved in the use, sale or distribution of drugs, but he does know the rap sheet (police record) of that person you picked up at the request of your friends. That person has a history of selling and distributing drugs. You give the Officer permission and he conducts his search of your vehicle. The Officer finds a plastic sandwich bag, which contains little plastic packets of cocaine (enough to be charged for sale and distribution) – definitely a felony amount. The Police Officer found the bag stuffed under the seat near where the stranger was sitting, but it isn't clear whether the plastic bag belonged to him or her because there were others sitting with him or her. The Officer asks whom the bag of cocaine belongs to, and all of you, including the stranger, claim you know nothing about the drugs.

The Officer and his backup arrest all of you. You're hauled off to jail, and, because you were the driver and owner of the vehicle that contained the drugs, your vehicle is now impounded and possibly confiscated. However, you still owe car payments and car insurance premiums on a vehicle that you no longer have in your possession and you may never get back. You now have to obtain legal services of an attorney, which is very costly, to get you out of the mess and to get your vehicle out of police impound.

Because you have your own apartment or home, are your so-called friends always showing up at your door to just hang out with you, to eat up all your food and drink, and to run up your electricity, order movies on your cable television service, and use your telephone like it's theirs? You had not planned on having company for the day or evening, but they just showed up. Then your friends ask you if they can all spend the night. They were not invited over in the first place, and now they want to spend the night at your home. They make long-distance phone calls and have lengthy conversations on your home phone, as if they were paying your telephone bill. You don't have the courage to tell them not to use your phone or to get out of your house.

Do your so-called friends invite other people into your home, who you do not know, while they are visiting you? You allow these people to come into your home because of your friends' invitation to them, thinking that it's just for a visit. Your friends and these strangers bring cigarettes, alcohol and drugs into your home to smoke, drink and shoot-up without even asking your permission? You finally speak up and tell them that you don't want them and their friends smoking, drinking and doing drugs in your home. They are so high and spaced out that they pay you no attention. The next thing you hear is the Police banging on your door demanding entrance. You go to the door and the Police rush in to find your friends and their guests (who, unbeknownst to you, are drug dealers and drug users) jumping out of windows escaping, but leaving behind their drug paraphernalia. Since you're the only one standing in your home, you're immediately arrested and taken to jail. You try to contact your friends to put up funds to bail you out, but no one returns your two phone calls. Unless you are represented by a really high-powered and expensive attorney, you are tried, convicted, and will serve a substantial amount of time in prison. You have lost your freedom and your home.

Do your so-called friends bring other people to your home, or to your apartment, so they can have sex? Do you allow this? Do you join in? Do you question your friends as to why they want to have sex with people at your place rather than at their own place? Do you question your friends' motives, morality, and friendship?

Do your so-called friends come to your home asking you if they can store some of their stuff in your home for a little while? They tell you they will be back in a few days to pick it up. You don't know what the stuff is, or who it really belongs to, or whether it's illegal. It could be illegal drugs, stolen property, guns, money, anything! Do you allow this? Do you know why your friends are asking you to store their stuff at your place rather than at their own place? Depending on what you're storing for your friends, are you willing to go to jail or even die behind the stuff your friends ask you to store for them? Do you want the friendship that badly?

You may have great credit and some money in the bank. There is a man who recently came into your life. You like him so much that he knows it. He begins to take advantage of you because of your feelings for him. He feels comfortable enough in his conversations with you to ask where you work, whether you save like he does, or if you own your home or condo like he does. He asks you if you have any children or are you paying any child support. He asks what your credit score is to see if it's higher than his "fictitious" credit score.

Does he invite you to his home or is he always meeting you at your home or at some social spot? Have you seen his car or does he always want to meet you or have you pick him up on some corner near his so-called home because he says his vehicle is in the shop?

Does this guy you like so much tell you that he's got an investment in some big business venture, but he needs more money to see it come to fruition? Does he ask you to invest with him and offer you a part of the proceeds gained when the investment comes through? Is this offer in writing? Does he provide you any conclusive details on paper?

Does this guy you like so much ask you to contribute money so he can start a business, but does not show you a business plan or his bank statements referencing how much money (collateral) he plans to invest in his own business? Does he introduce you to his partners or associates? Does he show you his business license, his FICO score, his Fictitious Name Statement that was in the newspaper, and his incorporation papers if he's creating a corporation? Will he want your name and your signature to be on any of the initial business documents to be filed with the Secretary of State? If so, if things go belly-up, you could be responsible for part if not all of the debt of the business or corporation. You could also be sued; depending on what role you played on paper in his business. After he starts his business, will he provide you with his Dun & Bradstreet Report (business credit report)? Will you receive any of the profits derived from the business? Do you ask him for any of these things?

Does this guy you like so much ask to borrow your credit card because he left his at home and he doesn't have cash to pay for something that he wanted to purchase? You let him borrow your credit card, but then he does not return it to you. When you get up the nerve to ask him for your credit card, he hands it to you sheepishly and says he forgot. He conveniently forgets to pay you cash or write you a check for the charges he put on your credit card. Do you ask him to reimburse you for the charges he placed on your card?

When this guy you like so much takes you out to dinner, does he conveniently forget to bring his credit card or cash, and when the waiter brings the check to be paid, he asks you to pay the bill, stating that he will pay you back later? Does he ever pay you back? Do you ask him to pay you back? Do you go out to dinner with him again?

Does this guy you like so much ask to see your driver's license to see if you smiled on your picture, but he looks like he's memorizing your driver's license number?

Does this guy you like so much check your mail when he comes over to your home to visit? Does he look at any papers you have lying around in your home? Do you find him in your home office when you clearly left him in the living room when you went to answer the phone? Does he check your medicine cabinet when he goes to use your bathroom?

Does this guy you like so much tell you that he's a little short this month and can't pay certain bills, and he then asks you to pay them for him and states that he will pay you back as soon as his "so-called" check comes? He also states that he would do the same for you. Do you feel guilty or are you understanding of his situation and pay his bills? Does he pay you back? When?

Does this guy you like so much borrow your car after you have just filled the tank with gas? He doesn't return your car to you at the time he said he would return it. You finally get your car back and the fuel needle is on empty. Do you ask him to fill your gas tank?

Does this guy you like so much ask to spend the night with you, and then in the morning he doesn't leave? Do you find things missing in your home after he has left? Has your wallet and purse been rifled through and you see that some of your credit cards and money are missing? Are you missing pieces of valuable jewelry that was in your bedroom on your dresser and in your jewelry box?

Since you and this guy you like so much are friends, did you stupidly give him an extra key to your home? Did you give him the security code to your home "just in case"? Did you give him a key to your car?

Since this guy you like so much has rifled through your home, do you notice that money is now missing from your bank account?

Are you receiving notices in the mail from credit card companies requesting payment for purchases in your name, but with a different address, that was then forwarded to your correct address, when you never opened a credit card account with that company? Are you receiving utility bills in the mail, in your name, for addresses other than your own? Are you receiving cell-phone bills in your name, with your address, but you did not purchase any new cell-phone? Are you receiving bills for major purchases on-line via the Internet that you did not order or receive?

Are you receiving phone calls from women and men at all hours of the night looking for this guy who you like so much? Are you receiving calls from collection companies searching for this guy who you like so much? The bill collectors tell you that your address and phone number were given to them. The bill collectors even threaten to put liens on your home if they don't get paid.

Need I go on???????????!

All of the above scenarios are real and have real and harsh consequences. You must be aware of who you are dealing with; be it boyfriends, friends, strangers, and sometimes even unscrupulous family members.

Have you got what it takes to see through people and size up situations before they occur to ensure nothing bad happens to you? This is called having insight, wisdom understanding and discernment.

Are any of the above-referenced traits in your friends or are these traits in you? Are you using people/friends for what you can get out of them?

Have you got what it takes for God? Are you getting your direction from the world or are you getting your direction from God? The world will chew you up and spit you out if you're not careful about yourself, who you associate with, what you have, where you live, and how you live. Are you appearing to others as a strong, moral person with conviction, or do others view you as a victim to be used and abused?

If you're not careful, the world will destroy you, and the world will not care. Have you really got what it takes?

Apparel – What Are You Wearing And Where Are You Going Dressed That Way?

The cares of this world changes everyday, especially when it comes to physical appearance. These days almost everyone is obsessed with the physical appearance of themselves and of others. If you're not as beautiful as they are, you don't fit into the click and you cannot be with them. If you're overweight and they are thin, you don't fit their mold and you cannot be with them. If you don't show as much skin as they do, you cannot be with them. If you don't drink, smoke, or use drugs like them, they don't want you in their group.

One day, mini skirts are in; the next day they're out. One day, long hair is in; the next day it's out. One day, tattoos are in and the next day tattoos are in. One day, it's fashionable to do drugs, drink alcohol, hang out at parties until morning, and to have bags and dark shadows under your eyes to be in with the "in crowd." The next day, your health is disintegrating. You look and feel old, you feel used and worn out, and you don't understand why. Ask yourself if you're following the way of the world?

Is what you're wearing tight enough, high enough, short enough, low enough, or revealing enough? Is it too bright and flashy or too dull and drab? Does it have enough bling or does it have too much bling? What's going on?

What is the composition of your appearance; the whole package?

1) What does your countenance look like?

2) What clothes are you wearing? Why are you wearing that outfit?

3) How do your clothes fit?

4) How are you wearing your hair? Why are you wearing your hair that way? Why did you put that color in your hair?

5) What's up with all those tattoos?

6) How much makeup is enough? Why are you wearing so much?

7) Why are you walking that way?

8) Why are you talking like that?

9) Who are you trying to attract?

10) Who are you trying to fit in with?

11) Why are you such a Forward Girl, Forward Teenager, or Forward Woman?

The way we dress, which is comprised of all of the above, says a lot about us. The combination of all can be provocative or in good taste, and can attract the right people or the wrong people.

(1) What does your countenance look like? Your countenance is your overall appearance. When people look at you, do they see the whites of your eyes or are the whites of your eyes bloodshot, red or brown-spotted? Are the pupils of your eyes dilated (big) like you're coming off a high from drugs? Or, are your eyes clear and white? Do you have bags under your eyes from staying up late, drinking heavily, or from doing drugs? Does your hair look like it hasn't been combed, and does it smell? Do you have body odor? Do your clothes appear as though you slept in them? Does your overall appearance reflect a dull and dragging-through-the-mud person or a bright and bubbly person?

(2) What clothes are you wearing? Why are you wearing that outfit? Is the outfit appropriate for the function or the purpose for which you are wearing it? Are the colors you're wearing complimenting your complexion and your personality? Are you wearing neon colors in the wintertime and drab colors in the summertime? Are your clothes loud and calling the wrong attention? Are you wearing clothes in the office that should be worn in a nightclub? Are you calling negative attention to yourself because of what you're wearing? Are you attracting the wrong sort of men by what you wear?

If you wear your clothes in a provocative manner, you will attract provocative responses by the opposite sex. For example, don't be wearing thong underwear with hip-hugger pants or skirts, whereby when you bend over, the thong underwear shows above the hip-line of the pants or skirt. This gives a provocative appearance suggesting a provocative response. Don't wear hot pants where the edge of the pant is in a straight line with the crotch of your panties. Don't wear tight blouses that overly accentuate or give attention to your breasts. All of these pieces of clothing, for example, promote provocative suggestions to others, which will prompt a negative-type of reaction that you don't want, or maybe you do. A combination of the thong, hot pants, and the blouse, as described above, with stiletto high heels (for example), will definitely prompt negative attention while walking down a public street. If you're wearing this outfit, the Police may mistake you for a hooker and arrest you for solicitation. How can one tell the difference?

The word 'provocative' means to stimulate, provoke, or to incite something. Synonyms of the word provocative are: earthy, risqué, salty, off-color, spicy, suggestive, erotic, exciting, and alluring. So make the right choice to bring the right attention.

(3) <u>How do your clothes fit?</u> Is the outfit too tight or too short in the wrong areas on your body? Are you wearing a skirt that is too high on your hips and too tight around the waist and hips? Is the skirt hanging barely below the cup of your butt? If the skirt has slits (or small openings) in the front or the back of it, does it reveal the inside of your legs and your crotch (vaginal area) when you walk? Is your skirt telling you it's too short because you're constantly pulling it down as you walk? Do the clothes you wear flatter you in a lady-like way or in a "loose woman" way? What are your clothes really saying about you? Are you easy or hard to get? Have you left anything good to anyone's imagination? These are things to consider. You may be attracting the wrong type of attention from the wrong men by wearing the wrong outfit.

(4) <u>How are you wearing your hair? Why are you wearing your hair that way? Why did you put that color in your hair?</u> Do you wear your hair like you just don't care? Did you brush and comb your hair before you left home to go out in public? Do people notice that your hair has an odor after you pass by them? When was the last time you washed your hair?

If you're wearing braids, sister-locks, dreadlocks, or a natural, are there fuzz and lint in the hair? Can people still see the style or are they looking at the lint? Have you worn your braids so long that they are beginning to look like a poor replication for dreadlocks, although that was not your intention? Are you wearing unnatural and abnormal colors in your hair that do not compliment your complexion or the clothes that you wear (blue, deep strawberry red, orange, purple, green and yellow)?

Did you wear your hair spiked, wear neon colored hair, fuzzy braids, or curls dripping with oil to a job interview in an office and then wonder why you did not get hired?

If you have a hairdo that requires upkeep on at least a weekly basis, decide whether you can afford to pay for the upkeep before wearing the hairdo. If so, then make the financial commitment to have it done on a regular basis so that your hair looks good all the time. There's nothing worse than wearing a style that you cannot financially afford to keep up, and then being stuck with it until you get your paycheck and are able to afford to have it either updated or changed. Learn how to fix your own hair. The excuse of not being able to go to the beauty shop will only last so long.

(5) <u>What's up with all those tattoos?</u> Most mainstream companies shy away from people who have visible tattoos beyond their clothing, especially in customer service, healthcare, law offices, and other office-type environments. Most corporate industry management believes that one who is tattooed up to the gills reflects a negative image for their business, they will lose clients, and, hence, they will lose money. Depending on what tattoos are on the body that are visible to customers or other business associates or representatives, they tend to give an image of "born to be wild" or "hell raiser" or "non-conformity", which tend to frighten or turn off the customer/client. One is hesitant to discuss a business proposition or business transaction with company representatives who have skulls and cross-bones (for example) on their arms, neck, and head. They

will avoid that person because they are intimidated by the person's appearance. I am speaking about women as well as men.

In most business circles, tattoos are not considered art. However, in almost all other circles tattoos are considered artistic.

(6) How much makeup is enough? Why are you wearing so much? You can tell a lot about a person by the makeup she wears. Some women wear a lot of eye shadow because they wear glasses and they want to accentuate their eyes through their glasses. This is okay as long as it's in good taste where their eyes don't look like the eyes of a raccoon.

Are you wearing the right makeup for the right setting? Is your makeup too loud where you look somewhat like a clown? Is the makeup you're wearing enough to compliment your features – eyes, lips, cheekbones, etc.? Just because you're wearing a teal-blue dress doesn't necessarily mean you have to have the exact same color eye shadow above your eyes where all a person sees is the teal blue dress and the teal blue eyes – they don't really see you. It's distracting. Too much is really too much.

Men tend to identify types of women by how much makeup women wear. If a woman wears a lot of makeup, the man tends to wonder what she looks like under all that stuff. Sometimes men think that she looks trampish or sluttish with all that makeup caked on her face.

If a man married a woman who wore makeup, kept her hair nice, and dressed sharp all the time, but then she later stopped, it would be prudent for the husband to ask his wife why. Instead, most men start looking at other women. Most of the time, the wife is too tired to fix herself up because of the kids, maintenance of the household, and working a job outside of the home. If that's the case, the husband should recognize her situation and help her with whatever is needed to gain the time for her to rest and to start fixing herself up again. With his help, she would more than likely be able to take better care of herself. Instead, most men tend to seek out another woman who doesn't have family and home responsibilities.

Most men want their wives to look exactly like who they married years ago. It doesn't matter to them what they, themselves, now look like (fat, bald, double-chin, big belly, shorter, etc.), but it definitely matters to them what their wives look like. They generally don't say anything. Instead, they start looking at other women. If the wife gains weight, they look for someone else. If the wife doesn't keep herself up due to various circumstances, they look for someone else. If the wife becomes sickly, they look for someone else. If keeping the wife up costs them too much money, they seek someone else. Instead of helping their wives be all they can be, they'd rather spend more money on wining and dining someone else. They are fickle.

Some women who wear no makeup really need to wear it. They tend to look homely, matronly, and older than they really are. Most men will give these women little or no attention at all. However, some men like women without makeup. They feel the woman looks good in her natural beauty. That's okay as long as he's not looking at another woman who is wearing makeup. It's good to have natural beauty, but by doing nothing to improve your appearance when you don't have natural beauty is definitely a problem. Putting on makeup in the right amount and wearing the right colors that compliment the facial complexion will make a woman look good, feel pretty, and be more feminine.

If a man married a woman who was beautiful, slim and trim, he wants her to stay that way at all cost, sometimes at all cost to her. Whether it's done through cosmetic surgery, liposuction, gastric bypass, membership to a gym or health spa, etc., he will pay for whatever it takes to make his wife look beautiful. Some men won't, but instead look for another woman who meets his visible standards.

Men want good-looking women hanging on their arms at all times, and in all situations, to compliment themselves and to impress other men. It's an ego booster for them. They feel it gives them credibility amongst their peer group.

(7) Why are you walking that way? The way you walk reflects your body language. Your walk tells people who you are and what you are. Walking provocatively will attract the wrong type of attention. Accentuating your posture by shaking your head, swaying your hips from side to side in an extreme manner, protruding your chest, and bouncing your rear end will definitely attract the wrong type of attention. However, walking naturally will make the wrong person leave you alone.

(8) Why are you talking like that? Do you speak softly, timidly, authoritatively, angrily, loudly, obnoxiously, or arrogantly? Do you have a potty mouth, or are you quiet and demure? Is every other word coming out of your mouth a curse word? Do you intimidate people by the way you talk to them? Do people believe you when you speak, or do they not take you seriously and dismiss anything you say? Do you look people straight in the eyes when you speak to them, or do you look away or put your head down? Are you argumentative or are you conciliatory (appeasing)? Do you let your body do your talking? Do you speak with your eyes? How you speak to people is very important. It's not so much what you say, but it's definitely the way you say it.

(9) Who are you trying to attract? Let's face it ladies, we know what to wear, how to fix our hair and makeup, what to say and how to say it when we want attention from the opposite sex to get something from them. Our body language tells the opposite sex whether

to approach us or leave us alone. Our body language also tells who in the opposite sex should approach us, good or bad. You must consider who you're trying to attract, and why you're trying to attract them before you do anything. Do you want good attention from good people or bad attention from bad people? Do you want any attention at all? Think before you dress. Think before you open your mouth.

How's your attitude? Are you a bubbly person or a stick-in-the-mud person? Are you the sweetest little baby-doll or are you the witch of the century? Do you roll your eyes at people in a defiant manner? Do you give people intimidating stares? Are you mean to people? Do you speak kindly to people at all cost?

Are you carrying yourself in a manner that lets all people know you are honorable, have good character, and are a reflection of God's righteousness? Are people won by your countenance? Those who approach you will respect you if you carry yourself in a way that shows you respect yourself. The way you carry yourself will determine who comes into contact with you and for what purpose.

(10) <u>Who are you trying to fit in with?</u> Are you trying to fit in with the world and its ways? Can you stand on your own with your morals and scruples intact in spite of the majority who are against you? The world is trying to pull you one way, but your morals and Godly values are pulling you another way. The world's way will give you pleasure in the short term, but pain and suffering in the long term. God's way will give you peace and success throughout. There is a price to pay when trying to fit a square peg into a round hole.

You know right from wrong. You know what the Bible says about you. You must always remember who you belong to, and what your purpose is in your life. By going against what you know to be true will cause a lot of friction and a lot of heartache until you make the decision to recognize who you are, and then to stand for it. Once you make that decision and put that decision into action, life will smooth out and you will be at peace with yourself and with others.

(11) Why are You such a Forward Girl, Forward Teenager, or Forward Woman? It seems to be a trend these days for women to approach men for attention instead of allowing men to approach them. These forward girls, forward teenage girls, and forward women have no problem in approaching boys and men to engage in a social relationship leading to a sexual relationship. There is no shame in their game. If they find a boy or man attractive, they go after him. These women are called "Forward" because they approach the opposite sex first, if they are interested, rather than allowing the man to notice and approach them. This is unnatural.

The forward woman has too much self-esteem/confidence. She believes she's so good-looking that she's entitled to go get the man of her choosing for whatever purpose. There is no hesitation in her approaching a man. She's confident enough to entice the man to even have sex with her. She doesn't care whether that man is currently in a relationship or whether he's married. She wants him and that's that! She has no discretion. *Proverbs 11:22* states: *"As a ring of gold in a swine's snout, so is a lovely woman who lacks discretion."*

Most men are turned off by a woman approaching them because they believe it's unnatural, out of God's order, and it takes away from their manhood because they are built to chase, conquer, and to provide. Women are not built to hunt/chase, capture, and provide for a man.

Some men like women approaching them because they don't have to do the chasing. Because the woman approached him, he takes it as a sign that the woman will do other things for him without him even asking.

Guys who have little or no respect for women in general will definitely take advantage of a forward woman. This negative trait of being a forward woman translates to men that she is either stupid, desperate, has no self-esteem, lonely, or horny. If the forward woman is offering it (whatever it is) for free, these men will certainly take it. They have no commitment to a forward woman. They have no desire for any real future with a forward woman because the forward woman has already put out or is willing to put out everything and anything she has up front. He certainly wouldn't work to support her; he doesn't have to. There is no desire or urgency for him to do anything for the forward woman. She's taken away any interest, desire, or intrigue in her because she has already shown all of herself. He will use her as long as she allows it or until he gets tired of her. I'm sure you have heard the phrase, "Why buy the cow when the milk is free?" This is such a true statement that it ought to be labeled as a scientific fact. Why girls, teenage girls, young women and even older women who are forward don't get this point is beyond me. No man is really interested in a lifetime commitment with a forward woman. What for?

A real man will not marry a forward woman. If she was forward with him, who else was she forward with? Does she have a reputation? Is there any serious future with a forward woman? Men who are "players" believe that it's alright to have relationships with many different women, but when it comes to marriage, they always want the virgin, the reserved woman, the lady. They may "settle" for a woman who is not a virgin, but they would rather have the virgin. They definitely don't want a forward woman.

Forward girls, forward teenage girls, and forward women usually get exactly what they ask for – nothing they want. The consequences are not good if a woman continues to pursue this way of establishing a relationship with a man. There will be no respect, no future marriage, and no possibility of a healthy relationship because the forward actions of forward women are in direct contradiction to man's nature to pursue, conquer, and provide. Being forward is out of God's order.

The Golden Rule Of Thumb – The "Jesus" Test

The real test that will determine what your appearance should be like as a teenage girl, young lady or woman is this: If Jesus was standing in front of you, would you look like you look? Would you wear your hair and makeup like that? Would you wear those tight clothes that show your "all and all" – showing most of your skin where the nipples of your breasts show through your blouse, where your belly-button is showing, where the crack of your butt is showing; and where your skirt or dress or shorts are so high and tight that Jesus could see the imprint of your pubic hair? Would you have tattoos injected into your skin on the body that Jesus created for you? Would Jesus, who is the Creator and artist of all life, recognize you? Would you have all those rings pierced into your nose, in your tongue, in your eyebrows, in your nipples (ouch), in your belly button, in your ears and in your toes? Would you walk in a provocative way in front of Jesus? Would you speak in a provocative manner and curse like a street hoodlum in front of Jesus? Would you have a bad attitude, suck your teeth and roll your eyes in front of Jesus? What do you think your appearance would say to Jesus about you? What would your appearance in front of Jesus say to you?

Colossians 3:23-24 states: *"And whatever you do, do it heartily, as to the Lord and not to men, knowing that from the Lord you will receive the reward of the inheritance for you serve the Lord Christ."* This is a good rule of thumb. If you can do it, wear it, talk it, and walk it in front of Jesus Christ without any shame or guilt, either you're confident that your appearance is pleasing to the Lord or you don't care about what the Lord thinks about your appearance. *1 Timothy 2:9-10* states: *"In like manner also, that the women adorn themselves in modest apparel, with propriety and moderation, not with braided hair or gold or pearls or costly clothing, but, which is proper for women professing godliness, with good works."* Propriety means decency, graciousness, politeness, and respectability, where no one would question your position as a woman of God.

The Lord is always with you no matter where you go. He sees and hears everything you say and do. *Romans 12:1-2* states: *"I appeal to you, therefore, brothers [sisters], by the mercies of God, to present your bodies a living sacrifice, holy and acceptable to God, which is your reasonable service. And do not be conformed to this world, but be transformed by the renewing of your mind, that you may prove what is that good and acceptable and perfect will of God."*

God fearfully and wonderfully made you. In *Psalm 139:13-18,* David recognized who made him, and he states: *"For You formed my inward parts; You covered me in my mother's womb. I will praise You for I am fearfully and wonderfully made; marvelous are Your works, and that my soul knows very well. My frame was not hidden from You, when I was made in secret, and skillfully wrought in the lowest parts of the earth. When Your eyes saw my substance being yet unformed, and in Your book they all were written, the days fashioned for me, when as yet there were none of them. How precious also are Your thoughts to me, O God! How great is the sum of them! If I should count them, they would be more in number than the sand. When I am awake, I am still with You."*

Some people have defiled themselves so badly by indulging in the wrong things (drugs, alcohol, sex – to name a few) whereby over a period of time (season) they have heavy bags under their eyes, they have an enormous amount of wrinkles, dark circles around their eyes, and they just look so unhealthy that I doubt Jesus or God would even recognize them by their physical appearance. Others have mutilated their bodies with all sorts of piercings and tattoos that their parents, Jesus, or God would not even recognize them. And still others have dressed in such a way that Jesus and God might mistake them for prostitutes. The popular saying holds true: "If it looks like a duck, walks like a duck, and quacks like a duck, it must be a duck."

Although you may want people to see a Godly and wholesome countenance, a warm personality, and a kind and gentle spirit in you, it's hard to see those attributes when you're projecting something else. But have hope for all is not lost, and all can be changed by the Word of God. As you study God's Word, you will begin to blossom into the person He wants you to be. Although you want to change, He knows you cannot change on your own, and He will help you change. Ask Him and trust Him.

Conclusion

Remember that first impressions are lasting impressions. Again, if it looks like a duck, walks like a duck, and quacks like a duck, it's a duck. If you walk, talk and dress provocatively, calling the wrong attention to yourself, you will definitely get it. You cannot dress like a hooker, walk like a hooker, and talk like a hooker, and then expect and demand to be respected and treated like a lady. It just doesn't work that way. Men can somewhat get away with that, but women can't.

You are accountable to God. *1 Corinthians 10:31* states: *"Therefore, whether you eat or drink, or whatever you do, do all to the glory of God."* This includes how you dress and how you carry yourself before man and before God. It also includes who you associate with because you are known by the company you keep. God is always with you because He says it in His word. *Hebrews 13:5* states: *"Let your conduct be without covetousness; be content with such things as you have, for He Himself has said, I will never leave you nor forsake you."* So, Jesus is with you always when you accept the fact that He died on the cross for your sins and that He rose again and is seated at the right hand of God petitioning on your behalf. You are saved because you have accepted Him as your Lord and Savior. As a child of God, you don't want Him to see other than Himself through you. You are a reflection of Jesus Christ.

Chapter 3

Tough Enough For The Consequences of Sex?

Tough Enough For The Consequences Of Sex?

To Be Or Not To Be A Virgin – What's In It For You?

Virginity is a highly valuable, virtuous, and special attribute that all women have for a period of time. Women are born virgins. Some women will live out their entire lives as virgins.

Virginity is described in the medical realm as having the hymen intact, or the vagina has not been penetrated sexually. The hymen is a soft membrane that covers the opening of the vagina, and it can be found just inside the inner labia. However, if the hymen is penetrated sexually, virginity no longer exists, and the inside of the body becomes vulnerable to anything that enters through the vagina.

Some women are born without hymens, but they are still considered virgins until they have sex.

Some women's hymens are opened through gymnastics and other physical activities; however, they, too, are still considered virgins until they are sexually active.

Women can only give the gift of virginity one time to someone, so that someone should be extremely special. Once given, we can never ever get it back. Also, once virginity is lost through sexual intercourse, our physical bodies are open to possible pregnancy, sexually transmitted diseases, or other health disorders. If you are celibate, meaning you don't have sex, you don't have to be concerned about dealing with most of these possible problems.

It's vitally important to be sure you know exactly who you're giving your precious gift of virginity to. It's also extremely important that you know why you are giving your special gift to a person. It's not enough to give your virginity to someone because you like him or you just have that animal urge to have sex. Is the person special enough that he's worth receiving your one and only most precious gift? If so, why? What will you gain from giving **that** person your virginity outside of marriage? Do you feel he's really worth the possible consequences you will be subjecting yourself to that could last 18 years and beyond? Are you serious?

Virginity is valued very differently by the opposite sex. Unfortunately, virginity has lost its value to most women, too, and is currently viewed as "common" and "no big deal". If men can have sex as they please without strings attached, why can't women? The answer to this question is because women bear most of the consequences, not men. Although it's hard to find a guy who is a virgin or who will admit to being a virgin, it's becoming even more difficult to find a woman who is a virgin.

Most men who get married don't want to discover sex as a virgin with their virgin wives. They want to be able to 'perform.' Because of commercialism and locker room talk, they want to be well versed in sexual intercourse prior to getting married. They believe they need to discover how to have sex early on so they will know what to do when they get married. However, the question that still remains is: Who is he going to "use" to get his experience and find out how his equipment works?

Under what circumstances are you giving your most special gift to a man? The most ideal circumstance that is blessed by your parents and ordained by God, Himself, is marriage. Any other reason, such as casual sexual promiscuity before marriage (called fornication), is unacceptable to God and more than likely unacceptable to your parents.

If you give your virginity away before the honeymoon, you will have nothing special and exciting to offer your new husband on the wedding night and throughout the marriage. Statistics show that marriages have a lesser chance of survival if there was pre-marital sex.

If not given to your husband in the honeymoon, what's the point of giving your virginity away? What's in it for you? Only you possess it, and only you can give it. No one can take your virginity away from you, no one can give it to someone else, and no one can restore your virginity back to you. Once it's gone, it's gone. You are the sole owner, possessor, controller, and protector of your virginity.

A virgin is basically looked upon as having distinction, purity, excellence, self-control, honor and respect. Although some women who are not virgins would say otherwise, a woman who is a virgin knows she's special. She values and respects herself. She knows she is of great value to men. She is not led by other influences, but is saving herself for that special man who wishes to have her as his one and only wife, knowing no other man had her sexually.

The virgin is in control of her body. She doesn't allow her flesh (feelings and emotions) or outside influences to dictate or have power over her body. She also has power and control over her prospective husband's fleshly desire for her prior to marriage. The virgin knows what she wants, and she knows how she needs to keep herself to receive the best that God has for her in life. She doesn't haphazardly give her virginity to a man based on her feelings, his looks, his material possessions, or what she thinks he would or could do for her.

Having never engaged in physical sexual intercourse eliminates getting pregnant or getting a sexually transmitted disease and the emotional trauma that follows. It also eliminates various health issues, relationship issues, career issues, and immediate and future financial issues. However, not being a virgin can negatively affect your health, your relationships, your career, your finances, and your future.

The woman who is a virgin values herself. She's wise. She's thought about her future. She's thought about the lifestyle she wants. She's thought about what she wants in her marriage. She's invested in herself to make her attractive, appealing, and educated in the areas of appearance, good health, a Godly foundation, morals, career objectives, and finances. She's a great catch for a man with similar values looking for a wife to share his life with. She's thought about the type of man she wants to marry, and she's given her request for the right man to God. She plans out her life in her heart and in her mind, and she implements her plan in accordance with God's Word.

If you had something of great value, would you just give it away?

There Is No Such Thing As "He Took My Virginity From Me!"

This is an oxymoron, a contradiction, since all women are in control of their own bodies and their virginity. The only way a woman's virginity could be taken from her would be in an act of violence such as rape. Other than that scenario, a woman is in complete control of her virginity.

All men with pure and not so pure motives want to marry a virgin. Yeah, they will be sexually promiscuous with a non-virgin because they know they can. However, deep down inside, they really want to marry a virgin – someone who hasn't been "had" by other men. Back in the day, a young lady who gave her virginity away without thinking about the consequences was known to be either plucked, spoiled, deflowered, used, busted, or had. She was not looked upon as being as valuable or as having the integrity of a virgin. She was not as respected as a virgin, except in the midnight hour, which is commonly known these days as a "booty call."

A young lady, sixteen years of age, was very distraught after being dumped by a boy she was sexually involved with. She thought he liked her and she thought she loved him because of the way he made her feel each time she saw him. We will give her the name Delia. Her mother tried to calm her down, but when she found out why Delia was so upset, her mother became enraged and hurt at the same time.

Delia liked this guy so much that she literally chased him, pleaded and begged him to spend time (any time) with her. She wrote love letters and notes to him in class, purchased gifts for him, gave him money, ditched school so she could see him, and constantly phoned him and sent text messages to him. Then she did the unthinkable – she sent all sorts of sexually provocative and naked pictures of herself to him through her cell-phone.

On a Saturday, while Delia was shopping with her girlfriends at the local mall, Delia's mother found her cell-phone that she unintentionally left at home. Her mother was gathering up dirty clothes in each room of the house to do laundry when she came upon Delia's cell-phone. Delia's mom read all the text messages and scanned through all the provocative photos on the phone. She was distraught and she turned the room upside down searching for any other evidence of Delia's misdeeds. She broke down and cried on the bed. In reviewing what was on Delia's phone, she knew her daughter was no longer a virgin, she felt her daughter deceived and lied to her, and she knew her daughter had disrespected the family home. She felt her daughter acted like a tramp, a prostitute, and a whore. She was deeply hurt by the child she carried in her womb for nine months, delivered, and whom she raised for over 16 years. She realized she didn't even know her teenage daughter anymore. She began to blame herself. She didn't know what she or her husband did to make their child do such bad things. She felt betrayed. She and her husband were not only good to their children but they were good examples to them. She couldn't figure out why her child desired to chase this boy to make him have sex with her. She then wondered whether her daughter had sex with other boys, and whether it was done in their home.

What happened to their family values? What happened with the sermons that were taught in church? When and why did their daughter lose her faith in God? Did their daughter believe that what she learned in the Bible did not apply to her? What happened?

Delia's mom began to second-guess herself, and she went through a mental checklist of what could have made her daughter change, but she could only think of the media that made promiscuity appear fun and without consequences. She also thought about her daughter's peer group at school. She knew nothing about what went on during the day at Delia's school. She thought her daughter was faithfully attending each and every class, and not ditching. She thought her daughter was a virgin.

Randy, the boy Delia was having sex with, was seventeen years of age and in the twelfth grade in high school. His parents were Christians, and they raised him with Christian values. His whole family went to church. Randy had a girlfriend in the church he attended, and she was a virgin. His parents approved of her. Randy did well in school. After graduation, he planned to join the military. His parents were very proud of him, and they saw a bright future for their son.

When Delia's dad arrived home from work Saturday afternoon, his wife informed him of the awful news and showed him the text messages and provocative photos. Needless to say, he was devastated. When Delia arrived home from shopping, her parents confronted her. They expressed how upset and disappointed they were. They wanted to know where the boy lived so they could confront him and his parents. She told them where he lived and they all went to Randy's home.

Randy's parents were shocked after hearing the news from Delia's parents. They called Randy to come downstairs to discuss the situation. Randy admitted to having sex with Delia, but he stated that she was constantly after him, and she forced him into having sex with her. He also said he didn't even like Delia; she was ugly, aggressive, and that he wasn't about to give up his girlfriend for her.

Randy stated that he weakened from the constant advances by Delia. Instead of talking to his dad and/or mom, or even to his pastor about the advances by Delia, he chose to seek advice from his peer group – his friends. Of course, they told him to go for it, it was free, and that he could get practice because sex was being thrown at him from all different directions by this girl. And so he took their advice. He made a conscious decision to involve himself with Delia. Delia invited him to her home while her parents were at work, and he had sex with her in her bed. He also had sex with her in his bed in his parents' home while they were at work. Then they both engaged in sex in the boys' bathroom stalls in the gymnasium after school. Afterwards, he was done with her. Maybe his conscience kicked in? Who knows?

Needless to say, Delia was crushed and she cried profusely. Randy's father stated that he planned to have a stern discussion with his son after Delia and her parents left.

Delia's father stated his wife was taking Delia to the doctor to be checked and, upon examination, if Delia was found to have a sexually transmittable disease or found to be pregnant, Randy's parents would be informed and bear half of the responsibility, financially and otherwise. Delia's father also said that charges could be brought against Randy for having sex with his daughter, who was a minor. Randy's parents understood and were cooperative with Delia's parents.

Delia cried all the way home, and she kept murmuring that Randy **"took"** her virginity away from her. When they arrived home, Delia ran up to her bedroom sobbing. Her mother later came into her room and saw her sprawled out on the carpeted floor kicking, screaming, and crying out that Randy took her virginity away from her, he snatched it from her, he used her, he stole it from her, she could never get it back, and she could never be whole again. She cried hysterically.

Delia's mom picked her up off the floor and sat her on the bed. Delia was told that since she did a very adult thing, it comes with adult responsibilities and consequences. Delia's mother told her that: (1) she, herself, gave her virginity away; (2) she was not forced or raped; (3) her virginity was one of her most precious gifts; (4) she cheapened herself and discounted what her virginity meant to her and to the man who wished to marry her in the future; (5) she gave up her virginity freely, willingly, and aggressively; (6) any boy or man who wasn't honorable would accept free sex from anyone; (7) it was too late to think about "if I would have, could have, should have"; (8) she and the boy were both irresponsible for not using any kind of protection to avoid pregnancy or an STD; (9) their actions showed they did not believe and trust what the Bible said about sexual purity and the consequences of sexual promiscuity; and (10) they didn't think about the consequences of their actions, but now they have to deal with whatever comes from it. Delia's mother scolded her for disrespecting herself, her family, her home, and Randy's family and home. Her mother expressed her total disgust concerning her escapade in the boys' bathroom at school. She demanded that Delia stop crying because she brought it on herself. She told Delia that Delia would take full responsibility and accountability for her actions.

Delia's mother felt sorry that Delia did not think as much of herself as she and her husband thought of her. She was sad that Delia ignored all of the teaching and training she received on the subject of sex through her and her husband, through church, and through school. Delia's mother and father thought the world of her and tried to show her in so many ways, but Delia chose to go a different direction that caused harm to herself, her family, and to others.

Delia's mom asked her what was it about the boy that made her want him so badly, even to the point of chasing him and engaging in sex with him. She wanted to know if Delia thought about her future. All Delia could say was that she was in love with the boy. So Delia's mom asked what was her description of love. Delia replied that he was cute and that she just wanted to be with him. Her mom asked her if she knew that he had a girlfriend, and Delia stated she did not know nor did she care; she just wanted to be with him. Delia's mom asked what happens next. Delia had no answer.

Delia's mom asked her what would she do if the doctor tells her that she's got an STD. Delia said she would cry. She asked Delia if she would be angry, and Delia replied that she would be. She asked Delia what she would do if the doctor informed her she was pregnant, and Delia replied that she would have the baby.

Fortunately, when Delia's mother took her to the doctor, he informed Delia that she was not pregnant and she showed no signs of having a sexually transmitted disease. However, he stated that it would take a few more weeks for symptoms of any STDs to show up.

Now, after all the sneaking around, after all the lying, after all the pursuing, after losing her virginity, after being found out by both sets of parents, after all the embarrassment, after learning the boy didn't even like her, after learning the boy had a girlfriend, and after being examined by the doctor, did Delia learn her lesson?

Delia's consequences were light compared to what could have been.

A Regretful Decision

Almost 18 years ago, I met a young African American woman who was about 28 years of age. She looked like she was 16. She was stunning to look at. She had that little boy figure that fits all styles of clothes, and she had long beautiful legs. Her long hair was straightened and hung down the middle of her back. She looked like a model out of any and all fashion magazines. Her complexion was caramel chocolate cream. She looked like what all women aspire to look like according to the worldly view of beauty. Her name was Suzanne.

Suzanne was invited to speak to those of us who attended a lunch hour seminar on AIDS at the firm where I worked. On a monthly basis, the firm brought in speakers from different charities and groups promoting saving humans, animals, and the environment. The firm was very supportive of these organizations, and donated large sums of money on behalf of all of its employees.

Suzanne was asked to tell her story about how she became HIV positive. She represented a small group of women fighting for the cure for AIDS and fighting against discriminatory practices by individuals, companies, and even some hospitals. Suzanne's purpose was to tell us how she became HIV positive; what her health, living and financial status was; and what her future plans were.

Suzanne spoke very humbly and candidly. She explained that after graduating from college with a Bachelor's Degree in Business and Accounting, she landed a job at a major company. She had a title and she made very good money for her young age. She moved into the city from the suburb where she lived while growing up. She got a nice apartment in a nice area of town.

Suzanne met a guy at a jazz concert she and her girlfriends attended. His name was Joe. Joe was very good looking, almost as good looking as she, and they seemed to have a lot of things in common. The relationship between Suzanne and Joe grew over a period of 9 months. He first asked her out for coffee, then dinner with friends, and then dinner by themselves. They went to concerts, walked on the beach, and played golf. He even took her shopping on occasion. She found it a bit strange that Joe did not try to get intimate with her right away, and he only kissed her after a few dates.

During the relationship, Suzanne found Joe to be distant yet wanting to talk to her more deeply at times. She figured he had pressure from his job. She felt that if Joe wanted to talk to her about whatever the problem was, she would be open to him. She really liked him and found herself wanting more from him emotionally and sexually. She knew he was attracted to her, too, but she didn't know why he held back.

Suzanne was doing very well on her job and she received promotions. She met a good-looking man who was very much into her. She was happy. Life was good!

One evening Joe went to Suzanne's apartment to take her to dinner, but he didn't feel very well and he had a fever. She decided they should stay in for the evening, and she fixed a light dinner for them. Joe had no appetite and he left after a couple of hours. She called him later that evening to see how he was feeling and he stated he would live. They exchanged pleasantries and she hung up. They continued dating.

After a few months of dating, they ended up in bed together. Joe insisted on using a condom for protection, and she had no problem with that. However, during sexual intercourse, the condom came off, but she thought nothing of it. He didn't do anything nor say anything about it as they continued to make love. Apparently he, too, thought the condom coming off during intercourse was no big deal. Afterwards, he went home.

Suzanne stated that after that night, Joe became very distant from her. He did not readily return her phone calls. When she did speak to him, he was either too busy or too sick to go out with her. She asked him if he went to the doctor and what the diagnosis was, but Joe became very evasive concerning his illness.

After a couple of months of little or no contact, the relationship ended. However, Suzanne was becoming ill. She developed flu-like symptoms, and she went to the doctor to get checked out. Based on her symptoms, all the doctor could determine was that she had the flu. By her appearance, he never considered she would be HIV positive. However, over a period of three months Suzanne was going to the doctor frequently because she was constantly sick. The doctor decided to run a series of different tests on her. He checked her medical history and found that she being constantly sick was not the norm for her. After the results of all the tests came back, the doctor informed Suzanne that she was HIV positive. She was shocked and mortified by the news.

The doctor advised Suzanne to contact her sexual partner. When she attempted to contact Joe, she learned that he was in the hospital. Joe died a few months later from AIDS.

At the time Suzanne spoke to us at the lunch hour seminar, she was undergoing treatment for HIV. She lost her job because she was away from the job too much because of her illness. All her employer knew was that she was sick beyond company policy. She was too ashamed to inform him that she was HIV positive, and she feared a backlash from her employer if she told the truth. She lost her apartment and moved into a women's shelter. She lost all of her savings behind paying for treatment and medicine. Her school loans were in default, and her medical bills were still rising. She believed the medications she received have helped her not only to get better, but also to enable her to look toward having a future. However, the jury was still out on the 'future' issue.

When I first met Suzanne at this lunch hour seminar, I thought she was going to speak about someone else who was HIV positive and their struggles. She looked like she was on top of the world. I had absolutely no clue she was going to speak about herself and her own struggles being HIV positive. Even though she looked like the picture of health, it isn't the sickest looking person who dies first sometimes. In that meeting, all of us learned that it only takes one time to alter one's life dramatically. We were grateful that our firm provided financially to support her organization for treatment of women who were HIV positive and who had AIDS.

Ignorance, Disobedience & Low Self-Esteem – A Bad Combination

Now, I'll just give you a little insight into what happened to me so you won't think that I'm "all that and a greasy bag of chips." My promiscuity did not garner the same results as Suzanne, but could have. Nonetheless, there were still consequences to pay for having low self-esteem, being disobedient, ignorant, and just plain stupid.

I don't recall my mother ever telling my sister or me about the subject of sex, the "do's" and the "don'ts", or the consequences that come from having sex out of God's order. The only thing she did do, when we became teenagers and started our menstrual cycles, was to show us our gravesites in a gully that was located at the far end of our backyard. She pointed to different spots in the gully and stated that if we got pregnant, we would be in those graves. That was her way of dealing with the situation – to put the fear of God and of her in us. Believe me, we feared her and God in that order. Naturally, neither one of us got pregnant while we lived at home. My mom never told us what pregnancy entailed. She never told us about the medical, emotional or moral issues and related consequences of those issues concerning getting pregnant out of wedlock.

My mother never asked us what we wanted to do with our lives. She never asked us what we thought about various things. She never discussed with us how to make our dreams come true. In fact, at that time we had no dreams. We were just striving to survive; that's all we had time for and that's all we knew. My mom only threatened us with death – the ultimate consequence – if we disobeyed her.

My mother had her own problems that she was dealing with while raising us four kids (two boys and two girls) as a single parent. She actually had six children, but she lost the first two children – one died stillborn and the other was a miscarriage.

Before my mother married my father, she was studying to be an opera singer. She had a beautiful soprano voice. Her competition was a famous opera star who also had a soprano voice, and who realized her dream. She was born around the same time my mother was born. She went to college, received her Bachelor of Arts Degree, and then she studied at the Julliard School of Music. She traveled around the world and gained fame for her beautiful performances in operas. She had the desire, tenacity, and family support to stay with the task and reach her dream. Although there were some hardships, she became what she always wanted to be. She was content and her life was full.

As my mom told the story of her family, her parents made her marry my father because his father was the first Black Police Captain where they lived. His mother was a schoolteacher, his brothers were police officers, and his sisters were schoolteachers. So, her parents believed my father would amount to someone prominent and worthy, too, but that was not the case. He, however, turned out to be the "black sheep" of the family.

My father married my mother right before he got out of the Marine Corps, and she had to beg his commanding officer to give him an honorable discharge because he was such a "bad ass." After marrying my mother and leaving the Marine Corps, he moved her to California where he would not be accountable to his family or her family for his actions. By moving my mother to California, which was over 3,000 miles away, he took away her support and protection system within her family.

My father worked in construction, and he belonged to a construction union. He became a union representative and went up in the ranks of the union. He then thought he was slick enough to embezzle the union and he went to jail.

Back in the 1940's, 1950's and early 1960's, women, especially minority women, did not have much of a chance to make a decent living for themselves and their children. Most women had a very hard time in general. Some women were able to work in the factories during World War II, but after the war was over, their jobs went to the men who were now veterans returning from the war. Minority women worked where they could during that time.

My grandmother's philosophy concerning my mom was that 'you made your bed, now lay in it.' However, my mother's bed was already made for her by her parents because she honored their wishes by agreeing to marry who they selected for her. Back in those days children honored their parents' wishes.

My mother never got the opportunity to make her dreams become reality. She became very bitter for a number of years, for a number of reasons, and the marriage to my father was the chief reason. It was not until fifteen years before she died that she mellowed out and was content with herself and her life.

My mother believed in God, but did not necessarily have a church home. She did not go to church on a consistent basis. She did find some stability and consistency in the Catholic Church, so she sent us to a parish in the neighborhood. She went with us a few times, but most of the time we went to mass Sunday mornings without her. I think it was her way of getting a break from us four kids. The mass was always in Latin, and only the announcements of the parish activities were in English and Spanish. We only spoke English in our household. Go figure.

We attended Catechism (Catholic Bible Study) after school one day a week for a few years, and fortunately it was taught in English. We learned Catholic prayers through the Rosary, but I do not recall the nuns ever opening a Bible or reading scriptures to us from the Bible. We believed in God through the Catholic Church, but we did not learn enough of God's Word to apply it to situations in our lives.

I was molested when I was about 13 years of age, but my mother did not believe me. One Saturday afternoon, she had her girlfriends and their men friends over to the house. They were all drinking, smoking, talking loud and laughing way into the night. One of the men came into the bathroom while I was in there. I asked him to leave, but he would not. He put his hand over my mouth, held me, and molested me. He then threatened me not to tell my mother while he was there or else he would find me and hurt me. I told my mother after all her company left, but she did not believe me. She became angry with me and sent me to bed. I was angry that my mother didn't believe me. I was upset because I was physically violated. I felt worthless, dirty, and guilty at the same time because she didn't believe what I told her and she wasn't going to and didn't do anything about it. I felt the guy should have knocked on the door first before walking into the bathroom where I was. He should not have come into the bathroom when I told him it was occupied. I tried to leave, but he molested me. He would not let me go, and he threatened me. Since my mother did not believe me when I told her, and would not do anything about what happened to me, I was then afraid the guy would later harm me if he later found out I told my mother. No one cared about me and, I guess after a while, I didn't care either.

I did not get pregnant until a few years after I graduated from high school and left home.

I liked a guy in high school and he liked me. When he graduated a year before me, he asked me to go steady with him, I accepted, and he then gave me his class ring. My mother only allowed me to go out with him a few times. He joined the U.S. Navy and served aboard an ammunitions ship (the USS Vesuvius) loading and unloading bombs and ammunition for guns and other weapons to and from smaller ships during the war in Viet Nam. During his tour of duty, we lost touch with each other. It turned out that my mother withheld his letters from me because she didn't like him. His complexion was too dark for her taste (candy bar chocolate), and she didn't want any dark people in her family. What can I say! I thought he was no longer interested in me since I no longer received letters from him. I thought he found someone else.

After I graduated from high school, I left home and moved to North Hollywood. I rented a room from a lady who was the accountant for a number of famous jazz artists and blues celebrities. Her home was near the junior college I attended, and my part-time job on campus paid for my room and board. She was very nice to me. She treated me like I was one of her daughters. I lived with her almost two years.

When my high school boyfriend completed his tour of duty, he received an honorable discharge from the Navy, went back to live at home with his family, and landed a job in the aerospace industry. He then searched for me and found me through my girlfriends. We began dating again.

My boyfriend wined and dined me constantly. He told me he loved me. After a short while, he proposed marriage to me. As we began making plans to get married, he seduced me and made love to me. Although I did not know what I was doing, I loved him, trusted him, and **"I"** allowed him to take my virginity from me. I got pregnant immediately – very fertile, I guess. Because I did not know any better, I didn't think this was a big deal, but it became a big deal later on. We got married, and I was looking forward to living happily ever after.

Wrong, Wrong, Wrong!!!!!!!

One of the problems in my marriage was that I didn't really enjoy having sex because I didn't know what I was doing. I was never told how and what to do. If it comes naturally, it's supposed to be enjoyable, but it wasn't. My husband didn't tell me what to do, but he enjoyed doing what he did. No one ever told me about the functions of my physical equipment and I didn't really explore or investigate. I did not ask anyone how to have sex because I didn't want people, especially my girlfriends, to know I was having sex. I didn't want anyone to think I was stupid, and I certainly didn't want anyone to put my business in the street. I didn't know what exactly my boyfriend-turned-husband was doing while having sex with me, and I didn't know what to do to please him or what he was suppose to do to please me. I knew nothing about sex, and I didn't even know what to ask. I felt good as he kissed me, but that was about it. I just had no clue.

The sexual act in itself was intimacy to my husband. As long as he was happy and fulfilled, I guess I was happy, too. That was all. He had no clue about what to do to please me sexually, and he didn't know or care that he should be interested in pleasing me emotionally and then sexually. He certainly was not interested in asking me how he could please me or in telling me how to please him. He got his sexual satisfaction, and then he was done. No more, no less.

We used "no" protection against me getting pregnant or getting a disease. We didn't even discuss birth control. Although I knew I should have had some type of protection, especially since it was readily available at the time, I just thought pregnancy would not happen to me. I thought wrong.

My boyfriend didn't see the big deal about me getting pregnant. He was very happy that I was pregnant. He had proposed marriage to me, I was engaged to him, and we would be married soon. Case closed.

When we began to make love/have sex, we really had no place at the time to "do it" except in his mother's brand new 1970 black and white Chevy Monte Carlo that he purchased for her when he got out of the military. We made love in that car at night in the neighborhood park or in the local drive-in movie. On one occasion, we were caught by the Police while making-out in the parking lot at the park. (Thank God we were caught before most of the clothes came off. What in the world was I thinking???!!) The Police Officer told my boyfriend to step out of the vehicle, and then the Officer reprimanded him. The Officer then told him that he could at least take me to a motel and not be so cheap and sleazy to do it in a car in the park.

That night we both were ashamed and, needless to say, we did not continue in our lovemaking for a while. As he brought me home that night, we both were silent. I thought to myself how stupid I was, how cheap, how dirty, and I asked myself why I did not seem to care about myself like I should have. Why did I put myself in that situation? I knew my boyfriend loved me, but why didn't he think about these things, too? Why didn't my boyfriend think more of me? Why didn't I think more of myself? Why did it take a Police Officer, who didn't even know me, to tell him what he should and should not be doing with me? Yeah, that night was a revelation for us both. It was just as much my fault as it was his.

I kept asking myself why did I allow myself to be treated like I was less than I thought I was. Was I worthy to myself? Did I not know better? Did I not think more highly of myself? Did I think of myself at all? Was I respectable? Did he respect me? Why did I not respect myself? I didn't know what I was and, apparently, I didn't think about what I was doing, nor did I think about the consequences of my actions. What was wrong with me? Where was my self-esteem? Why did I go along with his agenda? What was my agenda? Why didn't I use some form of contraception? How come I didn't insist that he wear a condom? Why did I not think I would get pregnant? Why did I not think I would get a venereal disease? I knew the formula; it never changes. Why didn't I think about my future and what I wanted out of life? Why didn't I think about where I wanted to be in my life – two, five, or even ten years down the road? What about my college education? Was marriage all there was for me? What was wrong with me? Why was I doing this anyway? Deep down in my heart I certainly knew better. What was my problem? The Police Officer thought more of me than I thought of myself, and he didn't know me. What's up with that? I felt icky, sticky, dirty, guilty, and very uncomfortable. I did not feel worthy nor did I feel respected. I didn't respect myself. I felt I allowed myself to be molested again, this time with my consent.

Later on when the sting of what happened in the park wore off, we tempted fate again because this time I was wearing an engagement ring from my boyfriend, as if it justified our actions. Sure enough, I got pregnant. Too late! This was my consequence for being sexually promiscuous and having unprotected sex before marriage. Can you spell "B-R-A-I-N-L-E-S-S!"

Things could have been worse, although that's no excuse.

When you have unprotected sex, you are bound to get pregnant or get a disease, or something will always go wrong. The odds are always against you when you don't do the right thing. Although I never received this information in my home upbringing, in my education or in my religion, deep down inside I knew better and I was convicted in my conscience.

Now, I know things may be a bit different now, with some variation, but the formula is still the same and the consequences have not changed. My particular consequence was that I got pregnant before I got married, and, because of that, I was unable to fulfill my dreams. I didn't think it was such a big deal because I got pregnant by the man I loved and was going to marry anyway, so in my small mind (at that time) it was really sort of okay. I justified my actions in my mind. I put my future plans aside because of the unplanned reality I created when I became sexually active and got pregnant.

The saving grace of my pregnancy, in spite of all of my mistakes, was that I birthed a beautiful baby boy. This child was and still is a wonderful blessing to me from God. Four years later, I birthed a beautiful baby girl. Both children grew up very healthy and happy. I encountered other problems in my marriage that ended in divorce, but God blessed me and my ex-husband to forgive each other, and we are good friends today – for our sakes and for the sake of our children. We both love the Lord.

What Is Adultery All About?

Adultery involves a married person making a conscious and deliberate choice to have sex with someone other than her or his spouse. The other person involved in the adultery could be single or a spouse of another person. There are many names and terms for adultery such as infidelity, cheating, an affair, violation of the marriage bed, conjugal infidelity, extramarital sex, criminal conversation, unfaithfulness, philandery, non-monogamy, and unlawful consensual sex.

The measurement for how adultery is viewed in many cultures around the world ranges from a totally non-serious offense to a crime punishable by death. The method of causing the death of a woman who has committed adultery is horrific in some parts of the world. However, in those same parts of the world, a man who commits adultery is looked upon with a blind eye. The punishment for adultery could result in public beatings, castration, decapitation, mutilation, devouring by dogs, honor killings, murder, stoning, and a select crowd of people pushing the guilty offenders off cliffs. Additional inadvertent consequences of adultery include separation, divorce, unplanned pregnancy, abortion, sexual diseases, public humiliation, loss of health, loss of income, loss of financial support, loss of invested time, loss of relationships, and loss of property.

Here's a little history concerning adultery around the world:

In ancient Native American Indian cultures, the woman who committed adultery against her husband could receive severe punishment, including beatings and bodily mutilation.

The ancient laws of China required that the man be castrated (removal of the penis and testicles) for committing adultery against his spouse. The married woman who committed adultery was sequestered (isolated, secluded, set apart, or confined) for a long period of time or indefinitely. In China today, adultery is not punishable. However, it can be grounds for divorce.

In Judaism, the Torah demanded that those who committed adultery be put to death by a designated group of individuals who stoned the guilty parties or pushed the guilty parties off a cliff.

Under Islamic law, premarital sex was punishable by 40 or more lashes of a whip inflicted on the backs of the woman and the man. This is also known as flogging, flagellation, or thrashing. Adultery committed by women was punishable by stoning (lapidation), flogging, decapitation (beheading), mutilation, and "honor killing." These different types of chastisement are considered capital punishment, which is still in force to this day, but mostly against women "suspected" (not seen and not caught in the act) of being sexually promiscuous.

In ancient India, if a woman were charged with the act of adultery, she would be torn apart and eaten by dogs in the town square for all to see. Men were not prosecuted, but considered gods. However, these days when a man commits adultery with a married woman, without the consent of her husband, that man could be sentenced up to five years in jail if the husband prosecutes.

In most European countries, adultery is not considered a crime. However, retaliation by the injured party can be punishable by each country's laws, depending on the type of retaliation.

In many countries within South America, the courts upheld 'honor killings' by those marital partners who were wronged. However, some of the higher courts have outlawed "honor killings" by spurned husbands, stating that the husbands used this excuse to kill their wives for their own vanity. Christianity is now playing a larger role in matters concerning adultery in South America.

In the United States, adultery is punishable through the court systems via legal separation and divorce proceedings in family law courts. The laws vary from state to state, from life sentences in jail to the payment of small monetary fines. However, additional penalties outside the court systems can include unplanned pregnancies, abortions, unexpected child support payment requirements, and sexual diseases.

What Is Fornication?

Fornication is a conscious, deliberate, and a lot of times spontaneous choice of one single person to have consensual sex with another single person, or between two people – one of them not being married.

The ramifications for fornication in most countries are basically the same as for adultery. However, in the United States there are no legal penalties for having consensual sex unless one of the persons involved is under the age of accountability, a pregnancy develops, or a sexual disease is diagnosed.

In the United States, penalties for fornication can be accomplished through the court system should a pregnancy or a sexually transmitted disease develops. The inadvertent penalties also apply to fornication such as unplanned pregnancies, abortion, unexpected child support payment requirements, and sexual diseases.

Sexual Sin

"Nobody rides for free. Nobody!" Our society is deceived into thinking that sex can be had without any penalties. Most of the programs and commercials on television flaunt sexual promiscuity as if it's cheesecake and you can't gain weight from it. But, be not deceived, for there are definite consequences for operating outside of God's laws concerning sexual promiscuity. There are even some penalties for operating outside of man's laws regarding sexual promiscuity, but that's in Chapter 10 in this book.

Some teenage girls and women have sex outside of marriage because: (1) they feel lonely and want to feel intimate with someone; (2) they feel they don't fit in and need to be accepted, so they use sex as the vehicle for it; (3) they feel empty inside and need some type of fulfillment in their life through sex; (4) they believe they are less than what they should be and need to build up their self-esteem through sex; (5) they feel taken advantage of in a relationship with someone and use sex with someone else to get back at the other person; or (6) they need to make money (prostitution) to support themselves. All of these are the wrong reasons for having sex outside of marriage, and there are consequences following each of these wrong motives.

Sexual sin, like any other sin, begins in the mind. Sexual sin requires your desire, your will, and your consent – all done in the mind way before you actually perform the act. If you guard and control your mind, you will keep yourself from receiving the wrong consequences. Your thoughts control your decisions, your decisions control your actions, and your actions control what consequences you will subject yourself to.

Having sex outside of marriage for any reason is disobedience to God's laws, and causes significant emotional and physical damage. It eventually brings up emotions such as feeling empty, disappointed in oneself, let down, depressed, guilty, and feeling unworthy. Not only that, you're angry with yourself because you knew better, you've been there before, and you fell into that same old trap, **AGAIN!** The momentary act of sex did not sustain you; you still feel unfulfilled. Your low self-esteem has taken another dive downward. You feel like a hypocrite because you have convinced others that you're innocent, pure and clean. You're fearful of receiving future repercussions, be it a sexual disease, or getting pregnant, or the person demanding to have sex with you again because you were so easy the first time, or you fear your name will be smeared as you are labeled an easy lay to other men (and, yes, men talk). You feel depressed because you know you've been dishonest with yourself. You feel you have destroyed your image of yourself to yourself and to others. You feel anxiety about your future and the consequences that are ahead. You feel pressure and confusion in your mind.

You cannot have sex out of the will of God and expect to get away with it. There is no immediate pleasure without some penalty on the horizon. We are to flee sexual immorality because there are consequences. The consequences will come; it's inevitable. *1st Thessalonians 4:8* states: *"Therefore, he [she] who rejects this [God's Word] does not reject man, but God, who has also given us His Holy Spirit."* When you reject God's word on a subject, you are out of His order and out of His protection. *1 Corinthians 6:18-20* states: *"Flee sexual immorality. Every sin that a man [woman] does is outside the body, but he [she] who commits sexual immorality sins against his [her] own body. Or do you not know that your body is the temple of the Holy Spirit who is in you, whom you have from God, and you are not your own? For you were bought with a price; therefore, glorify God in your body and in your spirit, which are God's."* Sexual sin will take you much further than you want to go, it will keep you longer than you ever intended or wanted to stay, and it will definitely cost you more than you thought you would pay in almost all areas of your life.

There are three major examples in the Bible of the consequences of what happens because of sexual immorality: David and Bathsheba *(2 Samuel 11:1 – 24; 12:1-18)*; Samson and Delilah *(Judges 16)*; and the cities of Sodom and Gomorrah *(Genesis 19)*. "Talk about the good, the bad and the ugly!" These verses in the Bible give clear and comprehensive details concerning sexual promiscuity and the ensuing consequences because of disobedience to God.

Dating

Back in the day, a man who was interested in a woman would ask her out on a date, and this is how the date would go: On a Wednesday, the man would call the woman and ask to take her out to dinner. She, being somewhat interested in him, would accept the dinner invitation. He would ask her what type of food she liked to eat, and she would tell him. He would then recommend a couple of restaurants. She would select one of his suggestions or would recommend a restaurant she liked. He would accept. By the type of restaurant, they both determined how they would dress. He would then ask what day and time she would be available to go out on the date. She would tell him that she would be available on Saturday at 7:00 p.m. He then made the dinner reservation. If the restaurant selected required a shirt and tie, the man would wear a shirt and tie. The type of restaurant selected would also let the woman know what to wear – either a nice dress or pantsuit.

In preparation for the dinner date, the woman would select a dress of a certain color that flattered the best part of her body (maybe her legs) and that enhanced the color of her skin. She selected jewelry to match the dress, select the shoes and matching handbag, and she selected that special expensive perfume to wear. She would get her hair done at the beauty parlor, and get a manicure and pedicure if needed. The man would generally shower, shave and wear a suit.

The man would be on time to pick the woman up for the date. He would open the car door for her as she got into the car and as she got out of the car at the restaurant. He would compliment her on her attire and she would do likewise. The conversation at the restaurant would be light and fun. After dinner, he would pick up the check and pay for the dinner. He would then take her home. When he brought her to her door, she may or may not give him a signal to kiss her. She would go inside her home and he would go home.

Dating these days is far less formal for teenage girls and women. There are many variations of dating, but most are centered around promiscuous activities. There are the "booty calls" where the guy calls the woman in the late hours of the evening or in the early morning hours asking to come to her home to have sex with her. He doesn't even want to take her out to dinner. He just wants to get in, get laid, get up, and get out. He may put up money for a dinner or a gift, but only if she puts out in the bed. Then there's the dinner date or club date where the guy will pay for dinner, but he will be expecting to have sex with the woman when he brings her home. He figures he paid for the dinner so she should pay in the bed. Then there's the sex date, where two people get together for the sole purpose of having sex, and then they go their separate ways – no muss, no fuss, no commitment.

Some teenagers call their dating "hooking up", which means having sex with a bunch of other teenagers. Very little money is spent on this type of dating amongst them. There may be a run to fast-food joints and liquor stores for some beer or alcohol, but mostly the dates involve having sex with multiple partners (boys with girls, boys with boys, girls with girls, and girls with boys). They all alternate with each other in oral, anal, and vaginal sex. After everyone has had everyone else sexually, they all go to their own homes and get in their own beds.

Then there are the married couples "swapping" or "swinging" with other married couples in which they all have sex with each other's partners. This, too, involves oral copulation, anal, and vaginal sex.

There use to be standard types of men to date. There's the strong, muscular, and handsome type who was more into his body-building than being sexually involved. He just wanted a cute female on his rippling arm. There's the shy type who is just happy that a lady is going out with him. There's the rich guy who wants to impress his lady date with his money, and he wants her to impress him with her good looks. Then there's the everyday, hard-working, easy-going type who is comfortable to be around all the time. There are many more standard types of men, but these are just a few.

These days, you really need to know who you're dating before you get sexually involved because there are now other categories of men who are out there dating, but these categories are deadly. You definitely need to be aware of and stay away from these men:

<u>The "Promiscuous" Man</u> – He's the one sleeping around with other women, aside from having sex with you. Some may even be married women. There's no telling how many bed partners he's had, is currently involved with, or will have, but you are definitely one of many on his list.

<u>The "Bi-Sexual" Man</u> – He's the one who is not only dating and having sexual intercourse with you, a female, but he's also having sexual intercourse with other men.

<u>The "Down-Low" Man (DLM)</u> – He's similar to the Bi-Sexual Man, but he's the man who is "married" and having sexual intercourse with his wife, with you, and with a man or other men.

Any of these types of men can increase your risk of getting a sexual infection, virus or disease by a thousand-fold. It only takes **"<u>one time</u>"** for you to be infected by someone who is already infected with a sexual infection, virus, or disease. Will any of these promiscuous types of men tell you they are sleeping around with others – be it male or female? I think not! Will any of these promiscuous types of men tell you they have a sexual infection or disease? Get real! Your life and your future are immediately jeopardized if you sleep around with them.

Unfortunately, women can be in the above categories, too, and present the same risks to men and to women.

Health Risks

Do you know that every person you sleep with becomes a part of you? Do you know that whatever the person has in the form of a Sexually Transmitted Disease (STD), your chances of getting it is 100%? Do you know that 1 out of every 4 people in the United States has an STD? Do you know there are **"Dead Women Walking"** because the sexual disease they have is incurable and these women have an expected expiration date? Do you want to be part of any of these statistics? This is not a game!

The health risks listed below are what should be discussed with all young girls, teenage girls, and all ages of women. Older women who want to have sexual encounters, flings, or affairs should also be aware of the vital health risks. Age does not make anyone immune to STDs. This is the information that should be, or should have been discussed with you by your mom, your big sister, or someone very close to you whom you trust and feel safe and comfortable with. You can and should even discuss this with your doctor if you feel uncomfortable discussing it with a member of your family.

You should do all you can to obtain as much information as you can before making that wrong decision to **"spread your legs"** and have sexual intercourse, which can affect your health, your future, and your life. Sorry to be so crass, but it is what it is, and it can be devastating. Again, it only takes **"one time!"**

Before you get married, you and your prospective partner should discuss your sexual histories with each other. You should both get tested for STDs and obtain and exchange medical reports on one another. You should then discuss the reports. You both should then resolve any and all issues reflected in the medical reports before you take that sexual plunge into marriage. If your prospective mate refuses to be tested, that should be a **"BIG RED FLAG"**, which indicates there's definitely a problem. If he really loves you, he will have no problem taking any tests for the sake of the relationship and the impending marriage. After all, honesty is part of the love relationship.

Just as you would not purchase a used car without knowing its' repair and accident history, you should not marry someone without knowing his medical/sexual health history, among other things. It's not out of line to ask and expect to receive **"sex facts"** about your partner, so you know exactly what you'll be dealing with. You should strongly reconsider whether you want to be involved with a person, especially to the extent of being sexually active with him prior to marriage, if he has a problem being tested for any kind of health wellness. The health risks involved go way beyond your emotional feelings and your belief that such a thing could never happen to you.

"Be smart and be informed!"

Once you review each of the below-listed sexually transmitted diseases, you will see why it's so important to abstain from having sex until you get married. These infections, viruses and diseases are very real, some even deadly, and they will be glaring reminders to you that you made the wrong choice because you did not do your homework, you did not insist that the man be tested, and you did not abstain from having sex with him. Remember, this will affect **your** life and **your** future, and **you** will bear the consequences. You are responsible for **"<u>you</u>"** alone. You only have one "life-suit" on this earth. There are no cures for some of the STDs that are discussed below.

<u>Center For Disease Control (CDC)</u>

The information provided comes from the Center for Disease Control (CDC). The information is real, current, accurate, and reflects the possible dangers as well as the damages. The listed diseases can be a death warrant for your life, so **<u>you must take this seriously.</u>**

Don't be foolish in thinking that this cannot happen to you. It happens to the best of us in the best of households, especially to the most naive and to the prettiest women and girls. It happens to all races on the face of the planet. It happens to the wealthiest family member as well as to the poorest family member. These infections, viruses and diseases are no respector of person, race, location, or financial standing.

<u>Sexually Transmitted Diseases – Bad To Worst</u>

(1) <u>Bacterial Vaginosis</u> – This condition exists when there is an abnormal amount of certain bad bacteria growing within a woman's vagina. This is usually caused by having sex with multiple partners and/or douching. There is a discharge that has a strong fish-smell odor, some pelvic pain, itching around the outer part of the vagina, possible burning during urination, and a general sense of being uncomfortable. If not treated, this could lead to additional problems in the uterus, pelvis, fallopian tubes and ovaries, and could lead to an increased risk of HIV.

Bacterial Vaginosis is treatable. You must have a pelvic examination where the doctor will take a sample of the fluid, have it tested, and then she will prescribe antibiotics. The partners you had sex with do not have to be informed or treated, but if you felt comfortable enough to sleep with the guys, you should have no problem in letting them know about your condition so they can get examined and treated. This can be avoided by abstaining from having sex with partners outside of marriage.

(2) Chlamydia – This is one of the most frequently reported sexually transmitted infections. Chlamydia is pronounced Clam-id-ia. The more sex partners you have, the more susceptible you are to get this infection. This infection can be transmitted through vaginal sex, oral sex or anal sex. It's known as a silent infection because symptoms are not quickly and easily detectable.

Chlamydia is very damaging to the reproductive organs of a female, causing irreversible damage, even infertility, if not treated quickly. It is a bacterial infection that first affects the cervix and the urethra (the urethra is the urine canal from the bladder). It can then spread to the fallopian tubes. It can cause Pelvic Inflammatory Disease (PID) in women. PID can damage the uterus, fallopian tubes and tissues within the pelvic area. There is pain in the pelvic area, a burning sensation while urinating, a bad odor, and an unsavory discharge that accompanies Chlamydia. It causes a lot of discomfort, lower back pain, bleeding in between menstrual periods, nausea, fever, and pain during sexual intercourse. Chlamydia can be found in the cervix of females who have vaginal sex, and it can spread to the rectum. It can also be found in the throats of females who have oral sex. It can be found in the rectum of females who participate in anal sex causing rectal pain, a discharge, and bleeding.

Chlamydia can be treated by an examination from a physician who takes a sample of the bacteria, has it examined by the lab, and prescribes antibiotics. Any sexual partner of the woman should be notified so that he can get examined and treated for the infection. It can be avoided by abstaining from having sex with partners outside of marriage.

Chlamydia can affect a woman's ability to have children in the future. If the woman gets pregnant and has Chlamydia, she can spread it to her baby and the baby can be born with physical problems related to the infection.

(3) Genital Human Papilloma Virus (HPV) – This is one of the most common sexually transmitted viruses. There are over 40 varieties of this virus that affect the genital areas of women and men. It infects the mucous membranes and skin of both women and men. In women, it affects the linings of the vagina, vulva, cervix, and rectum. HPV can cause a range of problems, and it is somewhat undetectable. It can be as low-risk as causing genital warts (small bumps or groupings of bumps in the genital areas) or as high risk as causing cervical cancer and other types of cancer. Cervical cancer may not be detected until it is in its advanced stages.

HPV is generally transmitted sexually through vaginal or anal sex. The cells become abnormal and can turn into cancer cells over a long period of time. The body's immune system fights off these cells, but if the immune system is unable to fight off these abnormal cells, the cells may become cancerous over a period of time. This cancer can be in the vulva, vagina, cervix and anus. Cervical cancer is the most common and most deadly.

Cervical cancer can be prevented by keeping a healthy immune system, by abstaining from having sex with partners outside of marriage, by regular pelvic examinations with cancer screening for cervical cancer through pap smears, and by use of an HPV vaccine that protects and treats some types of cervical cancer and genital warts.

(4) Genital Herpes – The HSV-2 Virus causes most of the genital herpes, which is a sexually transmitted disease that appears in the genital area in a blister-like form. The blisters burst causing sores that heal within two to four weeks after the outbreak. This is very painful in the vaginal and anal areas of a woman. The symptoms of the disease are the outbreak of a crop of blisters in the genital area and flu-like symptoms such as a fever and swollen glands.

The HSV-1 virus (Herpes Simplex) can also cause Genital Herpes, but is most commonly known for causing fever blisters of the mouth and lips.

The Genital Herpes disease can be easily spread from an infected partner, who does not have any visible outbreaks, to an un-infected partner. The HSV-2 virus infected person who has oral and anal sex with a person can also spread the disease to the mouth and to the anus. This disease can be transmitted to a baby if the female is pregnant during the time she contracts the disease.

It's rather easy to diagnose Genital Herpes because of its visibility in the genital area. The doctor can also take a culture sample from one of the sores and send it to the lab for testing. Or, the doctor can draw blood from the patient, who has no visible outbreaks, and have the blood tested in a lab to determine whether the person has Genital Herpes.

The infection/disease is incurable, but the outbreaks lessen over time. One out of every five adolescents and adults has Genital Herpes, and it's more common in women than in men. It can be avoided by abstaining from having sex with partners outside of marriage.

(5) Gonorrhea – Another sexually transmitted infectious disease is Gonorrhea (pronounced Gone-or-re-ahh). It is caused by a bacteria that grows in the cervix, uterus, fallopian tubes, and the urethra. It can also grow in the mouth, throat, eyes and anus. The disease is spread through contact with the vagina, mouth, penis or anus. A man does not have to ejaculate to spread gonorrhea.

The symptoms of Gonorrhea are mild in women and can be interpreted as a bladder infection or a vaginal infection. There is a burning sensation when urinating, increased discharge from the vagina, or bleeding from the vagina between periods. There may also be pain in the pelvic area, soreness, a rash, a puss-like discharge in the genital area, and diarrhea. Symptoms of Gonorrhea in the rectum or anus include anal itching, discharge from the anus, bleeding and soreness, and a painful bowel movement. Symptoms of Gonorrhea in the mouth and throat include soreness in both.

Gonorrhea causes PID (Pelvic Inflammatory Disease), abdominal pain and fever, puss-filled pockets (abscesses) in the pelvic area that are hard to cure, damage to the fallopian tubes, and the disease can cause an increase in the occurrence of an ectopic pregnancy (a fertilized egg growing outside the uterus). It can also cause chronic pelvic pain. Gonorrhea can contaminate the blood and spread to the joints of the body. Gonorrhea can also make a person more susceptible to contracting HIV, the virus that causes AIDS.

Gonorrhea can also be spread to a baby from its mother during delivery. This can possibly cause blindness in the baby, can also cause infection in the blood of a baby, and can cause a joint infection in the baby.

To determine whether you have Gonorrhea, you must be tested and treated by a doctor. He will take a "Gram stain", which is a sample culture from the cervix, urethra, rectum or throat. The doctor can also take a urine sample and send it to the lab for testing. There are several antibiotics, which can successfully treat and cure Gonorrhea in adolescents and adults, **BUT** there are drug-resistant strains of Gonorrhea.

Gonorrhea can be avoided by abstaining from having sex with partners outside of marriage.

(6) Lymphogranuloma Venereum (LGV) – This disease is a sexually transmitted disease caused by a particular type of Chlamydia trachomatis. Lymphogranuloma Venereum is pronounced Lympho-granu-loma Vene-reum. It's mostly found among men having sex with men, and in those who have been found to be HIV infected, leading to AIDS.

Some of the symptoms include rectal bleeding, anal discharge, constipation, genital or rectal ulcers, and anal spasms.

There is little information with respect to females carrying this disease and the affects on their bodies, but they can also carry this disease. Not enough is known about the disease, except that males are definitely affected. However, this disease can be avoided by abstaining from having sex with partners outside of marriage.

(7) Syphilis – Another sexually transmitted disease is Syphilis, pronounced sif-i-lis. It's caused by a bacteria which creates sores in the genital area through sexual contact with someone who has the disease. These sores appear on the vagina, anus or in the rectum, on the lips, and in the mouth.

This disease can be spread during vaginal sex, anal sex, or oral sex.

It can also be transmitted to the baby of a pregnant mother. The baby may be delivered stillborn (born dead), or the baby may die shortly after birth. The baby may also become developmentally slow, have seizures, and can die.

Syphilis starts out as a chancre (pronounced kan-ker) sore that is small, round and painless. The sore is infectious, and can make a person easily vulnerable to receiving or transmitting the HIV virus, which can cause AIDS.

If Syphilis is not treated, it can turn into a secondary stage of a rash on different areas of the body. The rash appears as reddish brown spots on the palms of the hands and the bottom of the feet. Along with the rash, a person can develop a fever, lose hair in different parts of the scalp, experience headaches and muscle aches, develop swollen lymph glands, develop a sore throat, and have fatigue.

If Syphilis is still not treated, the second stage of symptoms will go away, and the third stage of symptoms develops. The third stage of Syphilis damages the internal organs of the body, which include bones, heart, brain, nerves, eyes, liver, joints and blood vessels. There will be paralysis, numbness, gradual blindness, and dementia. This stage of the disease can lead to death. The infection can remain in the body for years unless treated.

Syphilis is only transmitted through sexual intercourse. The genital sores caused by syphilis can bleed easily. When the sores come into contact with the soft tissues of the vagina, anus, or mouth during sex, they are easily spread and make the body very susceptible to HIV.

Syphilis can be treated at an early stage by a visit to the doctor for examination. The doctor will prescribe an antibiotic such as penicillin or she will prescribe other antibiotics for those who are allergic to penicillin. Afterwards, the patient should be screened (checked) for Syphilis on a regular basis.

Syphilis can be avoided by abstaining from having sex with partners outside of marriage.

(8) <u>Trichomoniasis (A Penis To Vagina Parasite)</u> – This disease affects both women and men, but is more common in women. Trichomoniasis is pronounced trick-o-mo-nia-sis. It is an organism living within the vagina. It is sexually transmitted from penis to vagina (from man to woman) or from vulva to vulva (women to women) during sexual intercourse. Females can contract the disease from men or women.

The disease creates a foaming yellow-green vaginal discharge with a stinking odor. It causes irritation and itching in the genital area of the woman. There is great discomfort during sexual intercourse and during urination. There are small red sores on the vaginal wall or cervix. Lower abdominal pain may also be present.

Pregnant women who have this disease can cause their child to be born prematurely and have low birth weight.

The disease can be treated by a physician, who will take a sample of the discharge and send it to the lab for further examination. The physician will then prescribe antibiotics. This can be treated and cured by prescription drugs. Men can expel the parasite within a couple of weeks, but women must be treated with antibiotics to kill the parasite.

Trichomoniasis can be avoided by abstaining from having sex with partners outside of marriage.

<u>Proctitis</u> – This is the inflammation (swelling and irritation) of the anus (the opening of your rear end) and the lining of the rectum (the lower part of the intestines or tunnel that goes down to the anus; about six inches). Proctitis is caused by irritation to the anus and rectum by foreign objects placed in the rectum (such as a penis, sex toys, or other foreign objects), trauma to the rectal area due to receiving something larger than what it's designed for, by chemicals and antibiotics from treatment for other physical conditions, and by radiation from treatment of other physical conditions.

If you have a sexually transmitted disease in the anus, the symptoms range from itching and soreness in the anus and rectum to puss-like discharges and bleeding from those areas. You can have Herpes or anal warts around the anus. You have the constant urge to have a bowel movement or the constant feeling of constipation. You may have anorectal trauma in the anus and rectum (abscesses, deformation, bleeding, itching, etc.) in which the anus opening and rectal linings stretch and tear. You may have a painful spasm in the anus and rectum along with the urgency to urinate or have diarrhea.

The disease can be treated by a physician, who will perform a proctosigmoidoscopy, which means he will stick a lighted tube with a camera up through your anus and rectum and take pictures of the areas. He will also take a biopsy (tissue sample) and a culture of fluids (puss, blood, etc.) coming from your anus and rectum, and send them to the lab for testing. The treatment will depend on the findings by the doctor and the laboratory.

The most common cause of proctitis is sexually transmitted diseases. Antibiotics are generally prescribed, depending on how bad the condition or conditions. Proctitis can be avoided by abstaining from having sex with partners outside of marriage.

(10) HIV – Human Immunodeficiency Virus (a/k/a AIDS) – AIDS stands for Acquired Immunodeficiency Syndrome. HIV is a rare type of cancer that attacks the immune system of the human body. HIV seeks out and destroys particular white blood cells (T-cells) that the human body uses to fight off diseases and infections. Lack of these T-cells weaken the immune system of the body. This causes the body to be unable to fight off infections that attack the body.

HIV is found in the blood stream, in the semen of a man, or in the vaginal fluid of an infected woman.

A person can only contract HIV by one of four ways: (1) sexual intercourse with an infected person (vaginal sex, anal sex, or oral sex); (2) sharing needles and syringes with an infected person; (3) exposing a baby prior to birth through body fluids or after birth through breast-feeding; and (4) blood transfusion with blood infected with HIV.

The symptoms of HIV are very similar to having the flu. You can develop a fever, a rash can break out on your body, you can have swollen lymph nodes and swollen glands, and you feel weak and achy all over. You are very contagious during this incubation period. To avoid contracting HIV, one should abstain from sexual activity, drug activity, and should ensure that any blood transfusions are not tainted with the HIV virus.

If one plans to marry and has not been sexually active, but her partner has been sexually active, she should have her prospective partner tested for the disease. If one plans to marry, and is sexually active with her prospective marital partner, she and her prospective partner should be tested for the disease. If you are sexually active and are being treated for HIV, you should contact your sexual partner(s) and inform him/them of your situation so they can get tested and treated.

Reality Bites!

In order for you to receive any of the above viruses, infections or diseases, you have to be injected or infected by someone who is carrying the virus, infection, or disease. The virus, infection, or disease is either carried on the outside of the penis, vagina, anus, or mouth or carried inside the penis, vagina, anus or mouth. The infected fluid is transferred, secreted, or ejaculated inside of you.

Take Herpes, for example. What appears to be small bumps on a guy's penis can and does burst and ooze the viral infectious fluid inside of your vagina, anus or your mouth. When the guy ejaculates (injects fluids) inside of your vagina, anus, or your mouth, he has dispensed the virus, infection or disease inside of you. It only takes one time, and you're infected for life.

I have not mentioned **all** of the sexual diseases, but just some of the **major ones.** If the descriptions of the above infections, viruses, diseases, and how you can be infected are not enough to make you keep your legs, anus, and mouth closed and keep you from being sexually promiscuous, I don't know what is! Just consider how much time it takes to clear up some of these infections and viruses with medical treatment. You will definitely be uncomfortable for a while, and will suffer physically and emotionally. You will suffer the rest of your life with pain, suffering, and the decaying of your body from a sexual disease that has no cure, unless God, Himself, miraculously heals you. This is the real deal; it's not a joke!

"Are you tough enough for the consequences of sex?"

Contraception – Avoidance Of Pregnancy Or STDs

Let's face it, you just can't have your cake and eat it, too!

There are several options you have in birth control, and the risks are great, but you have only one option to avoid an STD. Can you guess what that is? **Birth control does not stop an STD!**

The options for birth control are discussed below in the ranking of the best method to the worst method.

Abstinence – This is ranked **NO. 1**! Abstinence is the safest, most foolproof method of birth control. It's the ultimate shield against an

STD. It's 100% effective! Would you believe that it works **EVERY SINGLE TIME**!!!!!!!!!!!!!!! You don't have to read an instruction guide or a book to find out how Abstinence works. It's simple. It works any place and for any reason. It works in the bedroom, the back seat of a car, in the corner in the dark, and in your bedroom of your parents' home. It works everywhere, every time, and anytime. It works in Summer, Fall, Winter, and Spring. Abstinence is weatherproof. It works in the rain, in the blazing heat, under water, and in the snow.

Abstinence is the No. 1 Best Seller of all time, and do you know why??????? **IT'S FREE! IT'S QUICK! IT'S EASY! NO MUSS, NO FUSS!** There are no prescriptions, no money involved, no taxes, no penalties, and no consequences! Abstinence even saves you money because it's free. You don't need to apply for credit or get a loan to obtain abstinence. It only takes a moment for Abstinence to work: **"JUST SAY NO!"**

There's no guesswork with Abstinence. You don't have to take any pills or mix any ingredients before taking it. You don't have to insert some device inside of you, or have some rubber balloon stuck inside of you. You don't have to check a schedule before taking it, or wear patches, or count days, or get shots.

Abstinence has no expiration date. No one is allergic to Abstinence. There are absolutely no worries with Abstinence. When in doubt, Abstinence leaves it out.

Abstinence has redemptive qualities, too! Abstinence is your insurance policy. It's the cure for the most common urges. Abstinence protects your future, your goals, and your dreams.

You have respect and clout with Abstinence. Your parents love and respect you. Your teachers praise you. Your peers envy you.

Your doctor admires you. Your co-workers wish they were you. And do you know why????? Because you can control yourself, your life, and your future with Abstinence.

Abstinence keeps you healthy and good-looking. It keeps your figure in shape. You won't need a gym membership. Abstinence fits all sizes and shapes. You can dress for success with Abstinence – new clothes, new hairdos, and new high-heal shoes with that new matching handbag. It's like putting on a pair of the most expensive silk stockings or putting on that special dress that just makes you look like a million bucks. You will always be in style with Abstinence.

You can travel with Abstinence, too! When you want to go to Hawaii or Paris, you can with Abstinence. If you want to go skydiving, snow skiing, hiking, river-rafting, or even break-dancing, guess what? You can! You can't go wrong with Abstinence!

Abstinence fills all of your emotional needs, too! It keeps you in a good mood because there is no pressure and there's no guilt. You have no worries. You feel good when you make the decision to **"JUST SAY NO!"** when that guy tries to pressure you into having sex with him. Saying the word **"NO"** takes the pressure off of you and puts the pressure on him to do the right thing by you. Isn't it great to know that someone wants you and you have the power over that person by saying **NO!** In essence, you control yourself and you control him at the same time. You control your world with Abstinence. What awesome power!

If I could bottle Abstinence and sell it, I certainly would!

Abortion – What could have been? Have you ever wondered what purpose God had for your child? He or she could have been the one who discovered the cure for cancer or AIDS. He or she could have led the world in peace and compassion like Mother Teresa, who won the Nobel Peace Prize in 1979, or he or she could have been like Ghandi, who shaped the history of his country, India. He or she could have served the Lord in a ministerial capacity and been one of the greatest teachers since the Apostles, such as Billy Graham or Dr. Martin Luther King, or my pastor (Tom Pickens at the Antelope Valley Christian Center). He or she could have graduated from college, got a fantastic job, and was able to help you in your needs in your old age.

If you have aborted your child, you will not know in your lifetime on this earth what could have been. However, one thing you should know is that you've got a loved one in Heaven waiting for you with open arms. Your loved one in Heaven is waiting for you to dwell and to share with them in all of God's glory. You will find out in Heaven what your child's purpose was on this earth. You have definitely got something wonderful to look forward to when you go to Heaven. Your loved one loves you, and God loves you, too. God will forgive you for aborting your child if you ask Him.

God sees the sin of abortion as He sees all sin, and He forgives all sin when asked. By accepting God's Son, Jesus Christ, as your Lord and Savior by asking Jesus to come into your life, by repenting (changing the direction you're going in and following God's direction), and by asking for the forgiveness of your sins, your name will be written in the Lamb's Book of Life and you will be given entrance into Heaven to be with your loved one.

All is not lost in an abortion; there is great hope. God forgives us all. He is a forgiving God. He is a merciful God. God is a God of many chances. You have a **"do over"** chance to turn a wrong decision into a right action, but it starts with forgiveness. Ask God for forgiveness, then forgive yourself, and forgive the one who got you pregnant. In the Gospel of John, Chapter 8, Jesus was approached by some scribes and Pharisees. They brought before Him a woman they caught in the act of adultery. Since the scribes and Pharisees were male, they conveniently did not bring the man who was engaged in adultery with the woman, but only brought the woman. That did not make the man any less guilty, who was involved in the act of adultery. There were consequences for him, too. However, the scribes and pharisees wanted to test Jesus, and they asked Him what He thought should be done with the woman. The Law of Moses stated that she should be stoned. However, Jesus began writing in the dirt, and He said to them in *John 8:7: "He who is without sin among you, let him throw a stone at her first."* Being convicted in their hearts by what Jesus said, they each went away quietly. *John 8:10-11* states: *"When Jesus had raised Himself up and saw no one but the woman, He said to her, 'Woman, where are those accusers of yours? Has no one condemned you?' She said, 'No one Lord.' And Jesus said to her, 'Neither do I condemn you; go and sin no more.'"* As the Lord forgave the adulteress, He will forgive you.

As many will attest to, there are lingering emotional, and sometimes physical consequences that follow an abortion, and they do not go away easily, if ever, unless you come to Jesus and repent. Only He can take away the pain, guilt, and the emotional scars that were left from an abortion. He will forgive you, He will comfort you, and He will give you a new joy for your life. However, God has also given you a purpose to fulfill, and it's not too late. It's a wonderful purpose. Seek Him to find out what your purpose is in this life, and trust in Him.

If you value the person enough to have sexual intercourse with him, you should use that same standard of value to the child if you get pregnant. Or else, why have sex with the person. What are you getting out of the sexual relationship that has value to you and to your future? Ask yourself if the value to you is worth the consequences you will encounter?

Everything has a value. God placed the highest value on us by sacrificing His Son, Jesus Christ, for our salvation. *John 3:16* states: *"For God so loved the world that He gave His only begotten Son, that whoever believes in Him should not perish but have everlasting life."* God loves you so much that He gave His only begotten Son to die on the cross for your sins of yesterday, today, and tomorrow. God loves you unconditionally – you didn't have to pay anything for Him to love you because He loved you first. But because of His love for you, He paid a price that none of us will ever be able to repay.

If you get pregnant and are contemplating an abortion, remember **"God has a purpose for every human being born."** Also remember what God said in *Genesis 1:26-28*, which states: *"Then God said, 'Let Us make man in Our image, according to Our likeness, let them have dominion over the fish of the sea, over the birds of the air, and over the cattle, over all the earth and over every creeping thing that creeps on the earth.' So God created man in His own image, in the image of God He created him; male and female He created them. Then God blessed them, and God said to them, 'Be fruitful and multiply; fill the earth and subdue it; have dominion over the fish of the sea, over the birds of the air, and over every living thing that moves on the earth.'"* He will make a way for your child.

Please think about the consequences of having an abortion, first, before you decide to go through with it. There is always another way to solve a problem. You must look at it objectively from God's standpoint, not just from your own perspective. He is a God of creation, not of destruction of what He has created. He is able to turn a wrong into a right. If God is able to part the Red Sea, make rainbows around the whole earth, which signifies His promise to never again flood the earth, He can certainly turn your mistake into a blessing.

You don't want to compound the mistake of getting pregnant out of wedlock by having an abortion. The consequences are so much worse.

If the one who got you pregnant wants you to have an abortion, and is insistent about it, remind him that he will be accountable, too, for his actions, good or bad. Don't back down on this point. You are not the only one who will bear the consequences for your actions. The one who got you pregnant will encounter his consequences, too. No one rides for free!

Just because a guy got you pregnant, then left you, and you haven't heard from him, doesn't mean his life will be all that great! God knows exactly where he is, and God will deal with him, accordingly. Your responsibility is to ask God for forgiveness of what you did, then to forgive yourself, and forgive the person who got you pregnant and then abandoned you. Leave the rest up to God.

You should know that there are alternatives to abortion. You can give the gift of adoption to a family whose heart is open to receiving and loving your child, and who will provide the very best for your child. You can take comfort in knowing that not only did you help bring a life into this world to fulfill God's purpose, but you also saw to it that the beautiful gift you give to a family will be well taken care of and raised up in the admonition of the Lord. You will have allowed God's purpose in your child's life to be fulfilled through the help of others. **This is a WIN-WIN situation!** There are no down sides.

You will definitely be blessed, although you may not see it early on because you're in the thick of your dilemma, but have faith in God. Time is precious, and in the vast expanses of time you will see the blossoming of the life you helped to create. God works all things out for good to those who love Him and who are the called according to His purpose. *Romans 8:28* states: *"And we know that all things work together for good to those who love God, to those who are the called according to His purpose."* It doesn't matter what circumstances existed at the time you got pregnant. Everything will fall into place the right way at the right time for God's purpose to be fulfilled. Don't forget that it takes three to make a baby: God, you, and the person who got you pregnant. If God didn't allow it, you would **not** have gotten pregnant. That means He had a purpose in your getting pregnant. Even though you didn't do things God's way, He will work things out for your good and for His glory.

God will also honor your decision to keep your child and to raise him or her. You will not be alone because God is always with you. *Hebrews 13:5* states: *"Let your conduct be without covetousness; be content with such things as you have, for He Himself has said, 'I will never leave you nor forsake you.'"* You may be fearful concerning this decision, but God does not want you to fear. *Isaiah 41:10* states: *"Fear not, for I am with you. Be not dismayed, for I am your God. I will strengthen you, yes, I will help you. I will uphold you with My righteous right hand."* Although you may get hostility from your parents, from the one who got you pregnant, or from your so-called friends, just trust that God will make a way for you and your child. *Psalm 32:8* states: *"I will instruct you and teach you in the way you should go; I will guide you with My eye." Proverbs 3:5-6* states: *"Trust in the Lord with all your heart, and lean not on your own understanding; in all your ways acknowledge Him, and He shall direct your paths."* Your child is your sole priority, and he or she is well worth all that you may go through because he or she belongs to God. All of the negativity concerning your pregnancy will truly turn into positive and be very fruitful. As time goes on, you will certainly be glad you made the decision to keep your child.

On another note, realize that it took three people to create a baby. The man involved in the process of sexual intercourse, which led to you getting pregnant, is just as accountable to God as you. The burdens of guilt and emotional stress are not to be carried by you alone. A man who advises a woman to have an abortion because "he" does not "want" the responsibility of getting married or financially supporting and/or raising a child is just as responsible and accountable to God for his actions. He compounds his own situation by contradicting God's word concerning abortion by advising you to get an abortion. **I know of no man who was ever blessed in life by encouraging a woman to abort his child. No, not one!**

Now, there are some men who did not know they impregnated a woman, but they are still accountable because they were not suppose to have sex out of wedlock in the first place.

There are some men who knew they impregnated a woman, but were denied in the decision process to raise and support the child or to abort the child. This may be because he treated the woman badly before, during, or after he had sex with her. It may be because after he had his fun with the woman, he disappeared from the woman's life. It may be because of a number of reasons. However, these men, too, are accountable to God, and they will reap what they sow. God is definitely involved in all these circumstances. God is omnipresent; He sees everything. God is also omnipotent; He is all-powerful.

Birth Control Pills –What a hassle? Is it effective? Are there any side effects? Are you consistent in taking them? When did you last take it? Can you afford to renew your monthly prescription? What happens if you cannot afford to renew your prescription? What does this tell you if he won't help you pay for your pills? Will the pill stop HIV or other STDs? And on and on it goes.

Is there a chance you will get pregnant having taken the birth control pills? With human frailty and error, **YES**, there is a chance.

Is there a chance that you may get a sexually transmitted disease even though you've taken birth control pills? **Definitely!** Birth control pills do not protect you from any sexual disease. A birth control pill is designed to protect you from getting pregnant – that's its job, its only purpose, and its sole function. But, even when used, the pill doesn't always work. It's just like a car; you never know when it will break down.

There may also be side effects to your body from taking birth control pills. Not everyone can take the pill and not have problems.

The pill has many other uses aside from preventing pregnancy. For example, doctors have prescribed birth control pills to aid teenage girls and women during their menstrual cycles (periods) in reducing the pain of cramps, heavy bleeding, PMS, and other related physically stressful symptoms.

The method of using birth control pills is 85% to 90% effective. Are you in the 85-90% group of those who won't get pregnant, or are you in the 10-15% group who will get pregnant?

IUDs (Intra Uterine Device) – The IUD is a small, plastic, T-shaped birth control device that is inserted inside the uterus of a woman. There are two types: One covered with copper to prevent the sperm from fertilizing with the egg. The other is coated with progesterone to prevent the sperm from fertilizing with the egg, and it prevents ovulation. The device has to be inserted by a doctor.

This method of birth control is advertised as being 90% effective. Are you in the 90% successful group or are you in that unsuccessful 10% group?

Birth Control Ring – This is a small ring that looks like a donut that is inserted into the woman's vagina where it emits small doses of hormones to prevent ovulation. Consequently there is no pregnancy. During ovulation in a woman, the egg is released from the ovaries to fertilize with the sperm of a man.

The female is to use the ring in line with her monthly cycle. Once inserted, it takes a while for the hormones to begin to release. She has to keep track of when her monthly cycle starts, insert the ring accordingly, keep track of the time it takes the hormones to release (approximately 7 days), wear a female condom until the hormones release, yada yada yada. She may very well end up pregnant.

This method appears to be effective 85% of the time, leaving 15% to get pregnant. Are you in the 85% successful group or are you in the 15% unsuccessful group?

Patches – A patch is convenient to use. It is a small beige patch that goes on the skin. It emits progesterone and estrogen hormones through the skin into the bloodstream to prevent ovulation. The hormones also thicken the mucus membrane in the cervix so sperm have a difficult time getting through to mate with an egg. However, a female has to use the patch in line with her monthly cycle, put a new patch on the skin on the same day of every week for three weeks, yada yada yada. She has to use another form of birth control until the patch kicks in and begins to release the hormones.

This method appears to be effective 85% of the time, leaving 15% to get pregnant. Which group are you in – 85% or 15%?

Birth Control Shot – This shot consists of progesterone, and a woman is to get the shot every three months. If she waits longer than three months to receive the next shot, there's a chance she may get pregnant. The purpose of the Birth Control Shot is to prevent ovulation so one cannot get pregnant.

Only 3 out of 100 get pregnant by this method. The odds are good, but which one will you be? Let's face it, you will either be one of the 97 who will not get pregnant or you will be one of the 3 who will get pregnant.

Female Condom – The female condom is made out of polyurethane and is tube-like with rings at both ends. One end of the condom has a ring around the perimeter that is closed so no semen can go up into the vagina. This part of the condom goes inside of the vagina. The other ring at the end of the condom is at the opening of the vagina. The walls or sheath of the female condom line the walls of the vagina. During sexual intercourse, no semen is able to go inside of the cervix through the vagina.

Statistics show that there is a 20% rate of pregnancy due to accidents with use of the female condom. Are you in the 80% group who will not get pregnant, or are you in the 20% group who will?

Male Condoms – Condoms for males work in a similar fashion as the female condoms, but the condoms are worn on the outside of the male's penis for birth control protection. Unfortunately, most men don't like wearing condoms.

There is a 20% rate of pregnancy due to accidents (the condom coming off the penis) during sexual intercourse with the use of the male condom. Again, are you in the 80% group who will not get pregnant or are you in the 20% group who will get pregnant?

Diaphragm – This is a dome made out of thin plastic that is placed over the cervix so that no sperm can enter into the uterus. Spermicide is put into the diaphragm before placing it high into the vagina. The diaphragm must be left in the vagina for six hours after having sex, but must be taken out, washed, rinsed, dried and placed in its case for the next use. It cannot be left in the vagina over 24 hours because there is a risk that it may travel further up inside of the body and have to be surgically removed. It must be replaced every two years.

Almost 20% of those who use the diaphragm will get pregnant. 80% will not get pregnant. Which group will you be in?

As you can see, the odds are against those who do not use Abstinence, which offers 100% protection against pregnancy. No time-sensitive shots or patches are necessary with Abstinence. Abstinence does not require any foreign objects to be inserted inside the body that could possibly get lost and have to be surgically removed. With Abstinence there's no possibility of any allergies or negative reactions by the body's tissues from the insertion of foreign objects.

Is having sex out of wedlock with a guy really worth popping pills, taking shots, wearing patches, and inserting plastic bags and plastic hardware inside you??????

Summary Regarding Contraception

The birth control products/methods discussed above are about 80% of what's available on the market. Only one of the above birth control methods has a dual function; it eliminates the possibility of pregnancy, and it eliminates the possibility of receiving a sexually transmitted disease. Abstinence is the method of choice.

Consequences Of Being Sexually Promiscuous

Let's first consider the emotional consequences. After the act of sex, you feel guilty, uncomfortable, and uncertain. The thrill is gone, and nine times out of ten, the guy is gone, too. Deep down inside you know better, but you're too stubborn to admit it. This feeling wears on you. You push the thoughts out of your mind. If you keep pushing the thoughts out of your mind, you become callous to your conscience and after a while will do it again, and again.

Then another consequence may arise. You're beginning to feel uncomfortable in your pelvic area. You don't know what's wrong, but you definitely know something isn't right. There are no over-the-counter pills or ointments to cure the problem, so you end up going to the doctor.

How embarrassing it is to have to make a doctor's appointment because you not only know that something is wrong with you, but you're pretty sure you know the reason. You're not only feeling uncomfortable physically, but emotionally. You're in a whole new territory of medicine that you never thought about and have no business being involved in. You heard about STDs, but you have not educated yourself about the consequences of sexual promiscuity prior to having sexual intercourse, so you're not informed.

You have a fear of the unknown, which can be very stressful. You have no prior knowledge about what you have opened yourself up to.

You can't talk to any of your so-called girlfriends about it because you know they will talk about you, condemn you, and label you behind your back. You know they can't keep a secret.

You can't talk to your family about it, either, because they taught you better, and they know you know better. You feel your family would be ashamed of you, and they would look upon you differently for the rest of your life.

You're angry with yourself because you put yourself in this position. You're embarrassed about going to the doctor to see what's wrong with you in your pelvic area.

You can't stand it any longer. You have put off calling the doctor for an appointment for as long as you could, hoping that this ailment would go away, but it hasn't. You feel worse. You finally go to the doctor.

You tell your doctor that you don't feel well, and that there is an odor and a discharge coming out of your vaginal area. You answer all the questions the doctor asks concerning your physical discomfort. He tells you to get undressed and to put on that skimpy smock that covers only one-third of your body. You get up on the cold examination table with that flimsy tissue paper covering the top of the table (known in the medical industry as a protective shield), and you wait for the doctor to come back into the room.

When the doctor comes back into the room with his medical assistant, he tells you to lie down on the table, put your feet in the cold steel stirrups (that appear to be so high up in the air), and to bring your knees up. He then tells you to scoot your bottom close to the edge of the table, and to spread your legs wide open so he can position that big bright light down on your pubic area so he and the medical assistant can clearly see into your vagina and your anal opening. He uses a cold steel vice-like contraption called a "speculum" to open your body cavity up as he takes a sample of the bad smelling discharge coming out of your vagina to send to the lab. He presses down on your pelvic area to find out where the discomfort is coming from to determine how far into your pelvic area the infection or disease has spread. This is very embarrassing, uncomfortable, and painful.

During the examination, the doctor may say what he thinks it is based on past examinations of others, but he will definitely have the sample sent to the lab for verification and confirmation. He writes you a couple of prescriptions, one general prescription to fight off the infection and the other to ease the discomfort. You then go to the pharmacy to have your prescriptions filled. The pharmacy assistant looks at you strangely as she hands you your prescriptions to treat the problem. At this point, you have paid for the doctor's visit and the prescriptions out of your own pocket. You feel uncomfortable, paranoid, embarrassed, dirty, and alone. At this point, you're wishing you could turn back the hands of time.

Let's go deeper with this concept.

Before you engage in sexual relations with a person or with many persons, think about the consequences.

For example, after the deed is done, **you are the only one** going to the doctor's office to get help. That guy you had sex with did not even go with you to the doctor's office. Did you contact him to let him know you were sick, and ask him to go to the doctor's office with you? No. Or, maybe for some reason you were too ashamed to tell him you were sick and wanted him to take you to the doctor. By the way, who will be paying your doctor bill, prescription cost, and possible lost time from work? Did you ever think of those things before you made the decision to sleep with that person?

You feel alone in the waiting room at the doctor's office. **You're** alone in the examination room before the doctor and his assistant come in. Where is that guy who told you he loved you? **You**, alone, have to explain to the doctor the symptoms you are having. The doctor asks you questions that are embarrassing to **you**, but he needs to know so he will not misdiagnose your condition and so he can help **you**.

You should always tell the doctor the truth about your medical condition – your life is at stake. [In fact, there are five people you should never lie to: (1) God, (2) your parents, (3) your pastor, (4) the doctor, and (5) the police officer. You should not lie to anyone, but most importantly, you should not lie to these five because they are the only ones who can and will actually help you.] Where is that scoundrel who should speak up and defend your honor, and tell the doctor that it's his fault, and not yours?

You feel embarrassed, awkward, and un-nerved that you have to undress, put on that tiny piece of fabric that the medical industry calls a smock, lay down on that freezer-cold examination table with that thin tissue paper shield, put both your feet up into the air and into those cold, steel stirrups attached to the examination table (make sure your feet are clean), and then you have to spread your legs wide open so the doctor, his assistant, and whoever walks in the room can see your all-in-all, as the doctor uses the speculum to see inside of your vagina, that very private area of your body that the guy you were messing around with sexually liked so much. He even told you that you were so beautiful, so sexy, and all that garbage. Where is he now? Where is he?!!! You weren't embarrassed to take your clothes off and show your all-in-all in front of the guy you were having sex with, so why be embarrassed or concerned now?

Just getting a yearly pelvic examination and pap smear to maintain good physical health are stressful enough for women, but it's even worse this time because of the circumstances under which you went to see the doctor. Again, there's no one there to support you, or to defend your honor, which, under the circumstances, may be questionable. There's no one there to say sweet things to you to make you feel better about the situation or about yourself. There is no one there to pay the bills or to take you home. You are alone throughout the whole process.

What you thought was fun, exciting, enticing, and felt so good at the time has now fizzled into a very embarrassing and physically uncomfortable moment that brings your physical and emotional future into question. Where is this guy, or where are these guys??????

After the lab notifies the doctor of what the sample contains, then comes the bad or worse news of your life.

Again, you are alone when you receive the dreaded phone call from the doctor. You have to accept the bad news alone. Where is this jerk that you played around with sexually, and who put you into this frightening situation you are now facing?

The doctor informs you over the phone that you have an infection or disease, that it is treatable, but that it could reoccur if you continue in sexually promiscuous activity. He calls in a prescription for you to go pick up. He schedules you for another appointment within a few weeks to see if what he prescribed has cured the problem. You are relieved. But, **are you relieved enough** to change your sexual behavior or are you going to tempt fate again?

Or, the doctor could call and ask you to come into his office as soon as possible. You go, and while in his office you sit in nervous wonderment and concern as to what he has to tell you to your face that he could not tell you over the phone.

The doctor finally comes into his office after attending to another patient. He greets you somberly, sits down at his desk, looks at you, and then he puts his head down in his hands (how many times has he had to tell bad news like this?). He then lifts his head up and informs you that you have an incurable sexually transmitted disease according to the findings from the lab. What do you do? What do you do? Where is this SOB who put you in this predicament and who you now want to take out back and castrate and/or shoot? **Where is he?**

Or, because you went to the doctor so late (thinking you could treat yourself with some off-the-shelf medicine from the pharmacy), the doctor may inform you that what you have is so life threatening, and possibly spreading to other parts of your body, that he strongly recommends you have a hysterectomy. He tells you that your female organs are so damaged by the infection, virus, or disease that it could cause problems throughout the rest of your body. Your life is threatened. This news rules out your having a child in the near future, unless you adopt. This news also informs you that you may not even have a future.

Should you have to go to the hospital to have a hysterectomy, will this same guy, whom you had sexual intercourse with, visit you in the hospital? Will he call you? Will he take care of you after you're released from the hospital after surgery? Will his medical insurance cover you? Does he have any medical insurance? Do you have medical insurance to cover you? Will this guy pay your rent, utilities, and your other bills while you're recovering? Will he purchase your prescriptions for you while you're recovering? Will he physically be there to help you recover during the next 3 to 6 months? Or, will you bear all of this alone?

It's a harsh reality to be alone when you're sick and have to bear the full brunt of the situation. You then ask yourself: Was it worth it? Was he worth it? Was all that you went through really worth it? If you are on your deathbed from AIDS or cancer as a result of your sexual promiscuity, can you really say and believe that it was all worth dying for? Was he or they worth dying for?

Did this man or did these men love you or use you? Where are they when you really need them? What can they do for you in your medical condition? Can or would they even pray for you?

First of all, you may say, which is an old cliché, "What's love got to do with it?" Well, you see now that love has an awful lot to do with it. It's whether you love yourself enough not to put yourself in this situation. It's whether the man loved and respected you enough not to infect you if he had an STD. It's whether the man loved and respected you enough not to want sex from you unless he married you before taking you to bed. Did you love yourself enough to put your future plans before your sexual promiscuity? Did you love those who care about you enough not to hurt them with this terrible news? What does love have to do with it? A whole lot!!!

Secondly, the guilt of what you have done wears on you, and you can't shake it off. The facts of the consequences are staring you in the face. You're remorseful, but you can't change what's done. You, alone, have to bear the physical, emotional and financial consequences. You, alone, have to deal with the guilt of the consequences, which affects you. The consequences can be life threatening. The consequences are very real. When the consequences come, and they will come, it will be too late to say, "If I would have, could have, should have."

Sexually Transmitted Disease Summary

It takes longer for boys and men to detect an STD in their bodies. However, the damage to you may already be done.

Most STDs are transmitted through sexual intercourse through the vagina, or through the anus, or orally (mouth). Can you imagine orally receiving an STD? Is anyone safe to even kiss if they are sexually active in any of these ways?

I hear it's very popular and very common for teenagers to go to group parties ("hooking up") that turn into sex orgies, using all three methods in having sex as described above. They exchange sex partners during the orgies, whether male or female or both. It happens so often, that everyone seems to be immune to what they did as if it's no big deal. Group sex is the new drug of choice, so to speak, outside of drugs and alcohol. Not only that, but when alcohol and drugs are mixed in, these add fuel to the sexual fire for everyone involved.

Can you imagine if one of the people involved in this orgy had some sort of STD, how quickly the STD would be transmitted, how many partners would be affected, and what the outcome would be for each and every one of them?

Can you imagine how shocked and devastated the parents would be when they take their daughter to the doctor because she doesn't feel well and the doctor informs them that their daughter has a sexually transmitted disease?

If you are pregnant, have you thought about how these diseases will affect your baby? If you become pregnant, would you know which boy was the father?

As a female, one of the most important things to remember concerning having sexual intercourse is that YOU are the RECEIVER. So, you must be careful what you receive in your body, and be careful about which opening you receive sexual intercourse. Your mouth was not made for sexual intercourse, and neither was your anus (your rear end). Once your anal opening is stretched out, you need surgery to fix it. However, not all surgeries are successful. Not so sensual and sexy, is it?

If you have sexual intercourse in your anus (your rear end, your ass), there are certain things that happen to that muscle and tissue area that degrade its natural function and opens up a vast array of other physical health problems that can follow you for the rest of your life.

The infections, viruses and diseases described in this chapter have no feelings – they all hurt, they all can cause you physical and emotional damage, and some can even kill you. It doesn't matter that you feel dirty, used, unworthy, alone, and you just want to give up because you've put yourself in this position. These infections, viruses and diseases have no conscience, no remorse, and make no apology.

Let's look at a few more things that are important to note:

Testing

Recently, I was in a conversation with a young man who was in his late twenties. We discussed sexual promiscuity. Even though he was not married and he knew the Bible said that being sexually active without being married was wrong, he admitted that he still engaged in sex with his current girlfriend. He also admitted he had sex with all of his former girlfriends.

I asked him what his feelings were concerning the possibility of contracting a sexual disease based on his sexual practices. He stated that he goes to the doctor regularly to get tested. He stated that he also goes to the doctor to get checked after he breaks up with each girlfriend. He said that so far the tests have been negative – no diseases. I asked him if he thought he was gambling because just being tested would not prevent him from contracting a sexual disease, that it only told him whether he was infected, and that it was not a form of prevention of a sexual disease. He thought about it a few moments and then stated he wears protection and that he was very clean about himself. So, he believed (like many others) this helped him not contract a sexually transmitted disease. He stated that his sexual promiscuity did not bother him, and that he and his girlfriends wanted it. He also stated that because he has not contracted any STD or got a girl pregnant, he was okay with it.

Was he tempting fate?

Kissing

Kissing is a physical expression of emotion toward the other person. It can be an expression of affection, kindness, family love and romantic love. There are different emotional kisses for people who hold different titles in a person's life. For example, you would not kiss your mom the same way you would kiss your boyfriend. A kiss where both you and your boyfriend press your lips together, open your mouths and suck the life out of each other's tongues (French kissing) is supposedly a kiss of passion. However, discretion must be used when kissing because the use of the mouth and/or the lips can be the "kiss of death" when it comes to an STD.

Let's talk about the anatomy of the physical body of a female and the art of kissing. Each part of the body has specific purposes. For example, the purpose of the mouth is four-fold: (1) to speak; (2) to eat food and drink liquids for the nourishment of the body; (3) to smile; and (4) to kiss with the lips to show affection.

If you kiss someone who has the Herpes virus/disease, as reflected by visible sores on or around the mouth and lips, which look like blisters, the disease can easily be transferred from that person to you by physical contact through kissing. **It only takes one time.** You're not immune.

There are also health and moral boundaries as to who and what one kisses on the human body. At the very least, your mouth and lips are for kissing another human on the mouth and lips, preferably the one you plan to marry. Your lips and mouth are not to be used to kiss another person's genitals. STDs are found mostly on the genital area of the body, and can easily be transferred to the lips and inside of the mouth.

Animals can carry all sorts of diseases, too, so it's not a good idea to kiss animals on or in the mouth, especially a dog or a cat. Dogs tend to sniff and lick everything, including their own genitals, their own vomit, their own feces or the feces of other animals, and other disgusting things. You don't know where your dog's nose, mouth, or tongue has been. Cats are always cleaning themselves with their tongues all over their bodies, and you don't know what the cat is cleaning off himself/herself. Cats and dogs don't brush their teeth or use mouthwash.

Kissing during courting for marriage and in marriage, itself, is probably safe in most cases, but check to make sure the kissing area of the mouth and lips of the one you're planning to kiss are clear and free from any suspicious bumps, or open and oozing sores. If you see something unusual, don't be shy or hesitant to ask what it is. It's your body and your health that you must protect. **Only you can prevent an STD!**

In "French kissing", which is very popular, where one person tries to suck the tongue and the kitchen sink out of the other person, the same safeguards apply. If the person who you're French-kissing does not brush their tongue when they brush their teeth, if he brushes his teeth at all, you may encounter his halitosis (bad breath) in addition to whatever infection or disease is going on in his mouth. That kiss will not taste very good. The person you're going to kiss should think enough of you to want to have fresh breath and a clean mouth. You should do the same.

Personal Hygiene

We should be very sensitive about our personal hygienic cleanliness, especially during the menstrual cycle. Being clean in all parts of our bodies makes us feel good, pretty, confident and comfortable. When we are not clean, we are generally unhappy and very uncomfortable. When we were growing up, my mom use to tell us kids before we left for school everyday: "Make sure your bottoms (genital areas) and your feet are clean, and make sure you're wearing clean underwear and clean socks." She didn't care much about our faces and other parts of our bodies, just our bottoms and feet. It didn't make sense then, but it does now.

In general, most men's personal hygiene is not equal to women's personal hygiene. The hygienic standards of teenage boys and men are very different from women. Have you ever seen a guy go to the bathroom to urinate? Although I've never been in a public men's bathroom to investigate this issue, I have interviewed men and teenage boys asking them questions about their hygiene in public restrooms and in their personal bathrooms. I have also observed and timed men and teenage boys going in and coming out of public, private, office, and home restrooms. Some men go in and come out of restrooms way too quickly (in a matter of seconds) to be able to do their business and wash and dry their hands. In my questioning, I've learned that they do not wipe their penises with tissue or anything else after urinating. When urinating, most men hold their penis with one hand. When they are through urinating, they shake off the excess urine from their penis, place their penis back in their underwear inside their pants with one hand, zip up their pants with the other hand, and go out of the bathroom. Although they should, very few men wash their hands after urinating. They, instead, go back to whatever they were doing, such as handling papers, eating a sandwich, or handing something to you. Their bathroom germs are all over their hands. You have no clue as to where their hands have been or how long those germs on their hands survive.

If you think the above scenario is bad, consider when a man goes to a public restroom to have a bowel movement and to urinate. The man pulls his pants down by his knees, and he sits on the toilet.

Hopefully, he will use a butt-gasket (sanitary liner or sheet protector for the toilet seat). He may or may not have a toilet sheet protector to place on the seat in the bathroom stall, and he certainly won't do what most of us women do when there's no sheet protector (we make our own sheet protectors out of toilet tissue). He may or may not even use the sheet protectors if they are available. When he sits on the toilet, he makes sure all of his genitals (including his penis) are inside the toilet bowl as he makes his bowel movement so that he can urinate at the same time – convenient. When done, he wipes his anus with toilet tissue and gets up. Since he doesn't use toilet tissue to wipe his penis when he urinates, I doubt he uses toilet tissue to wipe his penis after a bowel movement. Anyway, he stands up in the bathroom stall, pulls up his underwear (if he's wearing any) making sure he gets his penis inside his underwear, he pulls up his pants, pulls the zipper up on his pants with his hands, opens the bathroom stall door with his hands, and hopefully he will go to the sink to wash his hands. Or, maybe not. After he leaves the restroom, he goes back to whatever he was doing, which may include handing you something with his hands, eating a sandwich with his hands, or even holding you with his hands. He may even want to have sex with you (a quickie) someplace where there is no disinfectant to decontaminate him.

Some men don't wipe their buttocks well enough after having a bowel movement. Many wives have testified to having to wash their husbands' underwear separately from the rest of the laundry because of grossly soiled and stinky jockey shorts, boxers, briefs, thongs, etc., which constitutes failure of their husbands to use enough toilet tissue to wipe their asses. This is a major complaint by most wives. We won't even talk about the underwear of single men in this area.

I said all of the above to say to you girls, teenagers and women who like to have quickie sex and oral sex with boys and men in obscure places, in the corner in the dark, and at irregular times – you better think about what you're dealing with in the area of cleanliness, let alone the possibility of contracting a sexually transmitted disease. Are you positively sure he washed his hands after leaving the restroom? Be sure his hands and his genital area are clean before you allow him to touch you. However, with abstinence, this would not be a problem.

Who Has A Conscience?

Do you really think a teenage boy or a man would tell you up front whether he's infected with a sexually transmittable infection or disease? Do you really? Would you, the RECEIVER, tell someone you were interested in having a sexual relationship with that you have a sexually transmittable disease and that you are in the "active" state? Would you really? Would you tell him that you had a sexually transmitted disease, although you don't have it anymore? Really? Would he tell you he had a sexually transmitted disease? Really?

For a couple about to get married, this would definitely be one of those "Come To Jesus Meeting" discussions that they should definitely have, which should include other issues related to married life. In this meeting, both parties would lay **ALL** their cards (issues) on the table to discuss and resolve prior to saying "I DO." This would include, but not be limited to, "**THE WHOLE TRUTH AND NOTHING BUT THE TRUTH"** about each of their lives – medical history, financial status, employment, ex-wives/ex-husbands, baby-mama or baby-daddy drama, child support issues, criminal records, IRS problems, and anything else that would possibly jeopardize the growth and success of the impending marriage. Failure to provide all information could also end a marriage relationship in mid-course. One should not assume anything about the other mate. The expectations/desires of each party should be satisfied prior to walking down the aisle to marriage. Those who are about to embark on a life together in holy matrimony should definitely have this discussion. After all, who in their right mind would want to encounter a bad surprise after the fact?

Would you still marry a person after he told you the bad truth about some parts of his life? Would he marry you? Is his love for you strong enough to overcome any negative issues, and would he promise not bring them up in the future? Is your love for him strong enough to overcome his negative issues, and would you promise not bring them up in the future? If both of you are able to overcome and/or work out an amicable solution to any and all of the negative issues without bringing them up in the future, you both are definitely worth marrying, **provided you both are telling the truth**, and you both keep your promise about not reminding each other of his or her past mistakes and frailties later on down the road of marital bliss.

If you found out that your married partner was not forthright and honest after you got married, what would you do?

What Are The Consequences Of Love?

The word "LOVE" is such a strange word in the world. It's used these days so cheaply and so frivolously, especially amongst young people – young girls in particular. However, if you really love someone and that someone really loves you, you find a way to work through each other's faults, mistakes, and frailties. You have to love the person enough to tell them the truth and risk the consequences, whatever they may be. This includes you informing your mate that you had a sexually transmitted disease that was cured, or you currently have a sexually transmittable disease that there's no cure for (such as having Herpes or being HIV positive), if you really love that person. That person should be just as truthful and honest with you. You must ask yourself if you love the other person enough to accept the possibility of contracting an infection or disease from the other person even if there doesn't appear to be any outbreaks – you know, take your chances!

Would you love the person enough to understand if they reject you after you tell them about your health condition? Would you reject them, although they told you the truth up front? Would you and he be willing to work through some of the ugly stuff? Would you love the other person enough to let them go if you could not deal with their medical situation?

Suppose you loved your mate enough to marry him and you accepted the possibility of receiving a sexually transmitted disease from him that was incurable (Herpes for example). After a period of time, you actually contracted the disease from your married partner. Then, later down the road, your marriage did not work out for other reasons and you end up divorced. Would you be able to tell the next potential mate you have an incurable sexually transmittable disease that you got from your former marriage partner? Would you? Would you be willing to infect your new prospective mate? Would you be able to accept his rejection?

What if you had sexual intercourse with a person that you cared deeply about, but he didn't tell you he had a sexually transmittable disease that was incurable (such as Herpes), yet you found out later after the doctor informed you why you were having problems in your genital and/or abdominal area. When you see this person again and confront him about it, he then tells you very casually that **"it's no big deal"** and walks away. What then? Look at the situation you allowed yourself to be placed in, although unknowingly. It really is a **"big deal"**, but now you're stuck with the consequences. If you sued the person, it wouldn't change your health condition.

Having a sexually transmittable disease such as Herpes may not have been a big deal to this guy because the affects on him are not quite the same as the affects on you. He probably did not even go to a doctor. Most men don't and won't go to the doctor about a few bumps on their genitals, so you know teenage boys won't. Instead, he will more than likely ask one of his buddies about the bumps on his penis. His buddy says very casually that by the description it sounds like he's got Herpes, but "it's no big deal." His buddy doesn't appear to be alarmed about it, and now neither is he alarmed, and he doesn't expect anyone who sleeps with him to be alarmed. Life goes on for him. The guy is assuming that life will go on for you, too! "No big deal, right?" **Wrong!**

Herpes can also be on the mouth and face. What looks like a blister or cold sore can actually be Genital Herpes. How would you know the difference? If you kiss someone else on the mouth, after you have been kissed by a person with the virus, you could probably transmit the disease to that person. If you have sex with someone else, you may very well transmit the disease to the next person who has no idea of what you are giving him. It may be a very big deal to that person.

If you have a conscience, it's a **BIG DEAL!** If you're the one physically affected, it's a **VERY BIG DEAL!** If you infect someone else, it could be a **VERY BIG DEAL** to him. He can sue you in court for damages and you could serve jail time. Depending on the other person's temperament, a lot worse could happen to you, including physical violence once he finds out you gave him an incurable sexual disease.

There are steps that a young girl endures when she is sexually active and contracts a sexually transmittable disease. We will use Herpes in this particular case:

She's feeling uncomfortable to the point of needing to go to a doctor. She notices bumps that are blistering on the vaginal area of her body. She informs her parent that she's not feeling well in her abdominal area. Her parent asks her if she wants to go to the doctor. By her actions, her parent makes an appointment with the doctor. Her mother takes her to the doctor, pays for the doctor visit, and is informed by the doctor that her daughter has a sexually transmittable disease.

One of the unfortunate things about this situation is that her parents had no clue she was engaging in sexual activity. What a shocker! Even after their discussion with her about the birds and the bees, after the health education classes she took in school, and after examples of pregnant girls at her school and in her neighborhood, her parents just knew she was not sexually active.

Another unfortunate thing about this situation is that her parents had to come out of pocket to pay for a situation neither parent had any knowledge of. Their daughter did not go to them to ask their permission to be sexually active with a boy, she's not financially able to pay for any expenses incurred as a result of the doctor's visit or as a result of being sexually active, and she is not mentally mature enough to handle the ensuing consequences.

The parents feel bad for their daughter, they are upset their daughter is sexually active, and they feel guilty they did not tell her enough about the ramifications of having sex before marriage. Maybe they did, and she just didn't listen to them. They probably feel guilty they didn't give her enough information for her to make the right decision to say "NO", or they feel rejection towards her because of the situation, and they now look upon her as if she's dirty and they no longer favor her. The teenage girl feels bad, but has no one to turn to but her parents.

Unfortunately, most boys and most men have no conscience about having sex with a teenage girl or a woman knowing that they, themselves, have contracted and currently have a sexually transmitted disease or some related disorder. Their other head (their penis) tends to overrule their conscience and they say absolutely nothing. Or, they figure someone gave it to them, so they have no problem giving it to someone else.

These boys and men transmit any and all types of sexually transmitted diseases. The man does not tell a young unsuspecting lady up front that he has a sexual transmittable disease, and the young lady doesn't do her "due diligence" by inspecting his genital area or requesting a recent medical report prior to casually slipping in bed with him. A few days, weeks, or even months later, she doesn't feel good in her pelvic area, and she has a discharge with an unsavory odor. She finds her way to the doctor, and she's alone.

Damaged Goods?

At this point, you probably feel like you're damaged goods if you have a sexually transmitted disease, and especially if it's incurable. You feel alone, unwanted, unworthy of any future marriage to anyone, and you feel lost. You feel you could never be cured and you will never be the same.

You are not damaged goods. God can restore you, and He can restore your future. If you could only see yourself as God sees you. If you repent by turning away from your past sexually immoral activity, and turn to God and ask Him for forgiveness and restoration, He can and will forgive and restore you. This gift of forgiveness and restoration comes through God's Son, the Lord Jesus Christ. Only God can heal your heart, heal your body, and save you from destruction. *John 3:16* states: *"For God so loved the world that He gave His only begotten Son, that whoever believes in Him should not perish but have everlasting life."* Jesus, Himself, says in *John 14:6: "I am the way, the truth, and the life. No one comes to the*

Father except through Me." Romans 5:12 states: *"Therefore, just as through one man sin entered the world, and death through sin, and thus death spread to all men, because all sinned."* By accepting Jesus Christ as your Lord and Savior, you have received God's gift of salvation. *Ephesians 2:8-9* states: *"For by grace you have been saved through faith, and that not of yourselves; it is the gift of God, not of works, lest anyone should boast."* If you will confess that Jesus Christ is Lord, you will be saved and you will be open to all of God's blessings, which includes your healing by faith in the Lord Jesus Christ. *Romans 10:9-10* states: *"That if you confess with your mouth the Lord Jesus and believe in your heart that God has raised Him from the dead, you will be saved. For with the heart one believes unto righteousness, and with the mouth confession is made unto salvation."* Jesus is not only our Redeemer, but also our Healer. *James 5:13-15* states: *"Is anyone among you suffering? Let him [her] pray. Is anyone cheerful? Let him [her] sing psalms. Is anyone among you sick? Let him [her] call for the elders of the church, and let them pray over him [her], anointing him [her] with oil in the name of the Lord. And the prayer of faith will save the sick, and the Lord will raise him [her] up. And if he [she] has committed sins, he [she] will be forgiven." 1 Peter 2:24* states: *"Who Himself bore our sins in His own body on the tree, that we having died to sins, might live for righteousness – by whose stripes you were healed." Psalm 103:3* states: *"Who forgives all our iniquities, Who heals all our diseases."* He is the only one who can. The Lord Jesus Christ is everything to the believer.

As a believer in the Lord Jesus Christ, you are now the daughter of the Most High God. Being a daughter of God has benefits: (1) You're highly favored. (2) Believing God's Word and standing on it gives you power to overcome any past, present, or future hindrances. (3) You're more than a conqueror; you have conquered. (4) You are healed by Jesus' stripes. (5) You're under the protection of God, Himself. (6) God shines His countenance upon you where others can see His light through you. (7) By being a child of God and highly favored, you know that all things are possible with Him. (8) You have a bright future and a wonderful hope. You have all these things by your faith in the Lord Jesus Christ.

Pain and Suffering

When you were sexually violated at an early age, God was there! When you were physically abused, God was there! When you were called everything but a child of God, He was there! When you were lied on and wrongfully accused, God was there! When no one defended or protected you, God was there! When you were dismissed, shunned, and ignored, God was there! When your feelings were hurt by people you allowed to get close to you, God was there! When you were alone with nowhere to turn, God was there! When you were abandoned by your parents, God was there! When you were used and abused, God was there! When you were incarcerated for being with the wrong people at the wrong place at the wrong time in the midst of the wrong elements, wrong substances, etc., God was there! When you were seduced, or raped, and ended up either pregnant or with a sexually transmitted infection or disease, God was there! When you were kicked out of your home, God was there! When you lost your job, God was there! When you were physically hurt, God was there! When you came into the knowledge that you had an incurable ailment or disease, God was there! When you miscarried a child that you wanted so much, God was there! When your married partner fell out of love with you and in love with someone else, God was there! When you were penniless and broke, God was there! When you lost your loved one to death by whatever means, God was there! When you felt like there was no hope because you made the same mistake over and over again, God was there! When the devil tried to kill you, steal from you and destroy you, God was there! When you were down and out, and the only thing you could do was to look up, God was there!

Although you may have felt abandoned by God while you went through an awful circumstance, He was with you and He used that circumstance to work out good for you. *Romans 8:28* states: *"And we know that all things work together for good to those who love God, to those who are the called according to His purpose."* It was God who brought you through, not you. You may have made a bad choice that got you into the problem, but God was there to bring you through the problem into victory. God is the One who will turn a wrong into a right, who will pick you up when you're down, who will change your bad into good, and He is the only One who can bring you from defeat into victory!

You've got to trust Him, and trust His word that He will do what He says He will do. God is not a man that He should lie, nor a son of man that He should repent. *Numbers 23:19* states: *"God is not a man that He should lie, nor a son of man that He should repent. Has He said and will He not do? Or has He spoken, and will He not make it good?"* In essence, God says what He means and He means what He says. Your faith and trust in Him will bring it to pass.

God is not the one who put you into bad circumstances, He did not tell you to be involved with the wrong people, nor did He give you any disease or strife. He did, however, give every man [woman] his [her] own free will. By free will, God allows you to make your own choices. He doesn't want robots; He wants you to love Him for Him. He allows things to happen in this world because of man's free will, but He isn't the one who causes negative things to happen. What would be the purpose of sacrificing His only begotten Son to save the world if He created all of the bad things of the world? God loves you too much to do such a contradicting thing. God does not contradict Himself and He is not the author of confusion. *1 Corinthians 14:33* states: *"For God is not the author of confusion, but of peace, as in all the churches of the saints."* When you or someone else made decisions to do things out of the will of God, bad things happened and the consequences came. But God brought you through those bad consequences, and He will continue to bring you through. Again, in *John 3:16*, the scripture says: *"For God so loved the world that He gave His only begotten Son (Jesus Christ), that whoever believes in Him should not perish but have everlasting life." John 3:17-18* states: *"For God did not send His Son into the world to condemn the world, but that the world through Him might be saved. He who believes in Him is not condemned; but he who does not believe is condemned already, because he has not believed in the name of the only begotten Son of God."* God wants you to come to Him of your own free will. He wants you to believe in His Son, Jesus Christ, who is able to set you free from any problem.

Sometimes the circumstances that you created are just so unbearable that you just see no way out, but God is in the midst of the circumstances. He knows right where you are, He knows what is going on, and He knows what He's going to do to turn the situation around. He knows just how much you can take. After you're done taking it and finally give it to Him, He takes over! He has been patiently waiting for you to give it to Him. God wants you to give all of your cares to Him so He can care for you and help you. *1 Peter 5:7* states: *"casting all your care upon Him for He cares for you." Romans 8:28* states: *"And we know that all things work together for good to those who love God, to those who are the called according to His purpose."* It's sometimes hurtful, but God knows what He's doing. He may not come to the rescue at the time that you want Him to, or maybe what you expected the resolution to be was something altogether different, but God always has our best interest at His heart. We are here for His purpose, and He will use our circumstances to fulfill His purpose. He is always on time. *Isaiah 55:8* states: *"For My thoughts are not your thoughts, nor are your ways My ways, says the Lord. For as the heavens are higher than the earth, so are My ways higher than your ways, and My thoughts [higher] than your thoughts."* He's working things out for our good and for His purpose.

God created us. If we are stubborn, He will allow trials in our lives to smooth us out. Through trials, we grow, we gain strength, we endure, and we overcome. We learn to have faith in His word. We use His word against all negative circumstances. We learn patience. We gain expectation that He will bring us through. Through our trials, we realize that God honors His word. We are then able to serve Him by serving others who are in the midst of similar trials. We are able to pray for, support, and encourage one another. We can praise God for what He is doing and what He will do for the person going through their trial because He did it for us.

You're not the only one going through a trial. You won't stay in the trial. The trial has **come to pass**, and the trial will pass. The operative word here is "pass." But God wants to show you who you are in the trial. What are you made of? Do you have faith that He will bring you through, or are you wallowing in the muck and mire of the trial? How you handle the problem and your attitude about the problem will determine how long you will stay in the problem. He is no respector of person. God always brings you to something better when the trial is over. He wants to grow you, He wants you to trust Him, and He wants you to be successful and to overcome the trial, no matter what it is.

I don't look at the past to review the negative, but to see how He brought me through the negative circumstances with flying colors, which encourages me in my current trial. We will be going through trials throughout our entire lives. Don't dwell on the past, but dwell on the future of God's promises and trust Him.

I cannot tell you the many times I have been able to minister to people who were going through similar trials that I had already been through, and I was an encouraging example to them of the wonderful ways God turned things around for me. He will do it for them and for you. He also says in *Isaiah 51:12: "I, even I, am He who comforts you. Who are you that you should be afraid of a man who will die, and of the son of a man who will be made like grass?"* God gives you comfort and peace. He's your protection – there is no fear with God. *Psalm 29:11* states: *"The Lord will give strength to His people. The Lord will bless His people with peace."* So, no matter what you're going through, trust Him and He will give you strength to endure and peace through it all. Praise the Lord for all that He is doing in your life, even if you don't readily see it.

Conclusion

Abstain from Sexual Promiscuous Activity!

There are almost a half million teen pregnancies reported every year in the United States alone. What happens with these pregnancies? Do some pregnant teens get married? Are some pregnancies aborted? Do some babies grow to full term, get delivered, and are kept? Are some babies adopted? Where are the dads of all these kids? Who bears responsibility for all of these pregnancies?

STDs are on the rise in the United States. Almost twenty million new infections occur every year. About ten million young people between the ages of 15 and 24 are infected every year.

If your parents are telling you to abstain, if the Center for Disease Control (CDC) is telling you to abstain, if the American Medical Association (AMA) is telling you to abstain, if the Bible is telling you to abstain, if you see the negative results of those who engaged in sexual activity, and if you have that gut-feeling that you should abstain, **ABSTAIN!!!** The consequences may be more than you care to bear.

1 Corinthians 6:18-20 states: *"Flee sexual immorality. Every sin that a man [woman]does is outside the body, but he [she] who commits sexual immorality sins against his [her] own body. Or do you not know that your body is the temple of the Holy Spirit who is in you, whom you have from God, and you are not your own? For you were bought at a price, therefore glorify God in your body and in your spirit, which are God's."*

You do not belong to yourself. Fornication means being sexually immoral, means having sex with a person out of wedlock, and this includes adultery. Adultery means a married person is having sex with someone other than his/her married partner outside of his or her own marriage. Fornication also includes incest, which means a biological parent is having sexual intercourse with one or more of his or her own children. Fornication also includes whoremongers, which means someone who solicits customers for whores; a pimp in today's terms. A whore is someone who accepts payment in exchange for sexual intercourse. Single people who commit sexual immorality by having casual sex are labeled as fornicators. Those living together and having sexual intercourse as though they are married are also considered fornicators and are accountable for God's consequences. *1 Corinthians 6:9-10* states: *"Do you not know that the unrighteous will not inherit the kingdom of God? Do not be deceived. Neither fornicators, nor idolaters, nor adulterers, nor homosexuals, nor sodomites, nor thieves, nor covetous, nor drunkards, nor revilers, nor extortioners will inherit the kingdom of God." Revelation 21:8* states: *"But the cowardly, unbelieving, abominable, murderers, sexually immoral, sorcerers, idolaters and all liars shall have their part in the lake of fire, which burns with fire and brimstone, which is the second death."*

Although it may seem or appear like everybody's doing it (having sexual intercourse, whether married or not), God's laws still stand and there are grave consequences for disobedience in the area of sexual immorality. In *Isaiah 55:11*, God says: *"So shall My word be that goes forth out of My mouth; it shall not return to Me void, but it shall accomplish what I please, and it shall prosper in the thing for which I sent it."*

The body you have does not belong to you. It belongs to the One who created you. You did not create yourself. God, the Creator, created you. Your body is the temple where He dwells in you through the Holy Spirit. *1 Corinthians 3:16-18* states: *"Do you not know that you are the temple of God and that the Spirit of God dwells in you? If anyone defiles the temple of God, God will destroy him [her]. For the temple of God is holy, which temple you are."*

God expects you to be a good steward over what He has created. Therefore, when you commit fornication, you are sinning against your own body, and you are sinning against God. If you're a Christian and committing fornication, you, too, are sinning against God, but also against the Holy Spirit who lives inside your body. *1 Corinthians 6:13-14* states: *"Foods for the stomach and the stomach for foods, but God will destroy both it and them. Now the body is not for sexual immorality, but for the Lord, and the Lord for the body, and God both raised up the Lord and will also raise us up by His power."*

To avoid sexual sin, abstain from committing sexual immorality. It's better for a man to marry a woman, and a woman to marry a man if they cannot abstain. In *1 Corinthians 7:1-2*, the Apostle Paul states: *"Now concerning the things of which you wrote to me; it is good for a man not to touch a woman. Nevertheless, because of sexual immorality, let each man have his own wife, and let each woman have her own husband."*

God wants the very best for those who are obedient to His Word. *Psalm 145:17-21* states: *"The Lord is righteous in all His ways, gracious in all His works. The Lord is near to all who call upon*

Him, to all who call upon Him in truth. He will fulfill the desire of those who fear Him; He also will hear their cry and save them. The Lord preserves all who love Him, but all the wicked He will destroy. My mouth shall speak the praise of the Lord, and all flesh shall bless His holy name forever and ever." So, if you believe that the Word of God is true, also believe that God is not mocked and that His Word stands above all. *Galatians 6:7* states: *"Do not be deceived, God is not mocked, for whatever a man [woman] sows, that he [she] will also reap."* God means what He says and He says what He means. To fear the Lord means to reverence, worship, and obey Him. To fear the Lord is also the beginning of wisdom. *Psalm 111:10* states: *"The fear of the Lord is the beginning of wisdom; a good understanding have all those who do His commandments. His praise endures forever."*

James 1:14 – 16 states: *"But each one is tempted when he [she] is drawn away by his [her] own desires and enticed. Then, when desire has conceived, it gives birth to sin; and sin, when it is full-grown, brings forth death. Do not be deceived my beloved brethren."* I learned the hard way from my own mistakes that although "I" was the one who consciously made bad choices and followed through with "my" actions, I was not in charge of making the choice of what my consequences would be. I had to accept whatever consequence came as a result of my choices, and there was no way of getting around it. The consequences will come – good or bad, based on the choices you make. You don't know what the consequences will be or how long they will last. So don't do anything in opposition to the word of God, because you cannot stop the consequences that you activated, you are not in control of the consequences, and you cannot alter the consequences. Only God, Himself, can alter the consequences if you are truly repentant.

To fornicate or to commit adultery is a conscious decision based on your flesh. Don't be led by your flesh, which includes your feelings, your emotions, and your senses. The Lord Jesus states in *John 6:63: "It is the Spirit who gives life; the flesh profits nothing. The words that I speak to you are spirit and they are life." Romans 8:5-8* states: *"For those who live according to the flesh set their minds on the things of the flesh, but those who live according to the Spirit, [set their minds on] the things of the Spirit. For to be carnally minded is death, but to be spiritually minded is life and peace. Because the carnal mind is enmity [enemy] against God; for it is not subject to the law of God, nor indeed can be. So then, those who are in the flesh cannot please God."* When you operate in the flesh, you are bound by the flesh. Flesh is corruptible. Diseases feed off of the flesh; they have no feelings, emotions, or senses.

Just say "NO" and avoid the physical, emotional, and spiritual consequences that can last a lifetime and beyond.

Are you tough enough for the consequences of sex?

Chapter 4

Is It Too Late To Start Over?

Chapter 4

Is It Too Late To Start Over?

It's never too late to start over. It's never too late to change your mind. It's never too late to change your decision-making process based on what God says about you, not based on your past or what others say about you. *Proverbs 3:5-6* states: *"Trust in the Lord with all your heart and lean not on your own understanding. In all your ways acknowledge Him, and He shall direct your paths."* If you trust God, He will make things turn out right for you. *Romans 8:28* states: *"And we know that all things work together for good to those who love God, to those who are the called according to His purpose."*

A New You

God's supernatural grace can change you if you allow yourself to be open to change. His grace is sufficient for us all. He can change what we are. It's time to step out in faith and allow God to make that change in you for a better, brighter, and more fulfilling life. Ask God to come into your life and be saved. *Romans 5:12* states: *"Therefore, just as through one man sin entered the world, and death through sin, and thus death spread to all men, because all sinned." John 3:16* states: *"For God so loved the world that He gave His only begotten Son, that whosoever believes in Him should not perish but have everlasting life." Ephesians 2:8-9* states: *"For by grace you have been saved through faith, and that not of yourselves, it is a gift of God; not of works, lest anyone should boast." Romans 10:9-10* states: *"that if you confess with your mouth the Lord Jesus and believe in your heart that God has raised Him from the dead, you will be saved. For with the heart one believes unto righteousness, and with the mouth confession is made unto salvation."*

This is now your opportunity, based on the above scriptures, to accept Jesus Christ as your Lord and Savior. You can say your confession of faith by stating the following: ***"Dear Lord Jesus: I confess that I am a sinner and I repent of my sins. I believe in my heart that You died on the cross for my sins and that God raised You from the dead. I ask You to come into my life, forgive me of my sins, wash me with Your blood, and fill me with the Holy Spirit. I make You my Lord and Savior, and I will serve You all the days of my life. You are my Lord. Amen."*** If you believe these things in your heart and speak your belief with your mouth, you will now be saved and you will be a new creation. *2 Corinthians 5:17* states: *"Therefore, if anyone is in Christ, he [she] is a new creation; old things have passed away, behold, all things have become new."* You are not who you were a moment ago. You get to do a "Do-Over" with your life, and you will be able to live your life the right way – living for Christ.

Begin your new walk in Christ. In *Matthew 6:9-13*, Jesus used this prayer as an "example" of how to pray for forgiveness. It states: *"Our Father in heaven. Hallowed be Your name. Your kingdom come. Your will be done on earth as it is in heaven. Give us this day our daily bread, and forgive us our debts, as we forgive our debtors, and do not lead us into temptation, but deliver us from the evil one, for Yours is the kingdom and the power and the glory forever, Amen."* So bring to God's attention your sins in your own words, and ask Him to forgive you ***"in the name of Jesus, Amen."*** You don't need a lot of fancy talk, but just speak to Him plainly and ask Him to forgive you. And He will! After you ask for God's forgiveness, have faith that He has forgiven you. *Mark 11:24* states: *"Therefore I say to you, whatever things you ask when you pray, believe that you receive them, and you will have them."* And in your prayer to God, while asking Him to forgive you, you, yourself, must forgive others who have done wrong against you. *Mark 11:25-26* states: *"And whenever you stand praying, if you have* *anything against anyone, forgive him [her], that your Father in heaven may also forgive you your trespasses. But if you do not forgive, neither will your Father in heaven forgive your trespasses."* This is very important. If you don't forgive others, you nullify your own request for forgiveness.

The above scriptures are very important. Yes, people have wronged you, people have lied to you, lied on you, and took advantage of you. Yes, you're not in the best of circumstances and those who put you there have not asked you to forgive them nor have they come to your aid. But, if you let God be God, knowing that He has forgiven you through His Son's sacrifice on the cross, and that you are now a new creation, you **can** and **should** forgive anyone who has done you wrong. That person's sin against you, whatever it may be, is between them and God, and no longer between them and you. God sees all, He hears all, He is everywhere (omnipresent), He knows everything and He is all-powerful (omniscient). He is able to handle all situations. He saw the person sin against you; He was there.

Don't look for God to take revenge on those who wronged you. Just make sure that you, yourself, are doing the will of God. *Hebrews 12:14-15* states: *"Pursue peace with all people, and holiness, without which no one will see the Lord; looking carefully lest anyone fall short of the grace of God; lest any root of bitterness springing up cause trouble, and by this many become defiled."* You can't expect God to forgive you for your sins and then expect Him to not offer forgiveness to the one who offended you. You can't expect God to forgive you and yet you cannot forgive the one who offended you. God's word says to forgive that person and pursue peace and holiness. You do not know the thoughts of God or His ways. His thoughts and His ways are higher than yours could ever be. You, as the creation, cannot tell the Creator what to do and who to go after to avenge you. God says in *Isaiah 55:8-9: "For My thoughts are not your thoughts. Nor are your ways My ways, says the Lord. For as the heavens are higher than the earth, so are My ways higher than your ways, and My thoughts [higher] than your thoughts."*

Since God has forgiven you, He wants you to go and sin no more. Just like the woman who was caught in the act of adultery, Jesus told the accusers in *John 8:7: "He who is without sin among you, let him throw a stone at her first."* Needless to say, the accusers were all guilty of sin, and slowly but surely they withdrew themselves from the scene. Then Jesus turned to the woman and said to her in *John 8:11: "Neither do I condemn you; go and sin no more."* This didn't mean that the accusers were not sinners themselves, but because they were sinners, too, they had no right to accuse her or anyone else, and that's why they removed themselves from the presence of Jesus and the woman. Based on what Jesus said to them, it also showed that they needed to repent, too. They went away condemned in their own hearts. In this passage, the issue was with the woman in her sin, and Jesus forgave her. It's the same for you. Jesus forgave you, so don't seek revenge or justice on those who wronged you. The Lord will deal with them as He has dealt with you, but on His time and in His way, not yours.

When you came to be a follower of Christ, God blotted out all your sins, not only for your sake, but also for His own sake. In *Isaiah 43:25*, God says: *"I, even I am He who blots out your transgressions for My own sake; and I will not remember your sins."* So if God can blot out your sins, as bad as they were, you can certainly blot out others' sins against you.

You may say, "Is there any justice for what was done against me?" Yes, there is, but that is no longer your concern. God forgave you when you came to Him and repented. He will also forgive those who wronged you if they repent to Him. God is no respector of person. *Colossians 2:13* states: *"And you, being dead in your trespasses and the uncircumcision of your flesh, He has made alive together with Him, having forgiven you all trespasses."*

Not only will He forgive you, but He will heal you from all of the painful memories that were left behind when you were wronged. Stand strong and be of good cheer for you have been forgiven.

Remember, too, that we all have to still deal with the consequences of our sins that we set in motion, even though we are saved and forgiven. By trusting in God, He will help you get through those consequences.

God Is A God Of Second Chances

God is a God of second, third, fourth, and many chances. His mercy endures forever. You may be that one who now has a sexually transmitted infection, virus or disease because of your sexual promiscuity. Now you are going through all of the related consequences. However, God is the forgiver and He is the healer. He is more than the sickness or the disease that is in your body. *Isaiah 53:5* states: *"But He was wounded for our transgressions, He was bruised for our iniquities; the chastisement for our peace was upon Him, and by His stripes we are healed." James 5:16* states: *"Confess your trespasses to one another, and pray for one another, that you may be healed. The effective, fervent prayer of a righteous man avails much." Psalm 103:1,3* states: *"Bless the Lord, O my soul; and all that is within me, bless His holy name! Who forgives all your iniquities, who heals all your diseases."* Pray to Him and ask Him to heal you. Forgive and pray for one another that you may be healed. God is able.

When you pray to God for your healing, believe that He is going to do what He says He's going to do. Believing means standing in faith and having confidence that God is a God of His Word. God does not lie. *Numbers 23:19* states: *"God is not a man, that He should lie, nor a son of man, that He should repent. Has He said, and will He not do? Or has He spoken, and will He not make it good?" Hebrews 11:1* states: *"Now faith is the substance of things hoped for, the evidence of things not seen." Mark 11:24* states: *"Therefore I say to you, whatever things you ask when you pray, believe that you receive them, and you will have them." Hebrews 4:16* states: *"Let us therefore come boldly to the throne of grace, that we may obtain mercy and find grace to help in time of need."* So ask in faith. Tell your Father in heaven of your need for healing in accordance with His Word, as referenced in the above scriptures.

While asking for your healing, also ask for the forgiveness of your sins. You must also forgive others. *1 John 1:9* states: *"If we confess our sins, He is faithful and just to forgive us our sins and to cleanse us from all unrighteousness". Mark 11:25-26* states: *"And whenever you stand praying, if you have anything against anyone, forgive him, that your Father in heaven may also forgive you your trespasses. But if you do not forgive, neither will your Father in heaven forgive your trespasses." Psalm 103:1, 3* states: *"Bless the Lord, O my soul; and all that is within me, bless His holy name! Who forgives all your iniquities, who heals all your diseases."* I cannot stress the **"forgiveness"** part enough to you because it is really important.

While praying and asking for your healing, have no doubt or fear. In *Mark 11:23*, Jesus says: *"For assuredly I say to you, whoever says to this mountain [issue, problem], be removed and be cast into the sea, and does not doubt in his heart, but believes that those things he says will be done, he will have whatever he says." Mark 11:24* states: *"Therefore, I say to you whatever things you ask, when you pray, believe that you receive them, and you will have them."* In *John 16:23-24*, Jesus says: "*And in that day you will ask Me nothing. Most assuredly, I say to you, whatever you ask the Father in My name, He will give you. Until now you have asked nothing in My name. Ask and you will receive, that your joy may be full."*

Do not let any negative thoughts enter into your mind while you're praying and standing on God's word for your healing. For the sickness, virus, or disease was not given to you by God, but by satan who is seeking to steal your life from you, and he's seeking to kill and destroy you. In *John 10:10, Jesus* states: *"The thief does not come except to steal, and to kill, and to destroy. I have come that they may have life and that they may have it more abundantly."* You cannot be second-guessing yourself or God, which is, by the way, a strategy satan uses to make you doubt your request and doubt that God's word is true for you. This battle always takes place in your mind and satan always tries to make you reason and argue with yourself, he gives you suggestions and theories and reasonings, he plots and schemes, and he tries to make you contradict yourself and contradict God's word. The devil tries to dispute all the good that God has done for you in your past so that you won't believe God's word for your future. *2 Corinthians 10:4-5* states: *"For the weapons of our warfare are not carnal but mighty in God for pulling down strongholds, casting down arguments and every high thing that exalts itself against the knowledge of God, bringing every thought into captivity to the obedience of Christ."* You have to recognize that any negative word, argument, or contradiction to God's word being said to you in your mind is not coming from God. Anything that contradicts or disputes God's word from the Bible is definitely not from God. So, don't let satan steal your blessings.

Ask God for what you need and He will deliver – whether it's for healing, financial guidance, relationship repair, etc. *Philippians 4:19* states: *"And my God shall supply all your need according to His riches in glory by Christ Jesus." In John 16:23-24, Jesus* states: *"And in that day you will ask Me nothing. Most assuredly I say to you, whatever you ask the Father in My name He will give you. Until now you have asked nothing in My name. Ask, and you will receive, that your joy may be full."* Don't be afraid to ask God. You are His beloved child. *2 Timothy 1:7* states: *"For God has not given us a spirit of fear, but of power and of love and of a sound mind."* So know your enemy. If you go to the doctor for treatment, go to God, too. Put this whole situation into God's hands and trust Him. God uses doctors to help in your healing or He will heal you directly. In *2 Corinthians 10:4*, we see that: *"For the weapons of our warfare are not carnal but mighty in God for pulling down strongholds."* You are not just dealing with a physical problem, but you're dealing with a spiritual problem as well, and you will need more than just what the doctor prescribes to overcome what you have which is designed to take your life.

Then, in your prayer to God, you count it as done! *John 16:23* states: *"And in that day you will ask Me nothing. Most assuredly, I say to you, whatever you ask the Father in My name He will give you."* You know that it's done in the name of Jesus. You thank God for what He has done and is doing in your life, in the restoration and healing of your body. *Psalm 9:1-2* states: *"I will praise You, O Lord, with my whole heart; I will tell of all Your marvelous works. I will be glad and rejoice in You; I will sing praise to Your name, O Most High." Psalm 103:1-5* states: *"Bless the Lord, O my soul; and all that is within me, bless His holy name! Bless the Lord, O my soul, and forget not all His benefits: Who forgives all your iniquities [sins], who heals all your diseases, who redeems your life from destruction, who crowns you with loving kindness and tender mercies, who satisfies your mouth with good things, so that your youth is renewed like the eagle's." Psalm 145:1-3* states: *"I will extol You, my God, O King; and I will bless Your name forever and ever. Every day I will bless You, and I will praise Your name forever and ever. Great is the Lord, and greatly to be praised; and His greatness is unsearchable."* Begin acting like the new creation that you now are because you have accepted Jesus Christ as your Lord and Savior. Praise Him for it, and don't look back!!!

God Is A Restorer

Have you lost all sense of yourself because you have been dragged down by the weight of your sins? You've tried on your own to be respectable and clean from your past, but you're getting nowhere? The problem is that YOU are trying to do the fix instead of allowing God to do it. Here's the good news! God restores! In *Joel 2:25-27*, the Lord says: *"So I will restore to you the years that the swarming locust has eaten, the crawling locust, the consuming locust, and the chewing locust, my great army which I sent among you. You shall eat plenty and be satisfied, and praise the name of the Lord your God, who has dealt wondrously with you; and My people shall never be put to shame. Then you shall know that I am in the midst of Israel; I am the Lord your God and there is no other. My people shall never be put to shame." Psalm 23:3* states: *"He restores my soul; He leads me in the paths of righteousness for His name's sake."* God knows that because of your sin, you are where you are, but He will also restore you to where you should be in all areas of your life. Trust Him.

In times of despair and loss through others, God has provided His promises of restoration through the Lord Jesus Christ in *Chapter 61* of the *Book of Isaiah*:

"The Spirit of the Lord God is upon Me [Jesus] because the Lord has anointed Me to preach good tidings to the poor; He has sent Me to heal the brokenhearted, to proclaim liberty to the captives, and the opening of the prison to those who are bound, to proclaim the acceptable year of the Lord, and the day of vengeance of our God; to comfort all who mourn, to console those who mourn in Zion, to give them beauty for ashes, the oil of joy for mourning, the garment of praise for the spirit of heaviness; that they may be called trees of righteousness, the planting of the Lord that He may be glorified.

And they shall rebuild the old ruins, they shall raise up the former desolations, and they shall repair the ruined cities, the desolations of many generations. Strangers shall stand and feed your flocks, and the sons of the foreigner shall be your plowmen and your vinedressers. But you shall be named the priests of the Lord. They shall call you the servants of our God. You shall eat the riches of the Gentiles, and in their glory (material wealth and blessings), you shall boast. Instead of your shame, you shall have double honor, and instead of confusion they shall rejoice in their portion. Therefore in their land they shall possess double; everlasting joy shall be theirs. For I, the Lord, love justice; I hate robbery for burnt offering; I will direct their work in truth, and will make with them an everlasting covenant. Their descendants shall be known among the Gentiles and their offspring among the people. All who see them shall acknowledge them, that they are the posterity whom the Lord has blessed. I will greatly rejoice in the Lord. My soul shall be joyful in my God, for He has clothed me with the garments of salvation. He has covered me with the robe of righteousness, as a bridegroom decks himself with ornaments, and as a bride adorns herself with her jewels. For as the earth brings forth its bud, as the garden causes the things that are sown in it to spring forth, so the Lord God will cause righteousness and praise to spring forth before all the nations."

The *Amplified Bible* says it this way:

"The Spirit of the Lord God is upon me, because the Lord has anointed and qualified me to preach the Gospel of good tidings to the meek, the poor, and afflicted. He has sent me to bind up and heal the brokenhearted, to proclaim liberty to the [physical and spiritual] captives and the opening of the prison and of the eyes to those who are bound, to proclaim the acceptable year of the Lord [the year of His favor] and the day of vengeance of our God, to comfort all who mourn, to grant [consolation and joy] to those who mourn in Zion – to give them an ornament (a garland or diadem) of beauty instead

of ashes, the oil of joy instead of mourning, the garment [expressive] of praise instead of a heavy, burdened, and failing spirit – that they may be called oaks of righteousness [lofty, strong, and magnificent, distinguished for uprightness, justice, and right standing with God], the planting of the Lord, that He may be glorified. And they shall rebuild the ancient ruins; they shall raise up the former desolations and renew the ruined cities, the devastations of many generations. Aliens shall stand [ready] and feed your flocks, and foreigners shall be your plowmen and your vinedressers.

But you shall be called the priests of the Lord; people will speak of you as the ministers of our God. You shall eat the wealth of the nations, and the glory [once that of your captors] shall be yours. Instead of your [former] shame, you shall have a twofold recompense; instead of dishonor and reproach [your people] shall rejoice in their portion. Therefore, in their land they shall possess double [what they had forfeited]; everlasting joy shall be theirs

For I the Lord love justice; I hate robbery and wrong with violence or a burnt offering. And I will faithfully give them their recompense in truth, and I will make an everlasting covenant or league with them. And their offspring shall be known among the nations and their descendants among the peoples. All who see them [in their prosperity] will recognize and acknowledge that they are the people who the Lord has blessed.

I will greatly rejoice in the Lord, my soul will exalt in my God; for He has clothed me with the garments of salvation, He has covered me with the robe of righteousness, as a bridegroom decks himself with a garland, and as a bride adorns herself with her jewels. For as [surely as] the earth brings forth its shoots, and as a garden causes what is sown in it to spring forth, so [surely] the Lord God will cause rightness and justice and praise to spring forth before all the nations [through the self-fulfilling power of His word]."

For all the pain, hurt, sorrow, humiliation, physical sufferings, deceit and betrayal that you encountered in your life, the Lord God will restore you. All losses will be restored to you double for your trouble, all those who have hurt you will receive the vengeance of God, Himself, all that was stolen from you will be replaced, you will be free from all of the burdens of the past, your heart will be healed, you will be given much joy for your sorrow, you will be blessed by and through your children and your children's children, your children and children's children will be blessed, and you will receive much honor and blessings through the Lord Jesus Christ.

Maybe you have not been able to have children 'YET' due to your health condition. God will restore you in accordance with the plan He has for you. *Joel 2:12-13* states: *"Now, therefore, says the Lord, Turn to Me with all your heart, with fasting, with weeping and with mourning. So rend your heart and not your garments; return to the Lord your God for He is gracious and merciful, slow to anger, and of great kindness; and He relents from doing harm."* God knows your heart and your desires. Remember Abraham and Sarah. Sarah was way, way, way past menopause, but God granted Sarah and Abraham a child in their latter years. *Genesis 17:19* states: *"Then God said [to Abraham]: 'No, Sarah your wife shall bear you a son, and you shall call his name Isaac.'"* God does great miracles. In *Genesis 18:14,* the Lord said: *"Is anything too hard for the Lord?"* Not only that, but God kept His promise to Abraham. *Hebrews 6:13-14* states: *"For when God made a promise to Abraham, because He could swear by no one greater, He swore by Himself, saying 'Surely blessing I will bless you, and multiplying I will multiply you.'"*

Your faith will bring you through to your healing, your restoration, and to the desires of your heart. Jesus said in *Mark 11:22: "Have faith in God."* If you have faith that God will do what He promised in accordance with His word, and you are doing your part in obedience to His word in accordance with His plan and purpose for your life, He will give you the desires of your heart. However, your knowledge of His word and your obedience to His word are key essentials to obtaining the desires of your heart.

He is already aware of your heart's desires because God is omniscient (all knowing, infinitely aware, and He has awesome insight). *Psalm 37:4* states: *"Delight yourself also in the Lord, and He shall give you the desires of your heart." Mark 11:24-26* states: *"Therefore I say to you, whatever things you ask when you pray, believe that you receive them, and you will have them. And whenever you stand praying, if you have anything against anyone, forgive him, that your Father in heaven may also forgive you your trespasses. But if you do not forgive, neither will your Father in heaven forgive your trespasses."* There are many reasons why women are unable to get pregnant, but one of the key reasons may be unforgiveness. If you are harboring anything against anyone, get rid of it now.

Romans 10:17 states: *"So then faith comes by hearing, and hearing by the word of God."* By hearing and understanding God's word, you will activate and increase your measure of faith. God has given each of us a measure of faith. *Romans 12:3* states: *"For I say, through the grace given to me, to everyone who is among you, not to think of himself more highly than he ought to think, but to think soberly, as God has dealt to each one a measure of faith."* So have faith that you are healed in your womb because Jesus took our infirmities and bore our sicknesses on the cross when He was crucified. *Matthew 8:17* states: *"that it might be fulfilled which was spoken by Isaiah the prophet, saying: 'He Himself took our infirmities and bore our sicknesses.'"*

There are many miracles in the Bible where Jesus healed people, and people are still being healed today who have faith in Jesus. Remember that Jesus is the same yesterday, today, and forever. In fact, *Hebrews 13:8* states: *"Jesus Christ is the same yesterday, today, and forever."*

God is always willing to bless us, but we tend to hinder ourselves from receiving our own desires being fulfilled. But, if we believe God's word, His word will be fulfilled in our lives. For example, in *Matthew 8:1-4: "When He [Jesus] had come down from the mountain, great multitudes followed Him. And behold, a leper came and worshiped Him, saying 'Lord, if You are willing, You can make me clean.' Then Jesus put out His hand and touched him, saying, 'I am willing; be cleansed.' Immediately, his leprosy was cleansed. And Jesus said to him, 'See that you tell no one; but go your way, show yourself to the priest, and offer the gift that Moses commanded as a testimony to them.'"*

The person who had leprosy was now whole. He believed the Lord was able to heal him if the Lord was willing. The Lord was willing and able. The leper had faith in the Lord that He was able and willing to heal him. The leper's healing was manifested because of his faith in the Lord and what the Lord could do. Although the Lord was willing and able, it was the faith of the leper that got him healed. God is always willing, but you have to step out in faith. Your faith is the key ingredient. Pastor Tom Pickens put it best in one of his sermons: "Faith is an action word." *Hebrews 11:6* states: *"But without faith, it is impossible to please Him [God], for he who comes to God must believe that He is, and that He is a rewarder of those who diligently seek Him."* In the Merriam-Webster Dictionary, some of the definitions of faith are (1) the firm belief in something for which there is no [visible] proof, (2) believing with strong conviction, (3) complete trust, and (4) belief and trust in, and loyalty to God. Pastor Tom Pickens also stated: "You have to believe to see, not see to believe." Faith is your confidence in the word of God. Then after you see it, you then know it, and your faith has brought it into being real and tangible. So, if you believe to see God do for you in accordance with His word, stand on that belief (faith/confidence). Your faith will bring whatever you need to come to completion.

Matthew 8:5-10 shows another step of faith: *"Now when Jesus had entered Capernaum, a centurion (head of many soldiers) came to Him, pleading with Him, saying, 'Lord, my servant is lying at home paralyzed, dreadfully tormented.' And Jesus said to him, 'I will come and heal him.' The centurion answered and said, 'Lord, I am not worthy that You should come under my roof, but only speak a word, and my servant will be healed. For I also am a man under authority, having soldiers under me, and I say to this one, go, and he goes, and to another, come, and he comes, and to my servant, do this, and he does it.' When Jesus heard it, He marveled, and said to those who followed, 'Assuredly, I say to you, I have not found such great faith, not even in Israel!'"* *Matthew 8:13* states: *"Then Jesus said to the centurion, 'Go your way; and as you have believed, so let it be done for you.'"*

The operative word here is "faith" (confidence) that the centurion had in believing that Jesus could heal his servant, even without being at the centurion's home, and even without laying hands on the servant. Jesus knew His ability and power. He didn't have to believe that He could heal the centurion's servant. But the centurion had to believe in order to make the healing come to pass. *Hebrews 11:6* states: *"But without faith, it is impossible to please Him, for he who comes to God must believe that He [God] is and that He is a rewarder of those who diligently seek Him."*

Here's another example of the Lord's healing power: *Matthew 9:18 – 33* states: *"While He spoke these things to them, behold, a ruler came and worshiped Him, saying, 'My daughter has just died, but come and lay Your hands on her and she will live.' So Jesus arose and followed him, and so did His disciples. And suddenly, a woman who had a flow of blood for twelve years came from behind and touched the hem of His [Jesus] garment. For she said to herself, 'If only I may touch His garment, I shall be made well.' But Jesus turned around, and when He saw her He said, 'Be of good cheer, daughter, your faith has made you well.' And the woman was made well from that hour. When Jesus came into the ruler's house, and saw the flute players and the noisy crowd wailing, He said to them, 'Make room for the girl is not dead, but sleeping.' And they ridiculed Him. But when the crowd was put outside, He went in and took her by the hand, and the girl arose. And the report of this went out into all that land. When Jesus departed from there, two blind men followed Him, crying out and saying, 'Son of David, have mercy on us!' And when He had come into the house, the blind men came to Him. And Jesus said to them, 'Do you believe that I am able to do this?' They said to Him, 'Yes, Lord.' Then He touched their eyes, saying, 'According to your faith, let it be to you.' And their eyes were opened. And Jesus sternly warned them, saying 'See that no one knows it.' But when they had departed, they spread the news about Him in all that country. As they went out, behold, they brought to Him a man, mute and demon-possessed. And when the demon was cast out, the mute spoke. And the multitudes marveled, saying, 'It was never seen like this in Israel!'"*

There are many scriptures throughout the Bible concerning healing by Jesus and healing by His apostles and by others who believe God's Word. *Acts 9:32-34* states: *"Now it came to pass, as Peter went through all parts of the country, that he also came down to the saints who dwelt in Lydda. There he found a certain man named Aeneas, who had been bed-ridden eight years and was paralyzed. And Peter said to him, 'Aeneas, Jesus the Christ heals you. Arise and make your bed.' Then he arose immediately." Acts 14:8-10* states: *"And in Lystra a certain man without strength in his feet was sitting, a cripple from his mother's womb, who had never walked. This man heard Paul speaking. Paul, observing him intently and seeing that he had faith to be healed, said [to him] with a loud voice, 'Stand up straight on your feet!' And he leaped and walked."*

In *James 5:16*, he being one of the Apostles, states: *"Confess your trespasses to one another, and pray for one another, that you may be healed. The effective, fervent prayer of a righteous man avails much." Psalm 103:1, 3* states: *"Bless the Lord, O my soul; and all that is within me, bless His holy name! Who forgives all your iniquities, who heals all your diseases."*

Did you notice that Jesus did not say that because many of these people were sinners they could not be healed. He fulfilled each and every request based on their faith. Also, the Apostle Paul was able to speak the Lord's word over people and they were healed based on their belief in the Word of God.

So trust in the Lord and be joyful. *Proverbs 3:5* states: *"Trust in the Lord with all your heart and lean not on your own understanding." Psalm 30:5* states: *". . . Weeping may endure for the night, but joy comes in the morning." Nehemiah 8:10* states: *". . . for the joy of the Lord is your strength." Romans 5:5* states: *"Now hope does not disappoint, because the love of God has been poured out in our hearts by the Holy Spirit who was given to us."* The joy of the Lord really is your strength. So rejoice!

Faith in God is extremely important in all areas of your life. *Hebrews 11:6* states: *"But without faith it is impossible to please Him, for he who comes to God must believe that He is, and that He is a rewarder of those who diligently seek Him."*

We are not called to be successful, but we are called to be **faithful**.

God Has Not Abandoned You In Your Pain And Suffering

When you were in negative circumstances in the past, God was there for you and He brought you through. Remind yourself how He was there for you, and how He brought you through. Praise Him for the joy and relief you had because He saved you through the negative circumstances. Remember His great love for you, and your great love for Him. Remind Him of His Word for He is true to His Word, He is not a respector of person, He will not let any of His words go unfulfilled, and His promises are real and true. When you do this, you're also encouraging yourself. *2 Corinthians 1:20* states: *"For all the promises of God in Him are Yes, and in Him Amen, to the glory of God through us."* Let God know that you know what He did, what He is doing, and what He will do for you because you belong to Him. Praise Him in everything, everywhere, and at every moment.

Rejoice in His Word, in His sovereignty, and in His grace. Tell Him how grateful you are and how blessed you are, even in the midst of the storm that you're currently in, because you know He will come through for you, because He has come through for you in the past, and He will continue to do so for those who diligently seek Him and do His will.

Look to Him, not to others, because it was He who got you out of hot water in the past, and He was the one who restored you. He can do it again.

Be still so you can hear His voice of encouragement to you. Be still and know that He is God, the Almighty One, the Creator of everything, the One who loves you like no other, the Healer, the Provider, the Protector, the All Knowing, the All Hearing, the One who has not and will not abandon you. *Psalm 46:10* states: *"Be still, and know that I am God; I will be exalted among the nations, I will be exalted in the earth."*

Remember and memorize *Romans 8:28*, which states: *"And we know that all things work together for good to those who love God, to those who are the called according to His purpose."* He has, He is, and He will work all things out for your good because you are His child. He cares for you even when you don't care about yourself.

Romans 8:37 states: *"Yet, in all these things, we are more than conquerors through Him who loved us."* God is here for you.

God can only be in control if you allow Him. He can't take the problem you're facing if you've still got your hands on it. So give that burden to Him and watch Him work it out for your good and for His glory.

Realize that although you're going through an ordeal, God is bringing you to something good, if you trust Him. The operative words are "through", "to", and "trust", which are action words. It means that you're not stuck where you are because God is bringing you through the problem into the solution. Stand in faith and trust Him, knowing that He is working on your behalf. Be willing to see what God is bringing you to. *Hebrews 10:38* states: *"Now the just shall live by faith; but if anyone draws back, My soul has no pleasure in him."* God has faith in you, and He wants you to have faith in Him. Therefore, don't waiver in your faith. He strongly dislikes lukewarm people. God says in *Revelation 3:16: "So then, because you are lukewarm, and neither cold nor hot, I will vomit you out of My mouth."*

In looking back over my life, I have seen myself get into situations that were not the best, and some even life threatening, but God brought me through. I have lived long enough to see God's hand at work in my life turning those situations around for my benefit and for His glory. The past was sometimes hurtful, and I thought I lost what I thought was worth keeping, but God knew what He was doing. It may not have seemed like I overcame at that time, but the end result was so much better and far outweighed anything I ever expected.

You are not the only one in life going through what you're going through, but remember that God is there for you like He was there and is here for me. He says in His word that He will never leave us nor forsake us. *Hebrews 13:5* states: *"Let your conduct be without covetousness; be content with such things as you have, for He Himself has said, 'I will never leave you nor forsake you.'"*

We may not understand in the midst of the circumstance, but His thoughts are not ours. He doesn't think as low as we think because we are mere mortals and He is God, our Creator. I am so glad and grateful that His thoughts are so much "**higher**" than mine.

In *Jeremiah 29:11*, God says: *"For I know the thoughts that I think toward you, says the Lord, thoughts of peace and not of evil, to give you a future and a hope." Numbers 23:19* states: *"God is not a man that He should lie, nor a son of man, that He should repent. Has He said, and will He not do? Or has He spoken, and will He not make it good?" Hebrews 11:6* states: *"But without faith it is impossible to please Him, for he who comes to God must believe that He is, and that He is a rewarder of those who diligently seek Him."*

God honors His Word. He does not lie. He knows what He's doing. He knows what He's thinking and what you're thinking. He knows what you need and He knows what you don't need. He is omnipresent, which means that He is with you all the time. He always has our best interest at His heart. If we are stubborn, He will allow trials in our lives to get our attention. Through trials, we look to Him, we trust, we grow, we gain strength, and we overcome. Through my trials, I have grown in such a way that I have compassion for anyone going through a trial, especially a trial that I, myself, have directly been through. I am able to offer God's Word and my own testimony as to how He brought me through. I assist a person in any way possible. Be it material (money or things that I have that they may need), physical (a helping hand), or spiritual (pray and stand in agreement with them for a need they have in line with God's will and His word). I am able to show that person God's love through my acknowledging how He brought me through the trial into victory, and He can do the same for them. I am able to show them through my patience, perseverance, and trust in His Word that they can have hope, too, if they do not faint.

We are not to faint in the day of adversity. *Isaiah 40:31* states: *"But those who wait on the Lord shall renew their strength; they shall mount up with wings like eagles. They shall run and not be weary. They shall walk and not faint." Proverbs 24:10* states: *"If you faint in the day of adversity, your strength is small." Ephesians 6:10* states: *"Finally, my brethren, be strong in the Lord and in the power of His might."* That's what being a woman of faith in God and in His Word is all about. We are ministers of God's Word, not just in speaking, but in doing also. We've got to walk the talk.

When you realize that you were taken advantage of and violated, do not avenge yourself, but give this to God to handle. *Romans 12:19-21 states: "Beloved, do not avenge yourselves, but rather give place to wrath: for it is written, 'Vengeance is Mine, I will repay,' says the Lord. 'Therefore, if your enemy is hungry, feed him; if he is thirsty, give him a drink; for in so doing you will heap coals of fire on his head.' Do not be overcome with evil, but overcome evil with good."*

The wrongs that others do to you is God's business, and no longer yours. Your business is to give the matter over to God, to forgive and pray for those who wronged you, and to do God's will so that you will be blessed. I know; it took me a while to get this, too. But I have been around long enough to see His handiwork, and no one could do it better than God. When someone wrongs you, that person has to now deal with God, for God is our avenger. Remember *Romans 12:19-21. Deuteronomy 32:35* states: *"Vengeance is Mine, and recompense [payment]; their foot shall slip in due time; for the day of their calamity is at hand, and the things to come hasten upon them."*

Let God turn things around for you. Let Him turn your mess into a message (testimony) to others to help and bless them. Be a blessing by giving your testimony to those who are in danger of making the same mistakes you made, which brought bad consequences. Since you know what the consequences will be, and the formula is always basically the same, you know what they are about to go through. Because you did not like what happened to you, don't let someone else go through what you went through without trying to help her see a better way before it's too late. See the bigger need.

As I am writing this book, I am going through a trial. It is probably one of the biggest trials I have ever been in, but I am faithful, hopeful, and excited in seeing how God is going to bring me through it! He has brought me through so many other trials in the past with wonderful results. The trials I have been through have always brought me to a better place, a better understanding, and peace in knowing that He is in control because I have cast all of my care upon the Lord for He cares for me. *1 Peter 5:6-7* states: *"Therefore humble yourselves under the mighty hand of God, that He may exalt you in due time, casting all your care upon Him for He cares for you."*

If you could only see yourself as God sees you. Remember your position. You're an heir and a daughter of the Most High God. Being a daughter of God has wonderful benefits: As stated in Chapter 3, you're highly favored, you have the power to overcome any obstacle, you're more than a conqueror, others can see His light through you, all things are possible with Him, and He is for you, not against you. *Romans 8:31* states: *"What then shall we say to these things? If God is for us, who can be against us?"*

Be Still And Trust In The Lord

Psalm 46:1 states: *"God is our refuge and strength, a very present help in trouble."*

The whole passage of *Psalm 46* is wonderful for teenage girls, young ladies, and women in general. I believe this passage was created just for us. This passage is for you who are in the flames of a trial; and you who may feel trapped, lost, rejected, guilty, dirty, broken and weary. Just knowing that God is behind the scenes working on your behalf to bring you through and out of your circumstances victoriously, no matter what they are, is a blessing to you.

Trust God and be still. *Psalm 46:10-11* states: *"Be still and know that I am God. I will be exalted among the nations, I will be exalted in the earth. The Lord of hosts is with us; the God of Jacob is our refuge."* If you are trusting God, you're being still. Just be still. He was there when you got into trouble, and He is still with you. He has not left you. He will see you through. He is working things out behind the scenes for your benefit and to His glory. Just be still and trust Him. No matter what your circumstances look like or feel like, just be still and let God handle it, whatever it is. Jesus healed the sick, opened the eyes of the blind, made the crippled walk, cleansed those who were diseased, made whole those who were mentally challenged, and He healed the broken-hearted. He did it when He walked this earth over two thousand years ago, and He can and will do it again for you. Just trust Him and be still. Don't get frustrated because you think He's taking too long. He says in His word not to be anxious for anything. *Philippians 4:6-7* states: *"Be anxious for nothing, but in everything by prayer and supplication, with thanksgiving, let your requests be made known to God, and the peace of God, which surpasses all understanding, will guard your hearts and minds through Christ Jesus."* If you overstep God, you will never know what a wonderful outcome He had for you. Anything that you do will be far less than what He can do, and it will not be as satisfying. You may even make things worse for yourself by not waiting for Him.

If you allow God to be in complete control, you should have confidence to face tomorrow and whatever it brings. *Isaiah 40:31* states: *"But those who wait on the Lord shall renew their strength; they shall mount up with wings like eagles; they shall run and not be weary; they shall walk and not faint."* Jesus says in *Matthew 11:28: "Come to Me, all you who labor and are heavy laden (weary, exhausted, weighed down), and I will give you rest. Take My yoke upon you and learn from Me, for I am gentle and lowly at heart, and you will find rest for your souls. For My yoke is easy and My burden is light."*

Fear will take you away from God's best. We are not to be fearful as we step out in faith to make that change for the better. *Isaiah 41:10* states: *"Fear not, for I am with you. Be not dismayed [discouraged] for I am your God. I will strengthen you; Yes, I will help you. I will uphold you with My righteous right hand."* "Fear" and "Faith" cannot occupy the same space, as discussed by Pastor Tom Pickens in one of his sermons at church. "If you're in fear, you are not trusting and believing in God. If you're in fear, you don't believe that God will do what He says He will do." God honors His Word. Speak His Word back to Him as you pray. As you're making that change for your better, remember that God is with you and He does not want you to be fearful, for He is in control. *2 Timothy 1:7* states: *"For God has not given us a spirit of fear, but of power and of love and of a sound mind."* The word "fear" encompasses worry, doubt, anxiety, stress, nervousness, depression, and failure. God did not make us to fail. If you're a child of God, you are automatically built "God-Tough" and you are resilient. You can withstand any obstacle that the enemy sets before you. You have the ability to remove any obstacle in front of you in accordance with *Mark 11:23*, where the Lord Jesus, Himself, states: *"For assuredly I say to you, whoever says to this mountain[obstacle, issue, problem], 'Be removed and be cast into the sea, and does not doubt in his [her] heart, but believes that those things he [she] says will be done, he [she] will have whatever he [she] says.'"* You're built to win!

So, is it too late to start over? Is it too late to change the direction you're going in? Is it too late to change what others say about you? Is it too late to change the consequences of your past actions? Is it too late to change your health? No. No. No. No. No! And, again I say a big fat "NO!"

As long as you are on this earth, living, breathing, and serving the Lord, it will never be too late to change. It wasn't too late for Rahab, who was a prostitute. *(The Book of Joshua, Chapter 2)* She was able to save herself and her family by helping the angels of God. It wasn't too late for Esther who saved her people [the Jews] and herself. *(The Book of Esther)* It wasn't too late for Ruth, who married Boaz and saved herself and her mother-in-law, Naomi. *(The Book of Ruth)* It wasn't too late for the woman with the issue of blood, who had the problem for many years. She believed that just touching the hem of the garment (Prayer Shawl – Tallit) worn by Jesus she would be healed – and she was healed. *(Matthew 9:20-22)* There are many other examples of women and men of the Bible who changed their course of life by believing and trusting in God. These were ordinary people, just like you and me, who trusted and had faith in God, and He made them extraordinary.

<u>Time To Grow Up</u>

Regret and guilt are terrible things to overcome, but overcome them you must because the Lord Jesus has overcome the world, He has forgiven you, and He has given you a future and a hope. *1 John 5:4* states: *"For whatever is born of God overcomes the world, and this is the victory that has overcome the world – our faith."* Jesus speaks to us through *John 16:33*, which states: *"These things I have spoken to you, that in Me you may have peace, in the world you will have tribulation, but be of good cheer, I have overcome the world."*

You have a responsibility both to Him and to yourself to put regret and guilt behind and press forward for the prize. In *Philippians 3:14, the Apostle Paul* states: *"I press toward the goal for the prize of the upward call of God in Christ Jesus."* As referenced in Chapter 3 of this book concerning sexual immorality, there are hard and sometimes lasting consequences for disobedience to God's Word in the area of sex and in other areas of your life. Although He has forgiven you, you cannot escape the consequences. Therefore, don't do anything that would cause you to suffer even more bad consequences. You know the old saying, "Don't do the crime if you can't do the time." This is such a profound statement. You must think about the possible ramifications and consequences before you make decisions and act on them, especially in the area of sexual promiscuity, because your decisions and actions can and will harm you and even kill you. The operative word here is **"YOU"** because you will be the one who suffers and bear the consequences. It really is all about **"YOU."**

You cannot claim ignorance because whether you know the Word of God or not, deep down inside you know right from wrong, and you know what you're doing is wrong. That signal from within is your conscience alerting you. Don't ignore your conscience because the consequences are the same, they are real and they are active. Your reasoning has to be in line with the Word of God. God's word is very clear concerning sexual immorality. *1 Thessalonians 4:3* states: *"For this is the will of God, your sanctification: that you should abstain from sexual immorality; that each of you should know how to possess his [her] own vessel [body] in sanctification and honor, not in passion of lust like the Gentiles who do not know God."* As a new creation, you're no longer a Gentile who does not know God or His Word. You are to study God's Word. *2 Timothy 2:15* states: *"Be diligent to present yourself approved to God, a worker who does not need to be ashamed, rightly dividing the word of truth."*

As a new creation, you are now able to carry yourself as an honorable person – a person of respect, a person not led by her passion and lust. As a new creation, you're not to be moved by your flesh, but by the Word of God. You have to change your way of thinking and have the mind of God in everything you do. To do this, you must renew your mind by meditating on the word of God. So you can't sleep around with boys or men anymore, you can no longer walk that worldly walk that attracted the wrong man to you, and you can no longer talk that street talk. As a new creation, you have put all of that behind you, and you must press ahead for God's promises and blessings to come true for you in your life. *2 Timothy 2:22* states: *"Flee also youthful lusts, but pursue righteousness, faith, love, peace with those who call on the Lord out of a pure heart." 1 Timothy 6:12* states: *"Fight the good fight of faith, lay hold on eternal life, to which you were also called and have confessed the good confession in the presence of many witnesses."*

You can't sleep with someone just because you "like" him or because he says he likes you. The risk is just too great! Your future and your eternity are at stake. You must weigh the risk, the guilt, and the consequences versus the temporary satisfaction or temporary reward. To do things God's way eliminates all risks. He will lead you and give you discernment and understanding so you can make the right choices **"if"** you believe His word is true and **"if"** you go to Him when confronted with the temptation. This is where your faith comes into play. *Mark 11:22* states: *"Have faith in God."* In situations like this, **"always"** remember *1 Corinthians 10:13*, which states: *"No temptation has overtaken you, except such as is **"common"** to man [woman]; but **God is faithful**, who will not allow you to be tempted beyond what you are able, but with the temptation will also make the way of escape, that you may be able to bear it."*

All sin is "common" (ordinary, familiar, nothing special, widespread, general, coarse). The person who tries to seduce you into having sex with him is "common" and the temptation by that person is "common." In the dictionary, the word "common", as used in a sexual or fornication-type approach, means falling below ordinary standards, lacking refinement, ordinary, and vulgar. Based on these descriptions, there is nothing special about having sex with a guy who has these negative attributes. If you do have sex with this person, you will be no better than he who seduced you.

The scriptures below references "man", which also refers to "woman." There are many scriptures in the Bible that refer to our bodies, who owns our bodies, and what we are to do and not do with our bodies. *1 Corinthians 3:16-17* states: *"Do you not know that you are the temple of God and that the Spirit of God dwells in you? If anyone defiles the temple of God, God will destroy him. For the temple of God is holy, which temple you are." 1 Corinthians 3:23* states: *"And you are Christ's and Christ is God's."* Since God is holy, you must be holy, too, because He lives inside of you through the Holy Spirit.

1 Corinthians 6:13-14 states: *"Foods for the stomach and the stomach for foods, but God will destroy both it and them. Now the body is not for sexual immorality but for the Lord, and the Lord for the body. And God both raised up the Lord and will also raise us up by His power."*

1 Corinthians 6:15-17 states: *"Do you not know that your bodies are members of Christ? Shall I then take the members of Christ and make them members of a harlot? Certainly not! Or do you not know that he who is joined to a harlot is one body with her? For 'the two', He says, shall become one flesh."* Don't think that only women are harlots; men who sleep around are harlots, too, because they are doing the same thing.

1 Corinthians 6:18 states: *"Flee sexual immorality. Every sin that a man [woman] does is outside the body, but he [she] who commits sexual immorality sins against his [her] own body."*

1 Corinthians 6:19-20 states: *"Or do you not know that your body is the temple of the Holy Spirit who is in you, whom you have from God, and you are not your own? For you were bought at a price; therefore glorify God in your body and in your spirit, which are God's."*

So, as you can see, it's never too late to change. God is waiting for you to change your heart and your mind and follow Jesus. The Bible has plenty of God's words on the subject of sexual promiscuity. He speaks to you through the scriptures in the Bible to encourage you to make that change, to let you know that He has got your back and He is with you through all of the hurt and pain. He tells you to fear not, and to have faith in Him and in His word. You don't have to be concerned about what others say about you, but only what God says about you. At some point in their lives, they will have to come to the Lord just like you. He can heal and restore them like He can heal and restore you. You do have hope for the future – your future with God.

Remind yourself that God is always thinking about you, and you should begin thinking what He thinks about you, too. *Proverbs 23:7* states: *"For as he [she] thinks in his [her] heart, so is he [she]."* What you think about you is what will either help you to overcome the negative darts sent by satan into your mind, or allow you to surrender to the negative darts sent by satan into your mind. Remember, everything you do begins in your mind. If you dwell on the love God has for you, the promises He made to you, what He says about you, how He has forgiven you through the sacrifice of His Son, Jesus Christ, how you have been made an heir to the throne of Almighty God, and how He has given you a future and a hope, you will definitely conquer the battle in your mind. But it all begins with you studying His Word, the Bible. You cannot begin to know how valuable you are and what He has in store for your future unless you read and meditate on His Word. Knowledge is power.

God loves you and wants your obedience. *Romans 5:8-9* states: *"But God demonstrates His own love toward us, in that while we were still sinners, Christ died for us. Much more then, having now been justified by His blood, we shall be saved from wrath through Him." John 3:16* states: *"For God so loved the world that He gave His only begotten Son, that whoever believes in Him should not perish but have everlasting life." John 14:15* states: *"If you love Me, keep My commandments."*

It's never too late to start over.

Chapter 5

What's Love Got To Do With It?

Chapter 5

What's Love Got To Do With It?

"For God so loved the world that He gave His only begotten Son, that whoever believes in Him should not perish but have everlasting life." (John 3:16)

You were born out of love. You were not born necessarily out of your parents' love for you. Maybe you were born out of two people's lustfulness that led to your being here, or born out of a crime of rape or incest where there was no love. You were, however, definitely born out of the love of God, and born out of His purpose for you at this time and in this place. You were meant to be here, born for God's purpose by His necessary means. *Ephesians 2:10* states: *"For we are His workmanship, created in Christ Jesus for good works, which God prepared before-hand that we should walk in them."* You were born on purpose for His purpose. It was not a mistake that you are here. You were born for such a time as this. You're not someone's bastard or unwanted child. You are definitely wanted and needed by God to fulfill His purpose through your life.

God created you for His glory and for your good. God made you. There is nobody like you on the face of the earth. Even if you were a twin, there is still no one like **you** on the face of this planet. God has inscribed you on the palms of His hands. *Isaiah 49:16* states: *"See, I have inscribed you on the palms of My hands; your walls are continually before me."* He knew your name before you were born. He knows where you are at all times. He knows everything about you, even more than you know about yourself.

You may have been born into a situation where both parents loved you before you were born. They were expecting you, and they made arrangements for you to come into their lives and share your life with them. They planned to take care of you, nourish you, provide graciously for you, protect you, educate you and encourage you. They even made out their life insurance policies and their Wills to ensure you are well taken care of in case something should ever happen to them. They have health insurance to provide medical attention to you if you get sick. They have dental insurance to ensure you get that award-winning smile. They have a home for you to live in, and they even decorated a bedroom just for you. They even have savings earmarked for your college education and/or a possible car in your future. They have taken pictures and videos of you through your years of growth that are in tons of scrapbooks and videotape/DVD libraries. They have proudly introduced you to all members of their family. They had you christened in a religious ceremony and presented you to God for His blessings. They are excited about you and have high hopes for your future. They affirm (believe in) you.

Or, you may have been born into a family where you did not look like the mother or the father, and although you were truly biologically theirs, they just did not want you. They were ashamed of you. They showed a difference between you and your siblings because your siblings looked more like them. Your complexion is dark and your siblings' complexions are light or high yellow. Your hair is kinky and your siblings' hair is wavy and curly. You have brown eyes and short eyelashes, but your siblings' eyes are hazel-green with long eyelashes. You are short and a little over-weight, but your siblings are tall and slender. You had to work twice as hard in school to get good grades, but your siblings seemed to breeze through school and get good grades. Your parents really favored and encouraged your siblings, but showed no interest in you and did not appreciate your struggle to achieve good grades. When company came to your home, your siblings were introduced, but you were not, and your mother and father did not want you around. In fact, after a little while, your parents shipped you off to live with other relatives, who lived far away from where your parents live, to be raised by them. Yeah, your parents sent money to provide financial support for you, but they did not keep in touch, nor did they give you any reason for sending you away to live with other relatives who you did not know. The relatives who are now raising you are indifferent toward you because you're not really theirs. They do not know you, nor do they want to. They treat you like a stepchild or a servant.

Or, you may have been born into a family that is in constant turmoil – drama going on 24/7 day-in and day-out. You see the father and the mother cursing each other, calling each other all kinds of disrespectful, condescending and destructive names. You see them physically fighting almost every weekend, and you see the police come on various occasions to break up the fights and to carry one, if not both parents, to jail for battering each other – whoever has the most bumps, bruises, and bleeding stays with the children sometimes because the Police cannot get a social worker to take you if both your parents are in jail. On occasion, you overhear what some of the arguing is about between your parents. It could be lack of money to support the household due to gambling it away by one of the parents, or it could be because of infidelity by one or both of the parents, or it could be because of money being used to buy drugs, or the money went for partying with friends. In essence, the money should have been used to pay the household bills and put food on the table. On and on it goes. You find that sometimes there is food in the house and sometimes no food is in the house. You find that some, if not all, of the utilities are cut off on occasion. You find yourself and your siblings alone in the house while both parents have taken a "time-out" away from home, forgetting or not even caring that they have children at home who need them. You find yourself taking the responsibility for keeping your siblings in line, keeping them safe, and keeping them out of trouble while your parents are physically out of the house and emotionally out of touch. You overhear one of your parents saying they wished they were not married or they wished they didn't have kids, or they would have had a better life with someone else. You find yourself hurting inside and feeling guilty for all the wrong reasons. You feel very insecure about your future and that of your siblings. You, yourself, become nervous and depressed. You just want to run away, but where?

Or, maybe you were born into a family where the father thinks your mother is too old and she's no longer physically attractive and desirable to him, but he thinks you're really cute and sexy because you're physically developing. You find your mother is afraid of your father as he takes you into the bedroom and molests you and has sexual intercourse with you. Your mother says nothing to you. Deep down inside you know something is dreadfully wrong, even though your parents have not taken you to church and you have no clue where to find the scriptures in the Bible that apply to this particular sin. When you try to talk to your mom to ask her to help you, she doesn't want to hear about it. She turns her back on you. You are now the enemy in her eyes. Your father grows a conscience every now and then, and when he does, you become disgusting in his sight until he changes his mind and molests and rapes you again. You feel dirty and ashamed. Your parents emphatically tell you what goes on in the home stays in the home. You are frightened, ashamed, and grow introverted. Kids at school think you're weird because of your reclusiveness. A few of your teachers think something is wrong, but they are too busy to pursue their instincts. There is no one to stop your father from committing incest on you again and again. There is no one to protect you. You feel violated and feel there is no hope.

Or, you may have been born in a single-parent family where the mother is left alone to raise you and financially provide for you. The man in her life used her; he never intended to marry her. You see her struggle and doing without to provide for you. She is unable to provide for you like other two-parent families provide for their children. She has to work, so she takes you to a babysitter who takes her money, but does nothing for you. She works long hours, and when she picks you up at the end of the day, she's too tired to even have a conversation with you. She changes your clothes, fixes a meal for you, and she then goes and sits down in front of the television and spaces out from the pressures of the day. The routine goes on for years until you're no longer sent to the babysitter, but come home alone, as a latchkey kid. You do your homework and your chores, and you wait until your mother comes home. You don't know who your father is. You don't know if he's providing any financial support to help you and your mother. All you see is your mother constantly working and struggling to make ends meet. She's too tired to oversee your schoolwork, or go see you participate in school activities. She's too tired to encourage you for your future; she's too tired for anything. She's bitter because of how she was treated in the past, and she sees no future for herself. If you make her angry or disappoint her, she tells you if it were not for you she would be living the life, whatever that life is.

Or, maybe when you came into this world, there was no mother or father to claim you, although it took both of them to help make you. You were not adoptable for whatever reason people had who were looking to adopt a child. So, you were tossed around in the foster care system. Some foster parents saw you as a dollar sign and used you to get extra income, but they did not care about you. Other foster parents abused you physically and emotionally until you were taken out of their homes. They had no interest in you and they treated you like a slave. After you performed work for them, you were sent to your room. You were not allowed to occupy any other place in their home, except to clean up something. The social worker came to the home to make sure you were okay, but you did not say anything for fear of retaliation after she left. The social worker couldn't interpret your quietness and withdrawal as you being threatened and mistreated. You ran away from some foster care homes, and after being caught, you now have a police record for truancy. You have not found that "right" foster home where the foster parents really care about you. You have no one to confide in because there is no one you trust. You know no one cares about you and no one wants you, so you don't care about yourself or anyone else. You don't even know how to care. You have no future to look forward to because you don't know what a future looks like. You know what you don't want in life, but you don't know what you do want, and you don't know how to go after it.

There are many other examples, and maybe you even fit into one of the ones described above. (I hope you fit into the first example.) However, what you need to do, from these negative examples and from the one good example noted above, is to take anything good that can be used in your life and leave out all the bad. For example, if one of the good things in the family was that your father did go to work, that's a good thing. Now what he did with the money he received after he worked was a bad thing, so you want to leave that part out of your life. You want to have a good work ethic, and you definitely want your husband to have a good work ethic. However, you do not want someone who works and does not support his family. *1 Timothy 5:8* states: *"But if anyone does not provide for his own, and especially for those of his household, he has denied the faith and is worse than an unbeliever."*

All of the examples of home life described above are dysfunctional, except for the first example. The problem of coming from a dysfunctional family is that your parents generally don't know they are creating the dysfunction. They are just surviving and are reacting to what life throws at them. They are not in control of themselves, and have difficulty being in control of you and your siblings in the right way. They don't act like they love you because they don't love themselves. They are also suffering from the consequences of their bad decisions and wrong actions. They don't realize they are experiencing their consequences – they think its just life and everybody goes through what they are going through. So, they are miserable and content at the same time for they figure that's the way it is. However, it doesn't have to be that way for you.

It is possible that you are dysfunctional, too, because you grew up in a dysfunctional family; they did not know how to create a healthy and functional family environment for themselves or you. You find yourself walking in their same footsteps to a certain extent, but you don't like the results you're seeing and you don't know how to break out of the pattern. But, you definitely know something is wrong in the lifestyle of the family and you don't want to live like your parents.

When you know something is wrong, but don't know exactly what it is, that's when you take a step of faith and look at other families and see how they operate. Look at what is working in a family that isn't working in your own. When you visit your friends, check out how they interact with their parents and siblings and how their parents interact with them. See if they live peaceably with one another. See if they respect and love one another. Take the good that you see and apply it to your life.

You want a better life, but you don't know how to obtain it. It will soon be your turn to call the shots for your life. All of the trials and hardships you have encountered can all be washed away if you realize that as an adult, as of the age of 18, you will have control over your own life. You will have control over what you think, what you do, and what you say. You will have control over the choices you make that will affect you directly. You will have control over your own future. However, you will also have control over the consequences based on what you think, what you do, and what you say. You will be the one, by your choices, who will determine whether you have good consequences or whether you have bad consequences. So, you must determine what works for your life and what doesn't. Don't use the dysfunction of your parents to be a justification for you to be dysfunctional, too. You do not want to re-invent a broken wheel, do you? No, you don't!

Self-Esteem

The negative examples referenced above create self-esteem (self-confidence) and misplaced values' issues that develop early in life in many girls, teenagers and young women. These self-esteem and misplaced values' issues are carried into adulthood with dramatic and costly consequences in all areas of one's life – be it in health, career, finances, relationships or marriage. How do you fix self-esteem issues?

Self-esteem is very powerful. It is a "make" or "break" issue in a person's life. Self-esteem is how a person views herself and how she values herself. A young girl who grows up being nurtured, loved, cared for and protected will develop a healthy self-esteem that will carry her through life and through almost all of life's obstacles successfully. All things being equal, where she has her biological parents raising and loving her, and she has a good relationship with her grandparents and other relatives of the family, she will be more stable and confident. No matter what happens in life, she knows she's loved, well thought of and confident she can do anything and overcome anything because this has been instilled in her since she was born. The parents make it a point at every turn to tell and show their love to their child. They will give her confidence and assurance as she grows into a young lady. They will encourage her in everything she shows interest in and does, and they will encourage her when she has disappointments in life as she grows up.

Those who love her do not degrade her, and they do not show a difference between her and her other siblings or other children belonging to other people. They love her for who she is, in spite of any physical, emotional or mental disabilities, in spite of lack of beauty in the world's eyes, and in spite of their own plans, dreams, and aspirations for her. They love her for who she is no matter what.

With the love and encouragement from those who care for her and care about her, she is able to blossom into whatever she wants to be in life. There is nothing holding her back. She has the strength and ability within herself to overcome any obstacle and disregard any negative thing said about her. She knows who she is and she knows of whom she belongs. She knows herself and is comfortable with herself. She is not looking to make up for any lack someone else may think she has. She is happy with herself and is not looking to please people for their sake. She is pleased with herself. Her morals, values, and emotions are in check and she is not insecure about anything. She's outgoing and happy. She knows she is valuable, worthy and loved, and she is able to give value, worthiness, and love to others easily. She's able to build people up and not tear them down. She cares about other people. She has a good and healthy self-esteem.

You can easily pick out the girls who have low-self esteem or no self-esteem because you see the hunger, the insecurity, the guiltiness of thinking it's their fault, and the non-caring attitude in them. Girls who grow up in dysfunctional families have little or no self-esteem/ self-confidence, they don't know whether they have any value, and they feel unloved.

Value! Importance! Worthiness! Love! What's that? Instead of knowing from their parents they have value and are loved for who they are, those who have low self-esteem look elsewhere to find it. When a young lady with low self-esteem, who does not value herself, is given attention by a stranger who does not have her best interest at heart and who wants to use her, she jumps into a situation with that person, feet first. Then she later finds out that the person did not value her at all, but used her and discarded her like she were a piece of trash. She's devastated. She becomes even more insecure, she feels guilty, she withdraws even more, or she develops a non-caring attitude concerning what happens to her because she was used and no one else cares about her or for her. She has been used before and expects to be used again. Over time, she becomes angry, bitter, callous and rebellious.

A young girl who does not have a healthy self-esteem can be given negative labels by people. Those negative labels or negative statements tend to stay in her mind. This could lead to very destructive behavior. If the ones who raised her have not given her a good self-esteem and value her, she will have a difficult time in life overcoming obstacles until she realizes, herself, that she is worthy and begins to value herself. For example, if her family tells her she's ugly, her friends or her peers tell her she's ugly, or if someone she respects tells her she's ugly, more than likely she will believe she's ugly, and she won't think much of herself. She will act ugly because she believes she is ugly. If a stranger comes along and gives her positive attention by telling her she's beautiful, she will be drawn to the stranger because she's craving the positive encouragement. Her negative self-image and low self-esteem are changed by the positive and encouraging attention shown by the stranger. However, if the stranger is not a worthy person, who just wants to use her, she will be burned in the process and her self-esteem will sink even lower.

This is where you need wisdom and discernment because you need to determine who it is who gives you value, worthiness, and self-esteem. You also need to know who it is that is tearing you down by giving you negative feedback. You must reach deep down within yourself and dismiss all of the negative things inside your mind people have told you that are not true. You need to dismiss statements like: (a) You're no good. (b) You will never amount to anything. (c) You're just like so-and so. (d) You're ugly. (e) You're fat. (f) You're too dark. (g) Your hair is nappy. (h) Why can't you be like your sister? (i) Why can't you be like your friend? (j) You're stupid. (k) You're an idiot. (l) I can't stand you. (m) I wish I never had you. (n) Get out of my sight. (o) You're a bastard. (p) You bitch. (q) You're nothing but a whore. There are many other negative statements, but none of these statements are who you are. They are statements made by other people that you allowed in your mind and you believed them. But those statements are not true. You are not to own any of the negative statements. Don't own anything about you that's negative and not who you are and not what God says about you. The statements are destructive, they are designed to tear you down, to control you, and to obliterate your self-esteem and your value. The statements, if you believe them, will keep you from living the life God has for you. People who make these statements to you are accountable to God. It's unfortunate that children have grown up with these labels/statements put on them throughout their years of growing up. I know, for I was the recipient of such negative statements and labels. I was called everything but a child of God at different times while growing up.

It takes a while to get rid of the negative junk in the mind and start believing and living out what God says about you. It took me a long time to identify and eliminate the negative statements and thoughts that I allowed people to put in my mind. The negative statements simply did not line up with the word of God. Once I knew what God's word said about me, my whole attitude and outlook changed. Every once in a while, some negative statement would float through my mind and I immediately rebuke it because I know it doesn't belong to me. It's not what God says about me. As you rebuke the negative junk that tries to invade your mind and replace that junk with what God says about you, you will win the battle in the mind in the area of self-esteem and begin to live out what God says about you.

The one who initially gave you your high self-esteem and value was God, Himself, who created you, who loves you, who gave you a purpose in your life, and who will help you fulfill that purpose and your dreams in life. God has a plan for your life. With God, it doesn't matter what anyone else says about you; His view of you is what counts now and in eternity.

God has a healthy and positive view of you. He calls you to be His righteousness. *Isaiah 51:7-8* states: *"Listen to Me, you who know righteousness, you people in whose heart is My law; do not fear the reproach [criticism] of men [women], nor be afraid of their insults, for the moth will eat them up like a garment, and the worm will eat them like wool; but My righteousness will be forever, and My salvation from generation to generation." Isaiah 54:14* states: *"In righteousness you shall be established; you shall be far from oppression, for you shall not fear; and from terror, for it shall not come near you." 2 Corinthians 5:21* states: *"For He made Him who knew no sin to be sin for us, that we might become the righteousness of God in Him."* You are God's righteousness.

The life you live at home, with or without parents, will either give you the security and confidence you need in order to make a productive, positive and rewarding life for yourself, or it will create in you insecurity, guilt, worthlessness, and self-destructive behaviors.

A lot of people's life's failures and bad consequences have been due to low self-esteem (lack of self-confidence) and lack of self-value (self-worth), and most of the time they project those negatives onto their children. If you're living in a dysfunctional home, you're not the one with the problem in the home. You did not cause the problems you encountered in the home. You did not make your family members act the way they acted or do the things they did. The problems of others (be it your parents, relatives, siblings, foster parents, or even others who were allowed into the home who caused problems) were projected on you. You did not create the dysfunctional family situation that you came from. It's not your fault. The dysfunctional members in your family do not love God and they do not love themselves. That's pretty much the crux of the problem.

You cannot allow the dysfunction of others to rule your future. It is not okay for you to give up and behave in a destructive pattern because of what you suffered from in your family. If you want a better life, you have to recognize where the negativity is coming from, dismiss it out of your mind and out of your life, and make better choices for yourself. If you don't know how to do this, seek counseling from your church or from someone in authority at your school who you respect and feel comfortable with in discussing your personal life.

Don't own the guilt, but recognize it for what it is and what it's not. It's not you. It's their problem and not your problem. They are accountable, not you. You have to endure it, though, until either your family comes to their senses or until you are able to live your life away from the nonsense. *1 Corinthians 14:33* states: *"For God is not the author of confusion but of peace, as in all the churches of the saints."*

There's a saying that holds pretty true in most situations, and it is this: **"If you want to be successful in life, do the things that successful people do."** This applies to a family situation as well. If you grew up or are growing up in a dysfunctional family, seek out those families that appear to have it all together – a normal family environment with no drama – a family who loves God, love themselves, and love each other. Use this family for your own pattern for dealing with life, and make sure they line up with God's word. Find a mentor to help guide you. Your mentor could be a counselor, a minister, a teacher, etc., anyone who has your best interest at heart and who you can trust.

When I was a child, I lived in a very dysfunctional family, but the inspirations I received for what I wanted my own family to be like were "Father Knows Best" and "Leave It To Beaver." I was also able to gain insight and understanding from one of my favorite teachers who saw something worthwhile in me, and she cared a great deal about me. Those were the only decent examples I had because my neighborhood was filled with all sorts of dysfunctional families with a variety of problems, from alcoholism to drug addiction to fighting to incest to police action, etc. My own family situation was bad enough, but after playing with the kids in my neighborhood and looking into their lives, I found my situation was not as bad as I thought. My situation was certainly not all that great, but in retrospect, it wasn't nearly as bad as other family situations.

However, when I got married and had my own children, I definitely knew what I did not want and I definitely knew what I wanted for my own family. The most important things I wanted for my family were peace and safety – sanctuary. I was very protective of my children and my family sanctuary. I was very cautious about who entered in. Needless to say, not many people came to my home for I was not having any nonsense at all, especially any craziness that would adversely affect my two beautiful children. I tried very hard to keep a stable, safe, and peaceful environment for my children, even though my marriage failed. But in spite of the failure of the marriage, I did all I could to provide a sanctuary for my children and me.

I found, as I grew up in a dysfunctional environment provided by my parents, that my parents' love for me had nothing to do with their dysfunction. I thought they loved me on GP (General Principle), and maybe deep down in their hearts they did. However, as I grew up and lived life for myself, I realized they did not even love themselves as individuals, nor did they love each other. Their love of my siblings and me was inconsequential, meaning that their love for us was a very low priority for them. Other things and other issues took precedence over their children. I would like to believe deep down inside my parents really did love their four children, but my parents' actions reflected otherwise. We got mixed signals some of the time and negative signals most of the time. I did not understand what they were thinking then. I did not understand why my father was in and out of jail so much. I did not understand when my father was home, why he was always raising hell, yelling, threatening, fighting my mother, and scaring us four kids half to death. We were extremely afraid of him. We tiptoed around the house and hid under our beds almost all the time. We hardly spoke. When we did speak, we stuttered out of nervousness and fear. Unless seen, most people never knew my parents had four kids.

How can a man say he loves his family, yet he turns around and beats his wife so badly (knocking her over furniture and picking her up like a rag doll and throwing her on the floor like she was an object and not even human), in front of his children, that she had to be carried to the hospital in a bloody mess. She would no sooner come home from the hospital that he would beat her again. This occurred on a regular basis; whatever regular is. We siblings were horrified and paralyzed by what we saw and heard. We were too young and too small to do anything. We did not know if all families were this way. We feared the unknown and definitely feared our father. I'm sorry, but that ain't love!

How can a man say he loves his family, yet he's in and out of jail frequently? When he's out of jail and at home, he's raising hell. There's no joy or peace in the home. The income for the family is inconsistent or totally lost, and the wife finds herself in a struggle to keep the rest of the family together emotionally and physically, keep a roof over their heads, and put food on the table. Does he really love his wife and family? I think not.

How can a man say he loves his family, yet he calls his wife every foul and degrading name he can think of, and not care that the children are watching and listening? I refuse to have anything at all to do with any person who calls me a bitch or a whore, or anything degrading and derogatory, who then expects me to fix him dinner and have sex with him at night – telling me that he loves me. What kind of mess is that?!!!.

How can a man say he loves his family, yet he disrespects, humiliates and physically abuses his wife in a public place, bringing such negative attention to himself and to his wife?

How can a man say he loves his family, but on payday he goes directly from his job to the casino or to the racetrack and gambles away all of his paycheck, leaving no money for the family bills to be paid or for food to be on the table so the family can eat?

How can a man say he loves his family, yet he drinks alcohol to the point of being out of control and over time becoming an alcoholic? He's so drunk that he doesn't show up for work on a number of occasions, and he ends up losing his job. He then gets so sick with alcohol poisoning that he has to be hospitalized, and then he has to recuperate at home with his wife having to take care of him as well as providing for the family. Is this what she expected when she got married? Is this what she deserves? Is this what the family deserves? Did she take the same liberties and not care enough about her marriage partner and family?

How can a man say he loves his family, yet he refuses to work to support his family and expects and demands that his wife provide financial support to him and maintain the children and the household? He lays up in the house all day and does not even take care of his own children. This was not agreed to prior to him and his wife getting married. What happened? *1 Timothy 5:8* states: *"But if anyone does not provide for his own, and especially for those of his household, he has denied the faith and is worse than an unbeliever."* In other words, men who do not support the families they create will not be blessed.

Real and true love are husbands and wives showing love, consideration, and care for each other as partners in marriage, and both partners showing their love for and to their children. The man recognizes that God is the head of him and he is accountable to God for the success or failure of his family. Being in line with God's order, the husband recognizes that God comes first, and his wife and children come second – both taking precedence over everything and anything else. He acknowledges that he is a servant to his family; he is to provide provision, protection, guidance, and love to his family. He recognizes his responsibility and accountability to his family because God allowed him to create his family. His wife did not ask for his hand in marriage, and the children certainly did not create themselves or ask to be in his family. Consequently, if the husband believes in God and studies God's word to learn how to be a man of God, a good husband to his wife, and a good father to his children, his application of what he has learned will end all dysfunctional behavior, which destroys the family. Following or not following God's word will determine the success or failure of the family.

A lot of children grow up with low or no self-esteem because of the dysfunctional family environment they live in, or they grow up in other dysfunctional-types of environments. Most adults who grew up in dysfunctional family environments end up creating and living in the same dysfunctional environment because they don't know any better, because it was so engrained in their heads, or because they saw no way out – they saw this destructive behavior to be the norm for them.

Some children grow up blaming themselves for the dysfunction of their families. They feel unworthy, unwanted, of no value, and they feel like they are trash. Some children act out in very destructive behavior patterns such as projecting promiscuous and lewd behavior with any and all who will give them attention, some get into drug addiction, some get into alcoholism, some are very angry and get involved with gangs to vent their frustrations, and some get involved in other criminal activities. Other children become very introverted, suffer from depression and other mental disorders, have major health issues, and some are suicidal. These are some of the consequences of having low or no self-esteem.

If you don't like the environment in which you are growing up in, or have grown up in, you have the opportunity and the choice to change it for yourself and for the family you intend to have in the future. But in order to make the right choices for your life, you need to know four things, which are extremely important in order for you to be successful in your life, in your future, and in your well-being:

(1) Know that it is not your fault.

(2) Know that God loves you.

(3) Know that YOU must love YOU.

(4) Love the person or the family enough to forgive them, let go of all the hurt and pain they may have caused you, and let God handle it.

You did not create the environment you grew up in. Your parents are accountable for your upbringing, your physical well-being, your safety, your healthy self-esteem, your healthy self-value, and your assimilation into this world. Your parents are responsible to teach you how to live this life in accordance with the word of God. They are responsible to be Godly examples before you in obedience to God's word. Your parents are accountable to God.

God loves you and He is absolutely crazy about you. God wants the very best for you, and He has provided a way for a better life for you through His word, the Bible. He has made promises to you that He will keep if you will love Him, trust Him, believe His word is true, and if you will act on His word. He will wash away all of the suffering, pain, and tears you shed behind what you went through. Also, the operative word is "through" – you went through, or, you are going through. You don't have to repeat what you went through, unless you just like to live that terrible and ungodly way. Remember, there are miserable consequences for a dysfunctional lifestyle.

God is offering you something far better than what you can even imagine. He is offering you a wonderful life, a life of all your needs being met, a life of peace, a life of protection, a life of joy, and a life of unconditional love. God loves His kids, and He definitely loves you.

You must also begin to love yourself. Don't think of yourself as others think of you if you know they think negative of you. Don't feel bad because you were treated badly. Don't feel bad or guilty because a difference was shown against you amongst your parents and siblings. Your siblings' prejudices came from your parents, and your parents are accountable to God for their discrimination. Don't feel bad or guilty because you were used and abused as a child or as a teenager. Your parents are accountable for all of that nonsense, not you. You must see yourself as God sees you. You must believe what God says about you. You are not a failure, you're not ugly or too fat, you're not stupid, you're not a piece of trash to be used and abused and then kicked to the curb.

Love the person, or the family, enough to release yourself from the dysfunction, put them in God's hands, forgive them, pray for them, and go on with your life. You are accountable for your life, not theirs. Cast all your cares upon the Lord for He really does care for you, and so He can care for you. This even includes your family members. Cast your family members upon the Lord. *1 Peter 5:7* states: *"Casting all your care upon Him for He cares for you."*

You are, however, the righteousness of God. God knew you and chose you before the foundations of the earth. He knew your name before you did. *Ephesians 1:3-4* states: *"Blessed be the God and Father of our Lord Jesus Christ, who has blessed us with every spiritual blessing in the heavenly places in Christ, just as He chose us in Him before the foundation of the world, that we should be holy and without blame before Him in love."* You are His creation, and He loves everything He has created, and that includes you. There is no one like you on the face of the earth. Even your fingerprints are unique.

You don't have to convince God to love you because He loved you before you knew you existed. You don't have to be concerned whether anyone else loves you because the only one who counts and who loves you immensely is God, the Father of creation. When you love yourself, and know God loves you, it will show in your manner and in your confidence that you love yourself (not conceit), and others will see God in you and appreciate you, too. By others, I mean the right people will give you the proper and respectful attention you deserve.

So, what's love got to do with it? A whole lot!

Love is the first commandment of God. In *Matthew 22:37-39*, Jesus says: *"You shall love the Lord your God with all your heart, with all your soul, and with all your mind. This is the first and great commandment. And the second is like it: You shall love your neighbor as yourself."*

Love is the major fruit of the Spirit of God. In *1 Corinthians 13:1-13*, the Apostle Paul states:

(1) *"Though I speak with the tongues of men and of angels, but have not love, I have become a sounding brass or a clanging cymbal.*

(2) *And though I have the gift of prophecy, and understand all mysteries and all knowledge, and though I have all faith, so that I could remove mountains, but have not love, I am nothing.*

(3) *And though I bestow all my goods to feed the poor, and though I give my body to be burned, but have not love, it profits me nothing.*

(4) *Love suffers long and is kind; love does not envy; love does not parade itself, is not puffed up;*

(5) *[Love] does not behave rudely, [love] does not seek its own, [love] is not provoked, [love] thinks no evil;*

(6) *[Love] does not rejoice in iniquity, but [love] rejoices in the truth;*

(7) *[Love] bears all things, [love] believes all things, [love] hopes all things, [love] endures all things.*

(8) *Love never fails. But whether there are prophecies, they will fail; whether there are tongues, they will cease; whether there is knowledge, it will vanish away.*

(9) *For we know in part and we prophesy in part.*

(10) *But when that which is perfect has come, then that which is in part will be done away with.*

(11) *When I was a child, I spoke as a child. I understood as a child, I thought as a child; but when I became a man [woman], I put away childish things.*

(12) *For now we see in a mirror, dimly, but then face to face. Now I know in part, but then I shall know just as I also am known.*

(13) *And now abide in faith, hope, love, these three; but the greatest of these is love."*

So, as a person operating in love, and who believes in love, you know love never fails. As a person operating in love, you will endure suffering just as the Lord Jesus endured suffering. You will be kind to others if you're operating in love. You will not be envious of other people no matter what they look like or what they have if you're operating in love. You will not be arrogant, conceited or prideful if you're operating in love. You will not be rude to others, regardless of whether they are rude to you if you're operating in love. You will not seek your own by demanding your own way or insisting on your rights if you're operating in love. You will seek God's will for you. You will not easily get angered or provoked to be angry if you're operating in love. You will not be trying to avenge yourself if you're operating in love. You will not be thinking evil of anyone or anything if you're operating in love. You will not celebrate in someone's downfall or defeat if you're operating in love. You will not celebrate sin if you're operating in love. You will rejoice and celebrate in the truth if you're operating in love. Again, love bears up against any and all situations that come about. Love hopes for the best in every situation and for every person. Love believes the best of everyone and for every situation. And, love endures every situation with the strength of knowing that all things will work together for good because you have love. *Romans 8:28* states: *"And we know that all things work together for good to those who love God, to those who are the called according to His purpose."*

In relationships with the opposite sex, "love" strongly applies. If a person really cares for you and loves you, he will not be asking you to do anything that goes against God's word. If the person loves you, really loves you, he will treat you like you're a queen, he will have great respect and consideration for you, and he will do the right things by you. If a person loves you, he will be honest with you. Instead of trying to get you in bed, he will be asking you for your hand in marriage and trying to get that engagement ring on your finger. He will fulfill all of your requests concerning possible marriage, like:

(a) Taking a health test for STDs and providing you the results. He will also inform you about whether he's currently infected with any STD or if he had an STD;

(b) Telling you the truth as to whether he is a "Down Low" man;

(c) Presenting you with his criminal record from the Police Department;

(d) Presenting you with his current credit report, which reflects his FICO score;

(e) Showing you all of the bills he is currently responsible to pay, and any judgments that are still outstanding against him;

(f) Showing you his last two income tax returns;

(g) Letting you know of any previous marriages and any children as a result of his previous marriages where he is responsible to pay child support;

(h) Informing you if he's paying child support either voluntarily or through the District Attorney's Office (court – wage assignment), and whether part of his wages are being garnished from his job to pay child support because of his lack of making child support payments on his own. He needs to tell you why his wages are being garnished; there may be a valid reason; and

(i) Letting you know if he has any children from any previous relationship(s) where he's providing child support, or not providing child support, and why he's not doing so.

You must be aware that if you marry this person, your combined income will be subject to increase his child support payment to his ex-wife for his children. His ex-wife may go into court to seek an increase in the child support payment once she finds out he has re-married. You will now be responsible for helping him to pay his ex-wife what he is responsible to pay for child support. If the increase in child support is granted, based on your added income, there is nothing you will be able to do about it. Do you love him enough to accept that? Also, by your marrying this person, you are inadvertently providing your income to help support children that are not yours. Do you love him enough to accept that? If you are in agreement with this arrangement up front, then it's okay. But, if you knew nothing about this issue prior to getting married, this could leave a very bad taste in your mouth and in your wallet for a long time because he was not honest with you up front.

However, if he really loves you, he will certainly tell you the truth, the whole truth, and nothing but the truth up front. By him telling you the truth about his child support situation up front, it means he loves you enough to risk losing you on the grounds that you may not want to marry him because you do not wish to use your income to pay child support for children that are not yours. He will be hurt, but he will respect you for it.

However, if you still marry this man who is paying child support, be aware of the laws of the state in which you live. You should definitely respect a man who is financially supporting his children. His children did not ask to come into this world, but since they are here, it's both parents' responsibility to make sure they are well kept.

Now, the same criteria applies to you before marriage. If you really love this person, you will provide the same information as noted above. This is what I call the "Come to Jesus Meeting" (CJM) where you both lay all your cards on the table to get a clear picture of what you both are getting yourselves into, and to determine whether the love you have for one another will withstand all obstacles presented in the CJM meeting.

Being up front and honest, accepting each other's obstacles, presenting and discussing a realistic plan of action to tackle the obstacles on both sides, and agreeing to work the plan together with God's guidance, you both will have a wonderful start in your marriage based on the truth between you. God will honor your efforts and your future will be bright.

If you love someone, you will respect him. If the person doesn't love you enough to respect you and be honest with you, **"YOU REALLY NEED TO LOVE THAT PERSON ENOUGH TO LET HIM GO!"** Leave them alone! Don't try to love them enough to change them. That's God's job. God has given every one of us our own free will, and unless the person, himself, sees the need to change his will, whatever you do will be futile. Too many women see a glaring problem in a guy, and out of desperation to be married, they discount the problem in hopes of changing the man. This is a disaster waiting to happen. You don't have time to try to change the person or have time to wait until he sees in you your wonderful qualities where he would eventually respect you and want to change for you. He needs to change for his own good, and because he, himself, feels he needs to change. By you wanting the person in spite of his problem, yet believing you can change the person, shows you're blinded and not trusting God.

God will send you only His very best and not someone who has a problem you know you cannot live with in line with God's word. Since the person has a problem, only God can fix him, not you. Get real!

Tomorrow is not promised to anyone. Somebody did not wake up today and someone will not wake up tomorrow, so you must make the most of today, right now, this moment. If the person you're interested in is not on the same page as you with God, you need to move on. Obviously, this person is not God's best, and God only wants the best for you. Love yourself enough to let him go, and remember God will only send His best to you.

Don't rush ahead of God in your search for a man. You should not be searching for a man for marriage anyway. You are out of God's will when you pursue a man. Men are the pursuers, not women. God knows what you need. *Matthew 6:8* states: *"Therefore do not be like them, for your Father knows the things you have need of before you ask Him."*

Living Together – Is It Love Or Is It Usury?

Think about it! Living together really means using each other for what you want and feel you need without any commitment, accountability, or responsibility. It's selfish and it's out of God's order.

I met a young lady a while back. She was simply adorable, very good looking, and she had a great personality. She had a lot going for her, but she didn't know it. She was laid off from her job and she wanted me to stand in agreement with her in praying for a new job. No problem.

She felt very comfortable with me, so she began to tell me about some of her personal problems. She told me her boyfriend lived with her; he was Christian, too. However, he would not work, and he refused to go to church with her or by himself. Excuse me! I believe she used the words "Christian" and "he would not work." I had a brain freeze at that point and almost choked on this piece of unfortunate information. I got TMI! (My son uses the term "TMI", which stands for 'Too Much Information.') However, she said she just wanted God to bless her with a new job so she could continue to support herself and her boyfriend.

LADIES, WHAT'S WRONG WITH THIS PICTURE?!!!!!!!!

Problem No. 1 – She is out of line and out of God's will for her life because she's living with and having sex with a man who is not her husband.

Problem No. 2 – Her boyfriend claims to be Christian, yet he's living out of wedlock with her.

Problem No. 3 – He won't work.

Problem No. 4 – She's asking that I stand in agreement with her to get another job to support herself and her boyfriend.

Problem No. 5 – She was providing financial support to an able-body man.

Problem No. 6 – The man she's living with refuses to go to church. I wonder why?

Problem No. 7 – She was not asking for God's forgiveness for living with this guy, but she did say she was disappointed her boyfriend would not go out and find a job, and he had not been working for a while.

There are other problems with this scenario, too, but I'm still trying to wrap my head around these seven issues that came from this young "Christian" female. Do you think her prayers for a job will be answered in the condition she's currently in?

The sad thing about this particular situation was that she said she was a Christian. I did not question her Christianity, but I did tell her she would have to stop living with her boyfriend, and she would have to stop having sex with him so her prayers would not be hindered. I prayed with her for a new job and for His guidance in her life. I suggested she study God's word to know what He has for her life. I showed her scriptures about answered prayer, and I suggested she seek counseling. I felt bad for her because as young and as cute as she was, she was not living the victorious life she should have been living because she was living out of line with God's word. The word of God does not condone living together out of wedlock, period! I surmised that what it all boiled down to was that she did not trust God, although she claimed to be a believer.

God responds to and answers His word, not our word, when we make prayer requests. You will not find anywhere in the Bible where God condones living together and having sexual intercourse out of wedlock. If you want your prayers answered, you have to be in line with His word in all areas of your life. Only then will your prayers be heard and answered.

Ladies, we've got to stop "playing house" with these men! We've got to clean up our own act, and do things the right way – God's way. Only then will our prayers be answered fully.

The reason why a woman may move in with a man or allow a man to move in with her may be that she's insecure and wants security quicker than waiting to be married, or she wants to belong to somebody because she's lonely, or maybe she wants to be able to have sex when she wants, or she's struggling financially and needs help to pay the bills and keep more money in her purse. Basically, she just doesn't trust God to get all her needs met. It really doesn't matter what the reason is because any reason that does not line up with the word of God is the wrong reason. By jumping into a situation that is not in line with God's order or His plan ties His hands and He is unable to help. We have no idea what blessings we will miss when we step out of line with God's word, and we will be facing negative consequences as a result of our disobedience.

When are we going to learn that there are consequences behind living with a man, which is out of God's order? What's it going to take for us to get this point?

Why are young ladies and grown women cheapening themselves in hopes of something better when they will get nothing good for their efforts by living with a man out of wedlock? The story is the same from any woman who has lived with a man. They have wasted their time, their bodies, their resources, their dreams and their future. They wasted all of themselves on the wrong person.

You are really with the wrong person if he wants you to violate your convictions to God and move in with him without being married. The old adage about the "cow and milk" still holds true to this day, unfortunately. The formula never changes, and you end up with the same result each and every time – nothing!

However, it is definitely more advantageous and beneficial for a man to be living with a woman because of the old adage: *"Why buy the milk when you can get the cow for free."* When a man lives with you, he has no desire to get married. What for? He gets an instant maid, an instant cook, an instant love-making machine, and an instant paycheck to ensure his well-being. If times get tough, you are there to bail him out. He knows you will take care of things while he decides what he wants to do. He will take his time, relax, and enjoy having the pressure off of him to provide because you have stepped into his role of being the **"provider."** You definitely will not be the fire under his feet to get him out the house to go look for a job. He's got it made in the shade. Why should he get married? Why should he marry you? What's love got to do with it? Think!!!

My pastor, Pastor Tom Pickens, discussed this problem quite thoroughly and directly during one of the marriage seminars he and his wife (Minister Donna Pickens) teach almost every year. The marriage seminars strengthen and solidify the relationships of married couples, and the seminars also educate the singles. The teaching on marriage is inspiring and enlightening. The church is packed out each time they teach on this subject. Pastor Tom and Minister Donna discuss issues together on various facets of marriage such as: (1) respect; (2) trust; (3) love; (4) finances; and (5) relationships between husband and wife, parents and children, family members and relatives, and between family members and friends. They are pretty thorough and don't hold back anything in their discussions. The marriage series has been rewarding and a blessing throughout the years. Pastor Tom and Minister Donna uphold God's word concerning living out of wedlock. The bottom line is that it's wrong and there are consequences.

What's love got to do with it? A lot!

Teenager/Young Adult Mothers With Multiple Babies By Multiple Men

I'm sure you personally know someone, or know of someone, who is young, unmarried, unemployed, and she has one, two, three or more children by one, two, three or more different men. The men who got her pregnant are nowhere to be found. She's on her own, on welfare, and her apartment or home is provided through the Section 8 Program (subsidized rent program). Only in America!

You ask yourself: What happened? How did she get to where she is – saddled with all these kids by all these 'different' men? Did she love each of these men so much to sleep with them, to get pregnant by them, to birth a child for them, and then raise that child all by herself? Was this love, lust, or insanity?

Did she ever consider marrying any of these men? Did these men consider marrying her before she got pregnant or after they found out she was pregnant? Did these men abandon her and their responsibility once they learned they were going to be dads?

What about birth control? Was it her responsibility to provide whatever defense against getting pregnant? Was it the men's responsibility to wear protection so they would not impregnate her?

Was there some sort of dating relationship period between these men and the woman before having sex, and before she got pregnant? Was there a serious relationship with even one of these men? Was she or he just a booty-call to one another?

Is this young woman leaving a door open for each man, who she conceived a child for, to come back into her life and into the child's life to create a relationship with his child and possibly with her?

Did she inform the man she was pregnant with his child and ask him what role he was going to play in her life and in the child's life? If so, what was his response? Is this young woman going after each father for child support for his child, or is she strictly relying on the government welfare program to take care of her and her children? Are these men getting a free ride?

What does the future hold for this mother and each of her children from all these different men? Will any of these men feel and be accountable? Will each man step up to the plate to take parental and financial responsibility for his child? Will any of these men even care about his child who is another human being that he helped to create; a child of his own blood? Will any of these men ever care about the mother of his child? Will he care about how the mother is raising his child?

If the child gets sick and is in the hospital, will the mother be able to reach the father? Does the mother even know where the father of the child is and how to reach him? Will she contact the father, if she knows where he is, to inform him that his son or daughter is in the hospital? Will she allow the father to see his child in the hospital? After knowing that his child is in the hospital, will the father visit his child, and will he donate an organ or blood, if necessary?

If the child dies, will the mother inform the father about the death of his child? Will the father of the child be remorseful and feel guilty because he did not do all he could to ensure that his child knew him and knew that he loved his child? Will the father assist financially in the burial of his child? Will the father go to his child's funeral?

What will the mother say to her children when they all grow into teenagers and young adults, when they realize they all look very different from each other, when they all realize they each have different fathers, when they all realize their fathers are not around and don't come around to see about them, when they all realize they have needs their mother is just unable to fulfill, when they all realize their fathers don't celebrate their birthdays or any holidays with them, and when they all realize their fathers don't care about them?

The children, when they mature and are able to reason things out (and they will), will ask hard questions of their mother such as:

(1) Who is my father?

(2) Where is my father?

(3) Why don't I have my father's last name?

(4) Why do I have your last name?

(5) How can I contact my father?

(6) Can I see my father?

(7) Why does my father choose to be out of my life?

(8) Was it a choice by my father to be out of my life, or was it your choice? Why?

(9) Is my father providing financially for me? If not, why not?

(10) Why do I have this medical condition and none of my other siblings have it?

(11) Why doesn't my father come to see me or see about me?

(12) Why does my father not care about me?

(13) Why does my father not love me, and what is the reason for him not loving me?

(14) What's going to happen to me?

(15) What did I do wrong?

(16) Mother, what did you do wrong?

The hardest questions the mother will face are these:

(17) What really happened between you and my father?

(18) How come you and my father didn't get married?

The unwed mother of multiple children from different fathers faces harsh ridicule by society. She's looked upon with contempt by some people when she goes out into public venues with all of her children because one can clearly see there is no resemblance in any of the children of one father or of each other. More than likely she's not wearing a wedding ring on her finger. She looks like she's struggling financially. The biggest questions from society are: Why did she allow herself to get pregnant in the first place? Why didn't she stop having babies after the first child was born out of wedlock? Why couldn't she control herself? Why do I have to financially support her mistakes through my taxes?

Somewhere, early on, along the road of life, these young teenage girls/women had no focus or they lost their focus. They had no real plans for their futures. They were just in the world, going through the motions. They didn't think about or take anything seriously. They thought this could never happen to them. They didn't understand what it meant when their mothers told them to 'leave those boys alone.' They didn't quite understand and believe their mothers when they were told not to get pregnant. Their mothers did not go into detail as to what constitutes getting pregnant or getting a sexually transmitted disease, and the ensuing consequences.

These young teenage girls/women went to school because they were told to go, not realizing the education they were receiving was for their own benefit, their future, and not for the benefit of their parents. They were having fun in school and outside of school. Their plans for what they wanted to do in life went out the window at a very early age because they got pregnant while in high school or even while in junior high.

Teen mothers and young adult mothers, because of their pregnancies, suffered through their parents' anger, ridicule, and disappointment. Maybe their mothers didn't care, and even expected them to get pregnant because they did the same thing when they were their daughters' ages. The cycle just continues.

The teenage girls suffered through having to leave high school to attend a continuation school until they gave birth to their children. They suffered through their classmates' and former friends' ridiculing and laughing at them for being so stupid because they got pregnant. Some girls went to group homes for pregnant teens because their parents threw them out of their homes because of their pregnancy. They suffered knowing that the guys who got them pregnant no longer cared about them or never did care about them. These guys went on to use other girls. These guys certainly did not provide any kind of support to them (emotional, marriage offer, financial, housing, transportation, etc.). Most teenage girls suffered through having to secure financial aide for their baby or babies through the state welfare system. They were left holding the bag – the baby bag!

These girls all started out the same. They liked the boy, or boys, they were messing around with, even to the point of sleeping with them, giving up their ultimate gift – their virginity. They knew they were not forced to engage in sexual activity with the opposite sex (it takes two people to make that decision). They even knew about contraception, but, like most of us, they didn't think it could happen to them, or didn't think about it at all. Contraception is no longer a factor in the equation now that they're pregnant.

As time went on, these teenage girls became young women who lost their self-esteem, self-respect, their hopes, and their dreams. They gave up. As time continued and as other men became interested in them for whatever reason (but not the right reason), they gave themselves fully to the men, forgetting about abstinence and birth control. Their hopes and expectations of a decent relationship, possible marriage, and a better future for themselves and their children became even more distant with each man they met and slept with. Their self-esteem tumbled further and further down, even to the point of them being numb to their plight.

These young teenage girls and young women didn't know what they wanted to do in life, or what their purpose was. They were never affirmed by their parents, and they didn't have enough conviction about themselves to make a plan for their lives and to stick to it. They followed bad patterns of bad behavior, and they ended up repeating the same mistakes that others made in the past (including some of their mothers) concerning sexual promiscuity.

The end result for these women was raising many children by many different men, with far too many heartaches, sacrifices, and struggles along the way. They did not plan for this to happen to them, but it did.

Great thought should be given to the above issues relating to unmarried teenagers and women with multiple children from multiple men prior to engaging in sexual promiscuity.

As mentioned in previous chapters, every child born on the face of the earth has a purpose in his or her life – God's purpose. God makes a way for them and for their mothers and fathers who care for them. God is true to His word in that each child is a blessing to any parent, no matter the circumstance. It's the parents' responsibility to love and raise their children in the admonition of the Lord, and to help their children find out and fulfill their purpose in life.

The good news is that God will work with the unwed mother, for the sake of her children, if she is willing to ask for forgiveness and repent (change her ways and walk in the love of the Lord) so that she can provide a better life for her children and herself, so she can begin to love herself because God loves her, and so she can gain or regain her self-esteem. God will see to it that she will be able to love her children and help them fulfill their purposes in life, which will complete her own purpose in life. This is in accordance with *Romans 8:28: "And we know that all things work together for good to those who love God, to those who are the called according to His purpose."* Also, in accordance with *Proverbs 3:5-6*, we are to trust in the Lord. *Proverbs 3:5-6* states: *"Trust in the Lord with all your heart, and lean not on your own understanding; in all your ways acknowledge Him, and He shall direct your paths."*

Again, what's love got to do with it?

<u>Mature Women Be Aware</u>

Something happened to me not too long ago that tested my faith and my strength in the Lord. By the way, I passed the test.

I met a man a few years ago. He was very nice and a very good-looking man. You know the type: Tall, dark and handsome – big guy/ football player body – definitely my type. He worked in my home doing plumbing, electrical, and carpentry. Over time he began to make conversation with me while he worked in my home. I learned he was a Christian, he was married (his second), and he had two children (son 16 and daughter 8) from the first marriage. He stated he had sole custody of the children from his first marriage, and his second wife was helping him raise his children. Each time in our conversations, he would give me a compliment (small but worth remembering) about my appearance, my hair, or my weight loss.

On one occasion when he came over to make a repair, he complained about his wife not going to church with him, not applying what she learned in church when she did go, not studying the Bible, and not working with him in their marriage as he felt a wife should in accordance to the Bible. Of course, the first thing in my mind and out of my mouth was whether he was in obedience to God's word as a husband and not to hinge on the part where it says that his wife should obey him. He laughed a little and then said it was quite the contrary. He went on to say she always complained about his first wife, as if she was jealous of her. She would throw his first wife in his face every time they had an argument. He also stated she spent money without consulting with him, yet she did not work outside the home to help with the expenses she created. He worked very hard and picked up extra jobs where he could, but he felt he was always in debt and could never break even due to her financial irresponsibility. I told him to pray for his wife and I would pray for him and for her. I also told him to get counseling from the elders of his church, and he said he would do so.

In a subsequent conversation with him when he came over to make another repair, he told me his wife was sick. He took her to the emergency room and she was admitted. She was in the hospital for a week. A lot of tests were taken and she was treated for her illnesses. She was then released from the hospital with the doctor's instructions to continue her healing. She didn't do what the doctor told her to do nor did she take any of the medications that were prescribed that her husband paid for. He stated that the prescriptions cost a lot of money, but she would not take them. Consequently, she relapsed, but refused to go back to the doctor. He demanded she return to the doctor, but she refused, stating she would only go if he brought her to the doctor and stayed with her. He had taken so much time off from work when she was in the hospital earlier that he feared he would lose his job. He also needed to work to pay the family bills as well as the additional bills created from her illness. He went on to state she was antagonistic, uncooperative, and that he was tired, very tired.

I encouraged him again to speak to the elders of his church, and he stated he did. He said they offered to send women counselors to his home to minister to his wife and to stand in agreement in prayer for his wife's healing. However, he did not want anyone from the church to come to his home because it was in such a mess. He said she and he were embarrassed to have anyone come to their home in its current condition. I told him they were coming to his home to minister to his wife and pray for her healing, not to check out the condition of his home. He told me he would ask them to come to his home and pray.

Over the months of coming to my home making repairs, he felt very comfortable telling me about his problems with his wife. I was becoming a bit uncomfortable, so I told him he should really be speaking to his pastor or fellow elders instead of me, but he said he did. He said I was a good listener and I understood what he was going through. In my conversations with him, I tried to be encouraging and I always centered our conversations on the word of God.

In one of our latest conversations, he told me he felt he wanted to leave his wife because he felt his relationship with her was deteriorating. He said everything was a struggle when he came home from work. He said she humiliates him every chance she gets. He stated he was tired and felt his marriage was not moving forward as it should. He was definitely not happy. He stated her sickness was getting worse, she still refused to go to the doctor, she had an odor from her sickness, the home was a mess, and he was just tired of trying. He was especially tired of her throwing his ex-wife up in his face. He stated he felt unworthy and unappreciated, and he found himself withdrawing from her emotionally and physically.

I encouraged him again to continue to pray for his wife and his marriage, and to have the church female counselors come to his home and minister to his wife. I told him to seek additional counseling from the elders of his church. I reminded him that he was the priest and servant of his home based on the scriptures in the Bible.

I didn't know whether he was telling the truth, I didn't know him that well, and I certainly did not know his wife. The one thing I did know was that there were three sides to his story. There are at least three sides to every story, especially when it comes to a husband and wife who are in marital conflict. There's the husband's side, the wife's side, and God's side. Yes, God is there in the midst of them. He never leaves us nor does He forsake us, so He is definitely involved. He sees and knows everything, and He knew the real truth about this situation.

I sympathized with him and told him that I would lift him and his wife up in prayer. I teased him a little bit to uplift his spirits because he was so unhappy and his eyes watered. I think he was about to cry. I told him that in California there were at least 30 women to every one man, and that his wife should appreciate him because it's hard to find a godly man who works. He laughed and thanked me for my encouragement.

[Now, this is how the devil creeps in and tries to destroy your relationship with God.]

As the conversations progressed, he told me he noticed that I lost some weight and I looked good. I thanked him. I was telling him about a segment of a chapter in a book I was reading, and, out of the blue he asked me if he could hug me. I told him "NO!" He asked if things were different, would I go out with him. I told him he was married and he needed to honor his marriage and do all he could to keep his marriage together because of his vows to the Lord and to his wife. At this point, I felt it was definitely time for him to go because I really felt uncomfortable, and I did not want him to pursue me. He had definitely overstayed his welcome.

He finished up his work at my home; there was no further need for him to stay, not even to chitchat. As he headed to the door to leave, he asked if he could shake my hand to thank me for my advice and prayers. He extended his hand. I shook his hand and thanked him for his work, but instead of releasing my hand, he held it and caressed it. I had to snatch my hand back. I told him he was a bad boy. He grinned a little, and then he put his head down as he walked out the door. He stayed parked outside my home for several minutes and then he left.

Now, had I given him that hug he asked for earlier, he probably would have kept me in his arms. This is based on his caressing my hand. I would then be in trouble. He was tall, dark, handsome, great body build, he spoke softly and had a nice manner about him. He was definitely pleasing to the eye and very comfortable to be around. In all honesty, the thought crossed my mind (satan implanted the thought) for a hot second and I rebuked it immediately with the word of God. I knew he was unhappy at home, but I knew I was not the answer to his problem. Was he telling the truth? I don't know. And, even if he was telling the truth, I could not allow myself to be involved. If I involved myself with this person, I would be committing adultery and I would be out of the will of God. Neither one of us would be blessed by God, and we both would suffer the consequences of our actions. Although I realized he had a desire to be physically close to me, it would be a sin for me to encourage or engage him.

I think more of myself than to accept less than what I deserve as a child of God. I don't want a momentary cheap thrill, and I don't want to be some cheap thrill to anyone. I'm expecting the best from God, and with that expectation, I must be the best that I can be before God. I must honor His word. I want God's best for my life.

I tried to be helpful in my understanding and in my recommendations, but I think he took my kindness the wrong way, even with the Bible in my hand quoting scriptures to him. What's up with that? I should not have allowed the conversations about his wife to continue even though I asked him to stop talking about her.

I certainly don't want to stop my blessings behind an adulterous relationship with a married man. I truly believe God will send the right man to me, under the right circumstances, and for the right reasons with no attachments and no drama.

I somewhat understood how he felt, but trying to create a relationship with another person while already embroiled in what seemed like a turbulent relationship/marriage will not solve the problem. It only exacerbates the problem and creates other nasty problems. The formula is always the same. The problem needed to be fixed from within, and only their cooperation with God could fix it.

I should not have allowed the conversations to go in the direction they went. I was somewhat uncomfortable allowing him to talk badly about his wife and I told him so. I would not like it if my husband spoke poorly about me. He told me he appreciated me allowing him to 'get things off his chest.'

I thought I was being understanding, consoling, and encouraging – a friend. However, I find that single women cannot really be friends with married men. We can be acquaintances, but not friends because friendships between opposite sexes tend to bleed into relationships over time through emotions and physical contact.

Also, I should maintain a strict business relationship with people who are working for me. I don't need to know their personal business and they don't need to know mine.

I can't speak about his thoughts because I am not a mind reader, but his actions and his words were definitely headed in the wrong direction toward me – the request for a hug and the caressing handshake. He might have been sincere, but he was a Christian and he knew better just as I knew better. Even though he did a good job, I did not have him do any future work for me for my own sake. Just keeping it real.

I viewed this as a test for me, too, and I am glad I passed the test. God has given me the tools to pass all tests, trials, and temptations. I rebuked satan in the name of Jesus, and I told satan that it's written in *1 Corinthians 10:13* that: *"No temptation has overtaken you except such as is common to man [woman], but God is faithful, who will not allow you to be tempted beyond what you are able, but with the temptation will also make the way of escape, that you may be able to bear it."* The Amplified Bibles says it this way: *"For no temptation [no trial regarded as enticing to sin, no matter how it comes or where it leads] has overtaken you and laid hold on you that is not common to man [woman] [that is, no temptation or trial has come to you that is beyond human resistance and that is not adjusted and adapted and belonging to human experience, and such as a man [woman] can bear]. But God is faithful [to His Word and to His compassionate nature], and He [can be trusted] will not to let you be tempted and tried and assayed beyond your ability and strength of resistance and power to endure, but with the temptation He will [always] also provide the way out [the means of escape to a landing place], that you may be capable and strong and powerful to bear up under it patiently."*

So, even though the temptation came to me, sadly through another Christian, God's word quickly came to me, too! I immediately told the devil that I rebuke all of his fiery darts in the name of Jesus, and then repeated the applicable scripture to the situation. In this case, I used *1 Corinthians 10:13* (as referenced above). God's word told me this temptation is a **'common'** thing. There was nothing new about this – nothing new under the sun. The scripture stated it was a temptation from satan, and I was able to resist the temptation. God had given me the strength to resist the temptation with the use of His word, and, therefore, He provided me a way out of the temptation by just saying "NO" to the temptation. I was victorious in overcoming the trial that was set before me.

I realized that my senses (sight, hearing, touch, smell, and taste) played a part within the devil's fiery darts (thoughts implanted by the devil in my mind) that were in battle with my conscience and the Holy Spirit within me. Both sides were battling. With my senses, I saw that this guy was pleasing to look at, he spoke softly, and he had a caressing handshake. In my mind, the fiery darts from the devil tried to reason with me by making statements like: You're single, he's in your home alone with you. No one will ever know except you two. He looks good, he's attracted to you, and you're attracted to him. You need to sleep with him because your body needs the sex. Nobody else has expressed an interest in you. When was the last time you slept with someone? You're getting old and may not have another opportunity. And on and on the fiery darts will continue to attack if I allow them. The devil was trying to put fear into my mind that I should be sexually involved with this person because I may not have another chance, my body is in need of sex, I'm getting old, and other stupid stuff. I realized what satan was doing, and I remembered *James 1:14-16*, which states: *"But each one is tempted when he [she] is drawn away by his [her] own desires and enticed. Then, when desire has conceived, it gives birth to sin; and sin, when it is full- grown, brings forth death. Do not be deceived, my beloved brethren."*

However, I operate in faith. *Romans 10:17* states: *"So then faith comes by hearing, and hearing by the word of God."* By studying the word of God, meditating on that word, your faith will bring God's word to your mind quickly through the Holy Spirit to overthrow the devil's thoughts. Since I operate in faith, I am not operating in my fleshly senses. Also, God had not given me the spirit of fear, which included anxiety, nervousness, stress, doubt, unbelief, worry, depression, or defeat. *2 Timothy 1:7* states: *"For God has not given us a spirit of fear, but of power and of love and of a sound mind."* You cannot operate in fear and in faith at the same time. When faith shows up, fear has to go. When fear shows up, you've lost your faith. We must stay in faith at all times. My faith eliminated any and all fear.

You must be careful because the devil works very fast in instilling negative and contradictory statements in your mind so that you will make the wrong choice before you have a chance to allow God's word into your mind. But, if you are fully immersed in God's Word, immediately His Word blocks out satan's darts of sinful suggestions and thoughts. However, if you don't know what God says about sexual promiscuity, you're defeated at the start. You end up **"reasoning"** with yourself by the thoughts satan has quickly implanted in your mind, you commit the sin, and then guilt and shame immediately set in. The devil has won because he was able to make you sin against yourself and against God.

The Holy Spirit works with your conscience, and the Holy Spirit will immediately bring God's word to your mind. *Matthew 4:4* states: *"But He [Jesus] answered and said, 'It is written, Man shall not live by bread alone, but by every word that proceeds from the mouth of God.'" Luke 4:4* says the same thing: *"But Jesus answered him saying, 'It is written, Man shall not live by bread alone, but by every word of God.'"* This is mentioned twice in the Bible for us to take heed to what God is saying. The word 'bread' identifies all of the things that sustain a body such as food, water, air, sleep, exercise, etc. But God sustains and maintains us through His word. His word keeps us from carnal desires and appetites for the wrong things that will harm or kill us.

I immediately cut the devil off with the word of God when the wrong thoughts came into my mind. If I lingered on what the devil said in my mind, my thinking would have turned into the lust of the flesh by reasoning, and I would have committed adultery in my mind, then my body would soon follow my mind, and I would be defeated. That's how sin works. Remember that sin always begins in the mind.

We must remember that we are not wrestling or fighting another human being. Human beings are used by satan as vehicles to defeat us. *Ephesians 6:12* states: *"For we do not wrestle against flesh and blood, but against principalities, against powers, against the rulers of the darkness of this age, against spiritual hosts of wickedness in the heavenly places. Therefore take up the whole armor of God, that you may be able to withstand in the evil day, and having done all, to stand."* God's armor consists of (1) the helmet of salvation, (2) the breastplate of righteousness, (3) the sword of the Spirit (which is the Word of God), (4) the shield of faith which is able to quench all the fiery darts of the wicked one [thoughts contradictory to the word of God], (5) the gospel of truth which is girding your waist, and (6) the preparation of the gospel of peace on your feet. This armor is found in *Ephesians 6:12-17*, and it's to be worn everyday. This passage in the Bible is very important to remember. Once you know whom you're dealing with, it's easy to diffuse all of his (satan's) plots and schemes with the Holy Spirit bringing to your mind God's Word. You are to rebuke satan with the word of God. You're a conqueror and you are victorious, as stated in *Romans 8:37: "Yet, in all these things we are more than conquerors through Him who loved us."*

I used God's word against the devil, and he had no choice but to leave my mind. Immediately, that battle was over, done, finished. When you refuse to go along with the devil and stand firm on the word of God, the devil can't do anything else but leave. The devil has no power unless you give it to him. *James 4:7* states: *"Therefore, submit to God. Resist the devil and he will flee from you."* To resist means to defy, oppose, and stand firm against the devil's fiery darts (thoughts). We are to rebuke the devil at every turn, and we are to ignore our senses if it contradicts God's word.

God's words are words of action, so even though you may know the scriptures, you must use the scriptures that apply to situations as they come up. Speak God's word to the devil's darts of negative and contradictory thoughts to what you know to be true from God's word, and see how quickly those thoughts disappear. If you don't know what God says through the Bible about a situation, you're defenseless and helpless against the fiery darts of the devil, and you will soon succumb to the devil's thoughts in your mind, your body will follow, you will be in sin, and you will be defeated.

I have to keep *Matthew 4:4* before me at all times as a single woman, so that I don't sin against God and against myself. I have desires, but I cannot allow those desires to have me. *Matthew 4:4* states: *"But He [Jesus] answered and said, 'It is written. Man shall not live by bread alone, but by every word that proceeds from the mouth of God.'"* *James 1:14-16* states: *"But each one is tempted when he [she] is drawn away by his [her] own desires and enticed. Then, when desire has conceived, it gives birth to sin; and sin, when it is full- grown, brings forth death. Do not be deceived, my beloved brethren."* I could have blown it big had I not known what God's word says, means, and how powerful His word is. Had I not had God's word in my heart because I studied and meditated on it, I would not have been able to reject this person's subtle advances. So, I rebuked the devil in the name of Jesus, and said what was written in *Matthew 4:4*, *1 Corinthians 10:13*, *James 1:14-16*, and *James 4:7*. I resisted and I'm free.

It's the thought before the action that gets us in trouble. If we stop the thought in its tracks before it blooms into something that shouldn't be, we will be fine. Since this guy and I are Christians, we both would have lost our footing with God if we entered into an adulterous relationship. I believe I helped him and me not to sin by just saying 'NO.'

Apparently, he developed feelings for me (or was it lust????) based on our conversations about his home life, even though I injected God's word at every turn. He was sent to do repairs in my home. While in my home, I did not flirt with him or encourage him. Since he saw me studying my Bible, he told me about his walk in Christianity. I believed that to be safe to discuss. My intentions were right, but his intentions became questionable.

By his actions, his Christianity became highly questionable. *2 Timothy 3:6-7* states: *"For of this sort are those who creep into households and make captives of gullible women loaded down with sins, led away by various lusts, always learning and never able to come to the knowledge of the truth."* I have seen this in many older women who are captivated by a man's prowess and the attention he gives them. They are accepting of advances by men without a thought because they crave the attention of a man. These women end up lonely, feeling used, sad, discarded, and disappointed in themselves. Yet again, they've allowed another man to seduce them and load them down with yet another sin. They tend to be silly women of no interest in the true things of God (even though some be in the church), and they are constantly looking for love in all the wrong places.

1 Timothy 5:24 states: *"Some men's [women's] sins are clearly evident, preceding them to judgment, but those [sins] of some men [women] follow later."* God's wheel of judgment turns slowly and finely. His judgment of your sin may not come immediately, maybe not for years, but His judgment will come. I don't ever want to be this type of woman. God has forgiven me of my sins, I have a clean slate, and I want to keep it clean. I continually strive to be a woman of God. Yea, I know I can catch, but I don't want to catch just any ole thing. I want to catch God's best!

In Conclusion

God loves us, no matter what. His love is pure. We are not damaged goods in His eyes. We are the apples of His eye. He is a faithful and understanding God. He is a forgiving God. He is a God of second chances. He gives grace and mercy freely and daily. He washes away our sins, hurts and disappointments, and He keeps all our tears.

God's love is all we need. He is more than enough. We must be confident in God's love toward us, in His provision for our lives, in His redemption, in His promises to us, and in the future He has for us. If we are not married to a man and doing the will of God for that man, we are married to God and we are to do His will. We cannot allow ourselves to be caught up in anything less than God's best for us. We cannot jeopardize our future and our eternal life with God over a mere mortal's momentary lustful desire to be satisfied by us.

What's love got to do with it? A whole lot – for our future and for our eternity.

Chapter 6

Why Reinvent A Broken Wheel?

Chapter 6

Why Re-Invent A Broken Wheel?

Do you not know that fat meat is greasy? Do you not know what goes up must come down? Do you not know that what's done in the dark will soon come to the light?

There are many clichès to get your attention to make you think. Doing the same wrong thing over and over again is very bad, unwise, ungodly, and damaging to you in so many ways. However, no one seems to want to call it what it is – sin, and sin has consequences. Sexual sin is something that is repeated constantly by young teenage girls and women without any forethought about the consequences. This cycle must stop!

The commercialism, glamorization, sexualization and general acceptance of sexual promiscuity tell us that it's okay to have sex anytime we want and with whomever we want. In commercialism, there are no boundaries or consequences.

These days, sex is used to sell everything, including sex, itself. There are sexy commercials displaying and selling skimpy lingerie that say you can really get your sex on by wearing this or that. These commercials are very provocative and enticing to men and women alike. Unfortunately, these same commercials are shown during prime family time on channels earmarked for family programs on television where children see them. Impressionable little girls see the commercials and believe they need to dress skimpily to be sexy, too. The commercialism tells little girls what the definition of being sexy is and how to dress the part. Some mothers and fathers buy into the commercialism also, thinking their daughters would look cute dressed like that. They purchase the clothing, makeup, and jewelry for their daughters. Unfortunately, when their child is physically touched in a private area on her body, or molested, or even raped by an adult stranger, friend or relative because of being skimpily and provocatively dressed, the parents then want to kill the perpetrator. The parents fail to realize that they played a part in putting their own child in a position to be sexually violated. The provocative way the child was dressed provoked or enticed the perpetrator.

Little boys are affected by commercialism, too, and they are curious and enticed to find out more of what it means for them concerning sexy looking girls. If left unchecked, these boys grow up having a skewed outlook on girls, teenage girls, and women. They see all women as sex objects. Some boys try to molest and rape little girls in school and on the playground when left to themselves. They grow up molesting and raping women because no one ever explained to them the rights, the wrongs, and the consequences of their actions based on what they see in and through provocative commercialism.

Teenage girls want to be the models in the commercials and look like sexy vixens. They have no clue of what the consequences are for dressing in such a way, which entices and attracts the wrong person to them. Hence, they are not viewed as having any value, but viewed as an object to be used and discarded by the perpetrators. They are mistaken for loosey-gooseys, they are touched inappropriately in the wrong places on their bodies without their permission, and they are possibly molested, raped, and sometimes even raped and killed.

The parents think their daughters look cute, and they pay no attention as to how their daughters are viewed by others outside their home. Their daughters go out into the world as sheep to be slaughtered without recognizing the wolves that are watching and stalking them. These young girls, teenage girls, and young women don't understand why they have been targeted by unscrupulous, perverted, degenerate, and evil people.

Young women go jogging in the most remote of areas skimpily dressed in "hot pant" or "bikini" shorts and a tank top tee shirt, thinking that because they jog they can run away from or out-run whoever would be after them. Time and time again we hear on the news about a female jogger who was found raped and killed near mountain trails and in other remote areas.

Sin

Now, some people don't believe in the word "sin." They believe "their" truth, whatever their truth is, is what's right for them. They also believe it's an individual thing. They believe everybody has his or her own individual standards and rights. They don't even use the word "sin" in their vocabulary. They don't believe in consequences, although the consequences are attached to their actions (good and bad), and they are real. They believe if something bad happens to them or anyone else, it just happens. However, there are consequences for even having such views. It is what it is. No matter what you choose to believe, the consequences are real, they are the same for everybody, and no one can escape them – plain and simple. Consequences, good or bad, are attached to every decision and action.

The consequences are always the same – some variations in circumstances, but basically they're the same. You never know when the consequences will come because some consequences do not come instantly. It may be years before you experience the consequences of your past actions. It doesn't even matter whether you accept the consequences or not. You have no choice once the consequences are set in motion by your decision and action. They are coming and when they come, they will complete their cycle.

However, after the consequences begin, you have to make the best of the outcome, whatever that outcome turns out to be.

Here's a rough table of the consequences of sexual sin.

Description	***Sin***	***Consequences (Possibilities)***	***Damage (Possibilities)***
Marital Sex	No	None	None
Adultery	Yes	Guilt & Remorse Pregnancy Bacterial Vaginosis Chlamydia Genital Human Papillomavirus Genital Herpes Gonorrhea Lymphogrannuloma Venereum Syphillis Trichomoniasis Proctitis HIV (a/k/a AIDS)	Loss of Marriage Loss of Family Financial Support Loss of Peace of Mind Loss of Health Loss of Finances Loss of Future Loss of Life

Description	***Sin***	***Consequences (Possibilities)***	***Damage (Possibilities)***
Fornication	Yes	Guilt & Remorse Pregnancy Bacterial Vaginosis Chlamydia Genital Human Papillomavirus Genital Herpes Gonorrhea Lymphogrannuloma Venereum Syphillis Trichomoniasis Proctitis HIV (a/k/a AIDS)	Loss of Peace of Mind Payment of Child Support Loss of Health Loss of Finances Loss of Future Molestation Rape Loss of Life

Do you think you are so different, so special, and so smart that you can't possibly get pregnant from the first sexual encounter? Or, do you think you're somehow immune or have some sort of force field that protects you from contracting a sexually transmittable disease? Are you that arrogant that you think you cannot die from one single act of sexual sin that was done in the dark and behind closed doors where only you and one other person knew about it? Even with using protection (whatever that is), do you think you, especially you, will not pay a price for your actions?

For every sexual action there is a sexual reaction. Depending on the method or formula you choose before the act [birth control pills, condoms, Vaseline (I heard this works, too – go figure), immediate douching, 10-second in and out rule, etc.], there will either be no consequence "this time" or it will take a few days, a couple of weeks, or nine months for your undercover activities to be uncovered. But, believe me, whatever you do will surely come to light. Definitely be sure that your sins will find you out. We're not even discussing the other person's actions and his consequences; we're discussing yours. Oh, and, yes, he will reap his consequences, too.

Yeah, yeah, yeah – I've heard it all before, even said some of the stuff myself back in the day in the corner in the dark. "Oh, it felt so good." "He kisses so well." "I've never felt this way before about anyone." "No one has ever moved me like he did." "He told me he loved me." Yada, Yada, Yada!

Or, one could justify one's actions by the music of the day. There was one particular record that really stood out as a number one hit back in the early 1970's. It constantly played on almost all of the rock and roll/rhythm and blues radio stations. The lyrics of the record were so smooth and made so much "worldly" sense that people actually believed it was okay to be in an affair with a married person. Although most people knew it was wrong to have an affair, the song gave justification, comfort, and some sort of crazy entitlement to those who were either involved in or wanted to be involved in a marital affair. The music was great to slow-dance to, and the lyrics just made so much carnal sense. This song connected with every person in a difficult marital relationship; every person who wanted to have his or her cake and eat it, too; every person who was lonely even though married; and every person who did not want to put in the effort to make their marriage work. The song made so much "worldly" sense that having an affair just had to be okay.

In reality, the song promoted cheating on one's spouse, lying by deception and omission, and transference of family funds and family time to support the cost of the adultery (entertainment, restaurants, hotel rooms, clothing, gifts, etc.). **[How come some of the best sounding songs that all could dance to promote the worst sins?]** This particular song promoted being slick enough to scheme, connive, and defraud in order to commit adultery. The cheater/adulterer did not think to honor his or her vows to God or to his or her spouse. The song promoted total disobedience to God's word. I can't begin to tell you the number of people who fell for that song and fell into sin (including myself, unfortunately). We justified our reasoning, our decisions, and our actions by that song, and we just didn't think or care about the ensuing consequences. Oh, but there were definitely consequences to pay!

Oops! The laws of sowing and reaping have now set in. *Numbers 32:23* states: *"But if you do not do so, then take note, you have sinned against the Lord; and be sure your sin will find you out." Galatians 6:7-8* states: *"Be not deceived; God is not mocked; for whatsoever a man [woman] soweth, that shall he [she] also reap. For he [she] who sows to his [her] flesh will of the flesh reap corruption, but he [she] who sows to the Spirit will of the Spirit reap everlasting life." Job 4:8* states: *"Even as I have seen, they that plow iniquity, and sow wickedness, reap the same." Proverbs 6:32-35* states: *"Whoever commits adultery with a woman [man] lacks understanding; he [she] who does so destroys his [her] own soul. Wounds and dishonor he [she] will get, and his [her] reproach will not be wiped away. For jealousy is a husband's [wife's] fury; therefore he [she] will not spare in the day of vengeance. He [She] will accept no recompense, nor will he [she] be appeased though you give many gifts."* In essence, you will reap what you sow, you will reap later than you sow, and you will definitely reap more than you sow.

Those of us who fell into adultery fell into all sorts of consequences that followed. Families broke up; children were confused and displaced; emotional, mental, and physical health were compromised; finances were lost; homes were lost; jobs were lost; and futures were destroyed. Those of us who believed in that song lost our moral compasses, lost our families, lost our wealth, and some of us even lost our lives. Had I known what the consequences were going to be, when they were going to come, and how long I was going to suffer, I would never ever have taken this route to solve the problems I had in my marriage!

The reason for cheating on one's spouse does not even compare to the hellish consequences that will follow. The consequences far outweigh the momentary pleasure of having a marital affair. A tremendous amount of people went through hell and some even went to hell behind that one song. Would I do it again? HELL NO! Is fat meat greasy? ABSOULTELY!

The consequences of being disobedient to God by not honoring one's marriage vows to Him and to the spouse are devastating, no matter what your reasons or justifications. God's word says in *Deuteronomy 23:21-23: "When you make a vow to the Lord your God, you shall not delay to pay it, for the Lord your God will surely require it of you, and it would be sin to you. But if you abstain from vowing, it shall not be sin to you. That which has gone from your lips you shall keep and perform, for you voluntarily vowed to the Lord your God what you have promised with your mouth."* You made the choice to accept the marriage proposal, and you sealed it with your vows to God and to your marriage partner. So don't be slow in honoring your promises/vows to God for He expects you to keep them. God is expecting you to honor your word to Him, who is your Creator. Making promises to God and not keeping them may be the reason why things in your life have not worked out for you, or are not working out for you. Ask for forgiveness, repent (change your direction), and don't make any vows that you're not going to keep.

So, The Question Is: WHY?

You heard about people who were involved in some sort of sexual promiscuity and their resulting consequences, which were unlike what's shown in the various media (television, movies, newspapers, books and trash trades, etc.). In the various media, it looks like there is no accountability, and there are no consequences. However, you have friends who fell into sexual sin, and you saw first-hand the bad results they received from their decisions and actions. You probably know a family member who faltered, got caught, and who suffered the consequences of his or her sin. You probably even saw the devastating effects on their family. You know about the broken relationships, spiritual and moral regrets, emotional drainage, physical problems, and the lasting financial damage caused by being involved in sexual promiscuity in and out the realm of marriage. Yet, you take the chance anyway? Why?

It's not even about the possibility of getting caught in the act anymore. Because you think everybody else is doing it, it's okay for you to do the same. You're not afraid. Your health is good. You feel fine, and you look fine. You didn't get caught the last time, so you don't think you will get caught the next time. However, unbeknownst to you, you may have thrown your future, your dreams, and your hopes away, and don't even know it yet. You don't care enough about yourself, or about those who will be affected, to think about the consequences before you make that dreaded move. Why?

Nobody ever comes back to tell you the truth about what happened to them after they committed their sins. Do you know why? Because after experiencing the consequences and finding the consequences to be so destructive in so many ways and on so many levels, they are too ashamed to say anything to you, that's why!

What is it about having sex before getting married, or being in an adulterous relationship that makes you want to risk all that you are, all that you have, and all that you, yourself, hope to be? Is it temptation?

James 1:12-16 states: *"Blessed is the man [woman] who endures temptation; for when he [she] has been approved, he [she] will receive the crown of life which the Lord has promised to those who love Him. Let no one say when he [she] is tempted, 'I am tempted by God'; for God cannot be tempted by evil, nor does He, Himself, tempt anyone. But each one [person] is tempted when he [she] is drawn away by his [her] own desires and enticed. Then when desire has conceived, it gives birth to sin; and sin, when it is full grown, brings forth death. Do not be deceived, my beloved brethren."*

Remember, the consequences of sin may be immediate or later, but they are definitely coming. The consequences will be a heavy payment for the sin.

'Desire' is a craving, a yearning, and a wanting of someone or something by your flesh. It's the lust of your flesh, as stated in *1 John 2:16: "For all that is in the world – the lust of the flesh, the lust of the eyes, and the pride of life – is not of the Father, but is of the world."* The works of the flesh are referred to in *Galatians 5:19-21, which* states: *"Now the works of the flesh are evident, which are adultery, fornication, uncleanness, lewdness, idolatry, sorcery, hatred, contentions, jealousies, outbursts of wrath, selfish ambitions, dissentions, heresies, envy, murders, drunkenness, revelries, and the like; of which I tell you beforehand, just as I also told you in time past, that those who practice such things will not inherit the Kingdom of God."*

Seek God's word, first, before you make a decision that can ruin your relationship with God, your family, friends, and others. Your sin can negatively alter your health; annihilate your credit; and destroy your future plans, hopes, and dreams. You can literally and physically destroy your life and send yourself straight to hell by the decisions you make.

Is this man really worth it? Is he worth you going to hell for? Do the statistics lie? Are your parents, clergy, and true friends lying to you? Why would you not believe those who love and care for you enough to tell you the truth so that you won't get hurt? Although you may really like some of your friends who want you to do wrong with them, you won't even know their names or where they live ten years from now. However, the sin and its consequences will be with you long after your friends are gone.

Who Pays The Medical Coverage?

If you're a teenager under the age of 18, and you either get pregnant or get a sexually transmitted disease, your parents end up paying for your care. If your parents put you out of their home because they are so disgusted by what you did, you become a ward of the state and the taxpayers pay for your room and board, your medical treatment, etc. Or, your parents may decide to allow you to stay in their home, and they help you by keeping a roof over your head, still sending you to school so you can get your diploma, and paying for all of your healthcare through their insurance and their own money.

Your parents may even contact the parents of the person who got you pregnant or who gave you the sexually transmitted disease to solicit financial assistance for you. Your parents may even press charges against the person, have him arrested, or sue him on your behalf in civil or family court. Kids and diseases cost money; **SOMEBODY'S GOT TO PAY!**

If you're an adult and get pregnant, or contract an STD, from the one you were sleeping around with, who will help you? Do you have medical insurance to cover your treatment and other related expenses? Is the person who got you pregnant, or who gave you the STD, going to financially assist you? Is he going to take you to your doctor and lab appointments? Will he take care of you while you're sick? Will he help pay your bills while you are unable to work? Or, will you have to hunt him down to make him account for at least his half of the financial responsibility? Will you have to sue him in court for child support or for expenses related to him giving you an STD? Can you prove that he is the culprit in either situation? Do you have the money to get an attorney to take him to court? These are the things we all need to think about prior to getting sexually involved with a person.

Speaking Of Child Support?

Be you a teenager or an adult, are you really ready for the expense of having and raising a child on your own? What has seemed to elude most young people, male and female alike, is that **"KIDS COST MONEY",** lots of it, and for a long time! Once the baby has arrived, you can't put her or him back inside your body. Nature has a peculiar way of quickly closing the gap between your legs after you deliver your child.

"IT IS NOT YOUR PARENTS' RESPONSIBILITY" to raise you and your child at the same time if you're a teenager living under your parents' roof. If they do, it's strictly gratis (grace) because of their love for you. In all fairness, it is as much the responsibility of the guy, who impregnated you, as it is your responsibility. The child did not ask to come into this world, especially under such adverse circumstances. So, you and the guy who you slept with must bear the full financial responsibility as well as the responsibility of raising the child until the child is of adult age capable of taking care of itself. You need to do all you can for the child. Your own desires and goals are now secondary to the welfare of the child you helped bring into the world. The child is your number one priority. There is no more "me", "myself", and "I." It's no longer about you, but it's all about your child.

The child is the boss; she or he dictates what your priorities are from the time they are born and onward. There is only the child and his or her well-being that counts until he or she reaches the age of accountability – age 18. If the child decides to go to college, you may be financially bound an additional 5 to 6 years until he or she completes his or her college education.

It doesn't matter that the guy ditched you when he learned you were pregnant with his baby. The sexual relationship has now turned into a "business relationship", clear and simple. It would be nice if it turned into a family relationship, too, but most of the time it doesn't. Now, you are involved (stuck) with the guy who got you pregnant (financially and otherwise), until the child reaches 18 years of age and possibly beyond. That's a long time to be involved with someone who refused to wear a condom when you asked him to before you had sex with him, a guy who was upset that you got pregnant, a guy who wanted you to have an abortion (but you didn't), a guy who doesn't want the child, a guy who doesn't want to get married, a guy who doesn't want to financially support the child, and a guy who definitely doesn't want his life to be altered. Can you imagine dealing with this type of person for 18 years or more?

Baby/Daddy/Mama/Drama

Needless to say, having a child out of wedlock can cause a great deal of drama, namely "Baby/Daddy/Mama/Drama." Unless the guy really loves you and is willing and anxious to marry you in spite of your getting pregnant, believe me, you will have plenty of drama down the road.

Guys who won't own up to their responsibility after learning they got a woman pregnant tend to be very selfish and act very ugly toward the woman. A baby was not what they ever had in mind when they were fooling around sexually with the woman. They want to live their lives, keep their money, have their fun, date and fool around sexually with other women. They don't want to be responsible and accountable for their actions. They're ready for sex, but nothing else. Boys and men just want to have fun. They don't want to be tied down!

After all, you didn't ask him if it was okay for you to get pregnant. After all, it was your responsibility (not his) to use some sort of birth control protection. After all, you cannot expect the condom to stay on throughout the whole time you're having sexual intercourse with him. After all, it's your fault that you got pregnant. After all, it's your responsibility to get rid of the kid because he's not obligated, he didn't plan on it, nobody asked him prior to the act, and he feels no need to help you. After all, it's not his problem; it's your problem, and yours alone. After all, you are the one carrying the problem, not him. After all, he needs his money to maintain his car(s) with those twenty-inch chrome rims, etc., so he can catch other women. After all, he was not even thinking about you the same way you were thinking about him, and he certainly was not thinking about a possible future with you. After all, he was thinking about obtaining his own sexual satisfaction at that moment, and that moment only.

He now wants a DNA test conducted to determine whether or not the baby is really his. Since he's now facing a somewhat permanent connection with you financially and otherwise because of the situation, his view of you has changed dramatically. He now sees you as the enemy, you are now promiscuous in his eyes, and you tried to trap him. He's definitely not happy about being forced into something he didn't ask for. Or, did he ask for it?

It can be a horrible time for you after you have given all of yourself to a guy only to learn he really wasn't serious about you when he seduced you into having sex with him. He was just using you, although he'd never admit it. You now see another side of him – his ugly, selfish, heartless, and mean side. He may even accuse you of sleeping around with other guys, or call you all sorts of demeaning names to your face. His parents may even threaten you. Get it?!

Cora & Darlene

While growing up, I had two friends named Cora and Darlene who I met in the second grade. They were my friends in spite of me having the nicknames Jailbird Kid and Welfare Rat. True friends! We went through elementary, junior high, and senior high school together. We stuck together like glue. Both Cora and Darlene helped me through my hard times growing up at home with my family. I loved them like they were my own sisters.

After graduation from high school, I moved to a different town to go to college, and I rented a room from a lady who lived a few blocks away from the school. Darlene continued to live at home, and she got a job as a telephone operator for the local phone company. Cora also remained at home, and she went to Nursing School.

I don't know exactly when, but Cora decided to sleep with a guy who was part of the "in-crowd" in high school. His name was Billy. Billy graduated from high school a year before us. She had a crush on him all through high school, but he never really noticed her. He thought she was kind of cute when he finally did see her. He took her on a few dates that included a few house parties and fast food joints. He never took her out to restaurants or to any movies. Cora never questioned or suggested any other places to go while on dates with him; she was just happy to be with him. He didn't feel the same about Cora as she felt about him.

Why Cora decided to give her most precious and most valuable gift to Billy was beyond Darlene and me. Anyway, Cora ended up pregnant at the beginning of summer.

I didn't see Cora too often after we graduated from high school because I no longer lived in the area. When I did visit with Cora and Darlene a few times during the summer months, Cora acted a bit strange. Darlene finally asked me if I noticed anything different about Cora. I told her I did, but I couldn't quite put my finger on what it was that was different about her. All I noticed was that she was more quiet than usual in our friendship. It was then that Darlene informed me Cora was three months pregnant. Cora was such a slim girl. I was surprised I didn't notice the pregnancy. Darlene asked me if I thought it strange that Cora was wearing long, bulky, mohair sweaters in the middle of August where the temperatures were soaring well over 100 degrees almost daily. When it dawned on me, I was stunned. I didn't know why I had not noticed. I just saw Cora. I was not such a quick thinker about things back then. I was just glad to see both my friends, and I never really cared about what they wore.

One weekend, Cora came to Darlene's house while I was visiting. Cora was upset and told us that she told her mom she was pregnant because her mom was suspicious because she was acting so strange and wearing those big, bulky, mohair sweaters in the middle of a heat wave. Cora's mom was very upset, but told Cora she would have to tell her father. Her mother was not going to give the bad news to her husband about their daughter. Cora was afraid to tell her dad because she was his favorite child of all his children, and it would break his heart.

Darlene and I didn't know what to do. We were scared for Cora, too. We all talked about it for a long time. We decided that if Cora's dad threw her out the house, we would get an apartment together, pool our money from our jobs, and all three of us would raise and support Cora's baby. We were convinced our plan would work. Cora was relieved but still afraid to tell her dad. Cora eventually told him and, needless to say, he was outraged.

A couple of weeks later, I saw Cora and we walked to the park to talk. I asked her how she was doing. She told me that her dad blew up about her pregnancy. He was extremely upset and demanded that she have Billy come to see him. Cora said that she tried to talk to Billy, but he wouldn't have anything to do with her. He denied getting her pregnant, accused her of sleeping around with other guys, called her everything but a child of God, and even threatened her if she came near him again. Cora was devastated. By this time, Darlene met us at the park and joined in the conversation. Cora told Darlene what happened with her dad. Darlene suggested that we all go together to Billy's house to inform his parents. We agreed to go to his home the following Sunday afternoon.

When Sunday afternoon came, Darlene was nowhere to be found, so Cora and I went to Billy's home. We went up the steps and onto the porch, and Cora rang the doorbell. I stood by her side. Billy's mom answered the door abruptly and harshly asked us what we wanted. Cora told her that she was trying to speak to Billy, but he wouldn't have anything to do with her. Billy's mom asked Cora why Billy would not speak to her, and that's when Cora informed her that she was four months pregnant with Billy's baby. Billy's mom became incensed. She called Cora a liar and a few other choice names. She even called me some of those names. She yelled and demanded that we get off her property or she was going to call the Police. She then slammed the door in our faces.

Cora and I walked home with tears streaming down our faces. We were silent all the way to Cora's home. That evening, Cora informed her father what happened at Billy's parents' home, and he told her he would handle it.

A few months later, Cora delivered a beautiful baby boy, and she named him Wesley. I received the call about the baby's delivery that afternoon, and I went to see Cora and Wesley at the hospital when I got off work. While I was at the nursery admiring Wesley, all of a sudden Billy showed up with his friends pointing Wesley out as his child, saying, "There's my son!"

As the years went by, Cora lived in her parent's home with Wesley while she worked and continued her education to be a Licensed Vocational Nurse (LVN). She later got her own apartment for herself and Wesley. Cora raised Wesley on her own with the help of her parents. She later became a Registered Nurse (RN). Wesley grew up to be a fine young man, and everybody loved him. Wesley looked just like Billy.

Billy never provided any financial support to Wesley while he was growing up. Billy never married. He never accomplished anything worthwhile, except for Wesley, who he disowned. Wesley later died in his early twenties from an accident. Billy's last name was not carried on in life through his son.

This is a mild case of Baby/Daddy/Mama Drama. I've heard worse, but I knew about this situation first-hand.

The Court System

If you get pregnant and have a child out of wedlock (unmarried), if your parents will not finance the welfare of your child, and if your baby's daddy refuses to help in the financial well-being of the child, you will be entering the world of the Family Court system. The Department of Social Services and the District Attorney's Office will assist you in the court system. You will file papers with the court to obtain child support from the father of your child. You will have to provide a valid address for the child's father so that the court can serve him with an order to appear in court. You may have to prove the paternity of the father of your child because some men will not own up to being the father.

If the father cannot be served due to his ducking and dodging, the District Attorney's Office will also assist the court by tracking him down through his driver's license and social security number, then garnishing his wages where he works, and authorizing withholding of any income tax refund money to pay child support for the welfare of the child. If the father is still uncooperative, the District Attorney's Office will have his driver's license revoked until arrangements are made for payment of the child support. At the very worst, the father can be jailed. The laws concerning child support have come a long way.

Welfare System

If you have never been on welfare (i.e., receive federal government financial assistance), the process is very invading. You will have to reveal a lot of your personal business to the social worker. She leaves no stone unturned. She needs to know if you have an income aside from the financial assistance that will be provided you through Social Services. She will need to know who is living with you and if they are providing you and your baby any financial assistance. If you receive additional income in addition to what you're receiving from welfare for the support of you and your child, it may be deducted from what you receive from Welfare. I don't believe you can have a brand new Jaguar while receiving government financial assistance. The taxpayers would not like that.

Now, thank God the United States of America has financial assistance for those who are in need. The welfare system is temporary; it's not a permanent solution. Its purpose is to sustain you and your child until you're able to find a permanent job to support yourself and your family.

Married Men

Being involved with a married man is totally a LOSE/LOSE situation no matter how you look at it. You lose because it's a relationship that won't go anywhere; it has no future. You lose because you make yourself available to someone who will only see you when he has a little free time that he doesn't have to account for. You lose your moral compass and your dignity, and you spend your time in regret. You lose your expectation because there is absolutely nothing to expect from a married man. It is what it is, and he's comfortable with that. He can only share whatever time he can steal away from his wife, family, and job to fool around with you. (The operative words here are "fool around.")

Mr. Right could be coming around the corner to meet you, but he then sees you fooling around with 'Mr. Married Man' and he walks away. You just missed your chance of total happiness in life.

The married man is not interested in making a major change in his life, especially to be with you. He has too much to lose if he gets caught with you or if he leaves his wife and family for you. He's got way too much invested in his marriage, in his children, and in his money. He wants to keep his total lifestyle – the lifestyle that his wife helped him build. He wants to keep the respect of his family members and his associates on the job. He doesn't want to start a new household and pay double (bills, spousal and child support, half of his retirement and other benefits, plus the bills he creates with and for you). He certainly doesn't want any kids by you, and he doesn't want to bring home a sexual disease as a result of cheating with you or with other women. Oh, do you think he will just cheat on his wife with you, alone? Really? If he's cheating on his wife with you, you're not the first, and he will cheat on you. He may very well be cheating on his wife and you at the same time.

The married man is already accountable to one woman; why in the world would he want to be accountable to you, too?

Married men who cheat on their families just want to have fun on the side, a little excitement and pleasure, and a little boost to their egos letting them know they still have the charm and the prowess to conquer. They may be unhappy for the moment at home, but not unhappy enough to walk out of their relationships with their wives, which they know would cost them an arm and a leg. They may be feeling unfulfilled on the job and can't seem to make forward progress, so they look for something to stimulate them or for someone else to get them over the hump. Or, they may feel they're getting old (and they are), so if they play around with you, they will feel young again. But be not mistaken, it's all about them, not you, and it's all temporary. It's a fling, a mid-life crisis, or just a naughty little fun thing to married men. Married men have no remorse about the "other woman."

Sure, the married man will spend a little money on you, buy you nice things, take you out to dinner at restaurants in remote places on the other side of town, take you away for a weekend or two and tell his wife that he had to go on a business trip. He will put most of his expenses on that special credit card that his wife doesn't know about, and call you on a cell-phone that his wife or her attorney can't trace. Yep, he will cover his tracks.

Some married men have the audacity to think they own you and own all of your time. When they call or when they come over to your home, unannounced, you are to be there, and be happy and grateful to see them. They believe they have some sort of power over you because you have succumbed to their pursuit of you. By the same token, they expect you to be totally considerate and understanding of all their limitations in their relationship with you.

If you have a major financial problem such as needing extra money from him to pay a delinquent bill, or to pay for a major car repair, or to purchase a new car because your car is no longer reliable and costs too much to repair, the married man might not be there for you.

When you get sick and need care, the married man will not attend to you; he must care and attend to own his family.

When the holidays come around such as Valentines Day, your birthday, or Christmas, you will be alone because he will be celebrating with his family. When you want to go on vacation with the married man to some romantic place, he will not be with you because he can't take that type of time away from his family to be with you.

You finally realize clearly that your problems are yours to bear by yourself, they are not his problems to deal with, and he will not be able to help you even if he wanted to. He may sympathize, but he will not take care of your needs. Need I say more?

Is this the kind of life you want? Is this the type of relationship you want? What benefit can you possibly get out of a relationship with a married man that would justify being in it? Is it worth the time you spend that you can't get back? Don't you think you're worth more than spending your time 'waiting' for the married man to call you to set up a secret rendezvous subject to cancellation at any time? Is he worth you risking your health because of his sexual promiscuity?

The married man is not a bad person in general, he's just GREEDY!!!!!!!!!!!!!

God tells the married man directly to stay with his wife. *Proverbs 5:15-23* states: *"Drink water from your own cistern, and running water from your own well. Should your fountains be dispersed abroad (to another woman or women), streams of water in the street? Let them be only your own, and not for strangers with you. Let your fountain be blessed, and rejoice with the wife of your youth. As a loving deer (husband) and a graceful doe (wife), let her breasts satisfy you at all times, and always be enraptured with her love. For why should you, my son, be enraptured by an immoral woman (the other woman who he's not married to), and be embraced in the arms of a seductress? For the ways of man are before the eyes of the Lord, and He (the Lord) ponders all his (the husband's) paths. His own iniquities entrap the wicked man (unfaithful husband), and he is caught in the cords of his sin. He shall die for lack of instruction. And in the greatness of his folly he shall go astray."*

Chapter *5:15-23* in the *Amplified Bible* puts it this way: *"Drink water out of your own cistern [of a pure marriage relationship], and fresh running waters out of your own well. Should your offspring be dispersed abroad as water brooks in the streets? [Confine yourself to your own wife] let your children be for you alone, and not the children of strangers with you. Let your fountain [of human life] be blessed [with the rewards of fidelity], and rejoice in the wife of your youth. Let her be as the loving hind and pleasant doe [tender, gentle, attractive], let her bosom satisfy you at all times, and always be transported with delight in her love. Why should you, my son, be infatuated with a loose woman, embrace the bosom of an outsider, and go astray? For the ways of man are directly before the eyes of the Lord, and He [Who would have us live soberly, chastely, and godly] carefully weigh all man's goings. His own iniquities shall ensnare the wicked man, and he shall be held with the cords of his sin. He will die for lack of discipline and instruction, and in the greatness of his folly he will go astray and be lost."*

As you can see in the scriptures concerning a married man's fate for his disobedience concerning his marriage to his wife and family,

God is not pleased. Just think what consequences you will face for being "the other woman?" As it is, these scriptures call you a "seductress" and an "immoral woman", in spite of whether he pursued you or you pursued him.

Do the benefits of having a sexual relationship with a married man outweigh the consequences? What can a married man do for you on a permanent basis? What can you do for a married man on a permanent basis? Is he worth you going to hell for? You probably know of other women who have been involved with married men, and their unfortunate bitter results. The consequences are always the same, and they will be the same for you, too. God does not approve or accept any adulterous relationship outside of marriage. You will also clearly lose out on meeting "Mr. Right" who God had specifically designed just for you.

Mothers

Parents are the child's first introduction to God, and they represent God in their children's lives. If children grow up trusting and believing their parents, they will be more accepting of God in their lives. Mothers play a vital role in the lives of their children, especially in the lives of their daughters.

If you have a teenage daughter, establish a solid relationship with her early on. This includes love, trust, and friendship. If you don't, the outside influences on your teenager will override your influence. Your daughter doesn't care how much you know until she knows how much you care, so you must establish a trust with your daughter early.

We must listen to our daughters, and listen to what they're not saying, too (read between the lines). We can't discount what they say about situations. What they see and hear about is very real to them; whether it concerns their friends, someone they know, what they see in school or in the street, or what they see through the various media. They do not see all sides of situations, and they certainly do not associate the consequences that will come from those situations. We must fill in the blanks of what they don't know about or what they can't see for themselves.

Next to the Word of God, mothers must be the "No. 1" influence in their daughters' lives on every subject, but especially on the subject of sex. As mothers, we cannot afford to assume our daughters will learn the right information about sex and the consequences for being sexually promiscuous by just telling them not to have sex before marriage or by allowing others (be it school health classes, girlfriends, boyfriends, magazines, television, etc.) to tell them about sex because we are too busy, too embarrassed, or too shy to discuss the subject. We just can't afford to allow others to take our place with our daughters in explaining what sex is all about, and their responsibility and accountability.

We can tell our daughters about sex, but what does it mean to them? Do our daughters know that they are in control of their own bodies? Do our daughters know they have power and control of the reproduction equipment that God has installed in their bodies? Do our daughters know how sex fits into their lives as teenagers and as adults? Do our daughters know when it is appropriate and when isn't it appropriate to have sex? What value should our daughters place on sex in line with their plans for their futures?

We've got to help our daughters get to the right answers for these questions. We've got to go into detail and explain to them what sex is and what it's not, what love is and what it's not. We've got to show our daughters in the Bible what God says about sex. We've got to explain to our daughters how vulnerable their bodies can be to sexual diseases and to pregnancy. We've got to get our daughters to understand how powerful, how detrimental, and how life-altering their decisions can be regarding sex. And, we've got to explain to our daughters about the bad consequences of being sexually active outside of marriage.

There is an extremely strong influence from the commercial media such as television, teen magazines, movies, music, etc., that's constantly encouraging and persuading teens to be sexually promiscuous. A teenage girl's peer group is another competing influence in the area of sexual promiscuity.

Boundaries should already be established where your daughter knows right from wrong, and she trusts your judgment. She needs to know that you care about her, that you respect her, and you will always tell her the truth – **even about the mistakes you made in your life**. She needs to know that you're human, too, and not perfect. Then your daughter will appreciate you being her mom first, and then being her friend and mentor. She will then be open to you about everything. She will love and respect you more because you were honest about yourself.

When we look at our daughters physically developing into women, we cannot afford to assume that just because they are blossoming physically, they are at the same time maturing into women emotionally, mentally, and intellectually. Yes, boys and men will consider them very attractive and will want to interact with them as women, but this is where most of our teenage girls get into trouble. It takes more than good looks to be a woman. There needs to be correct insight, wisdom, discernment, guidance, understanding, and good judgment. The young teenage girl needs to know that because her body has developed, she's now responsible and accountable for how she carries herself and, if she doesn't carry herself in the right manner for her own good, there will be consequences to pay. A mother can help her feel comfortable with her new looks, and guide her in how to deal with new challenges as a result of her physical development.

A mother should never use her past mistakes or past experiences against her daughter. Your daughter was not around when you were young, and she had nothing to do with the choices you made that resulted in your negative consequences. She is not you. Stop blaming your daughter because you see something in her that reminds you of you when you were her age, or reminds you of what you did that led to bad consequences in your life.

Stop reminding your daughter of her past mistakes every time she does something to annoy or offend you. She is accountable to God, not you, and if God can and has forgiven her, you should, too. God does not hold grudges, He does not bring up past sins every time we sin or make a wrong decision. *Isaiah 43:25* states: *"I, even I, am He who blots out your transgressions for My own sake."* God is a loving and forgiving God. We, as mothers, need to emulate Him.

Have hope in your daughter. Give her the right information she needs to avoid the negative consequences that you went through. Based on your relationship with your daughter, she will more than likely make the right decision when situations present themselves.

When your daughter knows you are supportive of her, she will be more apt to make the right decisions. She will even consult with you before she makes a decision. She will appreciate you being her mom and not her judge and prosecutor. You need to win this battle with your daughter each and every day.

Your daughter needs to not only know you're her mother who is responsible and accountable for what you teach her and how you raise her, but because you were once a young girl and teenager, too, you know how she feels. She needs to know that you felt then what she feels now, that you hurt when she hurts, and that you rejoice with her when she deals with situations the right way – God's way. When she falls, she needs to know you will console her, lift her up, and not condemn and discard her. She needs to know that although you don't like what she did, you will tell her why you don't like it, but you also will let her know that what she did has nothing to do with the love you have for her.

She needs to know that you love her unconditionally.

Remind your daughter you have the same physical body equipment and emotions that she has. Remind her that you, too, have the same hormones racing through you that can be activated by a sweet-talking, good-looking guy, and that you have to control yourself and think about your choices and their consequences, too.

You daughter needs to be able to discern right from wrong, on the basis of her home-life foundation that you have established.

WE NEED TO OPEN OUR MOUTHS AND SPEAK to our daughters. We need to be strong and positive examples to our daughters. If our walk doesn't match our talk, we will confuse our daughters and lose them to the world. I can't tell you the number of second, third, and fourth generations of mothers, daughters, and granddaughters who have babies out of wedlock and suffer the same consequences as a result. If those mothers only took the time to communicate their love and their honesty to their daughters, and not condemn, criticize or ignore their daughters, future outcomes may have been a lot different. But, it's still not too late.

Even with good teaching and being good examples, our daughters can still make mistakes. Everyone is born with his or her own free will. Your free will is not your daughter's free will. Unbeknownst to you, at some point in your daughter's life, she will test her foundation and her boundaries with her will and her desires. She will make mistakes in contradiction to what you taught her. But, forgiveness is key. Forgive your daughter so God can work things out for you both. He will heal your hearts and work things out in amazing ways if you let Him. *Romans 8:28* states: *"And we know that all things work together for good to those who love God, to those who are the called according to His purpose."*

It may not have been what you wanted for your daughter, it hurts, and it wasn't what she or you expected, but the error has been made and you both must go forward. Now is not the time to concentrate on the mistake; it's time to give the situation over to God and trust Him with it. He will work it out for her good, for your peace, and for His glory. Remember, your daughter did not sin against you; she sinned against herself and against God. God offers forgiveness to her for her sins, and you must do the same. She may have disobeyed and disappointed you, but the sin belongs to her, and she will bear the consequences of her own sins. God uses **"all"** circumstances, good and bad, to accomplish His purpose in all of our lives. By your forgiveness and support, you will strengthen your daughter, your relationship with her, and God will bless you both.

If you do not have a good relationship with your daughter, where she doesn't feel comfortable coming to you to discuss everything and anything (especially sex), she will definitely find someone she can trust and confide in, and you will lose your daughter to that influence.

When your daughter makes a wrong choice and later realizes through the ensuing consequences that she's made a mistake, she may or may not come to you, depending on the type of relationship you have with her. If she doesn't come to you, she will be relying on someone else she trusts, someone else who has a stronger influence on her, someone else who she believes can and will help her through her crisis. This may be good or bad, depending on the one she goes to. Pray for your daughter and the person she's confiding in. Pray that the person is giving her Godly advice.

If your daughter does come to you, she may unwillingly do so. She may realize that her friends, or the ones she thought so highly of, were not sufficient enough to help her out of the mess she created for herself. This is not the time for you to condemn her, humiliate her, or disown her. This is an **"opportunity"** for you to turn an already negative situation into a positive one, and to turn a "not-so-good" relationship into a better one.

The Lord will forgive your daughter as He has forgiven you, so you have no right to persecute her. Yes, you had high hopes for your child, as we all do for our children, but we did not give birth to robots. We gave birth to people who were born with their own free will and their own frailties. Although we do our best to raise our children the right way, and be the best examples we can be before them, they make their own decisions and they must bear the consequences as a result of those decisions.

This is the time for you to pray to God for wisdom and guidance in dealing with your daughter and her situation, and to step out in faith to help her deal with her consequences. Going through the consequences with your support will help her to make better choices within the consequences. Yes, she will still have to make choices as she goes through the consequences. The choices she makes in the midst of her consequences will either exacerbate or ease the pain of her consequences. With you by her side, not being judgmental or angry, she will be better able to handle whatever consequence comes from her wrong decision. She will know you love and care for her, and she will be more apt to come to you prior to making any future decisions that will possibly create bad consequences that will harm her.

Now, don't help her through the consequences to the point you become an "enabler." Don't become such a protector to the point she doesn't learn her lesson. She needs to learn that lesson, and she will, if you don't interfere to the extent you become a cheerleader instead of a mom. If you help her too much, she may not learn the lesson and end up repeating her original mistake. Allow her to feel the heat of her consequences behind her wrong choice, but be there to guide her through.

For example, if she gets pregnant while still a minor, help her through her crisis as a loving mother. Be proactive with the boy's parents in ensuring that your daughter receives the best of care – financially and otherwise, even if it means going to the District Attorney's office to press charges against the boy if he and his family do not cooperate with you. Also, in being proactive with the boy's parents, see the situation from the boy's parents' side and do all you can to work with them and not against them. The boy's parents didn't have a say in the situation just like you didn't have a say. Both you and your husband should sit down with the boy's parents to come to an understanding of how you both will deal with the situation. If you're a single parent, still sit down with the boy's parents and work out a plan of action. You must be proactive.

Both sets of parents should come together as a unified front in dealing with both your daughter and the boy who got her pregnant, letting them know their responsibility toward the child they created. Also let them know what you, as parents, will do and what you won't do. After all, they've done a very adult thing, so you must help them be responsible and accountable as adults.

When the child is born, don't start raising the baby as if you're his or her mom. For example, when you hear the baby cry in the middle of the night, this is not the time for you to get up and take care of the baby's needs; it's your daughter's time. If she doesn't get up to go tend to her baby, wake your daughter up and tell her to go take care of her child. You've already paid your dues in this area. Remember that this is part of her consequences, not yours. This includes no babysitting on your part, except every once in a while when you want to. If your daughter asks you to baby-sit, she is to pay you. Your daughter has to learn and feel the full responsibility of nursing, bathing, and caring for her baby; it is her responsibility, as well as the boy's. The boy needs to share in the responsibility of caring for his child, too. Your daughter's and the boy's time schedules need to equally, fairly, and adequately adjust to accommodate the baby. The welfare of the baby is their No. 1 priority. Your daughter's and the boy's free time is no longer their own; any free time belongs to the baby. You are to teach and guide her and the boy in raising and caring for their child.

Lift your daughter, her significant other, his parents, your husband, and yourself up in prayer. Involve your daughter, the boy, his parents and your husband in joint prayers, so you'll all be in agreement when coming to God about this situation. The Lord says to cast your cares upon Him for He cares for you and so He can care for you. *1 Peter 5:6-7* states: *"Therefore, humble yourselves under the mighty hand of God, that he may exalt you in due time, casting all your care upon Him for He cares for you."* Allow Him to care for you, for your daughter, and for your extended family in this crisis. Be willing to listen to Him for understanding and guidance. By helping your daughter go through her crisis in this manner, you are giving her guidance, courage, and strength to handle it and to be victorious in anything that life throws at her.

However, if you choose to go in the other direction, you will more than likely lose your daughter to the world, and that can be disastrous.

1 John 4:7 states: *"Beloved, let us love one another, for love is of God; and everyone who loves is born of God and knows God.*

He who does not love does not know God, for God is love." He has given us the power of love and the power to love. He has given us the power through love to forgive our children, and to overcome all obstacles with our children. We must walk in love with one another throughout all circumstances. In *John 3:16*, God showed His love toward us all through His Son Jesus Christ, who made the ultimate sacrifice for our sins. *John 3:16* states: *"For God so loved the world that He gave His only begotten Son, that whoever believes in Him should not perish but have everlasting life."*

In *1 Corinthians 13:1-8*, the Apostle Paul states: *"Though I speak with the tongues of men and of angels, but have not love, I have become a sounding brass or a clanging cymbal. And though I have the gift of prophecy, and understand all mysteries and all knowledge, and though I have all faith so that I could remove mountains, but have not love, I am nothing. And though I bestow all my goods to feed the poor, and though I give my body to be burned, but have not love, it profits me nothing. Love suffers long and is kind; love does not envy; love does not parade itself; is not puffed up; does not behave rudely; does not seek its own; is not provoked; thinks no evil; does not rejoice in iniquity, but rejoices in the truth; bears all things; believes all things; hopes all things; and endures all things. Love never fails."* This applies to you and how you treat your daughter in the midst of her storm. No, you didn't want her to get pregnant, but it's a done deal and everyone involved must deal with it trusting that God will turn this situation around for good, as stated in *Romans 8:28*: *"And we know that all things work together for good to those who love God, to those who are the called according to His purpose."*

Even though a mistake was made, God has a purpose for the child, for your daughter, and for that young boy who got your daughter pregnant. He even has a purpose for you in this situation. God knows what He's doing.

Don't be selfish by being embarrassed and more concerned about what your friends, neighbors, colleagues, church members, or society thinks and says about what your daughter has done. You don't know the skeletons in their closets, in their glass houses, and they certainly have no right to point out your frailties. Mistakes are made in the best of homes, in some of the richest of families, and in some of the families of the highest held public offices on the face of the earth. You just don't hear about it. Money covers up a multitude of sin, but only for a little while.

This situation may not have been part of your plan, or part of your daughter's plan, but the child (who your daughter is pregnant with) is definitely part of God's plan. The child is not a mistake. In *Jeremiah 29:11*, the Lord says: *"For I know the thoughts that I think toward you, says the Lord, thoughts of peace and not of evil, to give you a future and a hope."* God knows exactly what He's doing. God is not a liar. *Numbers 23:19* states: *"God is not a man, that He should lie, nor a son of man, that He should repent. Has He said, and will He not do? Or has He spoken, and will He not make it good?"* In essence, God says what He means and He means what He says. If He said it, it will come to pass.

As parents, we all want and expect so much of our children that we sometimes lose sight of the fact that they belong to God, and we only have them for a very short period of time. He has a specific purpose for them. They have their own wills and their own minds; they are not like us and they don't have the same desires and needs that we do. We can't hold onto them too tightly. If we do, we'll either smother them and they will not grow into the people God wants them to grow into, or we will give them too much latitude and they become something that we really don't like. It's a fine line in the relationship between parents and children.

As mothers, we must trust God through everything, especially concerning our children. Our children will make mistakes, but they and you will get through them, recover, and grow. As moms, we are to stand in prayer for our children, lifting them up to the Lord. Having done all, we continue to stand to see God turn things around for good for our children, no matter what. *Romans 8:28* states: *"And we know that all things work together for good to those who love God, to those who are the called according to His purpose."* So, we are to trust God, work our faith in Him by continually thanking Him for working in our children's lives and in ours. We will overcome all adversities. *Romans 8:37* states: *"Yet in all these things we are more than conquerors through Him who loved us."*

The Precious, Amazing And Exciting Power Given Only To Women

In the human race, women are the **only** ones who have reproductive organs/equipment to take man's seed and make a baby out of it. Women have two ovaries, two fallopian tubes, a uterus, and a vagina – functioning together to create another human, a baby. No man on the face of the earth has this equipment, nor can he create another human being with the equipment he has been endowed with by God. The only thing a man can produce is the sperm that mates with the egg, which is produced in the ovaries of the woman, and that begins the reproductive process.

The reproductive organs/equipment God has given to women has also given women great responsibility, power, and authority in the area of sex. For example:

(1) Women are the only ones who can **choose** to have sex, not men. Men want sex all the time, and they even beg for it, but women are the ones who actually make the final choice.

(2) Women are the only ones who can **choose** to use some sort of birth control method so they will not get pregnant because they **choose** to have sex, not men. Men do not even believe it's their responsibility to use birth control. Most men are insulted if women ask them to wear a condom. Men don't generally think about birth control. In their view, it's the women's responsibility, not theirs. Men know they can't get pregnant, so it's not their problem. They believe they should bear no responsibility or accountability on their part. Men just want to have sex.

(3) Women are the only ones who can **choose** to have abortions, not men. It's not an easy decision for women whose current plans do not make accommodations for a baby. Women choose to have an abortion for many reasons, but the most common reason is that they realize the man has abandoned them. They feel trapped. They feel they are forced into making such a decision. Although a man who doesn't want to have a child with the woman may argue, insist, and pay for an abortion, but the final decision rests solely with the woman.

(4) Women are the only ones who can **choose** not to do their homework prior to sleeping with a man. Homework means to get the man's health checked out, first, to see if he's carrying any kind of STD. A man will never tell a woman he has an STD; it doesn't seem to be a part of his psyche. This makes it the woman's responsibility.

(5) Women are the only ones who can **choose** to allow men to woo and seduce them into having sex outside of marriage. Although the woman knows better, she uses every excuse to explain why she made the choice to allow herself to be seduced by the temptation of having sex with the man. The excuses most women use are (a) he took advantage of me while I was drunk; (b) he caught me at a vulnerable time in my life; (c) I was weak that day; (d) I've been through so much that I just needed someone to hold me; and on it goes.

In all honesty, a woman makes the **choice** to have sex. Why? Because most of the time, the woman doesn't think things through far enough before allowing the man to overcome her, and she ends up having sex with him. She doesn't control herself enough not to allow it to happen. She doesn't say "NO" loud enough or forceful enough to make him stop pursuing her sexually. She encourages the man because she, herself, wants to have sex with him, excluding any common sense she has. She just takes the chance on having sex with him, and at the same time hoping everything will turn out okay. But as we all know, it doesn't always turn out okay. Gambling is a game of chance and it has a price, and sex outside of marriage is like gambling. When we lose, we must pay up.

It's a whole different and unfortunate situation when a woman is raped by a man, and that has its own set of consequences. I'm not talking about that type of situation.

True, we make every excuse in the book for having sex the wrong way – out of God's order, but we don't want to face the consequences nor pay the consequences. Men, in general, don't want to face the consequences either; they just want to have fun. However, since women are the only ones who have the **"equipment"** that can produce a child, God has also given women the responsibility, authority, accountability, and the power to control their own bodies. *Romans 12:1* states: *"I beseech you therefore, brethren, by the mercies of God, that you present your bodies a living sacrifice, holy, acceptable to God, which is your reasonable service." 1 Thessalonians 4:3-5* states: *"For this is the will of God, your sanctification; that you should abstain from sexual immorality; that each of you should know how to possess his [her] own vessel [body] in sanctification and honor, not in passion of lust, like the Gentiles (who do not know God." James 1:14-16* states: *"But each one [person] is tempted when he [she] is drawn away by his [her] own desires and enticed. Then, when desire has* *conceived, it gives birth to sin; and sin when it is full-grown brings forth death. Do not be deceived, my brethren."*

Let's face it. Women are the bosses, chief executive officers, directors, managers, and supervisors of their own physical bodies concerning sex. Real bosses bear the responsibility for their actions. Since we bear the responsibility, have the authority, and we have the power to be the boss over sexual intercourse due to the reproductive organs/equipment God has blessed us with, we are the ones who decide whether to have sex or not. Since we control this power, we bear the consequences when we make the wrong decisions regarding this power. The consequences can go nine months and beyond. A man can say anything to get a woman into the bed, but the final choice and decision rest solely with the woman.

Although men bear responsibility for sexual intercourse outside of marriage because they are equipped with the mechanism to produce sperm, the majority of men do not take their responsibility seriously and, thus, women end up bearing the burden.

Instead of accepting the consequences that come with having sex outside of marriage, most women blame men for either getting them pregnant, giving them an STD, or for causing the physical problems sometimes encountered after having sex. These women want men to financially support the offspring they helped produce outside of the marriage, but these women didn't ask the men if they wanted to have a baby prior to engaging in sex. These women didn't ask the men for financial support for the baby or for expenses related to an STD prior to engaging in sex. Most men who are sexually promiscuous only want sex – not marriage, not responsibility (financial or otherwise), and definitely no accountability. Both sexually promiscuous men and women will bear the consequences for their actions.

Every consequence a woman bears because of having sex out of wedlock could have been avoided by the use of one little word – the word **"NO."** There would be absolutely no STDs, no abortions, no need for the variety of birth control methods currently on the market, and no need for governmental agencies providing financial support and medical care to pregnant teens and unwed mothers. There would be no need for the District Attorney's Office to seek financial support from the men who impregnated these women. There would be no need for DNA testing, no lawsuits for child support, and no lawsuits against men who gave women STDs, etc.

An honorable woman would carry herself honorably, and she would demand to be treated honorably. She would be married before engaging in sexual activity. An honorable woman would be offended at any approach by a man wanting to have sex with her outside of the realm of marriage. An honorable man would not even approach an honorable woman with intentions less than that of marriage. An honorable man would honor the honorable woman's wishes.

There has been a breakdown in our knowledge of God's word as it applies to us, in our responsibility and accountability with regard to our reproductive equipment, in how we value ourselves, and in our morals.

In Summary

As a teenage girl, young woman or older woman, you have been provided with a few examples of the consequences you will be dealing with if you do not think before you involve yourself in sexual promiscuity with men. You are the one who makes the choice. The man you may think is good enough to sleep with may turn out not to be good enough to support his own child that you gave birth to. Or, he may turn out not to be honorable enough to tell you the truth about his sexual health that you are now suffering the consequences from. Or he may turn out to be married and have no intention of leaving his wife and his family for you. A relationship with a married man is a total waste.

Yes, you, yourself, may think that just one time with a person in a sexual encounter will have no effect. But, what's done in the dark will soon come to the light. It only takes one time!

You mothers who are too busy to care enough about your daughters, who are enamored with how cute your daughters look in skimpy and provocative clothing, who may be too embarrassed to speak about your own sinful past mistakes and poor judgments, or who do not take the time to educate your daughters in how to operate successfully as a woman in this highly sexualized society, more than likely you will see your daughters repeat the same mistakes you may have made, if not worse. If you establish a good relationship with your daughters early on, tell them the truth about sex and its consequences, and establish a genuine trust relationship with your daughters, you will save many tears and years of regret in their futures and in yours.

We need to think more highly of ourselves. We need to think about the equipment God has blessed us with, and the responsibility, accountability, authority, and power that comes with it. We need to take responsibility for our own actions, and not blame everything on the man. We need to respect and take care of our own bodies; we only get one "earth suit" in this life. We need to realize that God has given us a purpose and a plan for our lives. We need to think about what kind of future we want that would be pleasing to God, and begin to work toward that end. We should also make sure that the man of our dreams fits into our lives the right way, not the wrong way. We are responsible and accountable for what God has blessed us with, for our choices, our decisions, and the ensuing consequences – good or bad.

If, what I have written will make you think of the possible consequences before you do the same dumb things that I and many others have done, experiencing the same devastating results, then it's worth it.

There is nothing new under the sun. The formula has not changed. *Ecclesiastes 1:9* states: *"That which has been is what will be, that which is done is what will be done, and there is nothing new under the sun."*

So, why reinvent a broken wheel?

Chapter 7

Don't Go There!

Chapter 7

Don't Go There!

Leave The Past In The Past

If you live in the past, you will never see the future. You don't have to wallow in the past, in the mistakes you made. Living in the past is a conscious choice. You can choose to live in the past and wallow in your sins, or you can choose to ask God for forgiveness, accept His Son Jesus as your Lord and Savior, and repent of your sins. To repent means to change your mind and go a different direction. Once you change your mind, your decisions and actions will follow.

Minister Donna Pickens, in one of her sermons, stated, "Don't let your past hold you hostage. Put your past under the blood of Jesus. Counter all of satan's negative messages (fiery darts) to your mind with the Word of God." If you will walk away from your past and trust God, He can bring you to a brighter future. But, if you don't let the past go, you will never be able to see and receive God's best for your future. *Isaiah 43:18-19* states: *"Do not remember the former things, nor consider the things of old. Behold, I will do a new thing, now it will spring forth; shall you not know it? I will even make a road in the wilderness and rivers in the desert."*

It's time for you to step out in your faith and look forward to your new future as a person forgiven and as a person of victory by your faith and your obedience to the Word of God. *Philippians 3:13-14* states: *"Brethren, I do not count myself to have apprehended; but one thing I do, forgetting those things which are behind and reaching forward to those things which are ahead, I press toward the goal for the prize of the upward call of God in Christ Jesus."* In *Joshua 1:7-9,* the Lord states: *"Only be strong and very courageous, that you may observe to do according to all the law which Moses My servant commanded you; do not turn from it to the right hand or to the left, that you may prosper wherever you go. This Book of the Law shall not depart from your mouth, but you shall meditate in it day and night, that you may observe to do according to all that is written in it. For then you will make your way prosperous and then you will have good success. Have I not commanded you? Be strong and of good courage; do not be afraid, nor be dismayed, for the Lord your God is with you wherever you go."* Based on what God has said, there is no need to remind yourself of where you've been, but look with good anticipation to where you're going – into a bright and better future. He says that He will make your way prosperous so you can have good success. God wants you to have courage and not be fearful because He is with you.

Dwelling on past mistakes will bring you down emotionally, mentally and physically. It takes a lot of energy to dwell on the past. We all have sinned, made mistakes, made wrong decisions, and were influenced by the wrong people. You're not the only one and you're not alone. In fact, that's why the Lord Jesus died on the cross. He died for all of our sins, including all of yours.

If you keep wallowing in your regret and sin, you are not trusting that Jesus sacrificed His life and died for your sins. You are putting Jesus back in the courtyard of Pontius Pilate where He was beaten (scourged) unmercifully, and then you're putting His beaten and bloodied body back on that cross at Golgotha. Jesus was beaten so badly where chunks of his skin and muscle tissue were gouged out and ripped away by each blow of the leather whip that had pieces of metal, rock and glass fastened to the loose straps attached to the whip. The scourging left Jesus unrecognizable as a human. Would you want Him to go through that type of death again?

But Jesus is not dead. He is risen, and He is seated at the right hand of the Father petitioning on your behalf and on my behalf. Jesus has forgiven you your sins already by the sacrifice He made for you over 2,000 years ago. He remembers your sins no more, so you must forget your sins, too, and move forward in His grace and in His love for you. *Isaiah 43:25* states: *"I, even I, am He who blots out your transgressions [sins] for My own sake; and I will not remember your sins."* In *Isaiah 44:22*, the Lord says: *"I have blotted out, like a thick cloud, your transgressions, and like a cloud, your sins. Return to Me for I have redeemed you."* So, accept what Jesus has done for you. He provided a way of salvation, a way to set you free from your sins, from the guilt, and from the shame. Accept Jesus as your Lord and Savior, and ask Him to forgive you for your sins. Then forgive yourself and be free!

Don't go back to your old ways. Don't be like the dog that returns to his own vomit or like the pig, which, after being washed clean, returns to wallow in the mud again. *2 Peter 2:21-23* states: *"For it would have been better for them not to have known the way of righteousness, than having known it, to turn from the holy commandment delivered to them. But it has happened to them according to the true proverb: 'A dog returns to his own vomit,' and, 'a sow, having washed, to her wallowing in the mire.'"* Why would you want to go back to your old ways, your old sins, after you have been forgiven? Your sins have hindered you from receiving the good things of God. *Jeremiah 5:25* states: *"Your iniquities have turned these things away, and your sins have withheld good from you."*

Things will be worse for you if you go back to your old ways. *2 Peter 3:17-18* states: *"You therefore, beloved, since you know this beforehand, beware lest you also fall from your own steadfastness, being led away with the error of the wicked; but grow in the grace and knowledge of our Lord and Savior Jesus Christ. To Him be the glory both now and forever. Amen."* The Amplified Bible states in *2*

Peter 3:17-18: "Let me warn you therefore, beloved, that knowing these things beforehand, you should be on your guard, lest you be carried away by the error of lawless and wicked [persons and] fall from your own [present] firm condition [your own steadfastness of mind]. But grow in grace [undeserved favor, spiritual strength] and recognition and knowledge and understanding of our Lord and Savior Jesus Christ [the Messiah]. To Him [be] glory [honor, majesty, and splendor] both now and to the day of eternity. Amen [so be it]!"

You already have first-hand knowledge of the consequences of bad choices you made in the past. Don't repeat them, especially after knowing God's word on the subject. God does not want you to backslide. *Galatians 4:9* states: *"But now after you have known God, or rather are known by God, how is it that you turn again to the weak and beggarly elements, to which you desire again to be in bondage?"* Sin is bondage. After you have been forgiven and have forgiven yourself, and have experienced a new freshness of life, don't go back. The sins you were involved in are not worth going back into, and for what? *Galatians 5:1* states: *"Stand fast therefore in the liberty by which Christ has made us free, and do not be entangled again with a yoke of bondage." Galatians 5:7-9* states: *"You ran well. Who hindered you from obeying the truth? This persuasion does not come from Him [God] who calls you. A little leaven leavens the whole lump."* Don't allow those, who you've sinned with in the past, to take you down that old road again. You know where that road leads. The formula is always the same. There are worse consequences for those who know better, who know God's word, and yet they go back to doing wrong. *Galatians 6:7-8* states: *"Do not be deceived, God is not mocked; for whatever a man [woman] sows, that he [she] will also reap. For he [she] who sows to his [her] flesh will of the flesh reap corruption, but he [she] who sows to the Spirit will of the Spirit reap everlasting life."* So, since you know better, do not backslide for the consequences are much greater than what you have already suffered.

Don't get stuck in a rut of discouragement, doubt, worry, unworthiness, disappointment, depression, or defeat. All of these things equate to the word "fear." God has not given you any of these negatives that all boil down to a spirit of fear. Fear encompasses doubt, unbelief, anxiety, stress, nervousness, anxiousness, depression and defeat. God has given you the power to change. He has given you encouraging love from above. He has given you a sound mind by giving you wisdom, discernment, guidance and understanding. *2 Timothy 1:7* states: *"For God hath not given us the spirit of fear; but of power, and of love, and of a sound mind."* God also states in *Isaiah 41:10*: *"Fear not, for I am with you. Be not dismayed [discouraged], for I am your God. I will strengthen you. Yes, I will help you. I will uphold you with My righteous right hand." Proverbs 3:5-6* states: *"Trust in the Lord with all your heart, and lean not on your own understanding. In all your ways acknowledge Him, and He shall direct your paths."* God will also give you strength and peace. *Psalm 29:11* states: *"The Lord will give strength to His people. The Lord will bless His people with peace."*

If you are confused and don't know where to turn, just be still and know that God does not create confusion. *1 Corinthians 14:33* states: *"For God is not the author of confusion, but of peace."* Confusion will cloud your mind to make you make even more bad decisions, which will affect your future negatively by the consequences of those decisions. You are responsible for what you allow your mind to think about. You have a choice either to allow the negative thoughts to take control or allow God's word to control your mind. When negative thoughts come into your mind and you know they are not of God because God is love, reject them immediately "in the name of Jesus." In accordance with ***Luke 10:19***, the Lord Jesus says: ***"Behold, I give you the authority to trample on serpents and scorpions, and over all the power of the enemy, and nothing shall by any means hurt you."*** This passage tells you how to reject satan and his fiery darts which attack your mind by using thoughts of your past sins and thoughts of doing wrong which he's trying to use against you. You are to reject those thoughts "in the name of Jesus." God has not only given you His word, but He has given you the power through His word.

Jesus tells us to cast down all those negative thoughts. *2 Corinthians 10:4-5* states: *"For the weapons of our warfare are not carnal but mighty in God for pulling down strongholds, casting down arguments and every high thing that exalts itself against the knowledge of God, bringing every thought into captivity to the obedience of Christ."* A stronghold is a fortified place; a place dominated by a certain group. In this case, the group would be of a satanic origin bringing up your past sins against you in your mind. The Amplified Bible states it this way: *"For the weapons of our warfare are not physical [weapons of flesh and blood], but they are mighty before God for the overthrow and destruction of strongholds, [inasmuch as we] refute arguments and theories and reasonings and every proud and lofty thing that sets itself up against the [true] knowledge of God; and we lead every thought and purpose away captive into the obedience of Christ [the Messiah, the Anointed One]."* This passage is a very good one to memorize and have in your heart.

Train your mind to think good, not bad. *Philippians 4:8* states: *"Finally, brethren, whatever things are true, whatever things are noble, whatever things are just, whatever things are pure, whatever things are lovely, whatever things are of good report, if there is any virtue and if there is anything praiseworthy – meditate on these things."* By meditating on these things, you won't have time to dwell in the past. *Romans 12:2* states: *"And do not be conformed to this world, but be transformed by the renewing of your mind, that you may prove what is that good and acceptable and perfect will of God."*

Also, don't allow yourself to be tempted to do anything that you know is wrong and may cause you to stumble, bringing more consequences and regrets to you in the long run. You have the power to resist and the ability to reject any temptation that comes your way. *1 Corinthians 10:13* states: *"No temptation has overtaken you except such as is common to man [woman], but God is faithful, who will not allow you to be tempted beyond what you are able, but with the temptation He will also make the way of escape that you may be able to bear it."* You're not the only one who is bombarded with temptations and suggestions to do wrong. These tactics are common to all men and women. You have not been singled out to be attacked. That's why we are to put on the whole armor of God to withstand in the evil day. We do not wrestle against humans. *Ephesians 6:10-12* states: *"Finally, my brethren, be strong in the Lord and in the power of His might. Put on the whole armor of God that you may be able to stand against the wiles of the devil. For we do not wrestle against flesh and blood, but against principalities, against powers, against the rulers of darkness of this age, against spiritual hosts of wickedness in the heavenly places."*

The Amplified Bible states it this way: *"In conclusion, be strong in the Lord [be empowered through your union with Him]; draw your strength from Him [that strength which His boundless might provides]. Put on God's whole armor [the armor of a heavy-armed soldier which God supplies], that you may be able to successfully stand up against [all] the strategies and the deceits of the devil. For we are not wrestling with flesh and blood [contending only with physical opponents], but against the despotisms (a system of government where the ruler has unlimited power), against the powers, against [the master spirits who are] the world rulers of this present darkness, against the spirit forces of wickedness in the heavenly [supernatural] sphere."*

God's word is very clear as to who you are fighting, and that's why you need to stand wearing His whole armor, as referenced in *Ephesians 6:13-18: "Therefore take up the whole armor of God, that you may be able to withstand in the evil day, and having done all, to stand. Stand therefore, having (1) girded your waist with **truth**, (2) having put on the breastplate of **righteousness**, and (3) having shod your feet with the preparation of the gospel of **peace**; above all, (4) taking the shield of **faith** with which you will be able to quench all the fiery darts of the wicked one, and (5) take the helmet of **salvation** and (6) the sword of the Spirit [Holy Spirit], which is the **word of God**; praying always with all prayer and supplication [to ask God humbly and earnestly] in the Spirit, being watchful to this end with all perseverance [urgency] and supplication for all the saints."* So, God has provided body armor for you, His soldier, to protect you and to ensure that you stand against the evil one, the one who is trying to steal from you, and the one who is trying to kill and destroy you.

All that satan can do is make suggestions for you to act on. Otherwise, his hands are completely tied. Without your help (by accepting his suggestions), he is inoperative. He has no power over you. Acting on a temptation or suggestion is what gets us all in trouble. But by obeying God's word and standing against all the fiery darts of the wicked one (satan), you will be triumphant in winning the battle of the mind, which is the real battlefield.

Remember, God is faithful. He's not only faithful, He is faithful to you. *1 Corinthians 1:9* states: *"God is faithful, by whom you were called into the fellowship of His son, Jesus Christ our Lord."* He is so faithful to you that He has provided the armor for you to wear to stand against the wicked one. (*Ephesians 6:13-18)* The armor fits all shapes and sizes, all colors, all genders, and all nationalities. He has also given you a sword, the sword of the Spirit – His Word, to use to fight against the wicked one. How faithful is that?!!!!!!

The Mind Is A Terrible Thing To Waste

You are a new creation in Christ Jesus. Therefore, you have the ability to change your mind. You must change your mind to match the **new you** that God has created. *2 Corinthians 5:17* states: *"Therefore if any man be in Christ, he is a **new creation; old things** have passed away; behold, **all things have become new**."* God has already changed His mind about you, but you have to change your mind about what He says about you, and about what you think about you. God has given you a free will, and you must change your free will to match His will for you. **Only you can change your mind**, so make that change because **you are a new creation**, and **you're worth it**.

The enemy wants you to wallow in your mistakes and in your past sins. He wants to keep you down and out, keep you feeling guilty, keep you feeling unworthy, and keep you feeling defeated and believing that you can never change. He wants you to believe that you have no good future ahead of you because he keeps bringing up your sins to you in your mind. On top of that, satan puts temptations in your mind; it's a constant bombardment. This line of thinking is definitely from the enemy. *1 Peter 5:8* states: *"Be sober, be vigilant; because your adversary the devil, is like a roaring lion, walking about, seeking whom he may devour."* Don't feed on what the enemy says about you. Don't let him bring you down. Only you can decide to accept or reject what the enemy has told you about you in your mind. This is why you are to change your mind because the battle begins in your mind.

Each time a negative thought comes into your mind, based on your knowledge of God's word, you will know it's from satan. God does not bring up your past sins, but satan does and will. God does not tempt you, but satan does and will. *James 1:12-16* states: *"Blessed is the man [woman] who endures temptation, for when he [she] has been approved, he [she] will receive the crown of life which the Lord has promised to those who love Him. Let no man [woman] say when he [she] is tempted, 'I am tempted by God', for God cannot be tempted by evil, nor does He Himself tempt anyone, but each one [person] is tempted when he [she] is drawn away by his [her] own desires and enticed. Then, when desire has conceived, it gives birth to sin; and sin, when it is full-grown, brings forth death. Do not be deceived, my beloved brethren."* You have got to take charge of your mind, reject those negative thoughts that come into your mind, and replace them with what the Word of God says. Rebuke that negative thought immediately "in the name of Jesus." *1 Corinthians 10:13* states: *"No temptation has overtaken you except such as is common to man, but God is faithful, who will not allow you to be tempted beyond what you are able, but with the temptation, will also make the way of escape that you may be able to bear it."*

You have regrets and you doubt yourself more and more when you don't learn from your prior mistakes. When you've been there and done that so many times, you should know that things never change unless you **change your mind** to do things the right way – God's way. Once you change your mind to do things according to the Word of God, you won't have any regrets. All the "if I would haves", "could haves", and "should haves" won't change anything. You must **change your mind**.

God Responds To His Word

When satan fires one of his fiery negative thought darts at you, just say: "I don't receive that thought in the name of Jesus." Then use God's Word against the fiery dart. The table below gives some examples of the fiery darts that satan tries to use against us, and how we are to use God's Word to quench those fiery darts. We cannot withstand satan in our own strength. We need God and His word to obtain the victory over what satan sends against us. Immediately when you receive the negative thought, speak God's Word over the thought and rebuke it 'in the name of Jesus." Remember, the battle begins in the mind.

Here are a few examples of what I'm talking about:

Satan's Thought Darts:	***Your Response with God's Word:***
You messed up again, you're no good.	I don't receive that in the name of Jesus because it is written that I am the righteousness of God in accordance with *2 Corinthians 5:21*, which states: *"For He made Him who knew no sin to be sin for us, that we might become the righteousness of God in Him."* I rebuke you in Jesus' name.
You can't do that, you're not able.	I don't receive that in the name of Jesus because in accordance *Philippians 4:13*: *"I can do all things through Christ who strengthens me."*
You're a failure.	I don't receive that in the name of Jesus for it is written in (*Romans 8:37): "Yet in all these things we are more than conquerors through Him who loved us."*

Satan's Thought Darts:	***Your Response with God's Word:***
You're sick. You won't be able to get rid of this sickness.	I rebuke that in the name of Jesus because it is written in *Isaiah 53:5: "But He was wounded for our transgressions, He was bruised for our iniquities; that chastisement for our peace was upon Him, and by His stripes we are healed."* Also, in accordance with *Matthew 8:17*, it is written: *" . . . He Himself took our infirmities and bore our sicknesses."*

Satan's Thought Darts:	***Your Response with God's Word:***
God's Word is not true, you know it's not true. His word won't get you out of this problem.	I don't receive that in the name of Jesus because it is written in *1 John 5:20*: *"And we know that the Son of God has come and has given us an understanding that we may know Him who is true, and we are in Him who is true, in His Son Jesus Christ. This is the true God and eternal life."* I have faith in God. I do not doubt His word, for Jesus said in *Mark 11:22-23*: *"Have faith in God, for whoever says to this mountain, be removed and cast into the sea and does not doubt in his heart, but believes that those things he says will be done, he will have whatsoever he says." 2 Corinthians 10:5* states: *"Casting down all arguments and every high thing that exalts itself against the knowledge of God, bringing every thought into captivity to the obedience of Christ."* Also, God does not lie, as stated in *Numbers 23:19*, which states: *"God is not a man that He should lie, nor a son of man that He should repent. Has He said and will He not do? Or has He spoken and will He not make it good?"* So, based on God's Word, I bind your powers in the name of Jesus.

Satan's Thought Darts:	***Your Response with God's Word:***
Kevin wants you to sleep with him again. It felt so good the last time, don't you remember? Do it again.	I don't receive that in the name of Jesus, for it is written in *1 Corinthians 10:13*: *"No temptation has overtaken you except such as is common to man, but God is faithful, who will not allow you to be tempted beyond what you are able, but with the temptation will also make the way of escape that you may be able to bear it."* [Put this scripture in the 'first person': "No temptation has overtaken **me** except such as is common to man, but God is faithful, who will not allow **me** to be tempted beyond what **I am able**, but with the temptation will also make a way of escape that **I may be able** to bear it."]

We must be strong in the Lord, and in the power of His might. We must be strong in the knowledge of His Word. That's why we must study and meditate on His Word continually so when the fiery darts come into our minds, we will be ready with God's ammunition (His Word) to fight against them. You have to fight satan with the Word of God. God's word has the power to quench/extinguish all the fiery darts (negative thoughts) that satan whispers in your mind.

Forgiveness Is Key

So you made a mistake; so you made many mistakes! God is a forgiving God. He forgave you when He had His Son, Jesus Christ, die on the cross for your sins. He has forgiven your yesterdays, todays, and tomorrows. But, you've got to go to Him and ask for forgiveness, acknowledging that He loved you so much that He sacrificed His only begotten Son (the Lord Jesus Christ) as payment for all your sins. *John 3:16* states: *"For God so loved the world that He gave His only begotten Son that whoever believes in Him should not perish but have everlasting life." Ephesians 2:8-9* states: *"For by grace you have been saved through faith, and that not of yourselves; it is the gift of God, not of works, lest anyone should boast." Romans 10:9-10* states: *"that if you confess with your mouth the Lord Jesus and believe in your heart that God has raised Him from the dead, you will be saved. For with the heart one believes unto righteousness, and with the mouth confession is made unto salvation."*

After confessing the above and accepting the Lord Jesus Christ as your Savior, you are now forgiven and saved. Now that you know you're forgiven and saved, don't continue to make the same mistakes because you're accountable to God. You now have the knowledge and the confidence that you're forgiven, so walk in your confidence.

With knowledge comes responsibility and power. You are responsible and you have the power to do God's will and not your own. You are also responsible to be a witness to others in your walk. Others should see the change in you without you even opening your mouth. They should see such a change in you, in your happiness, and in your confidence that they will ask you what's going on with you. At that point, you can give your testimony as to how God forgave you, saved you, and blessed you. Your walk and your testimony will be encouragement for others to make that change.

Forgive those who despitefully used you, who persecuted you, who threw you away like a piece of trash, and who called you everything but a child of God. These are not to be weights on you that you should carry around throughout your life, dragging you down further and further to your own destruction. If you allow these weights to overtake your mind, which is where the real battleground is (where you are believing what was done to you was okay because you were a bad person anyway, or what was said to you or said about you was justified in some negative way), you could eventually destroy yourself. Instead, win that battle in your mind. You should win all the battles in your mind, not the enemy winning, because God has given you His word to use to defeat all poisonous darts (negative messages) sent by the devil to your mind. If you don't win the battles in your mind, the enemy (satan) will continue to defeat you in life, and he will ultimately destroy you.

You have got to take a stand against the enemy who tries to burden your mind with negative thoughts about you – thoughts of unworthiness, bitterness, doubt, defeat, loss, and anger. These negative and destructive thoughts are from satan, himself, but God has not given you the spirit of fear (of defeat, of depression, of doubt, of worry, of nervousness, of stress, of bitterness, of despondency, of lack, of loss, and of all that other garbage). *2 Timothy 1:7* states: *"For God has not given us a spirit of fear, but of power and of love and of a sound mind."* He has not given you the spirit of defeat. He has not given you the spirit of depression. He has not given you the spirit of worry, etc. You don't realize how much power you have. You have the awesome power of God through the name of His Son, Jesus Christ. Rebuke all that negative garbage **"in the name of Jesus"** and in accordance with *Luke 10:19*. Remember that God responds to His word. God's word destroys any word that satan tries to use against you, but you must know God's word and **speak God's word back to satan**. When you rebuke any negative thought that comes into your mind by satan with the word of God, just see how quickly that negative thought will disappear from your mind. The enemy has no power over the word of God.

I have trials in my life, but just knowing that God is with me and that He will never leave me nor forsake me has carried me through, and continues to carry me through this life. *Hebrews 13:5* states: *"Let your conduct be without covetousness; be content with such things as you have, for He Himself has said, 'I will never leave you nor forsake you.'"* God's word is true and powerful.

I also learned to forgive myself. It took me a little while to realize that since God had forgiven me and no longer remembered my sins, I should forgive myself, too. If God thought so much of me to sacrifice His only begotten Son for my sins, I had no right to keep having the Lord Jesus Christ beaten unmercifully and put back up on that cross bloodied and beaten each and every time I thought about the wrongs I had done in the past. Did I not trust God? Of course I trusted Him. He came through for me in the past, He is currently working on my behalf, and I know He will come through for me in the future. Since I was forgiven by God and became a new creation, I changed my thinking to be in line with what God says about His children in the Bible. Consequently, my decisions and my actions also changed. I no longer do the worldly things I use to do. I am changed. I no longer feel guilty, unworthy, or dirty. I learned to leave the past in the past, and am at peace with myself. I am content.

God has a purpose in everything, good or bad, so no matter what you've been through or what you're currently in, He will work it out for your good and for His glory. I've lived long enough to see and know His word is true. *Romans 8:28* states: *"And we know that all things work together for good to those who love God, to those who are the called according to His purpose." John 16:33* states: *"These things I have spoken to you, that in Me you may have peace.*

In the world you will have tribulation; but be of good cheer, I have overcome the world."

Jesus said in *Matthew 11:28-30: "Come to Me, all you who labor and are heavy laden, and I will give you rest. Take My yoke upon you and learn from Me, for I am gentle and lowly in heart, and you will find rest for your souls. For My yoke is easy and My burden is light." Isaiah 43:18-19* states: *"Do not remember the former things, nor consider the things of old. Behold, I will do a new thing. Now it shall spring forth. Shall you not know it? I will even make a road in the wilderness and rivers in the desert."* God does not want you to carry the weight of your sins or the weight of the sins by others against you. He wants you to give it all to Him and be free. He will make you a new creation. He does not want you to remember the things of old, but be new in Him for He has created a new creation in you. *2 Corinthians 5:17* states: *"Therefore, if anyone is in Christ, he is a new creation; old things have passed away, behold all things have become new."* Since you are a new creation, you have no business carrying anything from the past into your future. God has wiped your slate clean. It doesn't matter that others may remember your past. What counts is that God doesn't remember your past once you become His creation. *Psalm 103:12* states: *"As far as the east is from the west, so far has He removed our transgressions from us."* Rejoice! You are to hand over all those bad situations and bad memories to God. You are no good to anyone if you hold onto the mistakes of the past. Be good to you. Believe what God says about you, which is all good! My pastor, Pastor Tom Pickens, stated in one of his recent sermons that "God has already determined your end in life and it's good." So be happy for you have a bright future ahead of you, if you don't give up.

Forgive those who wronged you, and walk in your new life trusting that God will make things right (not you make things right, but you allowing Him to make things right). Remember *Romans 8:28:*

"And we know that all things work together for good to those who love God, to those who are the called according to His purpose."

Justice means to right the wrong. Although wrong may have been done to you, you, yourself, cannot right the wrong. Although you may want to get back at the person who wronged you, two wrongs don't make a right. Your vengeance will not make it right. But, what you can do is to forgive that person who wronged you. God was there when that person wronged you. He saw what the person did to you. He knew that person's motives. The person who wronged you is accountable to God for his thoughts and actions, not you. You are accountable to God for how you handle the wrong that was done to you – your thoughts and your actions. If you give the situation to God and forgive the person who caused it, you will not be responsible or accountable. *Mark 11:25-26* states: *"And whenever you stand praying, if you have anything against anyone, forgive him, that your Father in heaven may also forgive you your trespasses. But, if you do not forgive, neither will your Father in heaven forgive your trespasses." Romans 12:19-21* states: *"Beloved, do not avenge yourselves, but rather give place to wrath; for it is written, 'Vengeance is mine, I will repay, says the Lord.' Therefore, if your enemy is hungry, feed him; if he is thirsty, give him drink; for in so doing you will heap coals of fire upon his head. Do not be overcome by evil, but overcome evil with good."* So, if you want to be free, don't want to carry any burdens, and you want your prayers answered, give everything to God and forgive!

Depending on what was done to you in accordance with the laws of man, that person who wronged you may also be accountable under man's laws. That being said, you have the right to pursue man's laws against that person. However, you can still forgive him.

Let those who devise evil things against you get trapped in their own doing. *Psalm 9:16* states: *"The Lord is known by the judgment He executes; the wicked is snared in the work of his own hands." Psalm 7:11* states*: "God is a just judge, and God is angry with the wicked every day."* However, this doesn't mean that you should allow that same person, or anyone else, to continue to misuse or mistreat you. Also, you should not allow yourself to be put in the same position that harmed you in the first place. God wants us to use wisdom, discernment, understanding, insight, and guidance in everything we do so that we do not get snared in any traps. God wants us to be as meek and as harmless as doves, but as sharp as serpents. *Matthew 10:16* states*: "Behold, I send you out as sheep in the midst of wolves. Therefore, be wise as serpents and harmless as doves." Psalm 111:10* states*: "The fear of the Lord is the beginning of wisdom; a good understanding have all those who do His commandments. His praise endures forever."* In gaining wisdom and understanding, you will live a happier and more peaceful life. *Proverbs 3:13-18* states*: "Happy is the man who finds wisdom, and the man who gains understanding; for her proceeds are better than the profits of silver and her gain [is better] than fine gold. She is more precious than rubies, and all the things you may desire cannot compare with her. Length of days is in her right hand. In her left hand riches and honor. Her ways are ways of pleasantness, and all her paths are peace. She is a tree of life to those who take hold of her and happy are all who retain her."* So use wisdom in any and all circumstances, and you will have a happier and more peaceful life.

We, too, have to be careful with what we say. *Proverbs 6:2* states*: "You are snared by the words of your mouth; you are taken by the words of your mouth."* You cannot say you forgive the person on one hand, and turn around and speak badly about that person on the other hand. Forgiveness is total. God didn't forgive you and then turn around and bad-mouth you. No, He forgave you totally, and that was that! You must do the same.

I am still a work in progress. I am not perfect. There are some things the Lord and I are still working on in me. But, He is faithful. *1 Corinthians 1:9* states: *"God is faithful, by whom you were called into the fellowship of His Son, Jesus Christ our Lord." 1 Corinthians 10:13* states: *"No temptation has overtaken you except such as is common to man; but God is faithful, who will not allow you to be tempted beyond what you are able, but with the temptation will also make the way of escape, that you may be able to bear it."*

So, sometimes when I am speaking with someone going through a situation that is similar to my past experiences, I share with that person what the Lord did for me in that situation, and I remind them that God is faithful and He is no respector of person.

Being forgiven, being made a new creation, and realizing that the past is in the past, washed away and no more, you will find relief and strength. *Psalm 103:12* states: *"As far as the east is from the west, so far does He remove our transgressions from us." Micah 7:19* states: *"He will again have compassion on us and will subdue our iniquities. You [God] will cast all our sins into the depths of the sea." James 5:15* states: *"And the prayer of faith will save the one who is sick, and the Lord will raise him up. And if he has committed sins, he will be forgiven." "Have faith in God."*, as stated in *Mark 11:22.*

In the circumstances that you may currently be in, you can change your mind for the good. Do not compound the circumstances by giving up, or by making more bad decisions. Give your concerns to the Lord. *1 Peter 5:7* states: *"Casting all your cares upon Him for He cares for you."* God does not want you to worry. You are to give **all** your cares to Him and let Him handle them. *Matthew 11:28-30* states: *"Come to Me, all you who labor and are heavy laden, and I will give you rest. Take My yoke upon you and learn from Me, for I am gentle and lowly in heart, and you will find rest for your souls. For my yoke is easy, and my burden is light."*

Even if what you have done in the past was a total disaster, don't still live in it. Don't allow satan to remind you over and over again about your mistakes. You've been forgiven, you don't want to hear it, and God certainly doesn't want to hear it after He has provided forgiveness for you through the death and resurrection of His Son, the Lord Jesus Christ. When you keep rehashing the same bad stuff, in essence you're telling God that you don't believe you were forgiven, you don't trust Him, and you don't believe He can change you even though His word says that He has forgiven you and that He is changing you into a new creation. This is where your faith comes in – believing that God's word is true. If you believe God's word is true, it's true about you, too. Act like God's word is true in your life. God thinks you're worth His only begotten Son dying on the cross for **YOU!** So you must be worth an awful lot to Him. Again, 2 *Corinthians 5:17* states*: "Therefore if any man [woman] be in Christ, he [she] is a **new creation**: old things are passed away; behold, **all things are become new**."*

God honors His word. He keeps His promises. God is a God of covenant, which means He is in agreement with His word. If you are in the will of God, doing the will of God, He will honor you and keep His promises to you. God does not contradict His word, and He is no respector of person, which means that you're no different than anyone else. He will forgive you as He has forgiven others. *Numbers 23:19* states*: "God is not a man that He should lie, nor a son of man that He should repent [change His mind]. Has He said and will He not do it? Or has He spoken and will He not fulfill it [make it good]?"*

Yes, you have suffered for your sins, but the good news is that God is faithful and He will restore you. *1 Peter 5:10* states*: "But may the God of all grace, who called us to His eternal glory by Christ Jesus, after you have suffered a while, [He will] perfect [you], establish [you], strengthen [you], and settle you."* So be happy in knowing that He has given you a great future and a great hope.

Don't be concerned that you may fall back into the same traps, for God has made a way of escape. Use His word to fight off the fiery darts (the negative thoughts) of the wicked one that come into your mind. Your battle with satan begins in your mind. However, God is faithful, He has given you His armor to wear, and He will guide you. *1 Corinthians 10:13* states: *"No temptation has overtaken you except such as is common to man; but God is faithful, who will not allow you to be tempted beyond what you are able, but with the temptation will also make the way of escape, that you may be able to bear it."* You've got to trust Him and believe that He can do what He says He will do. Work your faith! Meditate on God's word consistently. Get His word into your heart by meditating on it. Meditating on God's word will keep you from falling into the same old traps that got you into sin in the first place.

God has brought me through many trials during my life, and it could only have been Him who brought me through so smoothly because I put my trust in Him. Yeah, in the beginning when I was a babe in Christ, I cried many times, was prostrate on the floor crying out, pleading and begging for forgiveness, pleading for help, and begging for understanding. I was waiting on Him. I wore Him out with my prayers and tears. I wasn't crying because I did not trust Him, but crying was my only release for my hands were absolutely, unequivocally tied – the situation was completely out of my hands. I could do nothing. I could not even go to my family and friends because I dare not get that close to them to share my burdens for possible fear of ridicule by them, which would make my pain even greater. I just could not bear any more than what was already on my plate. My problems could only be solved by my Father in Heaven.

After I was done with my prayerful tantrum (so to speak), nothing had changed that I could see at that moment, but things were being done in the Spirit, which is invisible to the human eye. He was in control and He straightened everything out like no one on earth could because I gave my burdens to Him. I could not fix things in my own strength. I didn't see change immediately because I was in human time and God is in His own time. But, He was right on time.

It took me a while to realize that He was working in the background making the right things come to the forefront to bring me through the problem and into victory. I also realized that I had a peace like never before. I was not anxious. I was no longer worrying about what the outcome would be and when it would come. I slept great at night.

I only look back on occasion to remind myself about the many things God has turned around for me. I only look back to see how He turned those things into such wonderful blessings for me in my life, that He was faithful, and that I could trust Him. I am truly amazed at His handiwork. He loves me. He loves you, too!

It would be a good idea to keep a journal to write when and how God came through for you. The journal that you keep will reinforce your awareness of God's faithfulness to you and His love for you during each trial you encounter. It will also remind you that you have the victory through Him. Life is a series of trials, but it's the faith in God's word and the use of His word that will get you through the trial quicker and with success.

Have Faith & Believe

"Have faith in God." Jesus made this statement in *Mark 11:22*. Believe in God and believe in yourself. You can overcome any and all obstacles with God's help. You are not alone. He will never leave you nor forsake you. He is with you forever. *Hebrews 13:5* states: *"Let your conduct be without covetousness, be content with such things as you have. For He Himself has said: 'I will never leave you nor forsake you.'"* The Lord is your helper, you are strong in the

Lord, and you have the victory. *Hebrews 13:6* states: *"So we may boldly say: 'The Lord is my helper; I will not fear; what can man do to me?'"* *Isaiah 41:10* states: *"Fear not, for I am with you. Be not dismayed, for I am your God. I will strengthen you. Yes, I will help you. I will uphold you with my righteous right hand."* Also, *Isaiah 40:31* states: *"But those who wait on the Lord shall renew their strength; they shall mount up with wings like eagles. They shall run and not be weary. They shall walk and not faint."*

There are many examples in the Bible of women who stood and overcame the most difficult circumstances. These women of the Bible were obedient to God, and they became great leaders, warriors, providers, and protectors – all for the glory of God. He gave each and every one of them a purpose, and He gave them what they needed to overcome the obstacles set before them.

Remember Mary, the mother of the Lord Jesus Christ, who raised Him from birth only to see Him crucified. As a human mother, how she suffered greatly to see her firstborn child being persecuted, beaten mercilessly and cruelly, and then to see Him crucified on the cross. Mary knew that Jesus' situation was totally out of her hands and she had no power of her own to save her Son. But, Mary remembered how she was divinely impregnated, she knew her Son was a gift from God to all of mankind, and she knew God was going to use her Son to fulfill His purpose. Through Jesus Christ, God provided a way on this earth to save all sinners. God gave Mary supernatural and mighty strength to endure what she would see her Son go through. Her hands were completely tied, but she knew that God was in control. She received courage from above to stand against the greatest of odds. She was able to rejoice when she saw her Son, the Lord Jesus Christ, rise again in accordance with God's word. She saw God's faithfulness, and there was much rejoicing for her tears were tears of joy when she saw her son, the Son of God, the Savior of the world, alive forevermore.

In the Book of Ruth, Ruth lost her husband who was the son of Naomi, and Naomi lost her husband who was the father of Ruth's husband. When they lost their husbands, they lost their income, and they lost their sense of purpose in fulfilling the needs of their husbands. Ruth made the decision to stay with Naomi rather than going back to where she came from. Naomi and Ruth went back to Bethlehem where Naomi had come from. One of Naomi's relatives, Boaz, was very kind and very wealthy. He showed favor toward Ruth and later married her, and he took care of her and Naomi. What a wonderful outcome!

There was Abigail who saved her obstinate husband, Nabal, and her whole family from the sword of David in *1 Samuel 25:1-15*. Abigail was a very beautiful woman, and Nabal was arrogant, prideful, ungrateful, and obstinate with his land and his money that the Lord blessed him with. [By the way, the Lord is the One who blesses us with wealth and prosperity. We are to use it to spread His word and to help those in need, not be selfish and think that what we have is due to our own strength. That's called pride and foolishness. God, our Creator, owns it all.] *Proverbs 1:7* states: *"The fear of the Lord is the beginning of knowledge, but fools despise wisdom and instruction."* David and his men protected Nabal's shearers and property while they were dwelling there. David and his men asked for no payment for their protection of Nabal's property and employees. However, when David and his men were low on their own provisions, David only asked Nabal to grant him and his men some food to eat. Nabal did not appreciate what David and his men had done for him and his family, his servants or his land. So instead, Nabal denied David and his men. Nabal even went so far as to insult David. This infuriated David, and he gathered up his men and headed toward Nabal to kill him and his household.

Abigail was informed by her servants of Nabal's insults and David's subsequent wrath. Given wisdom from above, Abigail gathered up an abundance of food for David and his men. She went to David while he was on his way to destroy Nabal, and she pleaded for the life of her foolish, stupid and offensive husband. Abigail showed her appreciation to David and his men for their protection of what Nabal had. David's heart was softened and he refrained from his pursuit of Nabal. Because of Nabal's obstinance, the Lord struck him and he died. David later married Abigail for he found her to be not only beautiful in her appearance, but beautiful in her heart. David knew she was a blessing from the Lord.

Esther was married to the King Ahasuerus, but he did not know she was of Jewish descent. Haman, one of the King's high administrators, tried to persuade the King to kill all of the Jews in the land. But Esther, although fearful for her own life because she was a Jew, advised the King of Haman's plot to kill her people, the Jews. She also informed the King that she was of Jewish descent. Esther knew she could be killed, too, for not only being Jewish, but for approaching the King on her own for this was not the custom for one in her position. But King Ahasuerus loved Esther, and he had Haman and his sons hanged in Haman's own courtyard. The King appointed Mordecai, Esther's uncle, to take Haman's place in his counsel.

Rahab, the prostitute, hid and protected the two spies that Joshua sent to spy out Jericho before destroying the city. Rahab was able to save her family from the destruction that was brought on the city of Jericho.

There are many other women who God used in mighty ways to fulfill the purposes He gave them. Their circumstances did not always start out the best, but these women had faith and were obedient to God, and He brought them all through in great triumph. They were not perfect, but He worked perfection in their lives. They finished well. God can do the same for you.

Chapter 8

A Friend In Need Is A Friend Indeed

Chapter 8

A Friend In Need Is A Friend Indeed

There are all types of friends, for all types of reasons and seasons, but a friend in need is really a friend indeed. A true friend will help you to be all that you can be.

The Merriam-Webster Dictionary describes a friend as one who is attached to another by affection or esteem, one who is not hostile, one belonging to the same nation or party or group, one who favors or promotes something, or a favored companion. Anonymous ("anon"), an unknown writer, wrote: "Everyone hears what you say. Friends listen to what you say. Best friends listen to what you don't say." "A true friend knows when something is wrong even when you have the biggest smile on your face."

Proverbs 18:24 states: *"A man [woman] who has friends must himself [herself] be friendly, but there is a friend who sticks closer than a brother." Proverbs 27:6* states: *"Faithful are the wounds of a friend, but the kisses of an enemy are deceitful."* In *John 15:13–15, Jesus* states: *"Greater love has no one than this, than to lay down one's life for his friends. You are My friends if you do whatever I command you. No longer do I call you servants, for a servant does not know what his master is doing, but I have called you friends, for all things that I heard from My Father I have made known to you." James 2:23* states: *"and the Scripture was fulfilled which says, 'Abraham believed God, and it was accounted to him for righteousness.' And he was called the friend of God."*

When you're going through trials, that's when you find out who your friends really are, and you find out who you really are, too.

You also discover who you are as a friend when your friend is going through trials.

I find most people don't know how to be a friend. There is no class to take to learn how to be a true friend. I'm still learning, myself. I'm still working on being a good and true friend to people. I'm also learning how to forgive those who have failed me in friendships with the help of God's word. I did not realize it until I began studying the Bible, but the Bible has a lot of information concerning how to be a friend. Jesus Christ, Himself, was and is the best example, and He is the best friend a person could ever have.

I don't have many friends. In fact, I can count my friends on one hand, and this is by choice more than by any other reason. Over the years I have learned the hard way how to have a friend and how to be a friend. Therefore, I am very selective as to who I will share myself, my time, and my intimate feelings with – good and bad. *Proverbs 14:7* states: *"Go from the presence of a foolish man, when you do not perceive in him the lips of knowledge."* You want friends who will affirm, enhance and encourage you. You want friends who are themselves good examples for you to emulate, who do the right thing all the time, and who will tell you the truth in love no matter how bad it may hurt you. *Proverbs 27:6* states: *"Faithful are the wounds of a friend, but the kisses of an enemy are deceitful." Proverbs 27:17* states: *As iron sharpens iron, so a man [woman] sharpens the countenance of his [her] friend."* You want friends who believe the word of God is true. If God said it, that's it! My best friend is the Father God. I have no problem telling Him anything and don't have to worry about any gossip.

We are very vulnerable and sensitive when we make a mistake or when something happens to us. We want to confide in someone we trust to tell what happened, our feelings about it, and to seek a good solution. We want emotional support from our friends. We want good advice from our friends. We want our friends to tell us the truth. We want our friends to be there for us. But, most importantly, we want our friends to keep what we tell them to themselves and no one else. This includes them not telling our mutual girlfriends, boyfriends, husbands, or acquaintances. News Flash: Husbands gossip, too!

Unfortunately, some who we confide in disappoint us by telling our most deep dark secrets, our feelings, and our frailties to others. This is a flaw almost all of us have; we can't seem to keep things to ourselves. So, my rule of thumb is: "When in doubt, leave it out." In essence, keep it to yourself. However, the best friend you could ever have, who would not tell a soul, but talk directly to you, is God! He will never tell any other person, friend or foe, about you. He sticks closer to you than a brother. *Proverbs 17:17* states: *"A friend loves at all times" Proverbs 18:24* states: *"A man who has friends must be himself friendly, but there is a friend who sticks closer than a brother."* God is always with you, no matter what. *Hebrews 13:5* states: *"Let your conduct be without covetousness; be content with such things as you have. For He Himself has said, 'I will never leave you nor forsake you.'"* He will be there for you to comfort and console you no matter the circumstance or problem.

God also sees everything everyone does. *Hebrews 4:13* states: *"And there is no creature hidden from His sight, but all things are naked and open to the eyes of Him to whom we must give account."*

If your friend sees you going astray in the area of associating with the wrong person for romantic reasons, or in making poor financial decisions, or in creating new bad habits, would your friend tell you? Would you tell her? Would you tell your friend she's heading for trouble in such a way that she gets your message loud and clear? Or, would you express (couch) what you say in such a way to not hurt her feelings, yet being evasive, thereby causing your message not to be understood but ignored? Or do you distance yourself from her and allow her to fall? Would you do all you could to keep her from making a mistake and show her a better way? How much do you care about your friends, and to what extent will you go to turn them away from making life-altering mistakes?

Or, are you one of those "after the fact" friends who say after the devastating outcome: "Well, I tried to tell you!"? You ask them when did they try to tell you, and they smugly state they expressed early on that they did not "think" you should do what you were going to do, and they left it at that. When you asked them when it was that they expressed their disapproval, they can't seem to remember. Then after the damage was done, they had the audacity to tell you, "I told you so" or "I tried to tell you." That's not a good friend!

Being A Real Friend

There are 3 rules that a real friend abides by:

(1) I will never lie to you.

(2) I will never lie for you.

(3) I will never lie on you.

I had a girlfriend who was married and who was cheating on her husband. She and her husband were having a lot of problems in their marriage. Although they were Christians, she did not always accept and follow the teachings of God concerning her marriage issues. She didn't really trust God.

Evalyn and her husband were ministered to separately and as a couple by the pastor, by Christian and secular counselors, and even by me. However, she chose to go a different direction in solving her marital problems. She also involved a third party.

When asked by her husband about her whereabouts, Evalyn told her husband she was visiting me. However, one day her husband called me, and he asked me if I had seen her on particular days. I had not seen her on those days, so I told him. I thought it strange of him to ask me about her whereabouts, but I later figured she must have said she was with me.

I didn't appreciate Evalyn involving me in her adulterous affair by lying to her husband and lying on me. I was trying to help her stay in her marriage by reminding her of what God's word said in the Bible, reminding her of her vows, and reminding her of her commitment to her husband and to God. I didn't even know there was a third party involved. Why did she expect me to lie for her? Needless to say, I was disappointed, but I forgave her.

I work hard at being a trusted friend to my friends. Even though I'm aware of their weaknesses, I still work on maintaining the friendship because I'm not perfect, either. When I see them going astray or about to make a terrible decision, I become very candid, sometimes brutally honest, and very adamant in telling them why they shouldn't. I also let them know about the negative consequences. Sometimes when you tell your friends nicely, they don't always get it. Then you have to add a little cayenne pepper to the mix in small doses until they get it. Sometimes when they finally understand, they don't like it, and the friendship suffers. But I take that chance because I care about them. If it works out, fine, but if the friendship dissolves because of it, I did my best and have no regrets.

As a friend, I'm going to say what the Bible says to sway my friends from making bad mistakes. They come to me because they really want the truth. I back up what I tell them with the word of God, with my past experiences and my consequences. It's not about being right; it's about avoiding a wrong and the consequences of that wrong.

Types Of Friends

Women take pride in having girlfriends. We tell our girlfriends everything. We even tell our girlfriends what we won't even tell our husbands, and our husbands are supposed to be our best friends, next to God. If husbands are good enough to marry, why aren't they good enough for us to be intimate in all things with them aside from sex? Some women even tell their girlfriends intimate secrets in their marital relationships, which is a "BIG NO-NO!"

Girlfriends even know when women are about to break up with their boyfriends or husbands long before the husband or the boyfriend finds out. Girlfriends applaud and agree with the reasons given for breaking up with the husband or the boyfriend. There seems to be very little objectivity between girlfriends in this area; they tend to stick together when it comes to men.

Girlfriends discuss their innermost secrets and deepest of feelings with one another. Thoughts and desires that should be off-limits and immediately rebuked, because they come straight from the pit of hell, are discussed amongst girlfriends. Some girlfriends will even do dirt together and then brag amongst themselves about it. The dirt seems to be the glue that keeps them together.

The question is: Do you like your girlfriends enough to follow them or to lead them into hell? Or, do you care enough about your girlfriends to lead them away from hell? You're accountable for leading or following your girlfriends in the wrong direction, especially when you know better. *Romans 14:21* states: *"It is good neither to eat meat nor drink wine nor do anything by which your brother [sister] stumbles or is offended or is made weak." James 5:19-20* states: *"Brethren, if anyone among you wanders from the truth, and someone turns him [her] back, let him [her] know that he [she] who turns a sinner from the error of his [her] way will save a soul from death and cover a multitude of sins."*

If you do end up in hell, it will be by the choices **you** made. Your girlfriends won't be with you in hell. You will be there for eternity by yourself. Your girlfriends may be there, too, but I doubt you will see them or even care to see them. It will be too late to say "if I would have", "could have", and "should have." It will be too late to make better choices of friends. When you stand before God, you will not have your girlfriends with you to provide support or justify your actions. You will be standing by yourself, and you will have to account to God for your own actions. Your girlfriends will individually have to account for themselves. You won't be able to say your long-time friend encouraged you to do wrong when you, yourself, knew better. There are no rewards to those in agreement to do a wrong.

Most of us keep our girlfriends for camaraderie-sake, if nothing else. It's a form of social networking.

What do you consider a best friend to be? What type of girlfriend are you? What kinds of girlfriends do you associate with? Do you have friends like the ones listed below? There are many types of friends, but listed below are some of the most common types of friends:

411 Gossip Friend – If you want someone to know how you feel about something, but you don't want to be direct about it, just tell the 411 Gossip Friend. She will make sure your information gets to the right person, and to others. She tells everything. She has no shame in her game. She will even spice it up and elaborate on what you initially told her. If she talks about someone else to you, you know she will and has talked about you. She will put all your business in the street, and then deny she ever said anything or knew anything. She can't keep anything to herself. And, please don't use those magic words like "please keep this a secret" or "just between you and me." These phrases are like Kryptonite to her, and she's got to get rid of it or it will destroy her. There may be some redeeming value to having a friend like the 411 Gossip Friend, but I haven't found it. Proverbs 17:9 states: *"He [She] who covers a transgression seeks love, but he [she] who repeats a matter separates friends." Proverbs 18:8* states: *"The words of a talebearer are like tasty trifles, and they go down into the inmost body." Proverbs 20:19* states: *"He [She] who goes about as a talebearer reveals secrets; therefore, do not associate with one who flatters with his [her] lips." Proverbs 21:23* states: *"Whoever guards his [her] mouth and tongue keeps his [her] soul from troubles."*

The Judge – This is the friend who judges everything you say and do. She's condescending, condemning, critical, ridiculing, and she turns her nose up at you as if she's so perfect and you're the scum of the earth. She has no problem hurting your feelings and making you feel bad; in fact, she's good at it. She intentionally says hurtful things when you least expect it. She has no heart, and she's delighted when she sees that she's upset you. It's like she puts the knife in your chest and twists it with her manner, her poisonous words, and her attitude. She takes pleasure in seeing tears stream down your face after she's destroyed you by her toxic words of condemnation. She claims she's your friend and she's 'telling you for your own good', whether you asked for it or not. She has no problem putting you down for any reason or for no reason. Nothing you could ever do or say will enhance her view of you. However, the only real reason she's hanging with you is because you're the only one who will put up with her. *James 4:11* states: *"Do not speak evil of one another, brethren. He who speaks evil of a brother [sister] and judges his brother [sister] speaks evil of the law and judges the law. But if you judge the law, you are not a doer of the law but a judge."* Jesus, Himself, says in *Matthew 7:1-2*: *"Judge not, that you be not judged.*

For with what judgment you judge, you will be judged, and with the measure you use, it will be measured back to you."

Miss Deceptive – She's always smiling in your face while back-stabbing you at the same time. She's ruthless, conniving, scheming, but the underlying current is that she's jealous of you. She slanders you amongst your mutual friends without provocation. She misleads you. She allows wrong to happen to you, and then she claims ignorance. She takes joy in your stumbling and in your downfalls, but then pretends to be concerned about you. *Proverbs 16:28* states: *"A perverse man [woman] sows strife, and a whisperer separates the best of friends." Proverbs 27:6* states: *"Faithful are the wounds of a friend, but the kisses of an enemy are deceitful."*

You make the mistake of telling her you're interested in someone who has expressed an interest in you, but then you find out later the man you were interested in is no longer interested in you because Miss Deceptive went behind your back and told him untrue things about you. The next thing you know is Miss Deceptive has your man.

You get ready to go to a party with Ms. Deceptive, but your skirt is hunched up in the back as you walk through the door into the party. Does Miss Deceptive inform you before you go into the room filled with people? No.

You confide in Ms. Deceptive about something very personal only to later learn she's used it against you. When she gets angry with you or jealous of you, she talks about you like you're a piece of trash to everyone you and she know.

When you need help with something and ask for her help, Miss Deceptive tells you she will help. She never shows up; she always has an excuse. Miss Deceptive tells you she cares about you and your welfare, but her words are without action. Miss Deceptive claims to be your friend, but if something bad happened to you, she would not shed a tear. Miss Deceptive always tells you she will call you, but she doesn't call unless she wants something.

Ms. Me, Myself & I – This person is so self-absorbed (narcissistic) that it's a wonder she even notices you. You are just along for the ride, even though she may be riding in your car. It's really all about her. She has to stand out in a crowd, so don't get in her way or her view of herself. When she's feeling down or up, she wants your undivided attention and she wants you to stroke her (encourage her). When she's lacking, she wants you to provide for her, but she doesn't do the same for you because, again, it's all about her.

Ms. Competitive – She's always in competition with you. She's not satisfied until she beats you at everything. If you have something, she's got to have it. If you like someone, she's got to get him first. If you purchase a vehicle, she's got to go out and purchase a better vehicle than yours. She's always trying to out-do you and impress others. She can't relax and be herself or be happy with who she is – she's extremely insecure. You can't have fun with someone who is always competing with you.

Ms. Yes – Unfortunately, she does not have a mind of her own. She always wants to please everyone. Whatever you say, she will say yes to it. She agrees with you in everything – right or wrong. If you tell Ms. Yes you did something bad or immoral, she will be excited and happy for you instead of telling you it's wrong. She will even try to justify your wrong. If you tell Ms. Yes you're upset about something, she's upset about it, too, but does not know what to do about it to help you. Ms. Yes craves your friendship. She can't stand to be by herself. She cannot make a stand on any issue. She's agreeable to a fault. Ms. Yes offers no wise words of wisdom, she gives faulty comfort, and she has no moral foundation of her own. When circumstances get really tough, Ms. Yes gets real quiet.

Ms. Naughty – She will do just about anything, anywhere, and with anybody. She wants you to share in her fun. She likes being a bit saucy – a slut, and she dresses the part. She sleeps around with many men and even some women. She has sexual encounters with strangers in the bathroom of a bar or club, in an alley, in a motel, in the back seat of a car, in an office conference room, etc., because it's exciting to her. She involves herself with married men for the thrill of it. She tends to drink heavy and/or do drugs. She's always on the prowl, and she's always hunting to catch. When she's invited to a party of unknown origins, she doesn't turn the invitation down. Whatever she's asked to do immorally and sexually, she's okay with it. She wants you to not be a party pooper but join in her fun and intriguing adventures. She hangs around with you because being with you gives her some respectability, but she definitely wants you to lower your moral standards and hang with her. *Ephesians 5:5-7* states: *"For this you know, that no fornicator, unclean person, nor covetous man [woman], who is an idolater, has any inheritance in the kingdom of Christ and God. Let no one deceive you with empty words, for because of these things the wrath of God comes upon the sons [daughters] of disobedience. Therefore do not be partakers with them." Proverbs 5:3-4* states: *"For the lips of an immoral woman drip honey, and her mouth is smoother than oil; but in the end, she is bitter as wormwood."*

Ms. Best of Friends – She will stick by your side no matter what's going on. When the going gets tough, she will get going with you wherever you go. Having done all, she still stands with you, helping you and encouraging you. She will be friend enough to tell you if you're about to make a wrong decision. She will tell you when you're doing the right thing. She will also pick you up after you've fallen. Ms. Best of Friends cares about you. She's honest and fair. You always know where you stand with her. If she sees you going the wrong direction, she will stop you, let you know, and point you in the right direction. *Psalm 15:1-3* states: *"Lord, who* *may abide in Your tabernacle? Who may dwell in Your holy hill? He [She] who walks uprightly, and works righteousness, and speaks the truth in his [her] heart; he [she] who does not backbite with his [her] tongue, nor does evil to his [her] neighbor, nor does he [she] take up a reproach against his [her] friend." Proverbs 17:17* states: *"A friend loves at all times . . ." Proverbs 27:6* states: *"Faithful are the wounds of a friend, but the kisses of an enemy are deceitful." Proverbs 27:9* states: *"Ointment and perfume delight the heart, and the sweetness of a man's [woman's] friend gives delight by hearty [sincere] counsel."*

Ms. Best of Friends will lead you to the Lord, not away from Him. She will always be an example before you of the graciousness of the Lord and she will give you His word, not hers. She will tell you the truth whether you like it or not. There will be times when you just hate Ms. Best of Friends because you know deep down inside she's telling you the truth, and it agrees with what your spirit and conscience are telling you. You want to release her from being one of your friends, but because she's right, honest, and fair with you, you accept her and continue the friendship. You know if she didn't care about you, she would not say anything or be around you. *Proverbs 11:16* states: *"A gracious woman retains honor . . ."*

Ms. Best of Friends stands against all odds, even against all your other friends who are trying to sway you away from doing what's right. Ms. Best of Friends will tell your other friends they are wrong, too, in accordance with God's word.

Although Ms. Best of Friends will not be with you when you stand before the Lord, even He will remember what Ms. Best of Friends said to encourage you to do the right thing, and He will probably ask you why you didn't do the right thing after being advised by Ms. Best of Friends.

Jesus was very clear about friendships. He did not call just anybody His friend. We must be careful to recognize and do the same. Although Jesus knew his true friends' frailties, He still called them His friends – the Disciples. *In John 15:13-15, Jesus* states: *"Greater love has no one than this, than to lay down one's life for his friends. 'You are My friends if you do whatever I command you. No longer do I call you servants, for a servant does not know what his master is doing; but I have called you friends, for all things that I heard from My Father I have made known to you.'"* Jesus trusted His disciples and called them His friends. He confided in His disciples. He cared for his disciples. He blessed his disciples. He was very much aware of the deceptive disciple, Judas, and had insight as to what Judas was doing against Him.

Jesus is your best friend. *Proverbs 18:24* states: *" . . . but there is a friend who sticks closer than a brother."* His name is Jesus.

What kind of friend are you? Are you that "friend indeed" to your friend in need? Do you tell your friend the truth no matter how it hurts? Do you gossip about your friend to other mutual friends? Can you keep a secret? Are your jealous of your friend? Do your hurt your friend's feelings out of spite? Do you entice your friend to do wrong with you? Do you really care about and honor your relationships with your friends?

Do you need a friend? If so, you have a friend in Jesus. He is your best friend, your protector, your provider, your healer, your comforter, and your righteousness. *Psalm 23* states: *"The Lord is my shepherd; I shall not want; He makes me to lie down in green pastures; He leads me beside the still waters; He restores my soul; He leads me in paths of righteousness for His name's sake. Yea, though I walk through the valley of the shadow of death, I will fear no evil for You [Lord] are with me; Your rod and your staff, they comfort me. You prepare a table before me in the presence of my enemies;*

You anoint my head with oil; my cup runneth over. Surely goodness and mercy shall follow me all the days of my life, and I shall dwell in the house of the Lord forever." This passage is a clear picture of the Lord's love, friendship, protection and provision for us in all areas of our lives. He is more than a friend to you. He sticks closer to you than a brother. He is God, your Creator. God has His companions *"goodness"* and *"mercy"* that follow you all the days of your life. Although this scripture is used in other circumstances of life, it's also very appropriate concerning friendship. We should all see the Lord as our best friend, and we should emulate Him, as referenced in *Psalm 23*.

Evil Company

There are also those friends who want to do bad and immoral things and they want you, because you're their friend, to do bad and immoral things with them. You want to be their friend, but you know better. You feel the pressure of losing the friendship because you don't want to join them in doing something you know is wrong. Yet, you don't seem to have the backbone to stand against what they want you to do with them. You're afraid to tell them you think what they want to do is wrong and you will have no part in it. You're fighting fiercely with yourself, which happens to be your conscience. *1 Corinthians 15:33* states: *"Do not be deceived: 'Evil company corrupts good habits."*

If you know what your friend is asking you to join in and do is wrong, be a real friend and tell her "NO." Tell her that what she wants to do is wrong and immoral, and what she's asking of you is wrong and immoral. Would a real friend ask you to compromise your morals, and what you know to be flat out wrong, to do something bad with her? Not only will she pay the consequences for her actions, but you will, too, if you go along with her. *Proverbs 15:3* states: *"The eyes of the Lord are in every place, keeping watch on the evil and the good."* So neither she nor you will get away with anything wrong in God's eyes. *1 Corinthians 6:9-11* states: *"Do you not know that the unrighteous will not inherit the kingdom of God? Do not be deceived. Neither fornicators, nor idolaters, nor adulterers, nor homosexuals, nor sodomites (those engaged in anal sexual intercourse), nor thieves, nor covetous, nor drunkards, nor revilers, nor extortioners will inherit the kingdom of God. And such were some of you, but you were washed, but you were sanctified, but you were justified in the name of the Lord Jesus and by the Spirit of our God."* You know better, you know from God's word you will not enter heaven if you engage in such practices. Heaven is the ultimate wonderful reward for obedience to Him and for godly living on this earth. However, the consequences "in the here and now" are what you will initially be facing, and they are not good. Then, at death, there are the consequences we must face when each of us stands before God. There are consequences for every action – good consequences for good actions and bad consequences for bad actions right now and right here on this earth. The consequences you pay in eternity are forever and ever.

Some friends who were very promiscuous received consequences of either getting pregnant, contracting a venereal disease, or even contracting AIDS. Some received all three consequences. Some promiscuous actions have even cost people their lives – they made the wrong decision to be at the wrong place at the wrong time doing the wrong thing with the wrong person who was married, for example. They and the married person were caught by the married person's spouse, and the spouse killed them both. At this point, it was too late to ask for forgiveness and to change their ways.

Some friends take you with them to a stranger's home to engage in some form of entertainment only to learn that the stranger was really strange, and you both barely escaped with your lives.

Some friends drive their vehicles way too fast, always tempting fate, soon to end up in a horrific motor vehicle accident where either they get killed, or you get killed because you were with them, or they kill someone else. The consequences of being a speed demon are fatal; it's too late to fix things to make it right after the damage is done. They can't bring back someone they caused to be killed. They have to live with the consequences the rest of their lives. It's too late to say: "If I would have, could have, should have." It's too late to say you're sorry.

Good Company/Bad Company

Be selective and careful concerning the choices you make in the area of friendship, because you will be known by the company you keep. You have to use wisdom, understanding, guidance and discernment with those who want to be your friends and with those who you want to be friends with. Be friend enough to tell your friend about consequences while telling her you will not partake in any wrong she wants to engage in with your participation. *2 Corinthians 6:14-15* states: *"Do not be unequally yoked together with unbelievers. For what fellowship has righteousness with lawlessness? And what communion has light with darkness? And what accord has Christ with Belial? Or what part has a believer with an unbeliever?"* This applies to marriages, friendships, and business relationships.

You've got to be **"tough"** to be a real and true friend. Not everybody is going to like you, or like what you believe in and stand for. You have to love some people enough, who think they are your friends, to let them go. Pray for them if they won't respect you and do the right things by you and by themselves. *Proverbs 23:17-18* states: *"Do not let your heart envy sinners, but be zealous for the fear of the Lord all the day; for surely there is a hereafter, and your hope will not be cut off."* So, it may seem like your friends are having fun while doing wrong, and it may seem like you're missing out on something, but their fun in doing wrong is just for a season and there will be consequences at the end. *James 4:4* states: *"Adulterers and adulteresses! Do you not know that friendship with the world is enmity with God? Whoever therefore wants to be a friend of the world makes himself [herself] an enemy of God." Proverbs 3:32* states: *"For the perverse person is an abomination to the Lord, but His [God's] secret counsel is with the upright."*

God will send you the right friends because He knows your heart. You will know them by their walk. *Proverbs 3:5-6* states: *"Trust in the Lord with all your heart, and lean not on your own understanding; in all your ways acknowledge Him, and He shall direct your paths."* Ask God to send you the right friends and stand in faith believing that God will do what He says. *Psalm 37:4* states: *"Delight yourself also in the Lord, and He shall give you the desires of your heart." James 2:23* states: *"And the Scripture was fulfilled which says, 'Abraham believed God, and it was accounted to him for righteousness.' And he was called the friend of God."*

Chapter 9

Be The Woman God Created You To Be

Chapter 9

Be The Woman God Created You To Be

Why Not Be A Proverbs 31 Woman?

Proverbs 31:10-31 in the Amplified Bible reads:

"A capable, intelligent, and virtuous woman – who is he who can find her? She is far more precious than jewels and her value is far above rubies or pearls.

The heart of her husband trusts in her confidently and relies on and believes in her securely, so that he has no lack of [honest] gain or need of [dishonest] spoil.

She comforts, encourages, and does him only good, as long as there is life within her.

She seeks out wool and flax and works with willing hands [to develop it].

She is like the merchant ships loaded with foodstuffs; she brings her household's food from a far [country].

She rises while it is yet night and gets [spiritual] food for her household and assigns her maids their tasks.

She considers a [new] field before she buys or accepts it [expanding prudently and not courting neglect of her present duties by assuming other duties]; with her savings [of time and strength] she plants fruitful vines in her vineyard.

She girds herself with strength [spiritual, mental, and physical fitness for her God-given task] and makes her arms strong and firm.

She tastes and sees that the gain from work [with and for God] is good; her lamp goes not out, but it burns on continually through the night [of trouble, privation (hardship), or sorrow, warning away fear, doubt, and distrust].

She lays her hand to the spindle, and her hands hold the distaff.

She opens her hand to the poor, yes, she reaches out her filled hands to the needy [whether in body, mind or spirit].

She fears not the snow for her family, for all her household are doubly clothed in scarlet.

She makes for herself coverlets, cushions, and rugs of tapestry. Her clothing is of linen, pure and fine, and of purple [such as that of which the clothing of the priests and the hallowed cloths of the temple were made].

Her husband is known in the [city's] gates, when he sits among the elders of the land.

She makes fine linen garments and leads others to buy them; she delivers to the merchants girdles [or sashes that free one up for service].

Strength and dignity are her clothing and her position is strong and secure; she rejoices over the future [the latter day or time to come, knowing that she and her family are in readiness for it]!

She opens her mouth in skillful and godly wisdom, and on her tongue is the law of kindness [giving counsel and instruction].

She looks well to how things go in her household, and the bread of idleness [gossip, discontent, and self-pity] she will not eat.

Her children rise up and call her blessed [happy, fortunate, and to be envied]; and her husband boasts of and praises her, [saying]

Many daughters have done virtuously, nobly, and well [with the strength of character that is steadfast in goodness], but you excel them all.

Charm and grace are deceptive, and beauty is vain [because it is not lasting], but a woman who reverently and worshipfully fears the Lord, she shall be praised!

Give her of the fruit of her hands, and let her own works praise her in the gates [of the city]!"

In essence, the *"Proverbs 31 Woman"* has got it going on, so to speak. She praises, honors, and fears the Lord. She's wise. She's discrete. She's honorable. She has sound judgment because she consults with the Lord. She spends her money wisely and for the benefit of her family. She has an open heart to give to others in need. She makes sure all of her family's needs are met, and her family appears to the public to be well cared for and wealthy. She keeps her household in order, including her servants. She does not spend her time in idle gossip. She does not complain about the work that is before her. She does what it takes, even to the point of working in the wee hours of the morning, to create and provide things for sale in order to be able to give to her family. Her children praise and love her immensely. Her husband brags about his wife and how wonderful she is to him and his family. He tells his friends that although there may be charming and sophisticated women who look good, the looks go in time and the charm and sophistication are deceptions, but he has the real deal, the prize, the gemstone at home – his wonderful wife, who is a great benefit to him, who makes him look good in front of all of his peers, and who helps him prosper. We should all aspire to be the *"Proverbs 31 Woman."*

Women Of God

We, as women, are to be Godly examples to each other, to our families, and to others. *Titus 2:1-8* states: *"But as for you, speak the things which are proper for sound doctrine: that the older men be sober, reverent, temperate, sound in faith, in love, in patience; the older women likewise, that they be reverent (respectful) in behavior, not slanderers (insult others, defame others), not given to much wine, teachers of good things that they admonish (caution, warn, reprimand) the young women to love their husbands, to love their children, to be discrete (separate, disconnected, detached), chaste (pure, virtuous, innocent, unblemished, spotless, and faithful), homemakers, good (high quality, decent, skillful, well-behaved, enjoyable), obedient (compliant, conforming, acquiescent, which is agreeable and yielding) to their own husbands, that the word of God may not be blasphemed. Likewise, exhort the young men to be sober-minded, in all things showing yourself to be a pattern of good works; in doctrine showing integrity, reverence, incorruptibility, sound speech that cannot be condemned, that one who is an opponent may be ashamed, having nothing evil to say of you."*

God created you for His purpose, and you're here on this earth to accomplish that purpose. You are well equipped because He has equipped you. Why would God give you a purpose to fulfill, but not give you what you needed to fulfill that purpose? You are well able. He has also given you a future and a hope. He has provided forgiveness for all your sins and your mistakes. He has provided for you to have wisdom, discernment, guidance and understanding. He has given you mercy, grace and goodness. He has provided for you to be healed by His Son's stripes when He [Jesus] died on the cross.

He has blessed you with all that you could ask and believe for. God loves you. *Psalm 103:1-5* states: *"Bless the Lord, O my soul; and all that is within me, bless His holy name. Bless the Lord, O my soul, and forget not all His benefits: who forgives all your iniquities, who heals all your diseases, who redeems your life from destruction, who crowns you with loving-kindness and tender mercies, who satisfies your mouth with good things, so that your youth is renewed like the eagle's."*

We, as children of God, are not to walk as the world does. We have a much higher calling and a much higher responsibility. We, as women of God, must walk in the light of His blessings on us. He is a Holy God and He wants us to be holy. In *Leviticus 19:2*, the Lord speaks to Moses saying: *"Speak to all the congregation of the children of Israel, and say to them: 'You shall be holy, for I the Lord your God am holy.'" 1 Peter 1:16* states: *"because it is written, 'Be holy, for I am holy.'"* So, we must check (ensure, safeguard, and inspect) ourselves to make sure we are walking as "holy young girls of God", "holy teenage girls of God", "holy young women of God", and "holy women of God." We honor God by our walk and by our talk, which encompasses how we dress, what we say, and how we carry ourselves. We can't look at the world and what the world is doing because we are not of the world – we are just visiting for a time.

We are to live our lives with purpose. After all, God has given you a future and a hope. Our Father says in *Jeremiah 29:11*: *"For I know the thoughts that I think toward you, says the Lord, thoughts of peace and not of evil, to give you a future and a hope." Proverbs 24:14* states: *"So shall the knowledge of wisdom be to your soul; if you have found it, there is a prospect [future], and your hope will not be cut off."*

We are not to live our lives haphazardly, thinking that whatever we do has no bearing on our lives or on others' lives, because what we do and what we say really does affect our lives and the lives of others. You never know who is watching you and for what reason. Not only is your speech being dissected and analyzed, but your walk is, too. Does your walk match what you say? Are you an encouragement or a discouragement to others?

There are consequences for everything we do, everything we do not do, everything we say, and everything we do not say. There are good consequences and there are bad consequences, based on our decisions and our actions. To not make a decision **is** a decision in itself. Although God has forgiven us, He cannot erase the consequences of our actions. The consequences are what we must bear as individuals. The consequences can affect all areas of our lives – our health, our finances, our families, our dreams, our hopes, and our future.

Our attitudes guide our thoughts, which create our decisions, which drive our actions, which will create our consequences that create our destinies. If you change your mind [attitude] and think about yourself as God thinks about you, you will definitely change your thoughts, which will change your decisions, which will then change your actions, which will change your consequences, and which will definitely change your destiny. God wants the best for you, but He has also given you a **"free will."** It's up to you to make the right choice. It's up to you to change your mind.

We are not our own. We belong to God. It's foolish to say, "This is my life and I'll do what I want with it." You don't own your life. You did not create yourself. God created you. God is the potter and you are the clay. *Isaiah 29:16* states: *"Surely you have things turned around! Shall the potter be esteemed as the clay; for shall the thing made say of him who made it, 'He did not make me?'" Or shall the thing formed say of him who formed it, "He has no understanding?"* Your body was created from dust and to dust your body will return.

Genesis 2:7 states: *"And the Lord God formed man of the dust of the ground, and breathed into his nostrils the breath of life; and man became a living being."* God spoke to Adam for his disobedience in the Garden of Eden in *Genesis 3:19,* stating: *"In the sweat of your face you shall eat bread till you return to the ground, for out of it [the ground] you were taken; for dust you are, and to dust you shall return."* So we are not to do with our bodies as we wish.

Many parents have said to their disobedient children, "I brought you into this world and I'll take you out." Well, that may not necessarily be a true statement by the parents, but the One who has the power to do both is God, Himself. *1 Peter 1:24-25* states: *"All flesh is as grass, and all the glory of man [woman] as the flower of the grass. The grass withers, and its flower falls away. But the word of the Lord endures forever."* So, it pays to be obedient to His word and do what He says in His word. The Lord Jesus, Himself, says in *Matthew 10:28*: *"And do not fear those who kill the body but cannot kill the soul, but rather fear Him who is able to destroy both soul and body in hell."*

Deep down inside, we all know right from wrong – good from evil. It has been instilled in us from the time of Adam and Eve when they were in the Garden of Eden and ate of the tree of the knowledge of good and evil. In *Genesis 2:17*, God commanded Adam, stating: *"but of the tree of the knowledge of good and evil you shall not eat, for in the day that you eat of it you shall surely die."* Because of what Adam and Eve did, we have become like God in the sense that the 'knowledge of good and evil' has been instilled in each and every one of us, whether we know the Bible or not. Because we know right from wrong, we have no excuse, and we shall surely die just like Adam and Eve. *Genesis 3:22-24* states: *"Then the Lord God said, 'Behold, the man has become like one of Us, to know good and evil, and now, lest he put out his hand and take also of the tree of life, and eat, and live forever.' Therefore, the Lord God sent him [Adam and Eve] out of the Garden of Eden to till the ground from which he was taken, so He [the Lord God] drove out the man; and He placed cherubim at the east of the Garden of Eden, and a flaming sword which turned every way, to guard the way to the tree of life."*

So, we know right from wrong – good from evil, whether we have ever read the Bible or not. It's the sin nature of every person who is born on earth because of Adam's sin in disobeying God when he ate from the tree of the knowledge of good and evil. Adam knew better because God commanded him not to eat of that tree. Even though Adam instructed Eve not to eat of the tree, she disobeyed and ate of it anyway. However, the responsibility of the sin rested on Adam because when Eve gave him some of the fruit to eat, Adam did eat of it, too, when he definitely knew better. Adam had a choice, and he made the wrong choice. We bear the consequences of Adam's choice.

This sin nature is instilled in us from early on because of Adam and Eve, so we have no excuse for the wrong that we do because we instinctively know better, but the good news is that we can go to our Heavenly Father for forgiveness through the Lord Jesus Christ who died on the cross for our sins. In *John 14:6*, Jesus speaks to his disciple Thomas: *"Jesus said to him, 'I am the way, the truth, and the life. No one comes to the Father except through Me.'"* Through the death and resurrection of the Lord Jesus Christ, you can have salvation, the forgiveness of your sins, and you can be restored to a new creation.

We are not to abuse our bodies. We did not come into this world smoking cigarettes, guzzling down alcohol, snorting or shooting up drugs, tattooing or body-piercing ourselves, or infecting ourselves with venereal diseases. In some unfortunate cases, some pregnant women who had a venereal disease unintentionally passed the disease to their babies through birth. None of this was God's intention for His creation. However, consequences for wrong decisions and actions have a way of coming to the surface.

Forgiveness

Forgive people because God has forgiven you. Jesus died on the cross in forgiveness of all your sins over 2,000 years ago. So forgive those who despitefully used you, who persecuted you, who threw you away like a piece of trash. As stated in *John 3:16-18*: *"For God so loved the world that He gave His only begotten Son that whoever believes in Him should not perish, but have everlasting life. For God did not send His Son into the world to condemn the world, but that the world through Him might be saved. He who believes in Him is not condemned, but he who does not believe is condemned already, because he has not believed in the name of the only begotten Son of God."*

We are not to repay evil for evil. *Romans 12:17-18* states: *"Repay no one evil for evil. Have regard for good things in the sight of all men. If it is possible, as much as depends on you, live peaceably with all men."* This doesn't mean that you're to be a doormat, to allow yourself to continue to suffer the wrongs of people against you, but you are to pray to God to forgive those who wronged you, and leave them alone to allow God to do His mighty work in them.

We are not to harbor vengeance against those who wronged us in any way – no matter what was said or done. We are to pray for and forgive them. The Lord says in *Romans 12:19: "Beloved, do not avenge yourselves, but rather give place to wrath; for it is written, 'Vengeance is mine, I will repay,' says the Lord."* In *Matthew 6:14-15*, Jesus states: *"For if you forgive men their trespasses, your heavenly Father will also forgive you. But if you do not forgive men their trespasses, neither will your Father forgive your trespasses."* This scripture is also referenced in *Mark 11:25-26*, which states:

"And whenever you stand praying, if you have anything against anyone, forgive him [her], that your Father in heaven may also forgive you your trespasses. But if you do not forgive, neither will your Father in heaven forgive your trespasses." The Apostle Paul also emphasized his own forgiveness of others in *2 Corinthians 2:10-11*, which states: *"Now whom you forgive anything, I also forgive. For if indeed I have forgiven anything, I have forgiven that one for your sakes in the presence of Christ, lest satan should take advantage of us; for we are not ignorant of his devices."* The Apostle Paul knew that if we don't forgive, we open ourselves up to satan's devices, which lead to bitterness and revenge, and we fall back into sin. However, when we forgive others, we are released from carrying that burden, and we are free. God takes on our burdens and He avenges the righteous in His own time.

God is faithful to forgive us. *1 John 1:9* states: *"If we confess our sins, He is faithful and just to forgive us our sins and to cleanse us from all unrighteousness."*

Did you know there are many "Woes" in the Bible against those who do wrong, especially to those who do wrong to other people? The dictionary identifies a woe as a distress, a grief, a sorrow, or a regret. So, the Lord will cause distress or grief or sorrow or regret to come on those who cause harm. In the Book of Isaiah, the Lord spoke through the prophet Isaiah to the people of Judah who had sinned. *Isaiah 3:11* states: *"Woe [regret, distress, sorrow, grief] to the wicked! It shall be ill with him, for the reward of his hands shall be given him." Isaiah 5:20-21* states: *"Woe [regret, distress, sorrow, grief] to those who call evil good, and good evil; who put darkness for light, and light for darkness; who put bitter for sweet, and sweet for bitter! Woe [regret, distress, sorrow, grief] to those who are wise in their own eyes, and prudent in their own sight." Isaiah 29:15* states: *"Woe [regret, distress, sorrow, grief] to those who seek deep to hide their counsel far from the*

Lord, and their works are in the dark; they say, 'Who sees us?' and 'Who knows us?'" *Isaiah 33:1* states: *"Woe [regret, distress, sorrow, grief] to you who plunder, though you have not been plundered; and you who deal treacherously, though they have not dealt treacherously with you! When you cease plundering, you will be plundered; when you make an end of dealing treacherously, they will deal treacherously with you."* *Micah 2:1* states: *"Woe [regret, distress, sorrow, grief] to those who devise iniquity, and work out evil on their beds! At morning light they practice it because it is in the power of their hand."*

These scriptures reflect what people bring on themselves when they do wrong to others, thinking that God doesn't see them. God sees everything and He knows everything we do and what others do to us. *Hebrews 4:13* states: *"And there is no creature hidden from His [God's] sight, but all things are naked and open to the eyes of Him to whom we must give account."* No one is getting away with anything. It may look that way to you, but God is not blind or forgetful. So, forgive those who wronged you and despitefully used you because God has already set in motion their reward.

Also, **FORGIVE YOURSELF**. Don't be angry with yourself. *1 John 1:9* states: *"If we confess our sins, He is faithful and just to forgive us our sins and to cleanse us from all unrighteousness."* Since God has forgiven you, stop carrying the guilt of your sins because it weighs you down and holds you back from doing what He has for you.

God is the Great Equalizer. Don't be so concerned with what the other person did to you because he will answer to God and bear his own consequences. You will bear the consequences of your own sins. God will forgive your sins when you ask for forgiveness and repent (change your mind and go a different direction).

Faith

God, our Creator, has given you the measure of faith, the faith that believes in Him and what He will do to carry you through all your trials. *Romans 12:3* states: *"For I say, through the grace given to me, to everyone who is among you, not to think of himself more highly than he ought to think, but to think soberly, as God has dealt to each one a measure of faith."* He has given you faith to know that whatever you ask of Him, within His will, it will be done for you. The same faith that Abraham had, you have. The same faith that Esther had, you have. The same faith that King David had, you have. Although Abraham, Esther and King David lived long ago, the same faith that operated in their lives will operate in your life today. You are well able in the faith that God has given you. *Galatians 3:9* states: *"So then, those who are of faith are blessed with believing Abraham."* The Amplified Bible states: *"So then, those who are people of faith are blessed and made happy and favored by God [as partners in fellowship] with the believing and trusting Abraham."*

We must live by faith in God, in what He can and will do. The Apostle Paul wrote in *Romans 1:16-17*: *"For I am not ashamed of the gospel of Christ, for it is the power of God to salvation for everyone who believes, for the Jew first and also for the Greek. For in it the righteousness of God is revealed from faith to faith; as it is written. 'The just shall live by faith.'"*

Just as you used your measure of faith for salvation and got saved unto Jesus, it is that same measure of faith to be used in everything you do. *Romans 10:17* states: *"So then faith comes by hearing and hearing by the word of God."* You heard the word of God and your heart was open to receive the measure of faith to accept Jesus Christ as your Lord and Savior.

Mark 11:22 states: *"Have faith in God."* Do not use your own human knowledge and reasoning. Trust God and have faith. *2 Corinthians 5:7* states: *"For we walk by faith, not by sight."* Whatever you have a need for, God has already provided it for you. His work is already done. **It's your faith that will bring it to pass.** Remember that He is not on your clock, but He is always on time. He is working behind the scenes to bring about the right results.

God wants you to trust Him. *Proverbs 3:5* states: *"Trust in the Lord with all your heart, and lean not on your own understanding; in all your ways acknowledge Him, and He shall direct your paths."*

If God did not want you to operate in faith, He would not have given you the measure of faith. You have the same amount of faith that He has given to each and every one of us. Those who operate in their measure of faith see their faith grow. Remember that God is not a man that He should lie. In fact, *Numbers 23:19* states: *"God is not a man that He should lie, nor a son of man that He should repent. Has He said, and will He not do? Or has He spoken, and will He not make it good?"* It's your faith that activates God's word to bring about what you need.

The Word

God has given you His word, which is life to you. His word has endured throughout time. What He has said has come to pass. He means what He says. He is not one to lie, but His word will be done. There is great power in the word of God. There is great power in the name of Jesus, who is the Word, as referenced in the Bible. *John 1:14* states: *"And the Word became flesh and dwelt among us, and we beheld His glory, the glory as of the only begotten of the Father, full of grace and truth." John 1:1-5* states: *"In the beginning was the Word, and the Word was with God, and the Word was God. He was in the beginning with God. All things were made through Him, and without Him nothing was made that was made. In Him was life, and the life was the light of men, and the light shines in the darkness, and the darkness did not comprehend it."* All throughout *Genesis 1*, *"God said"*, *"God created"*, *"God made"*, *"God called"*, and *"God blessed."* He is the Creator of all. He spoke His word and it was done. We must speak God's word back to Him, letting Him know that we are in agreement with His word and with His will. God responds to His word.

Wisdom

God has given you wisdom and discernment to know which way you should go. *Proverbs 9:10* states: *"The fear of the Lord is the beginning of wisdom, and the knowledge of the Holy One is understanding."* By having wisdom, you will be able to discern and avoid the pitfalls in life, and you will make your way prosperous. *Proverbs 3:13-18* states: *"Happy is the man who finds wisdom, and the man who gains understanding; for her proceeds are better than the profits of silver, and her gain [better] than fine gold. She [wisdom] is more precious than rubies, and all the things you may desire cannot compare with her. Length of days is in her right hand. In her left hand [are] riches and honor. Her ways are ways of pleasantness, and all her paths are peace. She is a tree of life to those who take hold of her, and happy are all who retain her."* So get wisdom!

Courage

We are to be courageous. In *Joshua 1:9*, the Lord God spoke to Joshua after the death of Moses, encouraging him to continue to lead God's people to the Promise Land by stating: *"Have I not commanded you? Be strong and of good courage, do not be afraid, nor be dismayed [distressed/discouraged], for the Lord your God is with you wherever you go."* This same statement applies to us today because He is with us. We are not to be weak, fearful or discouraged.

In fact, *2 Timothy 1:7* states: *"For God has not given us a spirit of fear, but of power and of love and of a sound mind." Isaiah 41:10* states: *"Fear not, for I am with you; be not dismayed for I am your God. I will strengthen you. Yes, I will help you. I will uphold you with My righteous right hand."* We are also encouraged by *Isaiah 40:31*, which states: *"But those who wait on the Lord shall renew their strength; they shall mount up with wings like eagles. They shall run and not be weary. They shall walk and not faint."*

Strength & Protection

God has given you strength to do His will, to stand, and having done all, to still stand. He has given you strength to endure and strength to lift up those who are struggling. *Psalm 29:11* states: *"The Lord will give strength to His people; the Lord will bless His people with peace."*

You are also endowed with God's protection. *Ephesians 6:11-18* states: *"Put on the whole armor of God that you may be able to stand against the wiles of the devil. For we do not wrestle against flesh and blood, but against principalities, against powers, against the rulers of the darkness of this age, against spiritual hosts of wickedness in the heavenly places. Therefore, take up the whole armor of God, that you may be able to withstand in the evil day, and having done all, to stand. Stand, therefore, having girded your waist with* ***truth****, having put on the* ***breastplate of righteousness****, and having shod your feet with the preparation of the* ***gospel of peace****; above all, taking the* ***shield of faith*** *with which you will be able to quench all the fiery darts of the wicked one, and take the* ***helmet of salvation****, and the* ***sword of the Spirit****, which is the Word of God; praying always with all prayer and supplication in the Spirit, being watchful to this end with all perseverance and supplication for all the saints."* Without the armor of God, you are vulnerable to the worldly schemes and attacks of satan who tries to send thoughts of your past mistakes or weaknesses to you to weaken you and make you revert back to your past life and your past sins. However, with God's armor, you are protected coming in and going out, and protected wherever you are because you are wearing the full armor of God.

Security In Our Faith

God has given you security in knowing that He is with you and working on your behalf to bring about His best in your life. Be secure in Him and in His word. *Romans 8:28* states: *"And we know that **all things work together for good** to those who love God, to those who are the called according to His purpose." 2 Timothy 1:7* states: *"For God has not given us a spirit of fear [nervousness, doubt, anxiety, stress, depression, defeat], but of power and of love and of a sound mind."* You have security in knowing that you are saved. *Romans 10:9-10* states: *". . . that if you confess with your mouth the Lord Jesus and believe in your heart that God has raised Him from the dead, you will be saved. For with the heart one believes unto righteousness, and with the mouth confession is made unto salvation."* So rejoice in knowing you are secure in the Lord.

Romans 8:37 states: *"Yet in all these things we are more than conquerors through Him who loved us."* God is perfect and He never makes a mistake. You're not a mistake. You are an overcomer, you're a conqueror, and you're victorious. God can take the circumstances you are currently in, and He can use those circumstances to bring forth His objective, His purpose, and your good. God is God, and He can change the circumstances to accomplish what He wills. He will bring you through the circumstances (the operative word is "through"). Remember in 2 Corinthians 5:7: "For we walk by faith, not by sight."

Our faith calls those things that be not as though they are. *Romans 4:16-18* states: *"Therefore it is of faith that it might be according to grace, so that the promise might be sure to all the seed [us who believe], not only to those who are of the law but also to those who are of the faith of Abraham, who is the father of us all (as it is written, 'I have made you a father of many nations') in the presence of Him whom he believed – God who gives life to the dead and calls those things which do not exist as though they did; who contrary to hope, in hope believed, so that he became the father of many nations, according to what was spoken, 'So shall your descendants be."*

Grace

God has given you grace, which is His favor, His love, and His goodness toward you that you cannot earn and do not deserve. *Ephesians 2:8-9* states: *"For by grace you have been saved through faith, and that not of yourselves, it is the gift of God, not of works, lest anyone should boast."* So, grace is one of many gifts you receive from God. If it were not for the grace of God, we would all be totally lost and headed straight for hell. God, being merciful, has not given any of us what we really deserve. He has given us His grace. His grace and His mercy renew daily and are enduring. *Psalm 23:6* states: *"Surely goodness [unfailing love] and mercy shall follow me all the days of my life, and I will dwell in the house of the Lord forever." Psalm 103:1-5* states: *"Bless the Lord, O my soul, and all that is within me, bless His holy name! Bless the Lord, O my soul, and forget not all His benefits: Who forgives all your iniquities, Who heals all your diseases, Who redeems your life from destruction, Who crowns you with loving kindness and tender mercies, Who satisfies your mouth with good things, so that your youth is renewed like the eagle's." Psalm 84:11* states: *"For the Lord God is a sun and shield; the Lord will give grace and glory; no good thing will He withhold from those who walk uprightly."* If that's not grace, I don't know what is.

1 Peter 4:10 states: *"As each one has received a gift, minister it to one another, as good stewards of the manifold grace of God."* You are blessed with the grace of God who gives us all good things in our lives. God loves you and favors you greatly. His grace is pure. Even when we were walking in the world, He was merciful and gave His grace that we might be saved. We must be gracious to others so their hearts will be opened to receive the gift of God – salvation.

By His grace, we can come to Him with anything. *Hebrews 4:14-16* states: *"Seeing then that we have a great High Priest who has passed through the heavens, Jesus the Son of God, let us hold fast our confession. For we do not have a High Priest who cannot sympathize with our weaknesses, but was in all points tempted as we are, yet without sin. Let us therefore come boldly to the throne of grace, that we may obtain mercy and find grace to help in time of need."* The Lord Jesus is there for us. He has been tempted like we are, and He passed all the tests. He understands our weaknesses and He will guide us through by His grace. We, as His disciples, live under His grace. Grace is not beating us up, but loving us up. God loves us.

His grace is sufficient for us in all things. Jesus spoke to the Apostle Paul concerning grace. *2 Corinthians 12:9-10* states: *"And He said to me, 'My grace is sufficient for you, for My strength is made perfect in weakness. Therefore, most gladly I will rather boast in my infirmities, that the power of Christ may rest upon me. Therefore, I take pleasure in infirmities, in reproaches, in needs, in persecutions, in distresses, for Christ's sake. For when I am weak then I am strong."* So, as you go through trials and hardships, remember the words of the Apostle Paul. The hope that the Apostle Paul had in Jesus Christ brought him through **all** trials, tests, and tribulations. The hope you have in the Lord Jesus Christ will also bring you through **all** trials, tests and tribulations.

Peace

God has given you peace, the kind of peace that passes all understanding. *Romans 5:1* states: *"Therefore, since we have been justified through faith, we have peace with God through our Lord Jesus Christ."* There is no greater peace than the peace of God. You know that He is not the author of confusion, so where there is no peace there is confusion. You must dwell in His word to keep yourself out of the realm of confusion. *1 Corinthians 14:33* states: *"For God is not the author of confusion but of peace, as in all the churches of the saints."* We are not to be anxious about anything, but we are to trust God. *Philippians 4:6-7* states: *"Be anxious for nothing, but in everything by prayer and supplication, with thanksgiving, let your requests be made known to God; and the peace of God, which surpasses all understanding, will guard your hearts and minds through Christ Jesus."*

Discipleship

God has made you a disciple to go into all the world and proclaim the word of God through your speaking His word and through your actions (matching your walking with your talking). If you do this, you are truly His disciple.

God chose you before you were even born. *Ephesians 1:3-8* states: *"Blessed be the God and Father of our Lord Jesus Christ, who has blessed us with every spiritual blessing in the heavenly places in Christ, just as He chose us in Him before the foundation of the world that we should be holy and without blame before Him in love, having predestined us to adoption as sons [daughters] by Jesus Christ to Himself according to the good pleasure of His will, to the praise of the glory of His grace by which He made us accepted in the Beloved. In Him we have redemption through His blood, the forgiveness of sins, according to the riches of His grace, which He made to abound toward us in all wisdom and prudence."*

You have been called to serve God, and He has instilled in you special gifts that equip you to serve Him. *Romans 12:6-21* states: *"Having then gifts differing according to the grace that is given to us, let us use them: if prophecy, let us prophesy in proportion to our faith; or ministry, let us use it in our ministering; he who teaches, in teaching; he who exhorts, in exhortation; he who gives, with liberality; he who leads, with diligence; he who shows mercy, with cheerfulness. Let love be without hypocrisy. Abhor what is evil. Cling to what is good. Be kindly affectionate to one another with brotherly love, in honor giving preference to one another, not lagging in diligence, fervent in spirit, serving the Lord, rejoicing in hope, patient in tribulation, continuing steadfastly in prayer, distributing to the needs of the saints, given to hospitality. Bless those who persecute you; bless and do not curse. Rejoice with those who rejoice, and weep with those who weep. Be of the same mind toward one another. Do not set your mind on high things, but associate with the humble. Do not be wise in your own opinion. Repay no one evil for evil. Have regard for good things in the sight of all men. Beloved, do not avenge yourselves, but rather give place to wrath; for it is written, 'Vengeance is Mine, I will repay', says the Lord."* This is your discipleship.

The Promises Of God

With all that you have been through, stay faithful and receive the promises of God. He has sustained you and provided for you, and He has given you strength to endure so that you can see His promises come to pass in your life. *Hebrews 6:13-15* states: *"For when God made a promise to Abraham, because He could swear by no one greater, He swore by Himself, saying, 'Surely blessing I will bless you, and multiplying I will multiply you.' And so, after he had patiently endured, he obtained the promise."* So, after you have patiently endured, being faithful, standing and continuing to stand, you will receive God's promise. It is impossible for God to lie, so just as

He promised Abraham and kept His promise, He has also promised a good outcome for you. *Galatians 6:9* states: *"Let us not grow weary while doing good, for in due season we shall reap if we do not lose heart."* In *Jeremiah 31:25*, the Lord says, *"For I have satisfied the weary soul, and I have replenished every sorrowful soul."* So you must have hope, the hope in the Lord Jesus Christ. *Psalm 40:5* states: *"Many, O Lord my God, are Your wonderful works which You have done; and Your thoughts toward us cannot be recounted to You in order; if I would declare and speak of them, they are more than can be numbered."*

So as a Child of God, blessed with all blessings, knowing that you are well equipped to do His will, you're well equipped to endure all adversity and to overcome with victory. You're well equipped in the God-kind of faith, knowing that He will answer all your prayers, and He will change your circumstances for the better. As a child of God, He will use you, your circumstances and your life in a mighty and wonderful way to fulfill the purpose He has for you, and for you to have a good testimony. You are His beautiful creation; you were created for His purpose.

Remember that all things are possible with God for those who believe. *Matthew 19:26* states: *"But Jesus looked at them and said to them, 'With men this is impossible, but with God, all things are possible.'"* Remember, too, that God keeps His word. *2 Corinthians 1:20* states: *"For all the promises of God in Him are Yes and in Him Amen, to the glory of God through us."* You have the victory in all areas of your life!

Chapter 10

The Laws Regarding Sexual Promiscuity

Chapter 10

The Laws Regarding Sexual Promiscuity

Legal Consequences of Sexual Promiscuity

There are man's laws and there are God's laws that are active in the area of sexual promiscuity. Both sets of laws carry heavy consequences.

The Surgeon General of the United States, in his July 9, 2001, letter entitled "A Call To Action To Promote Sexual Health And Responsible Sexual Behavior" cited the fact that over 12 million people in the United States a year contract some type of sexual disease, and those cases were the ones that were reported. As of July 9, 2001, almost 800,000 people had AIDS, and almost 900,000 people were living with the HIV virus. He cites lifelong consequences for individuals, families, communities and the nation. The Surgeon General also stated that most of those infected are economically disadvantaged, racial minorities with different sexual identities, disabled, and teenagers. He mentioned that sexual heath is connected with physical health, mental health, and spiritual health of people. The Surgeon General stated that everyone must play a part in the sexual health of our country – parents, teachers, clergy, social service professionals, medical professionals, and policy makers. The Surgeon General believes that our country has serious health challenges in the area of sex.

MAN'S LAWS

With respect to man's laws, one can be charged with civil damages for rape, statutory rape and incest, and serve jail time. We now have laws enacted to punish those who commit sexual crimes that jeopardize the health of others.

Tort Law/Personal Injury Laws Regarding Transmission Of Sexual Diseases

A person who has a venereal disease, who knowingly transmits that disease to an unsuspecting person while having consensual sexual intercourse, with or without protection, can be prosecuted in court civilly under "tort law" and is subject to pay civil damages for infecting a person with a venereal disease. However, the burden of proof is on the victim and can be hard to prove if the victim is sexually active with other people.

It is against the law, a crime, to transfer a sexually transmittable disease to someone without his or her knowledge or permission.

Most sexual crimes fall under tort law. Tort law means that a person has the obligation to another person to act with care towards that person to not cause significant injury to the person. If a person causes careless or intentional injury to another person and/or their property, the person who caused the injury or damage is liable under tort law to pay monetary damages to compensate for the injury and/or damage caused to the other person. For example, in a car accident, if the cause of the accident is your fault, you are responsible to make the person and his property whole (in the condition they were in before the accident).

With regard to sexual promiscuity, if a person who is infected with an active sexual transmittable disease has sex with a person who is not infected, and the person who was not infected now becomes infected, that newly infected person (plaintiff) can prosecute for civil damages which bring monetary awards in court. The plaintiff can also bring possible criminal charges (for jail time) against the other person (defendant), and also sue for money damages.

Under Tort Law, a woman can prosecute (sue) for (1) negligence, (2) intentional infliction of emotional distress, (3) fraud, and (4) battery. The burden of proof is on the woman to prove "intent", "negligence", and "fraud" by the man. Here are some general definitions under Tort Law:

Negligence – Failure to use reasonable care through an act or omission that a reasonably careful person would use in a situation or circumstance, or somebody does something that a reasonable person would not do under the same circumstances. Proximate cause exists when the woman is injured as a result of negligent conduct of the man who caused the immediate injury. Criteria for negligence are: (1) the man owed a duty to the woman, (2) the man violated that duty, (3) the woman suffered injury as a direct result of the violation of the man's duty, and (4) the injury was a proximate result or consequence of the man's negligence to use reasonable care toward the woman. A woman who unknowingly had sexual intercourse with a man (who has an STD and who did not inform her prior to engaging in the act of sexual intercourse) could prosecute the man for negligence, among other crimes. The parents of teenagers can prosecute on behalf of their teenagers, too, with or without their teenager's consent or cooperation.

Intentional Infliction of Emotional Distress – This is the intentional conduct by a person that is so extreme that it causes emotional distress to another person. The criteria for the intentional infliction of emotional distress are: (1) the person's acts are intentional and reckless, (2) the person's conduct must be extreme and outrageous, (3) the conduct is the cause, and (4) the conduct creates severe emotional distress in the other person. The conduct of the person must be so disgraceful and severe that the conduct goes way beyond normal decency. The conduct is inexcusable. Extreme emotional distress is where no reasonable person in society should be expected to endure such conduct. In California, a person suffering from intentional infliction of emotional distress by another person can recoup money damages in a lawsuit. A woman who unknowingly has sexual intercourse with a man who has AIDS could suffer from intentional infliction of emotional distress, and she can prosecute the man civilly (money) and criminally (jail time).

Fraud – Merriman-Webster's Dictionary has a great definition. "Intentional perversion of truth in order to induce another to part with something of value or to surrender a legal right; an act of deceiving or misrepresenting." For example: A young man seduces a teenage girl to have sex with him. The teenage girl has something of value – her virginity. She asks him if he has an STD and he says that he does not. She goes ahead and has sex with him. She later finds out that she has an STD, and she got it from him. He perverted the truth in order to have sex with her. He committed fraud, he was deceptive, and he damaged her good health by exposing her to an STD. Fraud is a deliberate misrepresentation that causes a person to suffer damage.

Battery – The willful and intentional touching by a person of another person against that person's will is battery. Offensive touching, whether it causes harm or not, is considered battery. The touching of a woman by a man may or may not cause physical harm to her, but it's still considered an act of battery. However, if a woman gives consent to a man to commit a battery on her, she cannot bring a lawsuit against him. Use of an object or a substance placed on or in a person against that person's will or without that person's permission constitutes a battery. For example, if a person spits in another person's face, it's considered a battery. A man touching a woman in an inappropriate manner and without her permission can be charged with battery and be prosecuted.

A woman who was infected by a man who has a sexually transmittable disease can prosecute the man for negligence, intentional infliction of emotional distress, fraud, and battery. However, most of the time the case is very hard to prove, the litigation of the case is expensive, and the outcome is not rewarding because the woman still has to be treated by a physician to cure the disease, if the disease is curable. Unfortunately, the burden of proof is on the woman who was infected by the man. STDs take some time to show up, and if the woman was sleeping around with every Tom, Dick, Harry, Married and, in some cases, Mary, she would have a difficult time determining which person gave her the STD, and she would have a difficult time proving it in court. However, if the guy admitted that he had Herpes (for example) and admitted that he did not inform her before he and she engaged in sexual intercourse, he could be charged with battery and possibly serve time in jail. He could also be prosecuted civilly and be required to pay money damages to the woman. A man can also prosecute (sue) a woman for contracting an STD from her, too, and the same criteria would apply.

Felony charges can be filed against a person who has AIDS or who is HIV positive if the person did not inform his sexual partner prior to having sexual intercourse. He can be sent to jail for failing to disclose the information to his sexual partner. Health & Safety Code Section 120291 makes it a felony for a person who willfully exposes his/her sexual partner to AIDS or HIV through unprotected vaginal or anal sexual intercourse. The person who violates this law can serve up to eight (8) years in prison. A woman filing felony charges against a man who has AIDS or who is HIV positive can prove that he "willfully intended" to infect her because of his prior medical records which show he has AIDS or he's HIV positive, her medical records reflect that she did not have AIDS or was not HIV positive prior to having sex with him, and that he did not inform her prior to having unprotected sex with her.

Age of Consent

States vary regarding what the Age Of Consent should be. Age Of Consent means that until a person reaches a certain age (defined by the state in which she lives), she is incapable of consenting to sexual intercourse. Age Of Consent also means the age when an individual can legally consent to having sexual intercourse with another person. Both parties who are under the Age Of Consent and who are legally married fall under the umbrella of being legally within the Age Of Consent. The Age Of Consent also depends on the mental age of a person, whether she is mentally capable of making a decision to have sex, and whether she mentally understands what she's doing. The Age Of Consent throughout the United States ranges from the age of 14 to the age of 18. In California, the Age Of Consent is 18, unless the minor is legally married.

I believe there should also be a "financial" component to the "Age Of Consent." There are financial costs to consider when teenagers engage in sex prior to the Age Of Consent, and their parents end up bearing most, if not all, of the financial costs. If the teen contracts a sexual disease and cannot afford to take herself to the doctor for treatment and pay for the treatment, the parents must bear this burden for their teenage child. Some state-run clinics will bear the cost of contraceptives for prevention and a limited amount of the costs when a teenager is pregnant. The teenager should discuss with her parents her intention to have sexual intercourse prior to doing so, but we all know that doesn't happen in the real world. In the real world, teenagers don't think about the possible financial consequences, and they certainly don't ask their parents for permission to have sex out of wedlock. However, there are definitely financial costs related to having sex prior to and after the Age Of Consent.

In California, civil penalties can range from $2,000 to $25,000 for statutory rape of a female under the Age Of Consent. The amount of the penalty depends on the age of the offender and the age difference between the offender, who is 21 years of age or older, and the minor, who is under 16 years of age. The monetary penalties collected go first to the cost of litigation, and the balance then goes to the State Underage Pregnancy Prevention Fund.

California Misdemeanor – Anyone 3 years older or 3 years younger having sex with a female who is a minor is in violation of a misdemeanor and could serve up to one year in county jail or in state prison.

California Felony – A male engaging in sexual intercourse with a female who is a minor (being under the age of 18 and who is 3 years younger than the male), is guilty of a misdemeanor or a felony and could serve one year in county jail or be imprisoned in state prison for two or more years.

The biggest problem with these laws is that if the person is not prosecuted, the crime continues and children continue to be born out of wedlock and become a burden to society.

Statutory Rape – Sex Under The Age Of Consent

The term 'statutory rape' has changed in most states. Statutory rape is now currently identified as sexual assault, rape of a child, corruption of a minor, carnal knowledge of a minor, or unlawful carnal knowledge. A female minor is a person who is past the age of puberty, meaning that she has matured enough physically to have a menstrual cycle (monthly period), and she's physically capable of getting pregnant (usually around 12 years of age). A minor who has sexual intercourse with an adult (a person who is of the Age Of Consent) is considered to be, by law, coerced into having sex with the adult. The word "coerce" means to 'dominate by force' or to 'take advantage of' or "to force by threat", or to "compel by force." The premise is that the minor is legally unable to give consent to having sex with an adult. An adult having sex with a child, who has not reached the age of puberty (not yet having a menstrual cycle), has committed the crime of child molestation.

Romeo & Juliet Laws

Not all states have Romeo & Juliet Laws. These laws are for teenagers having consensual sex. An older teenager having sex with a younger teenager, who is considered to be a minor, would normally be arrested, prosecuted, jailed, and labeled as a sexual predator and/or a child molester. However, under the Romeo & Juliet Laws, the penalties are not as severe if there is at least a two-year difference in ages between the teenagers. The violation in most states would be considered a misdemeanor.

In statutory rape, both minors can be charged because they each have committed statutory rape upon the other. Depending on the anger of the parents, many charges can be racked up against the violators on both sides, and both teens can be prosecuted.

A minor can be charged with statutory rape according to California Penal Code Section 261.5. The term used in the Penal Code is "unlawful sexual intercourse", and the law uses the term "any person", whether minor or otherwise, who has sexual intercourse with a minor would be liable. The penalties vary for a minor having sexual intercourse with another minor, and most of these cases would be heard in a family law court.

Most statutory rape laws these days are gender-neutral, meaning that females can be charged for statutory rape the same as males, and they will bear the same legal consequences. Also, if a pregnancy results as a consequence of sexual intercourse between a minor and a minor or an adult and a minor, the defendant will be liable to pay child support and any related costs.

Criminal and Civil Charges For Persons Having AIDS Or Are HIV Positive

If the person being sued is found to have AIDS or is HIV positive, he can be prosecuted criminally as well as civilly. In order to prosecute the party that injured you after having sexual intercourse with that party, you must prove that the venereal disease the party had was not disclosed to you prior to having sexual intercourse with him. The burden of proof would be on you to prove: (1) You were diagnosed with a venereal disease that you did not have prior to having sexual intercourse with the other party; (2) the venereal disease has caused you physical pain and emotional distress as a direct result of contracting the venereal disease from the party; (3) the party was the proximate (or direct) cause of you having the venereal disease; and (4) there was money expended in your medical treatment and possible cure, loss of wages for loss of time on the job, and for psychological or psychiatric counseling.

The courts will seek to determine whether there was negligence on the part of the party who injured the other party: (a) whether he knew he had a sexually transmittable disease beforehand; (b) whether he knew he had the ability to infect another person with the disease; (c) whether he did not inform the other party that he had a sexually transmittable disease prior to the act of sex; (d) whether he consciously performed the act of sex knowing of his condition; (e) whether he falsely stated that he was sexually disease-free or whether he intentionally omitted the fact that he was infected with a sexually transmittable disease when the other party inquired prior to engaging in sexual activity; (f) whether he intentionally deceived the other party (lied) regarding having a sexually transmittable disease;

(g) whether he, knowing of the possible spread of infection, went ahead anyway and had sex with the other party; (h) whether the other party was aware that he was infected with a sexually transmittable disease prior to engaging in sex; and (i) whether he knew that it would cause the other party emotional and physical damage, and yet he committed the act of sex anyway.

Since the burden of proof is almost always on the woman, it would be most advantageous for you to really think, ask the other party, and verify/confirm the physical health of the other party before engaging in sexual intercourse outside of marriage. Otherwise, you're just gambling and the odds are definitely against you.

The court system is a whole different world within itself, and it can be very frustrating maneuvering your civil case (and possibly criminal case) through it to get some sort of legal relief and possible monetary relief for the wrong that has been done to you. However, it will not resolve the physical pain and suffering, the emotional scarring, the financial expenses involved in a lawsuit, the embarrassment of the court case because courts create public records that can be seen by everyone, and it will not resolve the possibility of putting your future and your life in danger due to your health condition. But, if you think about the potential consequences before you act, you will avoid the situation and its consequences altogether. **The life you save may very well be your own.**

Laws Governing Minor's Rights Relating To Sexual Health

In the State of California, the law states that minors may have access to any contraceptive services, prevention and treatment of STDs, and pregnancy services without parental notification or permission beginning at the age of 13. The parents of the minor are not allowed to have access to the minor's medical information from a doctor or the medical records relating to contraception, treatment of

STDs, or pregnancy unless given permission by the minor. Minors have medical confidentiality from the age of 13 and onward.

Doctors who treat minors/teenage girls are prohibited from disclosing (1) contraception, (2) treatment of STDs, or (3) pregnancy information of a teenage girl to her parents without her permission. Consequently, if the teenage girl is taken to the doctor by her parents and the doctor treats the teenage girl for any of these three conditions, it is the teenage girl's right not to have her condition disclosed to her parents. If the doctor discloses the information to the teenage girl's parents without authorization by the teenage girl, the teenage girl can legally prosecute (sue) the doctor. The doctor is allowed to disclose the teenage girl's condition in all other medical areas.

The California Supreme Court passed legislation that allows minors the constitutional right to have an abortion (terminate a pregnancy), aside from a medical emergency, without their parents' consent or notification. It is considered the minor's right to privacy. Health & Safety Code Section 123450 states that the minor has a right to privacy under the California Constitution.

By establishing the above confidentiality laws for teenage girls, this allows the teenager to seek out medical treatment for herself without hindrances.

GOD'S LAWS

Boundaries/Borders

God has set up borders for your protection. There are consequences for living outside of His borders because you are not operating within His laws, which are set up to protect you. When you operate outside of God's laws, you are literally tying His hands, and you're left to the devices of the world, which are controlled by satan.

If there were no rules or restrictions and we were left to ourselves, we would literally destroy ourselves.

Our real enemy is satan, and he wants to destroy us because we are God's creation. He will use whatever means necessary to steal our happiness and wholeness; steal our virginity and our chances of a good marriage; and he will totally destroy us either physically, mentally, financially, or spiritually. By some of the examples in this book, you can see how satan is using sexual promiscuity and sexual diseases to destroy those who are operating outside of God's boundaries. Jesus stated in *John 10:10: "The thief does not come except to steal, and to kill, and to destroy. I have come that they [women] may have life, and that they [women] may have it more abundantly."*

Satan is the thief who wants to destroy you by whatever means necessary. Sexual promiscuity is only one of the methods satan uses to seduce and destroy. The Bible even tells us what we are up against. *Ephesians 6:12* states: *"For we do not wrestle against flesh and blood, but against principalities, against powers, against the rulers of the darkness of this age, against spiritual hosts of wickedness in the heavenly places."* The Amplified Bible says it this way: *"For we are not wrestling with flesh and blood [contending only with physical opponents], but against the powers, against [the master spirits who are] the world masters of the present darkness, against the spirit forces of wickedness in the heavenly places [supernatural sphere]."* This is not a game. This is real!

That's the reason why we have to protect ourselves, and God gives us protection – the whole and full armor of God, as referenced in *Ephesians 6:13*, which states: *"Therefore take up the whole armor of God, that you may be able to withstand in the evil day, and having done all, to stand."* God gives you the armor to stand and fight the enemy in Ephesians 6:14-17:

(1) Gird your waist with **truth**.

(2) Put on the breastplate of **righteousness**.

(3) Shod your feet with the preparation of the gospel of **peace**.

(4) Take up the shield of **faith**, which is able to quench all of the fiery darts of the wicked one.

(5) Put on the helmet of **salvation**.

(6) Put on the sword of the **Spirit**, which is the Word of God.

Age of Accountability

Along with the Age Of Consent comes the Age of Accountability. When you come into the knowledge and understanding of right and wrong, you are accountable for your actions in the area of sex as well as in all other areas of your life.

God's Laws Regarding Sexual Promiscuity

The Bible has many scriptures relating to sexual immorality, sexual promiscuity, and sexual sensuality. There are moral, physical, and emotional consequences for being sexually promiscuous. Here are most of them, mostly from the New Testament.

> ***Exodus 20:14*** **states: *"You shall not commit adultery."***
>
> ***Numbers 32:23*** **states: *"But if you do not do so, then take note, you have sinned against the Lord; and be sure your sin will find you out."***

Proverbs 6:32-35 **states: *"Whoever commits adultery with a woman [man] lacks understanding; he [she] who does so destroys his [her] own soul. Wounds and dishonor he [she] will get, and his [her] reproach will not be wiped away, for jealousy is a husband's [wife's] fury; therefore he [she] will not spare in the day of vengeance. He [She] will accept no recompense, nor will he [she] be appeased though you give many gifts."***

Ecclesiastes 12:13-14 **states: *". . . Fear God and keep His commandments, for this is man's [woman's] all. For God will bring every work into judgment, including every secret thing whether good or evil."***

John 8:34 **states: *"Jesus answered them, 'Most assuredly I say to you, whoever commits sin is a slave of sin.'"***

Romans 6:12 **states: *"Therefore do not let sin reign in your mortal body, that you should obey it in its lusts."***

Romans 6:16 **states: *"Do you not know that to whom you present yourselves slaves to obey, you are the one's slaves whom you obey, whether of sin leading to death, or of obedience leading to righteousness?"***

Romans 13:13 **states: *"Let us walk properly, as in the day, not in revelry and drunkenness, not in lewdness (sexually unchaste, vulgarity and profanity) and lust (loose sexual desire), not in strife and envy. But put on the Lord Jesus Christ, and make no provision for the flesh, to fulfill its lusts."***

1 Corinthians 3:16-17 **states: *"Do you not know that you are the temple of God and that the Spirit of God dwells in***

you? If anyone defiles the temple of God, God will destroy him. For the temple of God is holy, which temple you are."

1 Corinthians 3:18-20 **states: *"Let no one deceive himself. If anyone among you seems to be wise in this age, let him become a fool that he may become wise. For the wisdom of this world is foolishness with God. For it is written, 'He catches the wise in their own craftiness', and again, 'The Lord knows the thoughts of the wise, that they are futile.'"***

1 Corinthians 5:11 **states: *"But now I have written to you not to keep company with anyone named a brother [sister], who is sexually immoral, or covetous, or an idolater, or a reviler, or a drunkard, or an extortioner – not even to eat with such a person."***

1 Corinthians 6:13-14 **states: *"Foods for the stomach and the stomach for foods, but God will destroy both it and them. Now the body is not for sexual immorality but for the Lord, and the Lord for the body. And God both raised up the Lord and will also raise us up by His power."***

1 Corinthians 6:15-16 **states: *"Do you not know that your bodies are members of Christ? Shall I then take the members of Christ and make them members of a harlot? Certainly not! Or do you not know that he who is joined to a harlot is one body with her? For 'the two', He says, 'shall become one flesh.'"***

1 Corinthians 6:18-20 **states: *"Flee sexual immorality. Every sin that a man [woman] does is outside the body, but he [she] who commits sexual immorality sins against his [her] own body. Or do you not know that your body is the temple of the Holy Spirit who is in you, whom you have***

from God, and you are not your own? For you were bought at a price; therefore, glorify God in your body and in your spirit, which are God's."

<u>*1 Corinthians 7:1-2*</u> **states: *"Now concerning the things of which you wrote to me: It is good for a man not to touch a woman. Nevertheless, because of sexual immorality, let each man have his own wife, and let each woman have her own husband."***

<u>*Galatians 5:19-21*</u> **states: *"Now the works of the flesh are evident, which are: adultery, fornication, uncleanness, lewdness, idolatry, sorcery, hatred, contentions, jealousies, outbursts of wrath, selfish ambitions, dissentions, heresies, envy, murders, drunkenness, revelries, and the like; of which I tell you beforehand, just as I also told you in time past, that those who practice such things will not inherit the kingdom of God."***

<u>*Galatians 6:7*</u> **states: *"Do not be deceived, God is not mocked; for whatever a man [woman] sows, that he [she] will also reap."***

<u>*Ephesians 5:1-7*</u> **states: *"Therefore be imitators of God as dear children, and walk in love, as Christ also has loved us and gave Himself for us, an offering and a sacrifice to God for a sweet-smelling aroma. But fornication (consensual sexual intercourse between two people not married to each other) and all uncleanness or covetousness (greediness), let it not even be named among you, as is fitting for saints; neither filthiness, nor foolish talking, nor coarse jesting (foul mouth), which are not fitting, but rather giving of thanks. For this you know that no fornicator, unclean person, nor covetous man [woman] who is an idolater, has any***

inheritance in the kingdom of Christ and God. Let no one deceive you with empty words, for because of these things the wrath of God comes upon the sons [daughters] of disobedience. Therefore, do not be partakers with them."

Colossians 3:5-6 states: *"Therefore put to death your members which are on the earth: fornication, uncleanness, passion, evil desire, and covetousness, which is idolatry. Because of these things the wrath of God is coming upon the sons [daughters] of disobedience."*

Colossians 3:17 states: *"And whatever you do in word or deed, do all in the name of the Lord Jesus, giving thanks to God the Father through Him."*

1 Thessalonians 4:3-8 states: *"For this is the will of God, your sanctification (to set apart for a sacred purpose; to purification): that you should abstain from sexual immorality; that each of you should know how to possess his [her] own vessel [body] in sanctification and honor, not in passion of lust, like the Gentiles who do not know God; that no one should take advantage of and defraud his brother [sister] in this matter, because the Lord is the avenger [punisher] of all such, as we also forewarned you and testified. For God did not call us to uncleanness, but in holiness. Therefore, he [she] who rejects this does not reject man, but God, who has also given us His Holy Spirit."*

1 Timothy 1:8-10 states: *"But we know that the law is good if one uses it lawfully knowing this: that the law is not made for a righteous person, but for the lawless and insubordinate, for the ungodly and for sinners, for the unholy and profane, for murderers of fathers and murderers of mothers, for manslayers, for fornicators, for sodomites, for*

kidnappers, for liars, for perjurers, and if there is any other thing that is contrary to sound doctrine,"

2 Timothy 2:19 states: *"Nevertheless the solid foundation of God stands, having this seal: 'The Lord knows those who are His', and, 'Let everyone who names the name of Christ depart from iniquity.'"*

Hebrews 12:14-16 states: *"Pursue peace with all people, and holiness, without which no one will see the Lord: looking carefully lest anyone should fall short of the grace of God, lest any root of bitterness springing up cause trouble, and by this many become defiled; lest there be any fornicator or profane person like Esau, who for one morsel of food sold his birthright."*

Hebrews 13:4 states: *"Marriage is honorable among all, and the bed undefiled, but fornicators and adulterers God will judge."*

James 1:12-16 states: *"Blessed is the man [woman] who endures temptation; for when he [she] has been approved, he [she] will receive the crown of life which the Lord has promised to those who love Him. Let no one say when he [she] is tempted, 'I am tempted by God', for God cannot be tempted by evil, nor does He Himself tempt anyone. But each one is tempted when he [she] is drawn away by his [her] own desires and enticed. Then, when desire has conceived, it gives birth to sin; and sin when it is full-grown, brings forth death. Do not be deceived, my beloved brethren."*

Jude 1:7 states: *"as Sodom and Gomorrah, and the cities around them in a similar manner to these, having*

given themselves over to sexual immorality and gone after strange flesh, are set forth as an example, suffering the vengeance of eternal fire."

The Law Of Sowing & Reaping

The consequences of sexual promiscuity are also within the Law Of Sowing And Reaping. If you're promiscuous with sex outside of marriage, you are a gambler and the odds are stacked against you. You are bound to get pregnant, get raped, catch an infection, or contract a disease. We all have said to ourselves when things happen, "Where did this come from?" Sometimes it's an expression of joy because we did things the right way and got the right results, but most of the time it's an expression of sadness, disappointment, grief and regret because we acted outside of God's laws and, in some cases, outside of man's laws. Had we known what we were going to reap (or harvest) before we sowed a seed of sexual promiscuity, our thoughts, decisions, and actions would have led to a better outcome or a better harvest.

The Bible gives clear guidance concerning the penalty for sexual promiscuity relating to sowing and reaping. *Galatians 6:7-8* states: *"Do not be deceived, God is not mocked; for whatever a man [woman] sows, that he [she] will also reap. For he [she] who sows to his [her] flesh will of the flesh reap corruption, but he [she] who sows to the Spirit will of the Spirit reap everlasting life."* This applies to how we use our bodies as well as in other areas of our lives. As long as the earth exists, you will have a harvest of what you sow in all areas of your life. *Genesis 8:22* states: *"While the earth remains, seedtime and harvest, cold and heat, winter and summer, and day and night shall not cease."* Although this law applies to agriculture, it also applies to how we live in the world today. *Job 4:8* states: *"Even as I have seen, those who plow iniquity and sow trouble reap the same." Proverbs 22:8* states: *"He who sows iniquity will reap sorrow, and the rod of his anger will fail."* Disobedience reaps a harsh harvest. *Hosea 8:7* states: *"They sow the wind, and reap the whirlwind."* Being disobedient to God's word in spite of knowing what His Word says will reap severe consequences. *Psalm 7:11* states: *"God is a just judge, and God is angry with the wicked every day."*

But if you sow good to your body, you will reap good from your body. If you turn from doing wrong and ask God for forgiveness and repent (meaning don't do it anymore, but do things in accordance with God's word), He will forgive, heal, and bless you. *Hosea 10:12* states: *"Sow for yourselves righteousness; reap in mercy; break up your fallow ground, for it is time to seek the Lord until He comes and rains righteousness on you." Galatians 6:9* states: *"And let us not grow weary while doing good, for in due season we shall reap if we do not lose heart."*

We only have one body. We can't exchange it for another body, and we can't go to a parts store and purchase new parts to replace the bad parts of our bodies. Although much progress has been made in the medical field, there is no guarantee that the part you need is/or will be available. There are six major human body systems within our bodies (the nervous system, the digestive system, respiratory system, circulatory system, lymph system, and the musculoskeletal system). There are also other systems within the body (the immune system, endocrine system, cardiovascular system, reproductive system, and urinary system). These systems run like separate engines and yet run in conjunction with one another in our bodies. God created these systems within our bodies when He created us. A lot of research has been conducted in all of these body systems; however, the medical field has not progressed enough to replace any of these systems to give you a new lease on life. A single cell within the body that has been altered by artificial means or destroyed by use of mind-altering drugs, abuse of prescription drugs, alcoholism, diseases and infections (including sexual transmittable diseases and infections), and physical abuse can create irreversible damage and possible demise of the human body. Only God can make you whole again.

Whatever you put into your body or however you use your body can and will affect any one of these systems, if not all of them. Depending on what you do, allow to be done to you, or what you allow to enter into you by ingestion, injection, or physically, the effects may be good and enriching or they may be bad, debilitating, or deadly. (Have you noticed that there are no old drug addicts?!) You will suffer the consequences if you misuse your body. *1 Corinthians 3:16-18* states: *"Do you not know that you are the temple of God and that the Spirit of God dwells in you? If anyone defiles the temple of God, God will destroy him [her]. For the temple of God is holy, which temple you are. Let no one deceive himself [herself]. If anyone among you seems to be wise in this age, let him [her] become a fool that he [she] may become wise."* This passage means that God lives inside of you. God is holy. Therefore you should be holy, which means that you should have the mindset of God, and God's mindset is love. If you love God, you will recognize that God is in you and you will not defile your body.

The Bible is telling you to not be fooled into thinking that God's word does not apply to you, that you're immune from any disease, that you are as smart as God, or that you can outsmart God. *1 Corinthians 3:18-20* states: *"Let no one deceive himself [herself]. If anyone among you seems to be wise in this age, let him become a fool that he may become wise. For the wisdom of this world is foolishness with God. For it is written, 'He catches the wise in their own craftiness', and again, 'The Lord knows the thoughts of the wise, that they are futile.'"*

God means what He says and He says what He means. *1 Corinthians 6:13-14* states: *"Foods for the stomach and the stomach for foods, but God will destroy both it and them. Now the body is not for sexual immorality but for the Lord, and the Lord for the body. And God both raised up the Lord and will also raise us up by His power."*

You will reap what you sow into your physical body. You can count on it!

God wants you to stay focused on Him, for there is peace, safety and good health in Him. His word is infallible and eternal. *Proverbs 4:20-27* states: *"My son [daughter], give attention to my words; incline your ear to my sayings, do not let them depart from your eyes, keep them in the midst of your heart, for they are life to those who find them, and health to all their flesh. Keep your heart with all diligence, for out of it spring the issues of life. Put away from you a deceitful mouth, and put perverse lips far from you. Let your eyes look straight ahead, and your eyelids look straight before you. Ponder the path of your feet, and let all your ways be established. Do not turn to the right or the left; remove your foot from evil."*

Reprobate/Degenerate/Backsliding Mind

You cannot keep sinning, asking God to forgive you, and not take His forgiveness seriously. Repentance involves four major actions: (1) Tell God of your sin. (2) Ask God to forgive you of your sin. (3) Thank God for forgiving you of your sin. (4) Repent of your sin, which means to stop doing the sin. When you stop doing the sin after you have been forgiven, this tells God that you believe He has forgiven you. He knows that bad habits are hard to break, but ask God to help you to not continue in the sin. Some say they can't help themselves. This is all the more reason you should ask God to help you. He knows you and all your weaknesses, and He will help you if you ask Him. However, you have no excuse if you don't ask Him to help you to stop sinning in areas of your life such as in sexual promiscuity. Yes, you can stop sinning with God's help, but you've got to trust Him to help you. This is where your faith comes into play. In *Mark 11:24*, Jesus states: *"Therefore I say to you, whatever things you ask when you pray, believe that you receive them, and you will have them."* This statement by the Lord Jesus is in present tense – it's in the "now." This means that when you pray to God to forgive you and to help you conquer the sin of promiscuity, He immediately begins to work on your weakness. But, you've got to believe that God's word is true, His word is real, and His word is active and it's working in you.

You can't just wait on God to fix the problem. His word is always in the present, and that means that He's already done His part. He's waiting on you to do your part. Your part is to say "NO" when the desire to commit sin comes. Your job is also to stay in faith that He is working in you. The more you say NO to the sin, the more you are exercising your faith, and the less of a temptation the sin becomes. This is where your faith in God's word is working with you, giving you more and more courage each and every time to overcome the sin nature.

We do not allow our flesh to rule over us. *1 John 2:16-17* states: *"For all that is in the world – the lust of the flesh, the lust of the eyes, and the pride of life – is not of the Father but is of the world. And the world is passing away and the lust of it; but he who does the will of God abides forever."* The world is satan's domain, but we are not of the world. Our flesh is part of our body, and we are to control our bodies. God has given us power to control our bodies. So when the fleshly urge, desire, or thought to commit a sexual sin comes, you must recognize that the urge, desire, or thought did not come from God, but from satan, and you are to immediately dismiss it in the name of Jesus. That urge, desire, thought is from satan telling your flesh (which is part of your senses) that it needs sex, but God does not operate in the flesh. The devil operates in the flesh and in your thoughts trying to get you to yield to your flesh. The devil sends thought darts that he implants into your mind. If that particular sin is your weakness, the devil bombards you with those thoughts until you succumb to the thoughts or you dismiss those thoughts with God's word. Don't try to reason with these thoughts when you know what God's word says. Tell satan that you don't receive that thought in the name of Jesus. Tell satan that "It is written", and speak God's scripture concerning the particular temptation. *1 Corinthians 10:13* states: *"No temptation has overtaken you except such as is common to man, but God is faithful, who will not allow you to be tempted beyond what you are able, but with the temptation, will also make the way of escape, that you may be able to bear it."* So, as you can see in this scripture, God has already given you the ability to escape the temptation. The battle and the decision begin in your mind where satan tries to tempt you through your thoughts, your desires, and through people who try to entice/seduce you into committing a sexual sin. Remember *James 1:14-15*: *"But each one is tempted when he [she] is drawn away by his [her] own desires and enticed. Then when desire has conceived, it gives birth to sin; and sin, when it is full-grown, brings forth death."*

When the opportunity to commit sin comes, you must recognize it and dismiss it with God's word (the sword of the Spirit, which is part of God's armor that He has given you). If you don't know His word, you will fail in this area. You must stand on God's word and refuse to budge. *Ephesians 6:13* states: *"Therefore take up the whole armor of God, that you may be able to withstand in the evil day, and having done all, to stand."* Having done all, stand, and the thought about committing a sexual sin will leave you, and so will the temptation to do so. I can't guarantee the thoughts and desires won't come back after you dismissed them the first time, but each time they do come back, continue to dismiss them in the name of Jesus. Each time you dismiss the thought or desire, the temptation lessens. After a while, they won't come back, but if they do, you will know what to do about them.

By not taking God's word seriously, and constantly going back into your sin after asking for forgiveness and for His assistance in helping you to change, you put yourself in jeopardy of searing [burning] your own mind of which there is no return. No one knows when this searing will occur or how many times one continues to commit sin before his or her mind is seared. The following scriptures clearly reflect that God will leave you to your own sins that will eventually lead you to your own destruction if you continue backsliding into your sins.

Romans 1:24-32 states: *"Therefore God also gave them up to uncleanness, in the lusts of their hearts to dishonor their bodies among themselves, who exchanged the truth of God for the lie, and worshipped and served the creature [satan] rather than the Creator [God], who is blessed forever, Amen. For this reason God gave them up to vile passions. For even their women [men] exchanged the natural use for what is against nature. Likewise also the men [women], leaving the natural use of the woman [man], burned in their lust for one another, men with men [women with women] committing what is shameful, and receiving in themselves the penalty of their error which was due. And even as they did not like to retain God in their knowledge, God gave them over to a debased [defiled] mind, to do those things which are not fitting; being filled with all unrighteousness, sexual immorality, wickedness, covetousness, maliciousness, full of envy, murder, strife, deceit, evil-mindedness; they are whisperers, backbiters, haters of God, violent, proud, boasters, inventors of evil things, disobedient to parents, unloving, unforgiving, unmerciful; who knowing the righteous judgment of God, that those who practice such things are deserving of death, not only do the same but also approve of those who practice them."*

Titus 1:16 states: *"They profess to know God, but in works they deny Him, being abominable [repulsive], disobedient, and disqualified for every good work." Jeremiah 6:30* states: *"People will call them rejected silver; because the Lord has rejected them." Proverbs 14:14* states: *"The backslider in heart will be filled with his [her] own ways." 2 Corinthians 13:5* states: *"Examine yourselves as to whether you are in the faith. Test yourselves. Do you not know yourselves, that Jesus Christ is in you, unless indeed you are disqualified?"*

God has already provided a way for you to redeem yourself through your confession of sin, asking forgiveness of sin, repenting of sin (changing your mind and going a different direction), and accepting that you have been forgiven because the Lord Jesus Christ already died on the cross for your sins. However, this does not mean that you can continue in your sin. Again, repentance means to stop doing the sin and to change direction in this area of your life. God is not mocked.

If you repent and return to the Lord, He will forgive you and restore you. *Jeremiah 3:22* states: *"Return, you backsliding children, and I will heal your backslidings."* However, Jesus says very clearly that if you have been forgiven and restored, but yet you go back to your wicked ways, you are not fit for the kingdom. In *Luke 9:62*, Jesus states: *"No one having put his hand to the plow, and looking back, is fit for the kingdom of God."* Jesus gives a further warning in *John 15:6* concerning reverting back to your old sinful ways after He has forgiven you. In *John 15:6*, Jesus states: *"If anyone does not abide in Me, he is cast out as a branch and is withered; and they gather them [withered branches] and throw them into the fire, and they are burned."*

The Lord gives a further insight concerning backsliding. Only a foolish person will dismiss the forgiveness and grace given to her, which she did not deserve in the first place, and return to her wicked ways. *Proverbs 26:11* states: *"As a dog returns to his [her] own vomit, so a fool repeats his [her] folly."*

The Laws Of God Are Perfect

The Bible is God's instruction book for you to read, meditate, and implement in your life daily so you can live a successful, blessed, and peaceful life. You will do well to follow God's instructions because there is great reward and great blessings in keeping His word. All your needs will be met. You will have long life and good health. You will be protected and shown favor. You will be blessed going in and coming out. *Psalm 19:7-11* states: *"**The law of the Lord is perfect**, converting the soul; **the testimony of the Lord is sure**, making wise the simple; **the statutes of the Lord are right**, rejoicing the heart; **the commandment of the Lord is pure**, enlightening the eyes; **the fear of the Lord is clean**, enduring forever; **the judgments of the Lord are true and righteous altogether**. More to be desired are they than gold, yes, than much fine gold; sweeter also than honey and the honeycomb. Moreover by them your servant is warned, and in keeping them there is great reward."*

Rights of Parents, Children & Teenagers

God's Laws regarding children and teenagers are the following:

- ***Leviticus 19:3*, God states: *"Every one of you shall revere his mother and his father, and keep My Sabbaths; I am the Lord your God."***

- ***Ephesians 6:1* states: *"Children, obey your parents in the Lord, for this is right. Honor your father and mother, which is the first commandment with promise, that it may be well with you and you may live long on the earth."***

- ***Proverbs 13:1* states: *"A wise son [daughter] heeds his [her] father's [mother's] instruction, but a scoffer [someone who shows contempt] does not listen to the rebuke [reprimand]."***

- ***Proverbs 15:20*** **states:** ***"A wise son [daughter] makes a father glad, but a foolish man [woman] despises his [her] mother."***

- ***Proverbs 17:25*** **states:** ***"A foolish son [daughter] is a grief to his [her] father, and bitterness to his [her] mother who bore him [her]."***

- ***Proverbs 19:27*** **states:** ***"Cease listening to instruction, my son [daughter], and you will stray from the words of knowledge."***

- ***Proverbs 20:20*** **states:** ***"Whoever curses his [her] father or his [her] mother, his [her] lamp will be put out in deep darkness."***

- ***Proverbs 22:6*** **states:** ***"Train up a child in the way he [she] should go, and when he [she] is old he [she] will not depart from it."***

- ***Proverbs 22:15*** **states:** ***"Foolishness is bound up in the heart of a child; the rod of correction will drive it far from him [her]."***

- ***Proverbs 23:24-25*** **states:** ***"The father of the righteous will greatly rejoice, and he who begets a wise child will delight in him [her]. Let your father and your mother be glad, and let her [your mother] who bore you rejoice."***

- ***Proverbs 29:17*** **states:** ***"Correct your son [daughter], and he [she] will give you rest; yes, he [she] will give delight to your soul."***

Parents ***'pay the costs to be the boss'*** in the home, not teenagers!

Parents are accountable to God for the children He has blessed them with. Parents are to be responsible for and consistent in the raising and caring for their children and their households. Parents hold a responsibility for the success of at least two generations of their family – their children and their children's children. *Proverbs 13:22* states: *"A good man leaves an inheritance to his children's children . . . ."*

Parents are not selfish. Selfish people are very stingy people. If parents were selfish, you, as a teenager, would not exist. You certainly would not be able to demand your rights. You would not have your own bedroom, but share it with a sibling or two or three. You would not have your own cell-phone or computer or television in your bedroom. You would not be taken shopping for clothes more than once a year, if that. You would not have spending money. You would not be taken to the doctor or dentist to ensure your good health. These are just a few creature comforts that most teenagers take for granted.

Parents give to their family before they give to themselves. In fact, providing for their family is providing for themselves because they know their children are gifts from the Lord. Parents love their family. Parents serve and sacrifice for the needs of the family. Parents know that their children are an inheritance from the Lord, and they are responsible to God to help their children fulfill the purpose that God has for each child. Children are like arrows in the parents' quiver, where the arrows are to be molded and shaped in such a way that when they are shot from the bow out into life (leave home and go on their own) they will land well. *Psalm 127:3-5* states: *"Behold, children are a heritage from the Lord, the fruit of the womb is a reward. Like arrows in the hand of a warrior, so are the children of one's youth. Happy is the man who has his quiver full of them. They shall not be ashamed, but shall speak with their enemies in the gate." Psalm 128:2-3* states: *"When you eat the labor of your hands, you shall be happy, and it shall be well with you. Your wife shall be like a fruitful vine in the very heart of your house, your children like olive plants all around your table."*

When teenagers get in trouble, parents are there to correct, protect, and help them. When teenagers have doubts, parents reassure them. When teenagers have a need, parents meet that need. When teenagers feel threatened or are fearful, parents protect them and console them. When teenagers get sick, parents take care of them, take them to the doctor or hospital, stay with them, and do whatever is needed to ensure restoration.

Parents put up with nonsense on the job just to get that paycheck to support their family. Parents will work overtime to ensure they have enough money to buy that special gift for their child. Parents tolerate all sorts of personalities and situations on the job to ensure they are able to provide for their family. Parents work all during the year to provide a family vacation.

Parents who work inside the home (father or mother) are Domicile Engineers (DEs). They work in the home to make it pleasant for the whole family. DEs multi-task to ensure a smooth and successful running of the household. They feed, bathe, and clothe their children. They comb, brush, cut and/or braid their children's hair. They wash and iron their children's clothes for school. They prepare lunches for their children, and drive their children to school or walk them to the bus stop to be picked up by the school bus. They help their children with their homework. They are the chauffer taking their children to soccer, baseball, basketball, football, ballet or music practice. They take their children to doctor and dental appointments. They clean the house, do the grocery shopping, and prepare family meals. They pay the bills of the family, and they oversee household repairs.

If DEs charged by the hour, no one could afford to pay them.

First and foremost, parents and God bring children into this world. Parents provide the roof over their children's heads, the clothes on their backs, and the food they eat. Parents provide physical protection as well as health protection to maintain the well-being of their children. Parents pay for the room their teenager sleeps in, which, by the way, is not off limits to parents because they are paying the rent or mortgage. Parents provide the bed that teenagers sleep on, the linen on the bed, and those posters teenagers have taped or nailed to the walls of their "temporary" rooms. The mere fact that parents allow their teenagers cell-phones so they can be in contact with them in case of an emergency is a privilege; it's not a right or an entitlement. Parents pay the cell-phone bills, but it does not give their teenagers the right to abuse their cell-phone privileges.

Parents who purchase a car for their teenagers or provide use of the family car for their teenagers do this as a gift. This act lets the teen know that the parents believe they have matured and can be trusted. Teenagers should not abuse their driving privilege by driving recklessly, getting a bunch of tickets, or driving under the influence of alcohol or drugs. The use of a vehicle, any vehicle, is strictly a privilege granted to teenagers by their parents because they care for them. More than likely, parents have included their teens on their car insurance policy, which is very costly. Teenagers have no clue what it costs to have a minor child on a family car insurance policy.

Unless a teenager has a part-time job while attending school to pay for her own phone, her own vehicle, her own car insurance, her own room and board somewhere else, and other related costs, she has no right to demand her rights within the family home. A lot of teenagers say they have the right to do with their bedrooms as they choose. They want to do whatever they want in a room that their parents have allowed them to inhabit while growing up. They feel everything in their bedroom is off-limits to their parents because their bedroom is their own private property. This is a disease known as "entitlement." Teens also believe their cell-phones and computers are private and not to be invaded by their parents. They feel they can have anyone they choose in their bedrooms within their parents' home. However, they fail to realize that what they have received from their parents is "temporary" while they are residing in the family home.

Parents want their children comfortable during their "temporary" stay, so many parents provide a lot of creature comforts. But, again, the parents ***"pay the costs to be the boss"*** in the home. Therefore, a teenager's bedroom is **never** off-limits to the parents. No parent should be afraid to enter any room of their own home that they are paying for. The parents have the right and responsibility to check **"everything"** in the bedroom of their teenager, especially if the teenager is acting out of the ordinary living standards of the family, especially if the teenager can negatively influence and contaminate the other siblings in the household, and especially if the teenager can damage the environment of the household in general. There is **"nothing private"** in a family home amongst children and teenagers.

Parents pay for everything, and they are responsible for their family's welfare and well-being. Parents are accountable to God and man's authority for their children. Parents are in control of everything in the home. If a teenager doesn't like it, she's free to move out when she reaches the Age of Accountability – generally age 18. The teenager can also ask the family court to grant her to become an Emancipated Minor if she's capable of providing for herself financially, and if she is mentally and emotionally mature enough to handle her independence.

Many teenagers say they have the right to do with their bodies as they choose because it's their own personal bodies. They want to be able to get body piercings, tattoos, color their hair in unnatural colors, and they want the right to be promiscuous. But the bodies of teenagers belong to God. Until the Age of Accountability (18 years old), it's the parents' responsibility to keep their teenagers' bodies healthy, which means no body piercings, no tattoos, and no right to be promiscuous. For example, if a teenager's body piercing gets infected, her parents will end up taking her to the doctor and paying for the doctor visit, prescriptions for antibiotics, and any other related costs because she is under the Age of Accountability. The teenager generally has no financial means of her own to cover these expenses.

Concerning body piercings, *Leviticus 19:28* states: *"You shall not make any cuttings in your flesh for the dead, nor tattoo any marks on you; I am the Lord."*

If a teenager, who is under the Age of Accountability, is promiscuous and ends up pregnant, the parents will bear the costs related to the pregnancy, not the teenager. The teen has no financial means of her own to undertake such an expense. Therefore, since the teen is not of the Age of Accountability, she should not be doing things that she is unable to account for – sexually, financially, mentally, and emotionally.

Some teenagers ditch school because they have absolutely no interest in learning. They'd rather hang out with their friends, drink, do drugs, or have promiscuous sex. If you're a teenager who believes you're wasting your time in school and not trying to learn anything for yourself (to help you in **your** future), you will have only **yourself** to blame when life's reality hits you. It won't be your parents' fault, and it won't even be your friends' fault. It will be your fault because you made the choice. You are responsible for you and for your future. Parents already have their education and are living their lives. You are in charge of your own education and your own future.

Parents don't want their children to be ignorant or unintelligent. Parents want their children to have better opportunities and choices so they can enjoy better lifestyles. That's the whole point, the only point of sending one's child/teenager to school. Uneducated parents, especially, send their children to school to obtain a better education, to secure better opportunities in life, and to not have to work as hard as they did to make a living.

The saying, ***"A Mind Is A Terrible Thing To Waste"*** is so very true. A lot of teenagers believe they can take drugs and alcohol without any consequences because, of course, everybody's doing it, it's fun, and it's their right. If you alter your brain, your mind, and the different systems working within your body by using drugs (marijuana, cocaine, heroine, PCP, LSD, Methamphetamines, etc.), which alter, damage and kill your brain cells and body cells causing your brain signals to be scrambled so you can't think straight; or you experience dysfunctions in your body; or one or more of your body's systems malfunctions; or you have organ deterioration causing loss of ability of an organ; or you get some sort of exotic cancer, etc., it will be no one's fault but yours, and you will bear the consequences of living a miserable, sickly, and painful life until the damage from the drugs ends your life.

Your body is not designed to ingest and process foreign matter not intended to be processed by the human body. But, be sure your sins will find you out. In *Numbers 32:23* the Lord speaks through Moses stating: *"But if you do not do so, then take note, you have sinned against the Lord; and be sure your sin will find you out."* You, yourself, cannot fix the damage you allow to be caused inside your body through drugs or other foreign matter. You have no idea what kind of damage the drugs or foreign matter will create in your body, when it will begin to surface, how to stop it, how to fix it, or how it will alter your life. By the time you realize you have damaged your body, it will be too late because the damage is already done. It has come to the surface, and now you're dependent on any help you can get to change your body back to the way it was. By the use of drugs or anything that could alter your health, you have created a situation and a destination that you cannot repair or reverse. All the doctors, psychologists, psychiatrists, medications, and advances in medical technologies cannot fix or reverse the damage; they may be able to slow the progress of the damage, but, in essence, you're toast. This also includes the damage from sexually transmitted infections and diseases; they work the same as drugs – ravaging the human body.

Parents deserve your respect, no matter what. You don't have to like them, but the time is coming sooner than you think when you will be totally in charge of yourself and responsible and accountable for your own actions. Let's see how well you do. Even after you leave home to go to college, the military, trade school, or to work two fast-food jobs, you owe your parents respect. Your parents are accountable to God, not you, for how they raise you.

God says what He means and He means pretty much what He says concerning all aspects of the family, which include the family structure with respect to children and teenagers. God doesn't lie. *Numbers 23:19* states: *"God is not a man that He should lie, nor a son of man, that He should repent. Has He said, and will He not do? Or has He spoken, and will He not make it good?"*

Adulthood

As a teenage girl, you may feel that being under age and pregnant is your right. But you have no rights until you reach the Age of Accountability. However, when you do adult things even though you're a teenager under the Age of Accountability, you enter into adulthood and adult responsibility. It is now your responsibility to raise your child. You are now accountable as an adult.

It's not your parents' responsibility to raise your child because they did not make that choice; you did. You did not go to them and ask if you could have sex with a boy to get pregnant. You did not ask them beforehand to take care of you and your child if you got pregnant. You made the choice, not your parents. At the time you made the choice to engage in sexual activity, which led to your pregnancy, you did not give any consideration to your parents. Maybe you subconsciously assumed that things would work out where your lifestyle would remain the same. Maybe you thought the guy who got you pregnant would marry you, move you into your own apartment or home, and all your needs and the baby's needs would be easily met. There would be no lack and no struggle. Or, if the guy dumped you, maybe you thought your parents would continue to raise you as a teenager, and they would help raise and take care of your child, too. But reality is never what you think or assume. Your choice to gamble by being involved in sexual promiscuity will affect your future.

In California and in some other liberal states, as a teenager, you do have the right to be tested to see if you are pregnant. You also have the right to receive birth control pills. It's your right to be tested for an STD or for HIV. You also have the right to have an abortion. You don't need permission from anyone in order to execute your rights. But you, alone, will bear the consequences for the rights given you by the State you live in. You will also bear the consequences for your decisions and actions by your disobedience to God's laws. You are accountable and responsible.

The one who impregnated you or gave you an STD is also accountable and responsible. Don't think he's getting away with what he did. He, too, will bear whatever consequences come from his actions.

Teenagers don't want to be accountable for adult-type responsibilities, nor should they be, if they don't engage in things or activities that would make them bear such heavy adult responsibilities. As a teenager under the Age of Accountability, you are incapable of handling adult responsibilities in the areas of medical care, housing, finances, food, etc. And why should you? You're a teenager! Your only responsibilities at home involve going to school, doing your homework, doing your chores, and being obedient and respectful to your parents so you can live a long and fruitful life. You have no other responsibilities, and you need no other responsibilities.

However, if you're pregnant, you've taken an unwanted turn and have rushed too soon into the adult responsibility/accountability area of your life. And, guess what? The life of being a carefree teenager is definitely over, and the hard adult reality sets in quickly. This hard reality will last until your child reaches her or his own Age of Accountability.

You can't be a teenager doing adult things, yet expect to still be treated like a teenager. When you do things that adults do, you are acting like an adult, you are accountable as an adult, and you are responsible as an adult – whether you like it or not. Not thinking and making wrong decisions forces you to grow up real fast, too fast!

In essence, rights are not free, and freedom to exercise those rights is not free. Freedom to do anything is earned; freedom is not an entitlement. Freedom on any level of life is earned.

Teenage Sexual Promiscuity In The Home

Parents are the only ones who have the right to have sex (make love) in their own home – not their teenage children who live in the home! Parents ***"pay the costs to be the boss"*** in their own home.

Aside from it being wrong to have sex as a teenager, it's also wrong to do it in your parents' home. To commit this sin in your parents' home shows lack of Godly wisdom, lack of respect for your parents, and lack of respect for yourself. The person you're having sex with in your parents' home definitely doesn't respect you or your parents. This is definitely a moral breakdown, and consequences are on the way.

You haven't paid for anything in the home, so you have no right to have sexual intercourse in your parent's home, in the bedroom they provide for you, on the bed they purchased for you to sleep in, etc. You just can't play house in your parents' home.

Obviously, any guy who has sex with you in your bed in your parent's home doesn't think much of you or your parents. He doesn't even think much of himself. He has no shame. He's like a dog that will do anything, anywhere, at anytime without any regard. He just wants to have his fun at your expense and at your parents' expense. Not only is he getting the sex free from you, but he's also violating your parents' home. Don't even say that it's alright because you two love each other. It's not alright! If the guy loved you, he, himself, would not defile you or your parents' home. He would honor and respect you and your parents. He would do things the right way. If you're not sure about this, I dare you to tell your parents that you had sex or are going to have sex in your bedroom in their home, and see what happens.

Is it really the boy's fault for having sex with you in your parents' home? You were in control of the situation. You had the keys to your home. You had a choice. You made the wrong choice. So, you can't even blame him although he bears his own responsibility for this choice, too. Do you think he would have sex with you at his parents' home? I doubt it. So, the question is: Do you have enough respect for yourself and for your parents not to allow this sinful activity to happen under your parents' roof?

Also, in the area of sexual promiscuity while living in your parents' home, your parents definitely have rights, too. Your parents have the right to press civil and possible criminal charges against the boy whom you were sexually active with. **Your parents do not need your permission or your cooperation to prosecute the boy.** If the District Attorney's Office (prosecution) finds grounds to go forward with your parents' charges against the boy, the prosecution will not even need your testimony for or against the boy.

Under man's laws and God's laws, it's your parents' right and responsibility to oversee your welfare and well-being until you reach the Age of Accountability, at which time you are considered an adult. Before you reach the Age of Accountability, your parents are responsible for your total package. Your parents are responsible for teaching you God's word; teaching you right from wrong; being good examples in front of you in line with God's word; and providing a roof over your head, clothes on your back, food on the table, and keeping you safe and healthy. If your parents continue to support you after you have reached the Age of Accountability, it is strictly a gift, and not an entitlement.

As a minor under the Age of Accountability, if you break the neighbor's window while playing baseball in your yard, your parents are responsible to pay for the damage you caused. If your parents allow you to drive the family car and you get into an accident, and it's your fault, your parents are responsible for restoring the other party's vehicle – not you. If you get into trouble with the law, your parents will intervene on your behalf with the Police. If your parents allow you to have a cell-phone or a credit card, they are responsible for paying the bills you create from the credit card and the cell-phone. You have no rights in the financial arena while you are under the Age of Accountability and living under your parents' roof. You can't even buy a car under the Age of Accountability. If a car dealership allows you to purchase a vehicle while you're under the Age of Accountability, the contract is **"voidable" because a minor cannot enter into a legal binding contract.** Even if you had a part-time job to help pay for your expenses, the ultimate financial responsibility rests with your parents until you actually reach the Age of Accountability.

Your parents are responsible for keeping you healthy until you reach the Age of Accountability. If you get sick and your parents cannot fix the problem with an aspirin or a band-aid, they will take you to the doctor to find out what's wrong with you. They will pay for the doctor's visit(s), the prescription(s), and anything else needed to ensure your recovery and restoration. If you break a leg and end up in the hospital, your parents will pay for the expensive hospital visit, the surgery, medical supplies, and prescriptions via their medical insurance and co-pays of "cash" out of their pockets. Your loving parents will even dote on you (serve you) until you are able to do for yourself.

Pregnancy Under The Age of Accountability

If you get pregnant before you reach the Age of Accountability, your parents share financial responsibility with the one who impregnated you. If the one who got you pregnant is also under the Age of Accountability, his parents will also bear half of the expenses involved, which include the obstetrician, hospital stay, pediatrician, parenting classes for you and your significant other, transportation to and from doctor's appointments, baby's medical care, baby's clothing, baby's supplies, baby's furniture, baby food, etc.

Your parents can sue the one who impregnated you because of the financial burden you and he have placed on your parents. If the boy is statutorily older than you (generally 18 years of age in most states – the Age Of Consent), it is your parents' right to have him arrested and charged with statutory rape (consenting sexual intercourse between two people, one being older than the other).

If your parents knew you were dating the boy who impregnated you, they could still make the statutory rape charge stand against the boy even if he were not at the Age Of Consent. As a parent, I may or may not press charges against the boy who got my daughter pregnant if I knew they were dating for a while, but I would definitely make sure the boy and his parents bore no less than half of the financial burden of the child being born into the world, as well as having the boy provide child support and half of the childcare and education while the child is growing up.

The responsibility changes when you and the boy reach the Age of Accountability. At the Age of Accountability, you and the one who impregnated you will be responsible and accountable for everything related to the care and needs of the child until the child reaches his or her Age of Accountability. If both sets of parents continue to help you both financially after you reach the Age of Accountability, it's not an entitlement, but strictly a gift out of the love they have for you two and the baby.

The one who impregnated you bears no less than 50% of all responsibility for your baby's welfare and well-being until the child reaches the Age of Accountability (18 years old in most states). However, a majority of the boys who get girls pregnant don't own up to it, and a majority of their parents don't even want to hear about it from you. In fact, in most cases, the boy's parents will accuse you of being the forward seductress who lured their son into bed. Get the picture? To avoid all of this baby-mama/baby-daddy/baby-grandparents drama, **keep your legs closed!** You have the power over what a boy or man can do to you sexually – it's your choice.

Don't allow any boy or man to take your future plans away by enticing you into a bad choice concerning sex that will affect the next 18 to 20 years of your life. It doesn't matter how good-looking they are; good looks tend to fade over time.

Curfews

Your parents are responsible for keeping you safe and out of danger. That's why they give curfews. They want to know where you are going when you go out on a date or out with the girls. They provide you a phone to communicate with them. They need to see who it is that you're going out with – his physical features and appearance. Parents are inquisitive; they want to know what the boy or man is all about. You are their gift from God, you're their responsibility, you're their baby, and no one loves and cares about you more than they do.

I just loved a particular scene in a fairly recent fast-action movie, which showed a teenage boy coming to the home of a detective to take his teenage daughter out on a date. The detective's partner answered the door, pulled out a gun to the boy's frightened surprise, and threatened the life of the boy if he mistreated his goddaughter on the date. The girl's father subsequently came to the door, too, and verbally backed up his partner with threats of harm if his daughter returned home violated. The wife of the detective brought their daughter to the front door to meet her date. The mother saw how frightened the boy was, and told him not to be intimidated by her husband and his partner. But by that time, the father and his partner made their point. That particular scene was rough and somewhat over the top, but it definitely got the correct attention of the teenage boy. The boy knew there would be 'hell' to pay if the detective's daughter returned home violated in any way. This scenario was extreme, but it showed: (1) the father cared deeply about his daughter; (2) there would be massive negative consequences if his daughter was mistreated; and (3) the father placed a tremendous value on his daughter's well-being, and the boy had better do the same. I wish more fathers were affirming their daughters by giving them value, confidence, and protection. I believe there would be fewer violations against teenage girls and young women if their dates would meet their fathers.

Parent Emulation

Parents are responsible to God for being good examples to their children. They are responsible and accountable to God for their children's upbringing (teaching them God's Word, instilling Godly values, promoting a healthy self-esteem/self-image/self-confidence, and walking the talk). They are responsible to provide for their children until their children reach the Age of Accountability. Children did not ask to come into this world; God has a plan and a purpose for them. It's the parents' responsibility to help their children discover God's plan and purpose for their lives.

Children and teenagers pick up the good, the bad, and the ugly habits of their parents in their homes. For example, if parents are irresponsible in drinking alcohol and their children pick up the habit, it's hard for the parents to chastise their children for doing the same. Parents cannot get away with the phrase **"Do as I say, not as I do"** because habits are mostly **caught** rather than **taught** in life. What the parents should do is admit they have a drinking problem to their children; apologize to their children, explain the "dos" and "don'ts" of drinking alcohol and its consequences, and then change from their own bad habit of drinking.

In summary, we are all responsible and accountable to man's laws and to God's laws. There are consequences for violating man's laws and God's laws.

Nobody rides for free!

Chapter 11

Conclusion

Chapter 11

Conclusion

"My people are destroyed for lack of knowledge."
(Hosea 4:6)

Knowledge is power – power to change. You now have the knowledge – from God's Word and His laws, from man's laws, and from real and true circumstances and consequences that were referred to in this book.

It's time to change the way you think about your role as a young girl, teenage girl, young woman, and woman. Change the way you think about what you mean to God, and what you mean to yourself. *Proverbs 23:7* states: *"For as he [she] thinks in his [her] heart, so is he [she]."* If you don't think right according to what God says about you, you will make the wrong choices that will create unnecessary hardships for you and for others. Your wrong choices will also tarnish and delay the bright future God has for you.

Change your thinking about God and about you. *Jesus says in Mark 12:29-31: "The first of all the commandments is: Hear, O Israel, the Lord our God, the Lord is one. And you shall love the Lord your God with all your heart, with all your soul, with all your mind, and with all your strength. And the second, like it, is this: You shall love your neighbor as yourself. There is no other commandment greater than these." John 3:16* states: *"For God so loved the world that He gave His only begotten Son, that whoever believes in Him should not perish but have everlasting life." Romans 5:8-9* states: *"But God demonstrates His own love toward us, in that while we were still sinners, Christ died for us. Much more than having now been justified by*

His blood, we shall be saved from wrath through Him." As you can see through these scriptures, God loves you so much that He provided a way for you to be saved. He has forgiven your sins. He loves you in spite of your past sins. He cares for you. He will restore you. He will love you to the end of your life on this earth.

However, God has given you a **"free will."** He abides by **your** choices through your free will. You cannot operate in life successfully without knowing and obeying His word for your life. It's impossible to be successful in all areas of your life without God. You cannot know His word and continue doing wrong.

In the beginning, God set up built-in restrictions and built-in consequences for us all. By ignoring those restrictions, you will tie God's hands by your own free will, and you will pay the ensuing consequences. It won't be His fault if you don't heed His word. Although He will still love you, He can't change the consequences you have set in motion. But, if you repent, He will get you through those consequences. To repent means to change your mind, change your ways, and change your direction.

Your heart may change, but your situation will not change until you change your mind. If you stay in the word of God, He will change your thinking which will change you from the inside out. *Romans 12:2* states: *"And do not be conformed to this world, but be transformed by the renewing of your mind that you may prove what is that good and acceptable and perfect will of God."* The way you think will change the decisions you make, the actions you take, the direction you go, and will determine the consequences you will receive.

Priorities

Get your priorities straight. Your relationship with God is first and foremost in your life. You cannot have a relationship with a person that supersedes your relationship with God. If you do allow a relationship with a person to take precedence over your relationship with God, that person becomes your god, and you will be out of God's will for your life. You will be out of order with God. *Exodus 20:5* states: *"You shall not bow down to them nor serve them, For I, the Lord your God, am a jealous God, visiting the iniquity of the fathers upon the children to the third and fourth generations of those who hate Me, but showing mercy to thousands, to those who love Me and keep My commandments."* If you keep your relationship with God in first place, He will let you know whether you should be in a relationship with that person. He will show you all sides of the person you are interested in. He will also show you whether the person has his own relationship with God, which is key to a successful relationship with you.

If you have a relationship with God and the person you're interested in does not, you're not equally yoked and you are out of order. God will show you if the person is genuine, and He will show or tell you whether you should be involved with the person. This goes for friendships as well as relationships leading to marriage.

God's word says not to be unequally yoked with people who do not have God in common with you. *2 Corinthians 6:14-18* states: *"Do not be unequally yoked together with unbelievers. For what fellowship has righteousness with lawlessness? And what communion has light with darkness? And what accord [partnership] has Christ with Belial [iniquity and lawlessness]? Or what part has a believer with an unbeliever? And what agreement has the temple of God with idols? For you are the temple of the living God. As God has said: 'I will dwell in them and walk among them. I will be their God, and they shall be My people.' Therefore, 'Come out from among them and be separate', says the Lord. 'Do not touch what is unclean and I will receive you. I will be a Father to you, and you shall be My sons and daughters, says the Lord Almighty.'"*

The temple of God means that God is inside your body and your body is His holy place. In essence, your body is His temple. So, as a temple of God, you should not defile His temple with unclean things such as having sex outside of marriage or abusing your body by the use of drugs, alcohol, or by any other means that would defile you and the temple of God inside of you. Also, as a temple of God, you should not be unequally yoked with people who do not esteem God as you do, with people who do wrong, or with people who are bad influences on you.

By being obedient to God, you will avoid many problems, many wrong decisions, and many undue consequences as a result of those wrong decisions, especially regarding relationships and friendships.

Don't seek out a man for marriage. God knows who you are, what your desires are, what your tolerances are, what your weaknesses are, and where you are. He knows what you need and when you need it. He also knows what you need in a mate and when you're ready to have a mate. God has to help you grow up to meet the standard of His man for you. This takes time and patience on your part. Remember that we are not on our earthly time, but we're on God's timing. Allow Him to send you that right person, and it will be the right time. Who knows, God may have already sent the right person your way, but because you involved yourself with the wrong person, that right person went away. It's up to you whether God will allow that right person to return to you.

Keep your priorities straight by staying in the Word of God (the Bible), to grow in His word, to give you peace and comfort, to give you security, to give you courage to stand, and having done all, to stand until the day of the Lord.

Our priorities in life should be (1) to love God first and foremost above everything, and to love our neighbors as ourselves; (2) to love and care for our families; (3) to work as unto the Lord because He is our source and provider, not the employer (the Lord is right there on our jobs watching us and watching those we work with because they are accountable to God, too); and (4) to always tell the truth because the truth will set us free and save us every time. If you follow this order, you will be prosperous in all areas of your life.

Convictions

Don't set aside your convictions and promises to God because of your fleshly feelings and emotions. Negative feelings of inadequacy, guilt, loneliness, unworthiness, loss, anger, pressure, stress, anxiety, doubt and fear should all be given to God. *1 Peter 5:7* states: *"Casting all your care upon Him for He cares for you."* God wants to care for you. You're a winner in Christ. You have overcome all obstacles in this world. You're more than a conqueror through Christ who strengthens you. *Romans 8:36-37* states: *"As it is written: 'For Your [Christ's] sake we are killed all day long; we are accounted as sheep for the slaughter.' Yet in all these things we are more than conquerors through Him who loved us."* Keep your convictions to God!

Don't let your feelings take you away from what God has for you. Don't compromise your convictions to God to satisfy a fleshly need to not be lonely, or to satisfy a sexual desire, or to fulfill any worldly or ungodly thing. Allowing these things to manifest in you means that you are allowing your flesh to rule over your body, your mind, and your emotions. God is with you, and He knows what all your needs are before you even realize what they are. He will fulfill those needs at the right time in the right order according to His will if you give them to Him.

It is God who completes you, not another person, and certainly not a man. No human can ever complete you and make you whole. It is God, and it is He, alone, who makes you whole.

Fear

You should fear no man. *Hebrews 13:6* states: *"So we may boldly say: 'The Lord is my helper; I will not fear; what can man do to me.'"*

God has not given you the spirit of fear, worry, doubt, stress, anxiousness, nervousness, emptiness, worthlessness, pressure, depression, or defeat. *2 Timothy 1:7* states: *"For God has not given us a spirit of fear, but of power and of love and of a sound mind."* So, if you have any fear from any source, that fear is not from God, and you should immediately dismiss it in the 'name of Jesus.' In *Isaiah 43:1-2*, God was speaking a message of hope through the prophet Isaiah to Israel, Judah, and the surrounding nations after they had sinned, and after God passed judgment on them, stating: *"But now thus says the Lord, who created you, O Jacob, and He who formed you, O Israel: 'Fear not, for I have redeemed you; I have called you by your name; you are Mine. When you pass through the waters, I will be with you; and through the rivers, they shall not overflow you. When you walk through the fire, you shall not be burned, nor shall the flame scorch you."* God forgave the nations in the Old Testament, and He still forgives in the New Testament. In this passage of scripture, God tells the nations of Israel and Judah to 'fear not' for He will protect and take care of them. God will do the same for you. He is the same yesterday, today and tomorrow. He does not change. God says in *Malachi 3:6*: *"For I am the Lord, I do not change: . . . "*

God also says in His word that He will never leave you nor forsake you. *Hebrews 13:5* states: *"Let your conduct be without covetousness; be content with such things as you have, for He Himself has said, 'I will never leave you nor forsake you.'"*

Hope

Don't look at where you presently are in your circumstances, but look at your situation through God's eyes to where He will take you. Have hope in God and in His Son, Jesus Christ. *2 Corinthians 4:16-18* states: *"Therefore we do not lose heart. Even though our outward man is perishing, yet the inward man is being renewed day by day. For our light affliction, which is but for a moment, is working for us a far more exceeding and eternal weight of glory. While we do not look at the things which are seen, but at the things which are not seen, for the things which are seen are temporary, but the things which are not seen are eternal."*

Temptation

Don't let temptation of any kind steer you away from your ultimate goal – being in Heaven with God! *1 Corinthians 10:13* states: *"No temptation has overtaken you except such as is common to man [woman], but God is faithful, who will not allow you to be tempted beyond what you are able, but with the temptation will also make the way of escape that you may be able to bear it."* So, you're not the only one who has ever been tempted to do wrong, but having faith in God will keep you away from the temptation and give you the strength to "**JUST SAY NO!**" to the temptation. It's easy after you make up your mind that you are not going to accept the temptation. The devil (satan) has to search for another angle to get you to sin. Oh, the devil will leave you alone for the moment or even a little while, but he always tries to come back through a different deception. He comes through your mind with thoughts (temptations) where you've sinned in the past. Whatever fleshly weakness you have, satan will use that weakness against you in your mind through temptation. The battle of any temptation begins in the mind. It's up to you to control what you will allow in your mind. If you dismiss/reject the temptation, it will shortly disappear. The quicker you recognize what the temptation is and who it's coming from, the quicker you will be able to delete it in the name of Jesus.

Past Sins

Don't dwell on the past; this is another ploy of satan. *Hebrews 9:14* states: *"How much more shall the blood of Christ, who through the eternal Spirit offered Himself without spot to God, cleanse your conscience from dead works to serve the living God?"* The past will keep you thinking negatively about yourself. It will hold you back from God's blessings for you. The past will not allow you to experience a good and healthy future. Remind yourself that you are a new creation, redeemed, forgiven, healed, blessed, prosperous, and beautiful. You're a winner, and you belong to God. Whenever this issue comes up, recognize that satan is the one who is trying to remind you of your past sins through your mind, and just rebuke him at every turn in the 'name of Jesus.'

Continually renew your mind (update/change your mind) by reading and studying (meditating) the Bible to be in line (in agreement) with the word of God. *Romans 12:2* states: *"And do not be conformed to this world, but be transformed by the renewing of your mind, that you may prove what is that good and acceptable and perfect will of God."* Study and meditate on God's word to get His word in your heart, because the word of God is your weapon against satan's tactics. When satan tries to plant a negative seed in your mind, your heart will bring up God's word to combat it in your mind.

If you believe Jesus Christ is your Lord and Savior, that He died on the cross for your sins, that He was resurrected from the dead and is now seated at the right hand of the Father God and continually petitioning on your behalf, then stop putting Jesus Christ back up on that cross to suffer **again** for your past sins by revisiting in your mind your past mistakes and believing that He has not forgiven you.

Again, the negative thoughts are not from God, but from satan. The devil is trying to hold you down by throwing up in your mind your past sins. You must immediately rebuke them 'in the name of Jesus.' You are forgiven! God says in His word that He will remember your sins no more. *Psalm 103:12* states: *"As far as the east is from the west, so far has He removed our transgressions from us."* So stop beating yourself over your past, and stop trying to repeat the death and resurrection of Jesus! No one on this earth could endure what He did to save us from our sins, let alone do it over and over again. You can't change it anyway, and what God did for you was done once and for all for all sinners.

God does not want you to keep making the same mistakes. He wants you to stay in His word so your mind will be renewed through His word. Studying His word will continually renew your mind so you will immediately recognize satan's thought darts when they come, and you can immediately dismiss them because they are not in line with God's word. This will keep you from making the same mistakes.

Forgiveness and repentance is an exchange. It's not a one-sided transaction. He will forgive if you will repent/change. No one on this earth had the power to forgive us and save us until the Lord Jesus came on the scene. He was and is the only one who can. If you truly believe He died on the cross for your sins, then you have faith that you are forgiven. *1 John 1:9* states: *"If we confess our sins, He is faithful and just to forgive us of our sins and to cleanse us from all unrighteousness."*

There is nothing that you did so bad that you cannot be forgiven by the One who has the power to forgive you – God. The devil has no power to forgive you of anything. The devil, himself, was thrown out of heaven because of his own disobedience, so he definitely has no power to save you. The devil wants you to perish and be with him in hell. Hell is his destiny; it doesn't have to be yours. The devil wants you to think he's as powerful as God, but he isn't. He is a defeated enemy, and he will receive his just reward in hell. Hell was made for the devil and his demons (fallen angels), not for humans. However, *Psalm 9:17* states: *"The wicked shall be turned into hell, and all the nations that forget God."*

Yes, although forgiven by God, there are still the consequences that we all go through because of our bad choices and wrong actions. Remember, the restrictions and consequences were already built into the system in the beginning. God will give you what you need to bring you through the consequences if you repent, continue to stay in faith in Him, and get grounded in His word. Trust Him. *1 Peter 5:10* states: *"But may the God of all grace who called us to His eternal glory by Christ Jesus, after you have suffered a while, [He will] perfect [you], [He will] establish [you], [He will] strengthen [you], and [He will] settle you."*

When you ask God to forgive you, He does, and He sees you as forgiven and blessed. He cannot see you any other way because He cannot look upon sin. *Isaiah 43:25* states: *"I, even I, am He who blots out your transgressions for My own sake; and I will not remember your sins."* You, too, must see yourself as forgiven and blessed – not as you were, but as you are now and what you will be in the future. You are a new creation. *2 Corinthians 5:17* states: *"Therefore, if anyone is in Christ, he is a new creation; old things have passed away, behold, all things have become new."* This means that God no longer sees your sins; He sees a new creation.

Control

Control means courage and confidence under fire. If you have given God permission to have complete control of your life, you should have confidence and courage to face tomorrow no matter what it brings. Since God is for you, who can dare be against you? *Romans 8:31-35* states: *"What then shall we say to these things? If God be for us, who can be against us? He who did not spare His own Son [Jesus Christ], but delivered Him up for us all, how shall He not with Him also freely give us all things? Who shall bring a charge against God's elect? It is God who justifies. Who is he who condemns? It is Christ who died, and furthermore is also risen, who is even at the right hand of God, who also makes intercession [mediation] for us. Who shall separate us from the love of Christ? Shall tribulation, or distress, or persecution, or famine, or nakedness, or peril, or sword?"* In essence, God has got our backs. We belong to Him. We're His kids! He is with us through thick and thin. *Romans 8:28* states: *"And we know that all things work together for good to those who love God, to those who are the called according to His purpose."* Since you are the called according to His purpose, trust that He will work everything out for your good and to His glory.

Trust & Believe

Trusting and believing God boils down to "**faith**." Having faith in knowing that He will do what He says He will do is what will bring you through. In fact, God has already done what He said He would do. The question is whether or not you know His word, believe His word, and accept His Word. There are many scriptures relating to trusting God and what He will do in your life in all the circumstances that you face, but the main emphasis is on your 'faith' in His Word. *Hebrews 11:1* states: *"Now faith is the substance of things hoped for, the evidence of things not seen." Mark 11:24* states: *"Therefore I say to you, whatever things you ask when you pray, believe that you receive them and you will have them."* However, the most wonderful thing to know is in *Hebrews 13:8, which* states: *"Jesus Christ is the same yesterday, today, and forever."*

Trust God with all your needs, insecurities, desires and decisions. *Matthew 6:8* states: *"Therefore do not be like them, for your Father knows the things you have need of before you ask Him."* In *John 16:23, Jesus says: "And in that day you will ask me nothing. Most assuredly I say to you, whatever you ask the Father in My Name, He will give you." Philippians 4:19* states: *"And my God shall supply all your need according to His riches in glory by Christ Jesus." Hebrews 4:16* states: *"Let us therefore come boldly to the throne of grace, that we may obtain mercy and find grace to help in time of need."* As a child of God, you have a right given to you by the Lord Jesus Christ to come boldly to the throne of grace and make your petition to God for whatever you need. Have no doubt in your heart that your petitions will be heard and granted in line with your obedience to God's Word.

<u>God's Armor of Protection</u>

As children of God, we are in a constant battle for our lives and for our eternity. We need to put on God's armor to protect us. What is God's armor? When we stay in His word, we learn what His armor is and its purpose. *2 Corinthians 10:3-5* states: *"For though we walk in the flesh, we do not war according to the flesh. For the weapons of our warfare are not carnal but mighty in God for pulling down strongholds, casting down arguments and every high thing that exalts itself against the knowledge of God, bringing every thought into captivity to the obedience of Christ."* Remember that our weapons are the whole armor that God has given us in *Ephesians 6:11-17*, which are: (1) the breastplate of righteousness; (2) the helmet of salvation; (3) the sword of the Spirit (which is the Word of God); (4) the shield of faith (which stops all the fiery darts of sinful ideas, wicked thoughts, unholy suggestions, and condemnations of the wicked one in our minds); (5) the truth; and (6) the gospel of peace. So cast down any negative thought that comes into your mind and hold onto God's promises for you. Hold onto His word.

We are not to strive with men [women]. *Proverbs 3:30* states: *"Do not strive with a man without cause, if he has done you no harm."* Anything or anyone working against you will not stand because God is for you and He is with you. *Isaiah 54:17* states: *"No weapon formed against you shall prosper, and every tongue which rises against you in judgment you shall condemn. This is the heritage of the servants of the Lord, and their righteousness is from Me, says the Lord." Psalm 25:3* states: *"Indeed, let no one who waits on You [Lord] be ashamed; let those be ashamed who deal treacherously without cause." Isaiah 48:22* states: *"There is no peace"*, says the Lord, *"for the wicked."*

Gratefulness

Be grateful and praise the Lord while in the midst of your crisis. Be grateful that God has brought you through past crises, problems, and issues, no matter what they were. By knowing that He has brought you through past problems, you should have confidence in knowing that He will bring you through your current problem and any future problems victoriously.

Whatever challenge, trial or temptation you have will pass. **IT HAS COME TO PASS. IT HAS NOT COME TO STAY!** We are to count it all joy when we come face to face with these challenges, trials and temptations knowing that God is blessing us through to victory. *James 1:2-4* states: *"My brethren [sisters], count it all joy when you fall into various trials, knowing that the testing of your faith produces patience. But let patience have its perfect work, that you may be perfect and complete, lacking nothing." Psalm 103:1-5* states: *"Bless the Lord, O my soul, and all that is within me, bless His holy name! Bless the Lord, O my soul, and forget not all His benefits; who forgives all your iniquities, who heals all your diseases, who redeems your life from destruction, who crowns you with loving-kindness and tender mercies, who satisfies your mouth* *with good things, so that your youth is renewed like the eagle's."* Someone said that gratitude is the attitude that sets the altitude for living. It's all in your knowledge of God's Word, your faith in His Word, and in your attitude as to whether you will stand on His Word and be victorious. Or, will you listen to the enemy and fall. It's your choice.

Everybody on the face of the earth is either going through a trial, has just gone through a trial, or is about to enter into a trial. Trials are part of life, and everyone goes through many different trials. It's all in how you deal with your trial. Will you grow and gain strength from it or will you succumb to it and fail. Our faith and trust in God and in His Word will give us the victory each and every time.

Help

Help those who are going through what you went through, and who are in the midst of the consequences of their sin just as you were. You will bear much fruit when you share with someone your testimony concerning what you went through, and encourage her to trust God and to stand while in her crisis. When you help that person, you will be blessed, too. *James 5:19-20* states: *"Brethren, if anyone among you wanders from the truth, and someone turns him back, let him [her] know that he [she] who turns a sinner from the error of his [her] way will save a soul from death and cover a multitude of sins."*

Don't be judgmental or condescending now that you've been redeemed, but uplift others in the love of the Lord. You will give them courage and strength to overcome. They will realize that if you went through what they are going through, and you overcame, they will believe they can overcome, too. In *James 5:16*, God's word states: *"Confess your trespasses to one another, and pray for one another, that you may be healed. The effective, fervent prayer of a righteous man [woman] avails much."* You're not alone, and they are not alone, for we are all sinners saved by grace, but that not of ourselves, it is truly a gift from God. *Ephesians 2:8-9* states: *"For by grace you have been saved through faith, and that not of yourselves; it is the gift of God, not of works, lest anyone should boast."*

There is not a soul on this earth who can turn his or her nose up at anyone as if they are better than anyone. Sin is sin. No sin is worse than another sin in God's eyes, and He cannot look upon sin. Rich people sin, poor people sin, educated people sin, uneducated people sin, all nationalities of people on the face of the earth sin, beautiful people sin, ugly people sin, fat people sin, skinny people sin, short people sin, tall people sin, and on it goes. Again, *Ephesians 2:8-10* states: *"For by grace you have been saved through faith, and that not of yourselves; it is the gift of God, not of works, lest anyone should boast. For we are His workmanship created in Christ Jesus for good works which God prepared before-hand that we should walk in them."* Never look down on anyone, or be condescending toward anyone, but pick her up and encourage her. Everyone experiences tough times, but tough people overcome tough times. When the going gets tough, the tough get going.

Be the **"Good Samaritan"** that God wants you to be. Show mercy and help the person as you are able to do, and the Lord will honor and bless you for it. Remember the story of the "Good Samaritan" as told by Jesus, Himself, in the Bible? *Luke 10:30-37* states: *"A certain man went down from Jerusalem to Jericho, and fell among thieves, who stripped him of his clothing, wounded him, and departed, leaving him half dead. Now by chance, a certain priest came down that road, and when he saw him, he passed by on the other side. Likewise, a Levite, when he arrived at the place, came and looked and passed by on the other side. But a certain Samaritan, as he journeyed, came where he was and when he saw him, he had compassion. So he went to him and bandaged his wounds, pouring* *on oil and wine, and he set him on his own animal, brought him to an inn, and took care of him. On the next day, when he departed, he took out two denarii [money], gave them to the innkeeper and said to him, 'Take care of him, and whatever more you spend, when I come again, I will repay you.' So, which of these three do you think was neighbor to him who fell among the thieves? And he [the lawyer] said, 'He who showed mercy on him.' Then Jesus said to him, 'Go and do likewise.'"* We are to do the same. Not only are we to pray for our sisters, but we are also to put action to our prayer of faith. We are to physically, monetarily, and materially help those in their need, as we are able. We are to be Good Samaritans! That's the God kind of faith.

Love

When we love God, we belong to Him. *1 John 5:1-3* states: *"Whoever believes that Jesus is the Christ is born of God [a born-again child of God], and everyone who loves Him who begot [offspring of God, born again children of God] also loves him who is begotten of Him. By this we know that we love the children of God when we love God and keep His commandments. For this is the love of God, that we keep His commandments. And His commandments are not burdensome." 1 John 4:8-10* states: *"He who does not love does not know God, for God is love. In this the love of God was manifested [evident] toward us, that God has sent His only begotten Son into the world, that we might live through Him. In this is love, not that we loved God, but that He loved us and sent His Son to be the propitiation [atoning sacrifice, reconciliation for our sins – payment for our sins] for our sins."*

Always remember that God loves you more than you love yourself. Before you were created, He knew your name, your personality, your quirks, what makes you laugh, what makes you cry, and the mistakes you will make. He knew what you would be and how you would serve Him. He knew when you were going to be born and He knows when you will die. He knew you before the foundations of the world. In *Psalm 139:13-18*, David is acknowledging how God made him. *Psalm 139:13-18* states: *"For You formed my inward parts; You covered me in my mother's womb. I will praise You, for I am fearfully and wonderfully made. Marvelous are Your works, and that my soul knows very well. My frame was not hidden from You. When I was made in secret, and skillfully wrought in the lowest parts of the earth, Your eyes saw my substance, being yet unformed, and in Your book they all were written, the days fashioned for me, when as yet there were none of them. How precious also are Your thoughts to me, O God! How great is the sum of them! If I should count them, they would be more in number than the sand; when I awake, I am still with you."* God tells the prophet Jeremiah He knew him before he was born, with all detail. *Jeremiah 1:5* states: *"Before I formed you in the womb, I knew you; before you were born, I sanctified you; I ordained you a prophet to the nations."* God knew that Jeremiah was going to be a prophet because He ordained it. God knew us before we were born.

He loves you more than your parents could ever love you, although they may love you greatly. He loves you more than your friends could ever love you. He loves you more than your husband and more than your children. God loves and cares for you.

God knows where you are at all times – spiritually, physically, emotionally, and mentally. He is omnipresent – He's everywhere. God is also omnipotent – He is all-powerful. He is omniscient – He has infinite awareness, understanding, knowledge, and insight.

You need not worry who God picks for your mate in life. Let God choose His man to find you; don't you go looking for him. God will select a man who serves and loves Him and, in turn, the man God chooses for you will honor, love, serve and care for you. God's man will know how to love and care for you as Jesus loved and cared for the church.

"Be anxious [careful – don't worry] for nothing; but in everything by prayer and supplication with thanksgiving let your requests be made known unto God; and the peace of God, which surpasses all understanding, will guard your hearts and minds through Christ Jesus." (Philippians 4:6-7) Trust God with all your needs, desires and decisions. When you have consulted with God first and wait for His answers, you will make the right choices each and every time. *Proverbs 3:5-6* states: *"Trust in the Lord with all your heart, and lean not on your own understanding; in all your ways acknowledge Him, and He shall direct your paths."*

Obey God and let Him be responsible for whatever happens to you. With that in mind, *"Be kindly to one another with brotherly love, in honor giving preference to one another." (Romans 12:10)*

Remember the **"Beatitudes"** [Latin Word – "Beatus" – meaning 'Happy' or 'Blissful']:

Matthew 5:3-11: "Blessed are the poor in spirit, for theirs is the kingdom of heaven. Blessed are those who mourn for they shall be comforted. Blessed are the meek for they shall inherit the earth. Blessed are those who hunger and thirst for righteousness, for they shall be filled. Blessed are the merciful, for they shall obtain mercy. Blessed are the pure in heart, for they shall see God. Blessed are the peacemakers, for they shall be called sons of God. Blessed are those who are persecuted for righteousness' sake, for theirs is the kingdom of heaven."

Luke 6:20-26: "Then He lifted up His eyes toward His disciples, and said: 'Blessed are you poor, for yours is the kingdom of God. Blessed are you who hunger now, for you shall be filled. Blessed are you who weep now, for you shall laugh. Blessed are you when men hate you, and when they exclude you, and revile you, and cast out your name as evil, for the Son of Man's sake. Rejoice in that day and leap for joy! For indeed your reward is great in heaven, for in like manner their fathers did to the prophets. But woe to you who are rich, for you have received your consolation. Woe to you who are full, for you shall hunger. Woe to you who laugh now, for you shall mourn and weep. Woe to you when all men speak well of you, for so did their fathers to the false prophets.'"

Your Image

You are created in the image of God. *Genesis 1:26-27* states: *"Then God said, 'Let Us make man [woman] in Our image, according to Our likeness; let them [man and woman] have dominion over the fish of the sea, over the birds of the air, and over the cattle, over all the earth and over every creeping thing that creeps on the earth.' So God created man [woman] in His own image; in the image of God He created him [her]; male and female He created them."* Therefore, you are beautiful in God's eyes. He's not looking at your physical appearance, as the world does; He's looking at you through and through because He is your Creator, not the world. He's looking at your heart.

David recognized the magnitude of God's love for the creation in him (David) in *Psalm 139:13-18*, which states: *"For You formed my inward parts; You covered me in my mother's womb. I will praise You, for I am fearfully and wonderfully made. Marvelous are Your works, and that my soul knows very well. My frame was not hidden from You. When I was made in secret, and skillfully wrought in the lowest parts of the earth, Your eyes saw my substance, being yet unformed, and in Your book they all were written, the days fashioned for me, when as yet there were none of them. How precious also are Your thoughts to me, O God! How great is the sum of them! If*

I should count them, they would be more in number than the sand; when I awake, I am still with you." You need to recognize and appreciate God's creation in you, too. David recognized how highly God thought of him, and you need to do the same. You are unique, even down to your fingerprints. No one has your fingerprints in all the earth. There is absolutely no one on the face of the earth made like you. You will not fit into any of the world's molds, so don't even waste your time trying. That's the way God meant it to be because He made you special, unique, and in His image. You belong to Him.

You don't need another human being to tell you that you're beautiful or to give you justification for being. You don't need someone telling you how to change yourself to fit into the world in order to be liked by the world. You are not of this world. *Romans 12:1-2* states: *"I beseech you therefore, brethren, by the mercies of God, that you present your bodies a living sacrifice, holy, acceptable to God, which is your reasonable service. And do not be conformed to this world, but be transformed by the renewing of your mind, that you may prove what is that good and acceptable and perfect will of God."*

You never have to worry or be concerned about what other humans think about you because there is no insecurity with God. God made you, He loves you, and He's for you. He loves His creation in you.

Salvation

In *John 14:1,* the Lord Jesus Christ states: *"Let not your hearts be troubled; you believe in God, believe also in Me."* The Lord does not want you to be troubled or worried about anything when you believe in Him. The operative meaning here is that you don't have to worry about anything when you are a follower of the Lord Jesus Christ. *John 14:6* states: *"Jesus said to him [Peter, one of the*

Apostles], 'I am the way, and the truth, and the life. No one comes to the Father except through Me.'" Since Jesus is the way, you will not get lost. Since Jesus is the truth, you will not be deceived. Since Jesus is the life, you cannot be destroyed by satan.

If you are reading this book and have not accepted Jesus Christ as your Lord and Savior, you can do so by praying the prayer below:

"Dear Lord Jesus, I acknowledge that I am a sinner and I need a savior. I believe You came to this earth and died on the cross for my sins. I believe God raised You from the dead, and whosoever believes in You will not perish but have everlasting life. I accept You as my Lord and Savior. I ask your forgiveness for my sins. Please come into my heart and live forever. Thank you, Lord. Amen."

Supporting Scriptures To Your Confession Of Faith:

Romans 10:9-10 states: *"that if you confess with your mouth the Lord Jesus and believe in your heart that God has raised Him [Jesus] from the dead, you will be saved. For with the heart one believes unto righteousness, and with the mouth confession is made unto salvation."*

Romans 5:12 states: *"Therefore, just as through one man sin entered the world, and death through sin, and thus death spread to all men, because all sinned."*

John 3:16 states: *"For God so loved the world that He gave His only begotten Son, that whoever believes in Him [Jesus] should not perish but have everlasting life."*

Ephesians 2:8-9 states: *"For by grace you have been saved through faith, and that not of yourselves; it is a gift of God."*

The next thing you need to do is to obtain a Holy Bible and begin reading and studying the word of God. [I recommend you begin in the New Testament.] Then you need to begin your search for a Bible/Word-based church and begin going to the services to worship, to learn the word of God being taught, and to take notes. The church you attend should be a classroom to you where God's Word is being taught, where you're referring to the scriptures in the Bible as the pastor refers to them in his teaching, and you're taking notes so you can apply what you learn in church to your daily living (you know, just like in high school). If you don't take notes, by the time you leave the church you will more than likely forget most of what you learned. This is satan's attempt to take the Word of God out of your mind and out of your heart by distraction. But, if you take notes and study them or get a recording of the sermon and listen to it, you will be able to keep what you learned in your heart and mind. Get into a good bible study group to continue learning, understanding, meditating, and applying His word in your daily living.

I know the above scriptures for your salvation will be a major blessing and a tremendous turning point in your life.

Scriptures For Rededication To The Lord:

Isaiah 1:15-19 states: *"When you spread out your hands, I will hide My eyes from you; even though you make many prayers, I will not hear. Your hands are full of blood. Wash yourselves, make yourselves clean; put away the evil of your doings from before My eyes. Cease to do evil, learn to do good, seek justice, rebuke the oppressor, defend the fatherless, plead for the widow. 'Come now, and let us reason together', says the Lord. 'Though your sins are like scarlet, they shall be as white as snow; though they are red like crimson, they shall be as wool. If you are willing and obedient, you shall eat the good of the land, but if you refuse and rebel, you shall be devoured by the sword.' For the mouth of the Lord has spoken."*

Psalms 103:1-5 states: *"Bless the Lord, O my soul, and all that is within me, bless His holy name! Bless the Lord, O my soul, and forget not all His benefits; who forgives all your iniquities, who heals all your diseases, who redeems your life from destruction, who crowns you with loving kindness and tender mercies, who satisfies your mouth with good things, so that your youth is renewed like the eagle's."*

Matthew 22:37-39 states: *"Jesus said to him, 'You shall love the Lord, your God, with all your heart, with all your soul and with all your mind. This is the first and great commandment. And the second is like it: You shall love your neighbor as yourself.'"*

Acts 3:19 states: *"Repent therefore and be converted, that your sins may be blotted out, so that times of refreshing may come from the presence of the Lord."*

Colossians 2:6-7 states: *"As you therefore have received Christ Jesus the Lord, so walk in Him, rooted and built up in Him and established in the faith, as you have been taught, abounding in it with thanksgiving."*

Romans 12:2 states: *"And do not be conformed to this world, but be transformed by the renewing of your mind, that you may prove what is that good and acceptable and perfect will of God."*

1 John 1:9 states: *"If we confess our sins, He is faithful and just to forgive us our sins and to cleanse us from all unrighteousness."*

If you are a Christian and need to rededicate yourself to the Lord, pray:

"Dear Father in Heaven, in accordance with Your word (*Isaiah 1:15-19, Psalms 103:1-5, Matthew 22:37-39, Acts 3:19, Colossians*

2:6-7, Romans 12:2, and 1 John 1:9), I repent of my sins and from turning away from You. I pray that You forgive me and have mercy on me. Please restore me. I will love You with all my heart, all my soul, and all my mind, and I will love my neighbor as myself. I will renew my mind and not be swayed by the world, but will conform myself to be acceptable to You. In confessing my sins, I know that You are a faithful God who will cleanse me from all my unrighteousness. I praise You for all of Your benefits, for forgiving all of my iniquities, for healing all my diseases, for redeeming my life from destruction, for blessing me with loving kindness and tender mercies, and for providing good things for me. I thank You for Your forgiveness. In the mighty name of Jesus Christ I pray. Amen."

If you are a believer in the Lord Jesus Christ, but have backslidden, the above scriptures for rededication will get you back on the right track to a rewarding and fulfilling life in Christ Jesus.

God wants the best for you in everything. *3 John 2* states: *"Beloved, I pray that you may prosper in all things and be in health, just as your soul prospers."* God said in *Hebrews 13:5*: *" . . . I will never leave you nor forsake you."* Let go of the past and head toward the future with God. God's way of living your life is better than any other way. He is faithful and He will bring you through. *Psalm 27:14* states: *"Wait on the Lord. Be of good courage and He shall strengthen your heart. Wait, I say, on the Lord."*

Remember that God is omnipresent, meaning that He is always with you, especially in the trials of your life. God is omniscient, meaning that He knows everything about you and He sees all sides of the circumstances you're in. And, lastly, He is omnipotent, meaning that He is all-powerful where He will bring you through all the trials and circumstances in your life successfully if you trust Him. Trust God because He is working a good thing in your life. *Romans 8:28* states: *"And we know that all things work together for good to those who love God, to those who are the called according to His purpose."*

Praise God at all times – through the trials and through peace. Keep in mind that when you go through trials, the operative word is 'through.' He's taking you through something to bring you to something better. He is building you in the trial and you will come out victorious. Remember that when praises go up, blessings always come down. You have a wonderful future ahead of you. You are a new creation. You are forgiven. You are victorious in Christ!

Chapter 12

My Prayer For You

Chapter 12

My Prayer For You

(Write your name in the blank space.)

Dear Father in Heaven, I pray that ________________ believes and trusts in Your Word for her life, and that she accepts Your Son, the Lord Jesus Christ, who died on the cross for her sins, as her personal Lord and Savior in accordance with the following scriptures: *Romans 5:12: "Just as through one man sin entered the world, and death through sin, and thus death spread to all men, because all sinned." John 3:16: "For God so loved the world that He gave His only begotten Son that whoever believes in Him should not perish but have everlasting life." Ephesians 2:8- 9: "For by grace you have been saved through faith, and that not of yourselves; it is the gift of God." Romans 10:9-10: "That if you confess with your mouth the Lord Jesus and believe in your heart that God has raised Him from the dead, you will be saved. For with the heart one believes unto righteousness, and with the mouth confession is made unto salvation." 2 Corinthians 5:17: "Therefore, if anyone is in Christ, he is a new creation; old things have passed away; behold, all things have become new." 1 John 4:15: "Whoever confesses that Jesus is the Son of God, God abides in him, and he in God." 1 John 5:11-13: "And this is the testimony: that God has given us eternal life, and this life is in His Son. He who has the Son has life; he who does not have the Son of God does not have life. These things I have written to you who believe in the name of the Son of God, that you may know that you have eternal life, and that you may continue to believe in the name of the Son of God."*

I pray that _________________ be led to a church that teaches Your Word, rightly dividing the word of truth so that she can learn how to live her life victoriously and in obedience to You.

I pray Dear Father that if _________________ has backslidden or turned away from You in the past, that she be renewed in her faith in You and that she begin again to walk in Your will, circumspectly and honorably, in accordance with the following scriptures: *Isaiah 1:15-20: "When you spread out your hands, I will hide My eyes from you; even though you make many prayers, I will not hear. Your hands are full of blood. Wash yourselves, make yourselves clean; put away the evil of your doings from before My eyes. Cease to do evil. Learn to do good; seek justice, rebuke the oppressor, defend the fatherless, plead for the widow. 'Come now, and let us reason together', says the Lord. 'Though your sins are like scarlet, they shall be as white as snow; though they are red like crimson, they shall be as wool. If you are willing and obedient, you shall eat the good of the land; but if you refuse and rebel, you shall be devoured by the sword'; for the mouth of the Lord has spoken." Jeremiah 3:22: "Return, you backsliding children, and I will heal your backslidings." Acts 3:19: "Repent therefore and be converted, that your sins may be blotted out, so that times of refreshing may come from the presence of the Lord, and that He may send Jesus Christ, who was preached to you before." Colossians 2:6-7: "As you therefore have received Christ Jesus the Lord, so walk in Him, rooted and built up in Him and established in the faith, as you have been taught, abounding in it with thanksgiving." Romans 12:2: "And do not be conformed to this world, but be transformed by the renewing of your mind, that you may prove what is that good and acceptable and perfect will of God." 1 John 1:9: "If we confess our sins, He is faithful and just to forgive us our sins and to cleanse us from all unrighteousness."*

I pray that _________________ ask for forgiveness of her sins and that she not harbor anything against anyone for what she has been through, but that she forgives them and trusts You to do the rest, in accordance with the following scriptures: *1 John 1:9: "If we confess our sins, He is faithful and just to forgive us our sins and to cleanse us from all unrighteousness." Matthew 6:12: "And forgive us our debts [sins], as we forgive our debtors [those who sinned against us]." Colossians 2:13: "And you, being dead in your trespasses and the uncircumcision of your flesh, He has made alive together with Him, having forgiven you all trespasses." Colossians 3:13: "bearing with one another, and forgiving one another, if anyone has a complaint against another; even as Christ forgave you, so you also must do." Mark 11:25-26: "And whenever you stand praying, if you have anything against anyone, forgive him, that your Father in heaven may also forgive you your trespasses. But if you do not forgive, neither will your Father in heaven forgive your trespasses." Ephesians 1:7: "In Him we have redemption through His blood, the forgiveness of sins, according to the riches of His grace."*

Dear Father in Heaven, I pray that every scripture in this book, that applies to ________________ and her situation, be grounded in her heart and that she apply those scriptures to her current situation or condition. I pray that she stands on Your Word for the resolution of her circumstances.

I pray Dear Father in Heaven that ________________ be healed by Jesus' stripes from the top of her head to the soles of her feet because Jesus took our infirmities and bore our sicknesses on the cross. I pray that she stand on Your word for the restoration of her body, soul, and mind in accordance with the following scriptures: *Psalm 103:2-5: "Bless the Lord, O my soul, and forget not all His benefits: Who forgives all your iniquities, who heals all your diseases, who redeems your life from destruction, who crowns you with loving kindness and tender mercies, who satisfies your mouth with good things, so that your youth is renewed like the eagle's."*

Isaiah 53:5: "But he was wounded for our transgressions, He was bruised for our iniquities; the chastisement for our peace was upon Him." James 5:15-16: "And the prayer of faith will save the sick, and the Lord will raise him up, and if he has committed sins, he will be forgiven. Confess your trespasses to one another, and pray for one another, that you may be healed. The effective, fervent prayer of a righteous man avails much."

I pray Dear Father in heaven that you bring the right people into __________________'s life to help her stay grounded in Your Word, and encourage her in her new life, in accordance with the following scriptures: *Proverbs 17:17: "A friend loves at all times." Proverbs 18:24: "A man who has friends must himself be friendly, but there is a friend who sticks closer than a brother." Proverbs 27:6: "Faithful are the wounds of a friend . . ." Proverbs 27:17: "As iron sharpens iron, so a man sharpens the countenance of his friend."*

I pray that __________________ develops self-esteem, that she leaves the past in the past, and that she go forward into a wonderful future that awaits her, not looking back but pressing forward, in accordance with *Philippians 3:13-14: "Brethren, I do not count myself to have apprehended; but one thing I do, forgetting those things which are behind and reaching forward to those things which are ahead, I press toward the goal for the prize of the upward call of God in Christ Jesus."*

I pray that __________________ knows whose she is and what her purpose is in this life in accordance with the following scripture: *1 Thessalonians 2:12: "That you would walk worthy of God, who calls you into His own kingdom and glory."*

I pray Dear Father that __________________ forgives those who wronged her, who made her believe that she was less than what You said she is, and I pray that You bring those who wronged her into the knowledge of Your Word for the salvation of their souls. I pray that they see Your countenance in _________________.

I pray Dear Father in heaven that _________________ love You and that she loves herself and love others because You first loved her and still love her through all her sins, through all her pain, through all her fears, through all her disappointments, and through all of her challenges in accordance with the following scripture: *Matthew 22:37-39: " Jesus said to him, 'You shall love the Lord your God with all your heart, with all your soul, and with all your mind. This is the first and great commandment. And the second is like it: You shall love your neighbor as yourself. On these two commandments hang all the Law and the Prophets."*

I pray that Your peace rule in _________________'s heart and mind through Jesus Christ, in accordance with the following scriptures: *Numbers 6:24-26: "The Lord bless you and keep you; the Lord make His face shine upon you, and be gracious to you; the Lord lift up His countenance upon you, and give you peace." Hebrews 12:14: "Pursue peace with all people, and holiness, without which no one will see the Lord."*

I pray that _________________ casts all her cares upon You because You love and care for her, and so you can care for her. I know You want the best for her, as referenced in *1 Peter 5:6-7: "Therefore humble yourselves under the mighty hand of God, that He may exalt you in due time, casting all your care upon Him for He cares for you."*

I pray that _________________ trust You and that she does not fear, or worry, or doubt, or stress out, or be anxious, or feel defeated for You have not given her any of these negative things that are within the spirit of fear, as referenced in *2 Timothy 1:7: "For God has not given us a spirit of fear, but of power and of love and of a sound mind."* I pray that she stands on Your word in *Isaiah 41:10,* which states: *"Fear not, for I am with you; be not dismayed, for I am your God. I will strengthen you. Yes, I will help you. I will uphold you with My righteous right hand."*

I pray Dear Father that ________________ pass every one of life's tests/trials triumphantly that are set before her, and that she is encouraged in Your Word, the Holy Bible, in accordance with *2 Corinthians 4:16-18* which states: *"Therefore we do not lose heart. Even though our outward man is perishing, yet the inward man is being renewed day by day. For our light affliction, which is but for a moment, is working for us a far more exceeding and eternal weight of glory. While we do not look at the things which are seen, but at the things which are not seen, for the things which are seen are temporary, but the things which are not seen are eternal."* Also, in accordance with *James 1:2-4,* ________________ is victorious. *James 1:2-4* states: *"My brethren, count it all joy when you fall into various trials, knowing that the testing of your faith produces patience, but let patience have its perfect work, that you may be perfect and complete, lacking nothing."*

I pray that ________________ prospers in accordance with *3 John 2: "Beloved, I pray that you may prosper in all things and be in health, just as your soul prospers."* I pray that ________________ does not lose hope and give up, but that she continues in her walk with You no matter what, in accordance with the following scriptures: *2 Thessalonians 3:13: "But as for you, brethren, do not grow weary in doing good." 1 Timothy 6:12: "Fight the good fight of faith, lay hold on eternal life, to which you were also called and have confessed the good confession in the presence of many witnesses." Joshua 24:15: "... But as for me and my house, we will serve the Lord."*

In the mighty name of Jesus Christ, I pray.

Amen.

Additional Acknowledgements

Additional Acknowledgements

I appreciate all of God's servants
who taught me the Word of God,
who guided me in my walk of faith
and who "walk the talk!"

Dr. Tom Pickens, Jr.
Senior Pastor & Founder
Antelope Valley Christian Center

Minister Donna Pickens
Women's Ministry/Women's Bible Study
Antelope Valley Christian Center

Pastor Tom Pickens, III
Executive Assistant Pastor
Antelope Valley Christian Center

Minister Al Andrews
Minister David Barnes
Minister Joey Brown
Minister Sherreé Pickens-Johnson
Antelope Valley Christian Center

Frederick K. C. Price (Dr.) (Apostle) & Minister Betty Price
Ever Increasing Faith Ministries/
Crenshaw Christian Center

Jack Hayford (Dr.)
Senior Pastor, Founder
Church On The Way

Chuck Swindoll (Dr.)
Pastor
Insight for Living Ministries

James Dobson (Dr.)
Focus on the Family

Paul Crouch (Pastor) & Jan Crouch (Minister)
Trinity Broadcasting Network (TBN Ministries)

Bishop T. D. Jakes (Dr.)
Pastor – T. D. Jakes Ministries/The Potter's House

Creflo Dollar (Dr.)
Senior Pastor & Founder
Minister Taffi Dollar
Creflo Dollar Ministries/World Changers Church International

Charles Stanley (Dr.)
Pastor – In Touch Ministries/First Baptist Church of Atlanta

Joyce Meyer (Dr.)
Pastor – Joyce Meyer Ministries

Joel Osteen
Pastor
Minister Victoria Osteen
Joel Osteen Ministries/Lakewood Church

James Merritt (Dr.)
Senior Pastor
Touching Lives Ministries

James MacDonald (Dr.)
Pastor
Harvest Bible Chapel

Michael R. Magasin, Esq.
Law Offices of Michael R. Magasin

Bibliography

Bibliography

BIBLIOGRAPHIC CITATIONS:

Nelson Bibles, ***The Holy Bible – New King James Version,*** 1982, Thomas Nelson, Inc., Publishers, Nashville, Tennessee 37214, ***<http://www.tomasnelson.com>*** – "Scriptures taken from the New King James Version, Copyright 1982 by Thomas Nelson., Inc. Used by permission. All rights reserved."

Zondervan, The Lockman Foundation, ***The Amplified Bible Large Print***, 1987, Zondervan and the Lockman Foundation, Grand Rapids, Michigan 49530, U.S.A., <http://www.zondervan.com>

WORLDWIDE WEB:

American Cancer Society: Information and Resources
<http://cancer.org>

Bible Resources, Online – King James Bible References
<http://www.bible.com>

California HIV/AIDs Laws
<http://californiaaidsresearch.org

Center for Disease Control & Prevention (CDC)
<http://cdc.gov>

Expert Law
http://expertlaw.com

Merriam-Webster Dictionary
<http://www.merriam-webster.com/dictionary>

National Center for Youth Law
<http://www.youthlaw.org>

SexLaws
<http://sexlaws.org>

The Surgeon General of the United States – July 9, 2001
A Call To Action To Promote Sexual Health And Responsible Sexual Behavior
<http://surgeongeneral.gov>

Wikipedia
<http://wikipedia.org>

CODES & STATUTES:

California Penal Code Section 261.5

Health & Safety Code Section 120291

Health & Safety Code Section 123450

Lightning Source UK Ltd.
Milton Keynes UK
UKHW010650160420
361757UK00001B/359